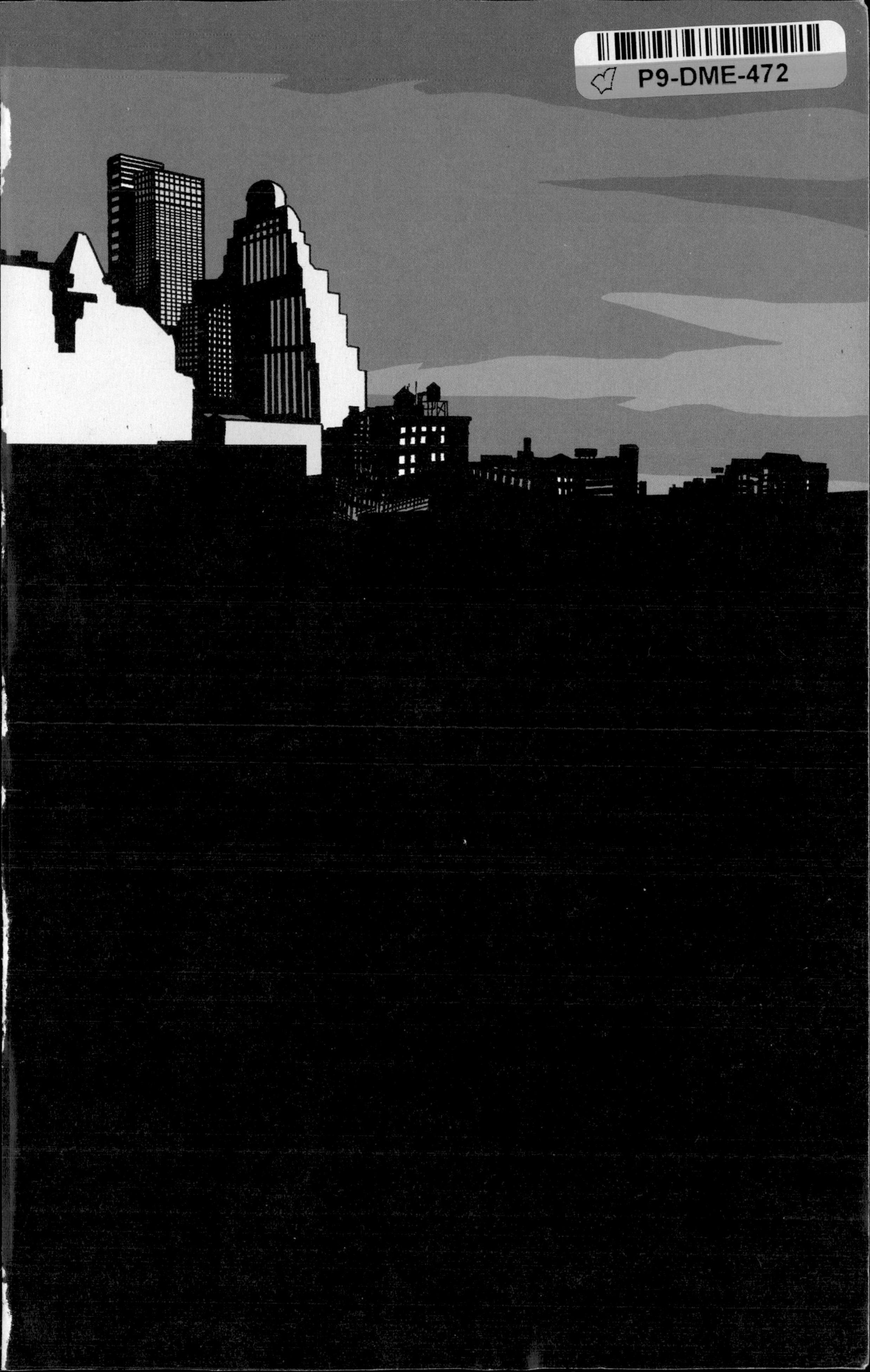

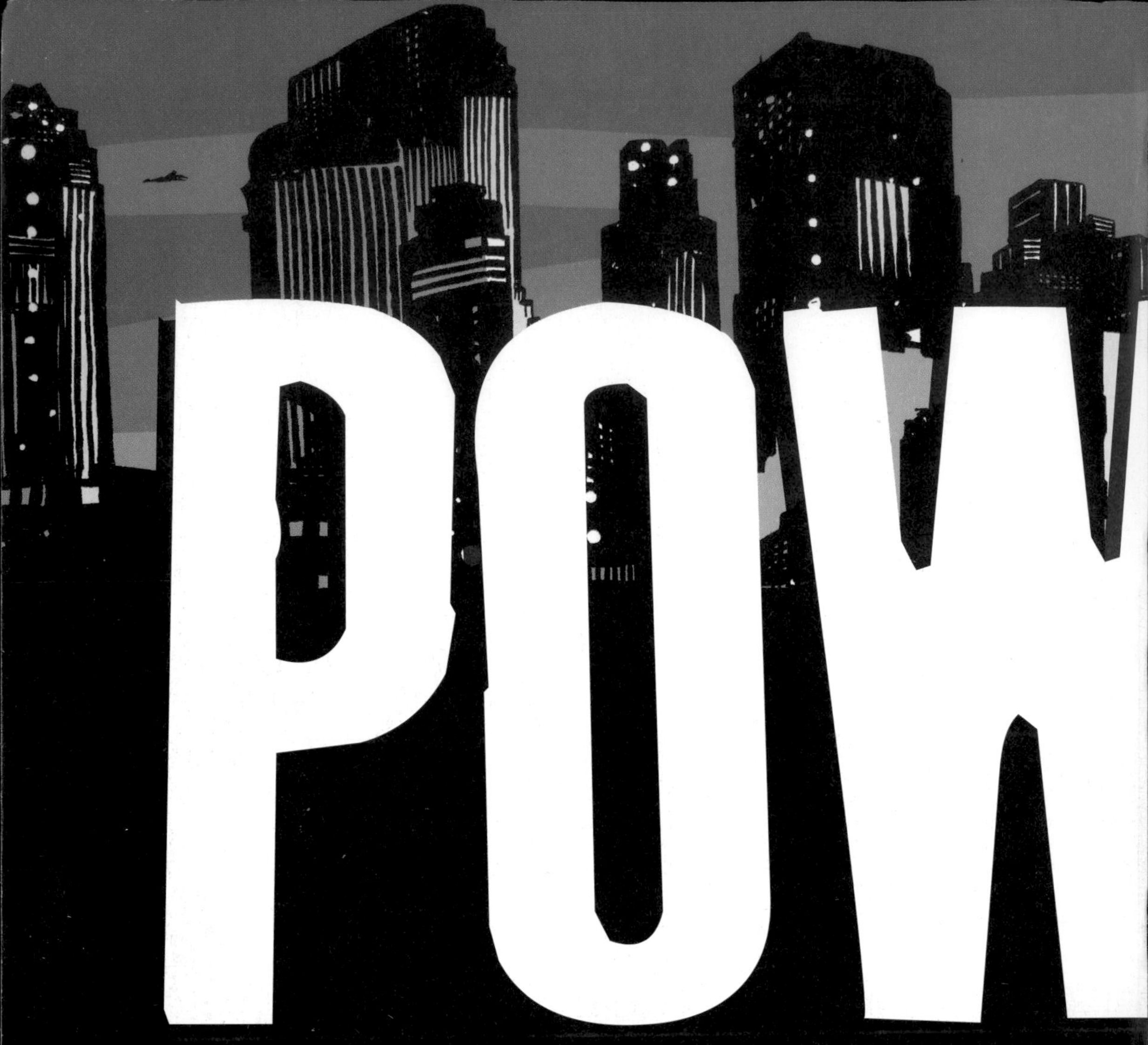
POW

CREATED AND PRODUCED
BY
BRIAN MICHAEL BENDIS
AND
MIKE AVON OEMING

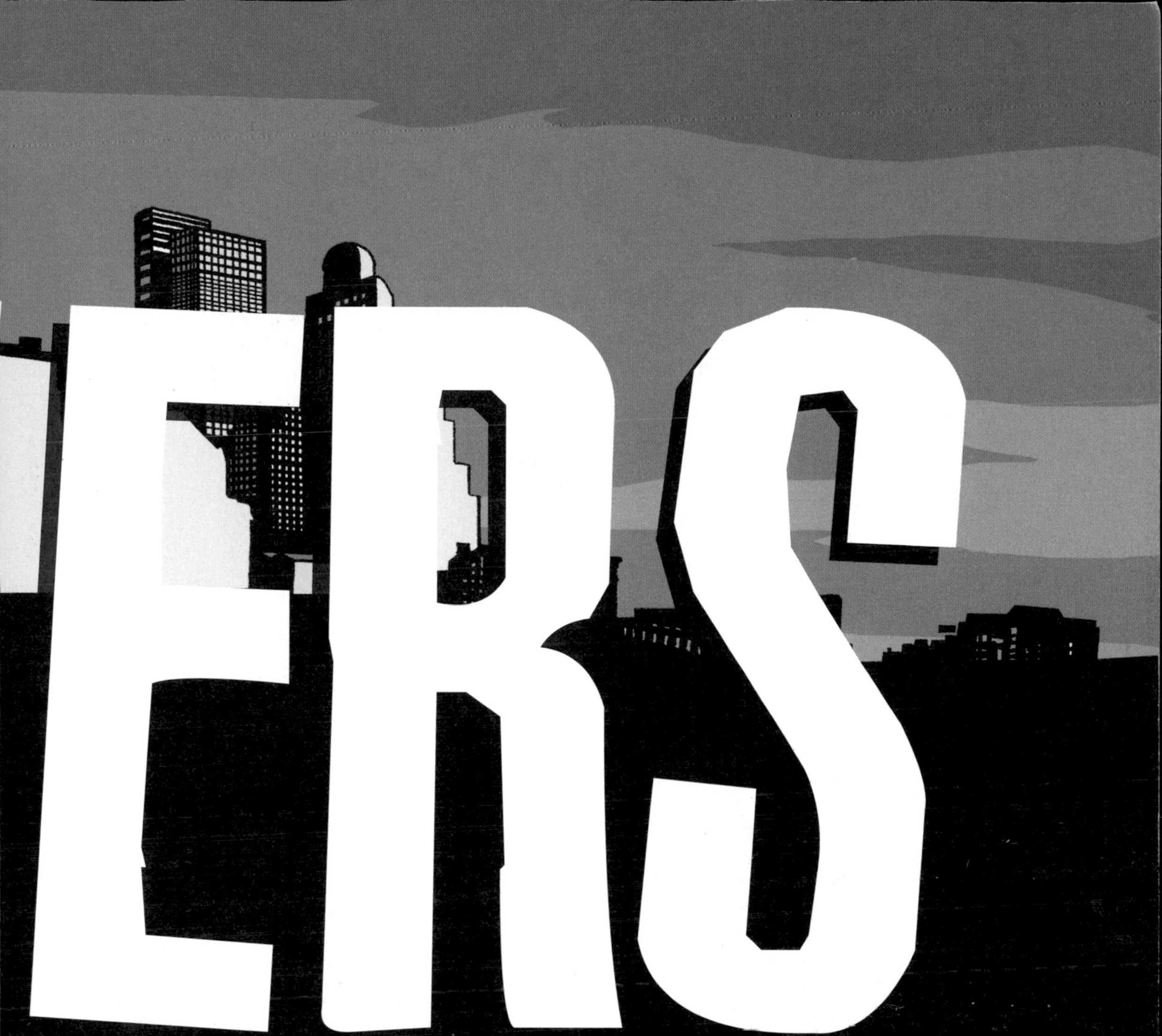
ERS

COLOR ART
PETER PANTAZIS

TYPOGRAPHY
KEN BRUZENAK

EDITED BY
JAMES LUCAS JONES

BUSINESS AFFAIRS
ALISA BENDIS

DESIGN AND PRODUCTION BY
KEITH WOOD

# Previously in Powers:

Homicide Detectives Christian Walker and Deena Pilgrim investigate murders specific to superhero cases... powers.

The damage brought on by this out of control power forced the world governments to declare all powers illegal. The city, reeling from a powers turf war, is in the worst shape it has ever been.

But shockingly, Retro Girl, one of the most beloved superheroes the world has ever known, has returned from the dead. Walker discovers that Retro Girl is someone he knows—A girl he rescued years ago named Calista. She has grown up only to develop powers and an unexplainable attachment to the Retro Girl legacy. Now she wants Walker to train her to be a superhero.

And Deena now carries a dark secret. She has mysterious, dangerous powers that she contracted from a villain. She doesn't know what they are or what they are doing to her...

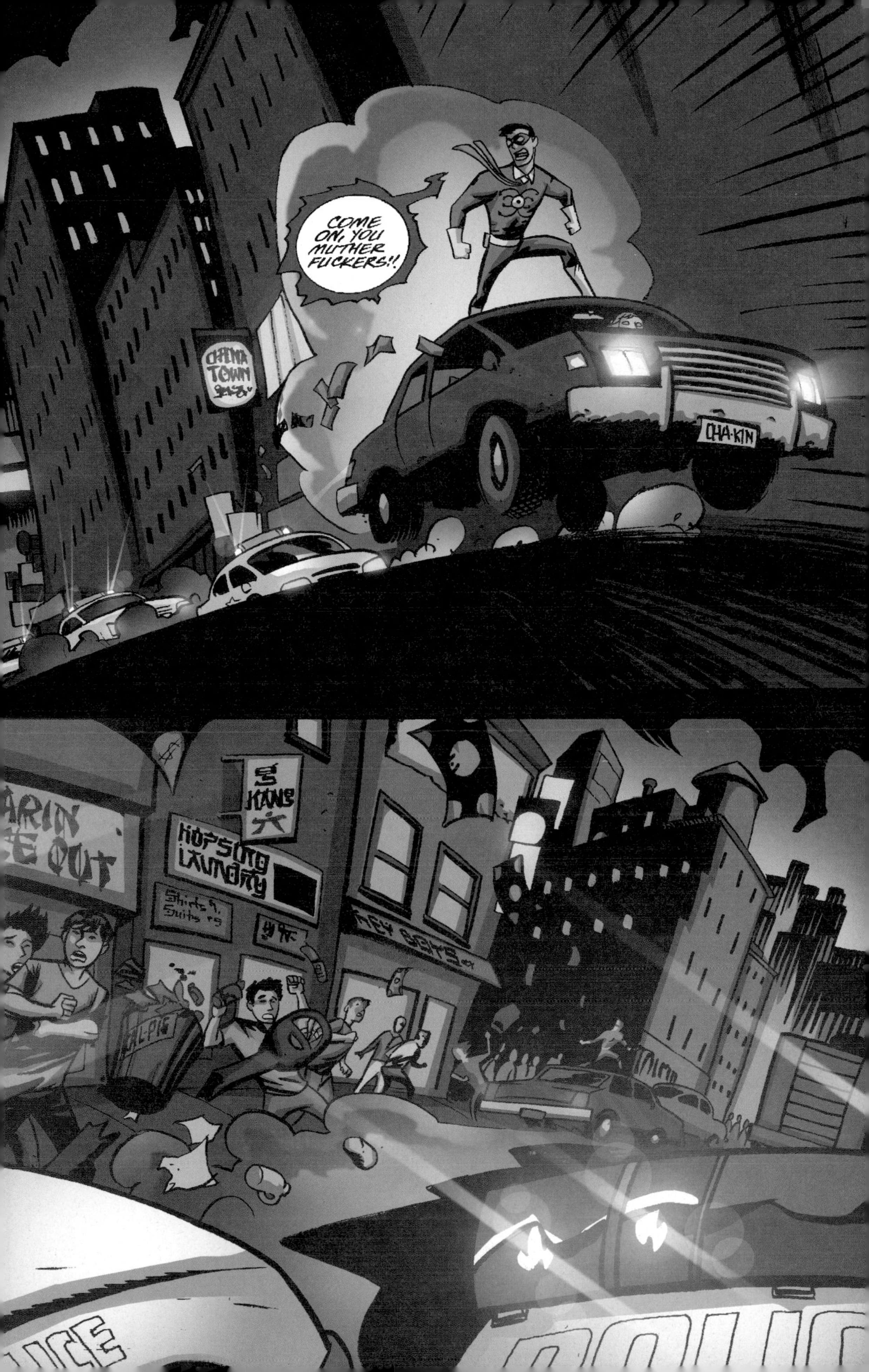
COME ON, YOU MUTHER FUCKERS!!
CHINA TOWN
CHA-KIN
HOPSING LAUNDRY

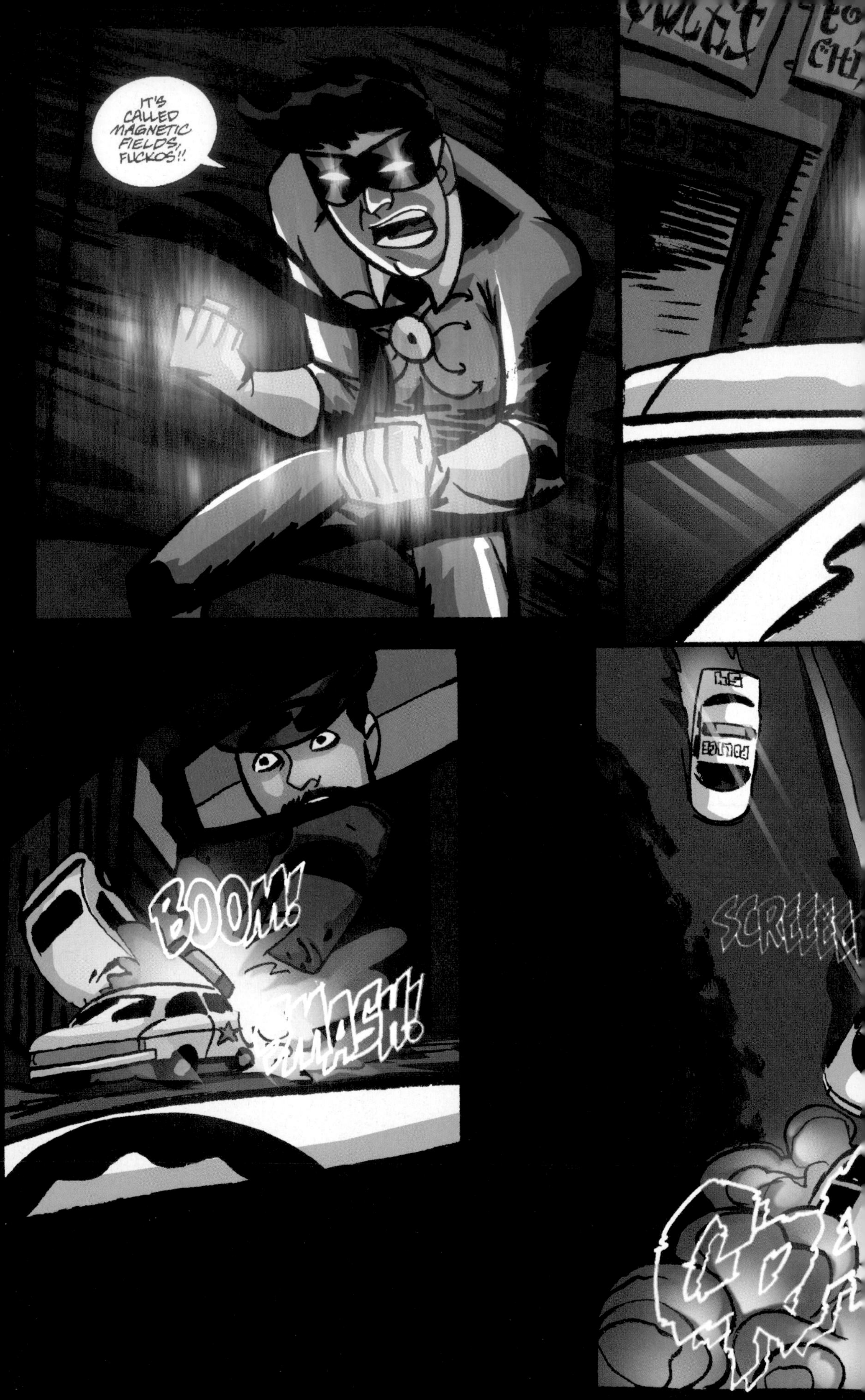
IT'S CALLED MAGNETIC FIELDS, FUCKOS!!
BOOM!
SCREEE

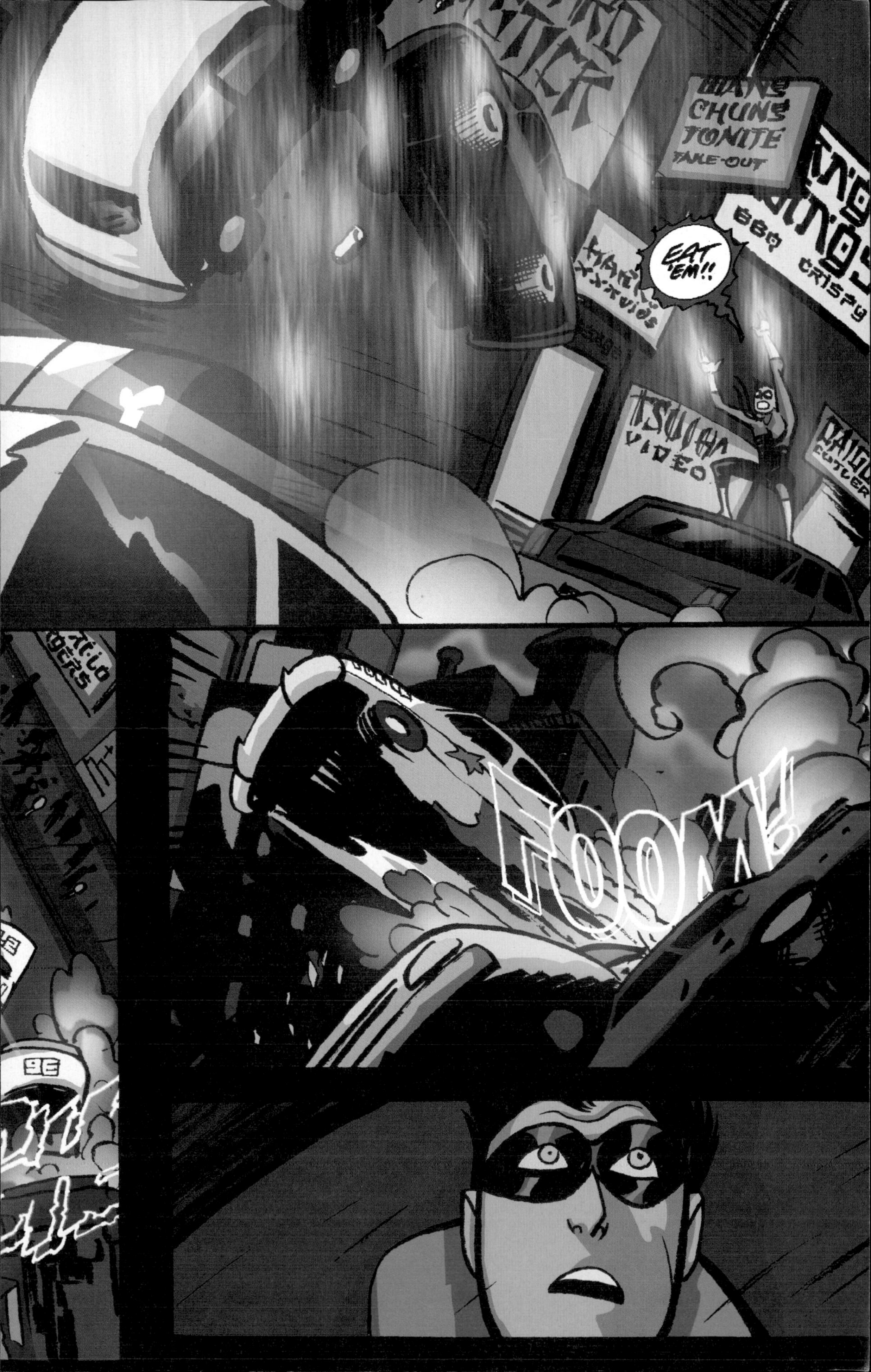
WANG CHUNS TONITE
TAKE-OUT
BBQ CRISPY
EAT 'EM!!
VIDEO
FOOM!

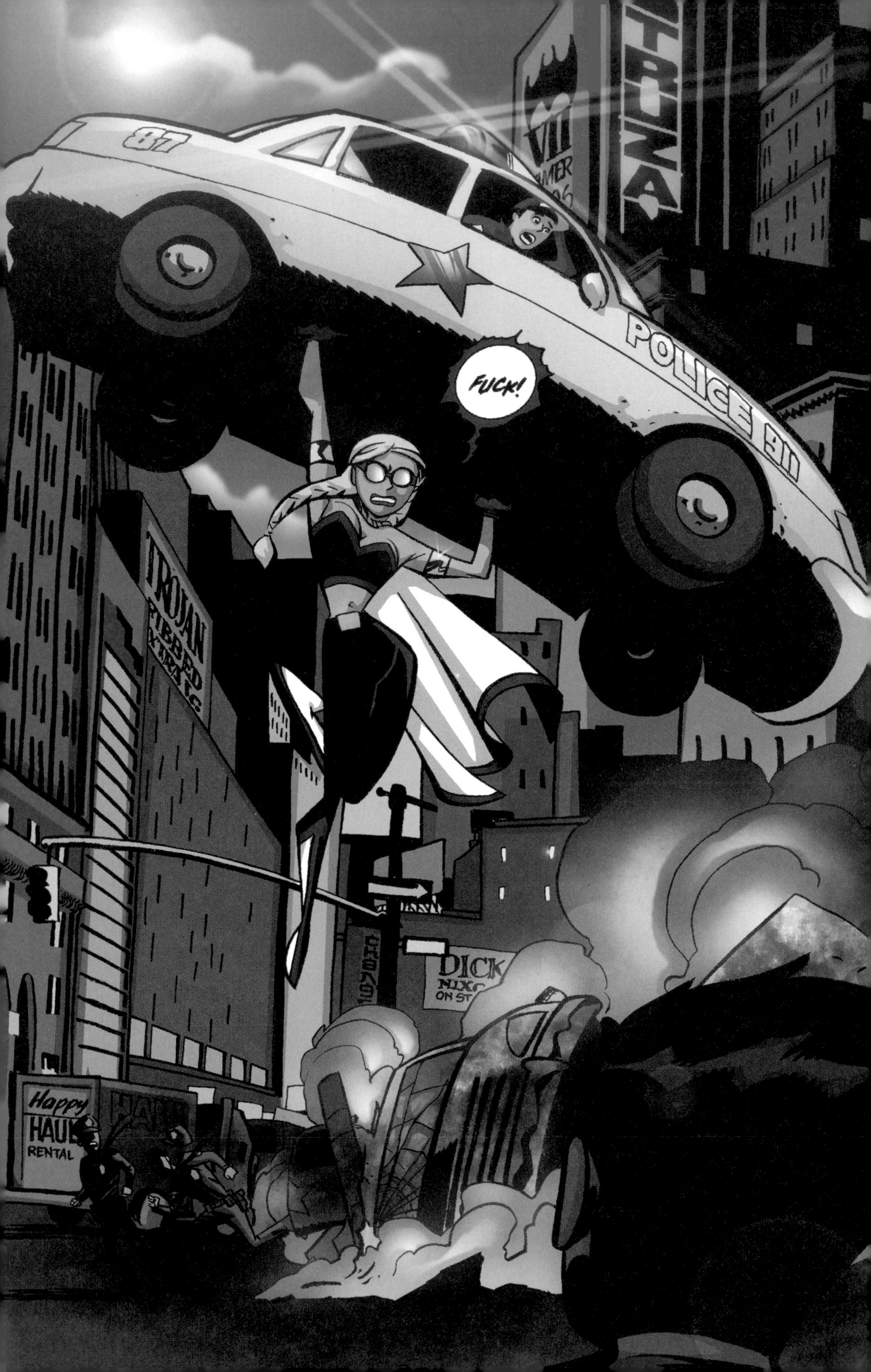
87
POLICE 811
FUCK!
TROJAN
Happy
RENTAL

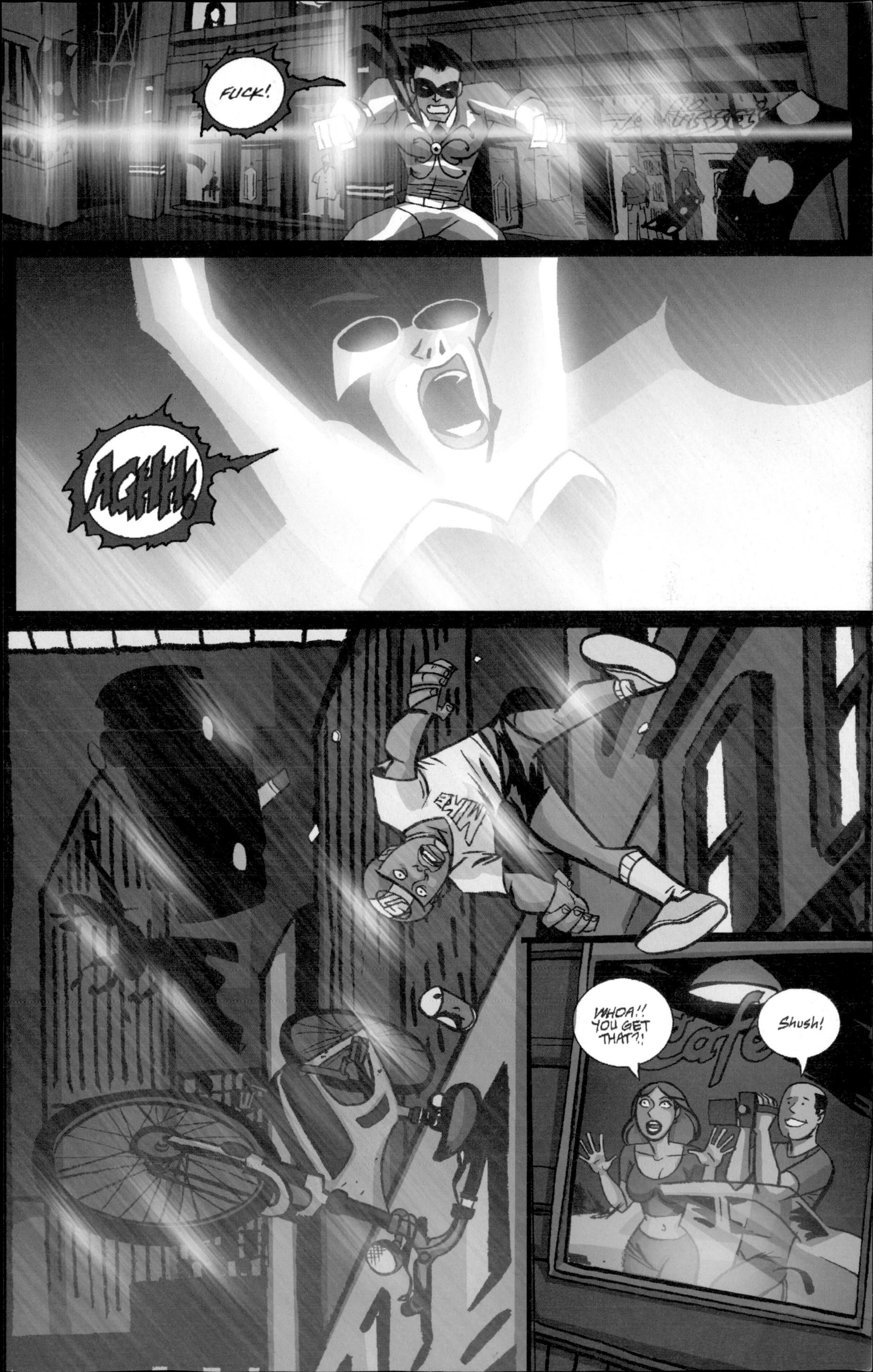
FUCK!
AGHH!
WHOA!! YOU GET THAT?!
Shush!

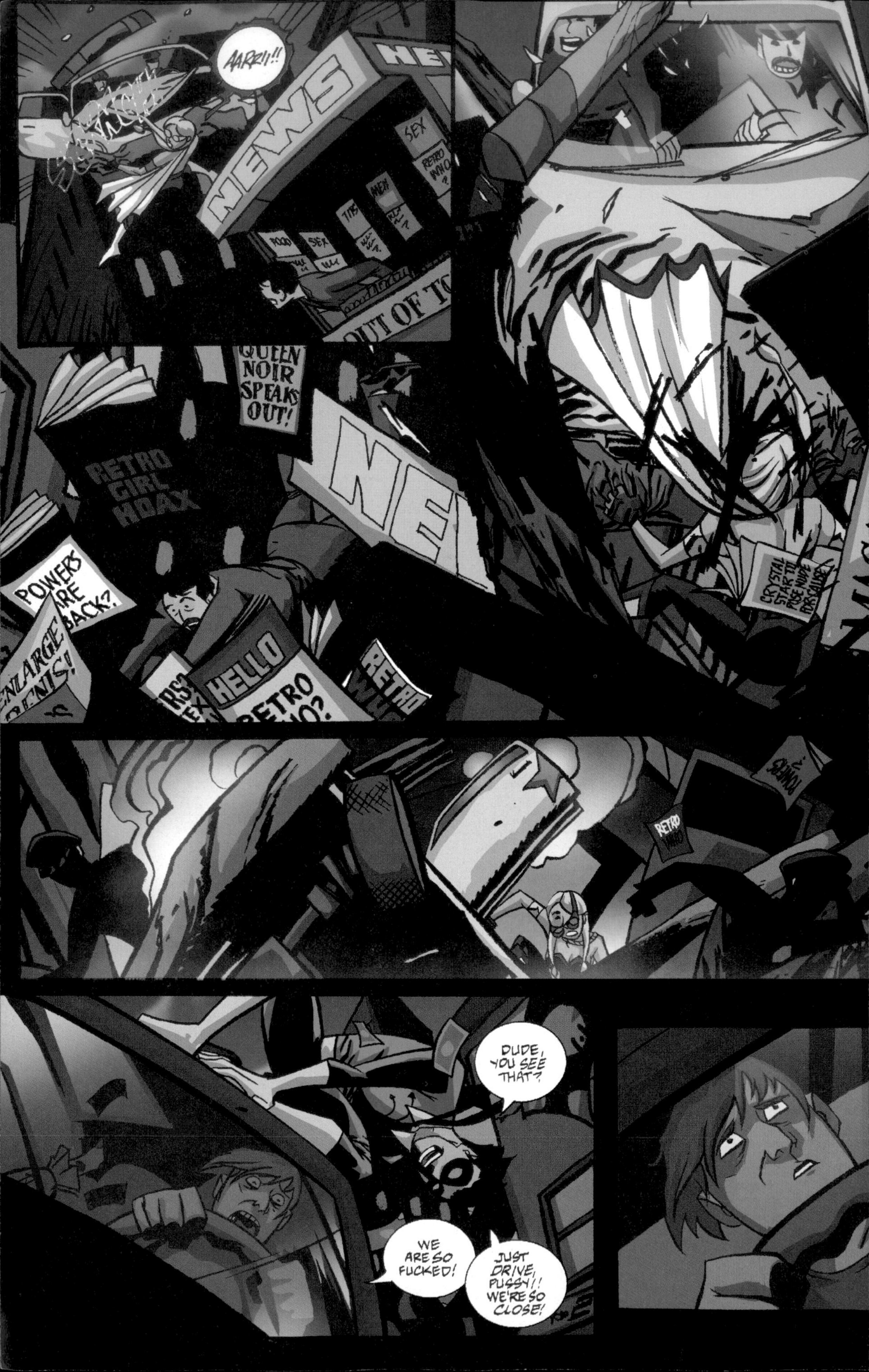

AARRI!!
NEWS
SEX
RETRO WHO?
TITS
FOOD
SEX
OUT OF TO
QUEEN NOIR SPEAKS OUT!
RETRO GIRL HOAX
NEW
POWERS ARE BACK?
ENLARGE PENIS!
HELLO
RETRO
CRYSTAL STAR TO POSE NUDE FOR CAUSE!
RETRO WHO
DUDE, YOU SEE THAT?
WE ARE SO FUCKED!
JUST DRIVE, PUSSY!! WE'RE SO CLOSE!

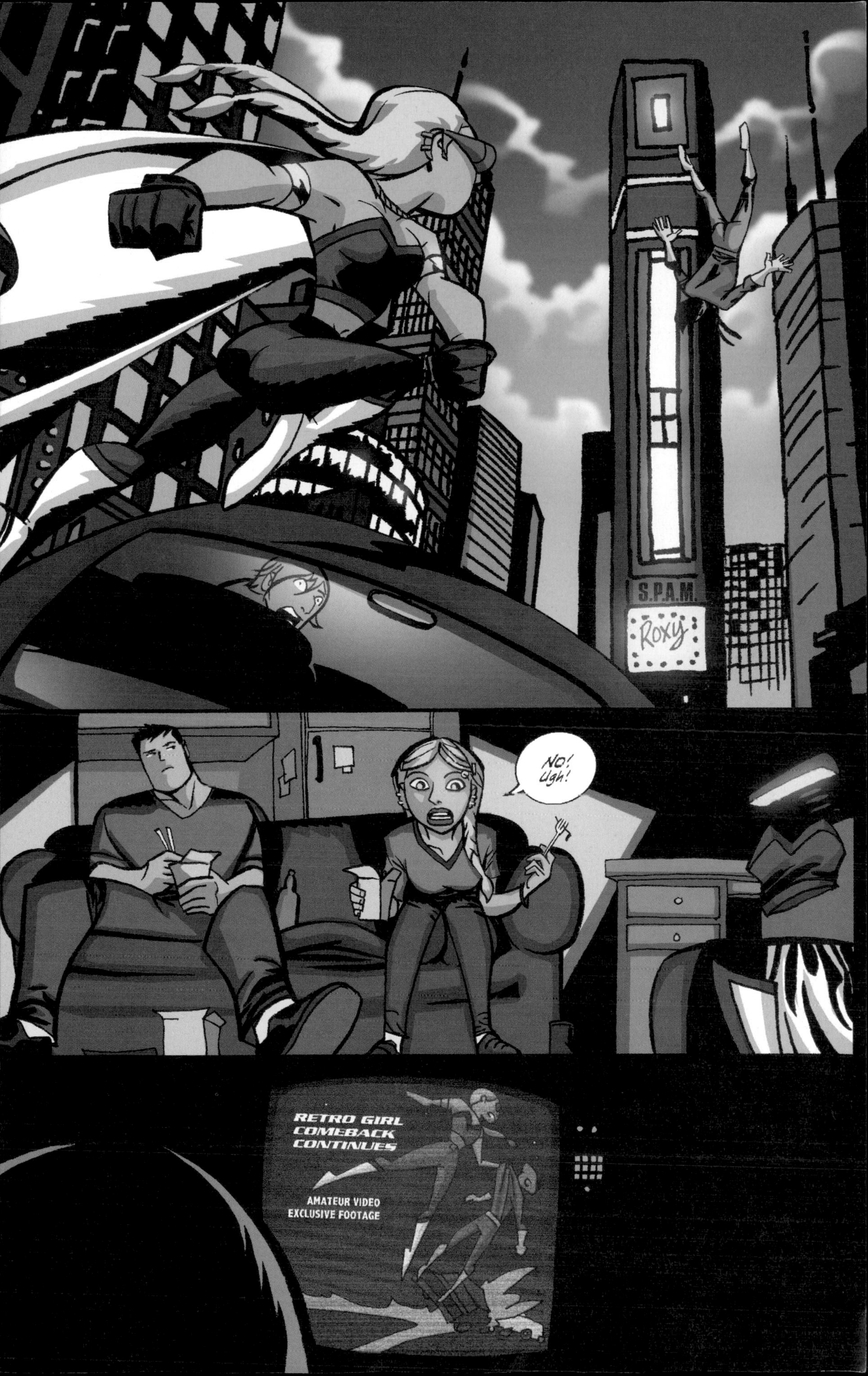
S.P.A.M.
Roxy
No! Ugh!
RETRO GIRL COMEBACK CONTINUES
AMATEUR VIDEO EXCLUSIVE FOOTAGE

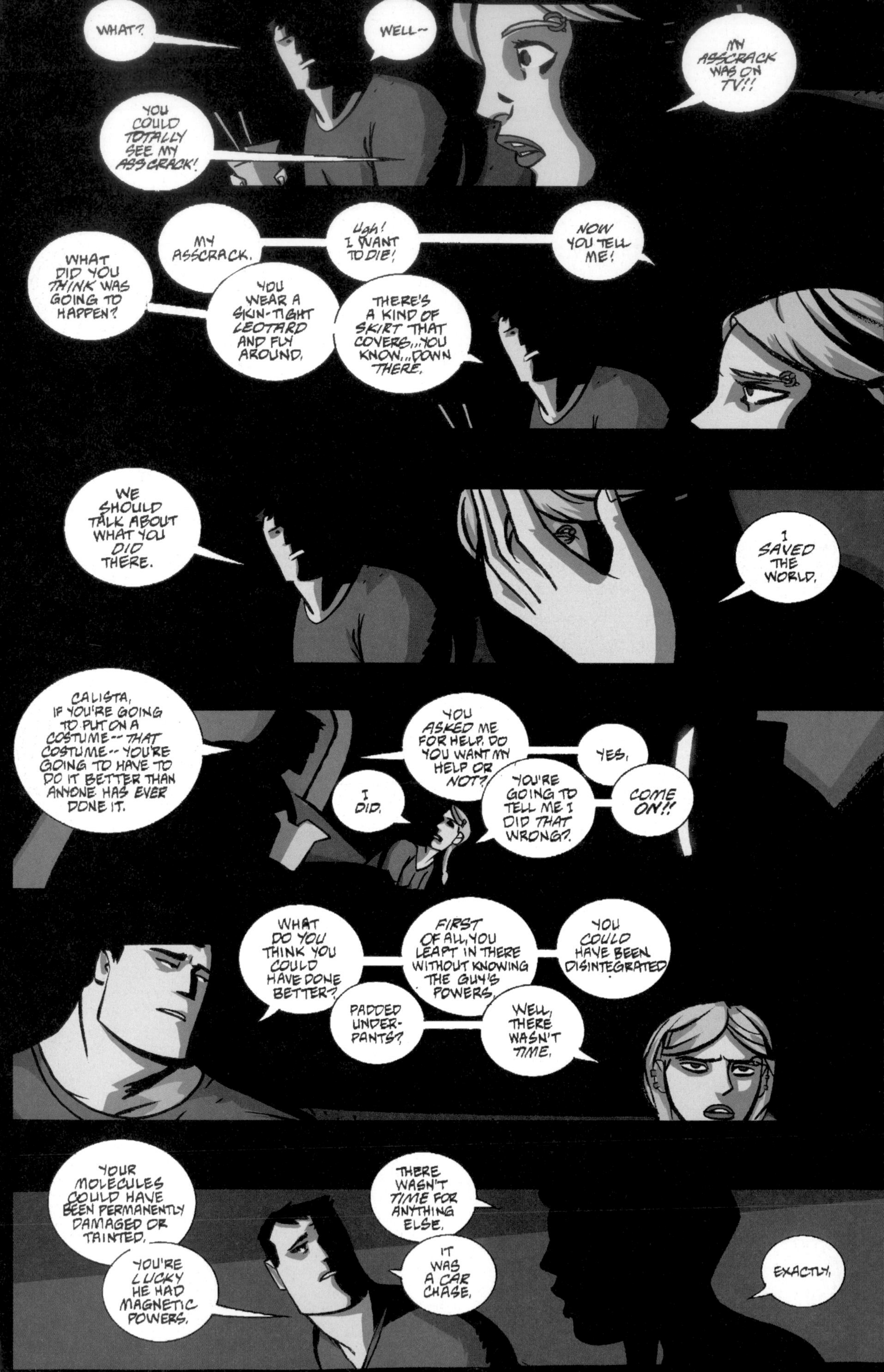
WHAT?
WELL--
YOU COULD TOTALLY SEE MY ASSCRACK!
MY ASSCRACK WAS ON TV!!
MY ASSCRACK.
Ugh! I WANT TO DIE!
NOW YOU TELL ME!
WHAT DID YOU THINK WAS GOING TO HAPPEN?
YOU WEAR A SKIN-TIGHT LEOTARD AND FLY AROUND.
THERE'S A KIND OF SKIRT THAT COVERS...YOU KNOW...DOWN THERE.
WE SHOULD TALK ABOUT WHAT YOU DID THERE.
I SAVED THE WORLD.
CALISTA, IF YOU'RE GOING TO PUT ON A COSTUME-- THAT COSTUME-- YOU'RE GOING TO HAVE TO DO IT BETTER THAN ANYONE HAS EVER DONE IT.
I DID.
YOU ASKED ME FOR HELP. DO YOU WANT MY HELP OR NOT?
YES.
YOU'RE GOING TO TELL ME I DID THAT WRONG?
COME ON!!
WHAT DO YOU THINK YOU COULD HAVE DONE BETTER?
FIRST OF ALL, YOU LEAPT IN THERE WITHOUT KNOWING THE GUY'S POWERS.
YOU COULD HAVE BEEN DISINTEGRATED.
PADDED UNDER-PANTS?
WELL, THERE WASN'T TIME.
YOUR MOLECULES COULD HAVE BEEN PERMANENTLY DAMAGED OR TAINTED.
YOU'RE LUCKY HE HAD MAGNETIC POWERS.
THERE WASN'T TIME FOR ANYTHING ELSE.
IT WAS A CAR CHASE.
EXACTLY.

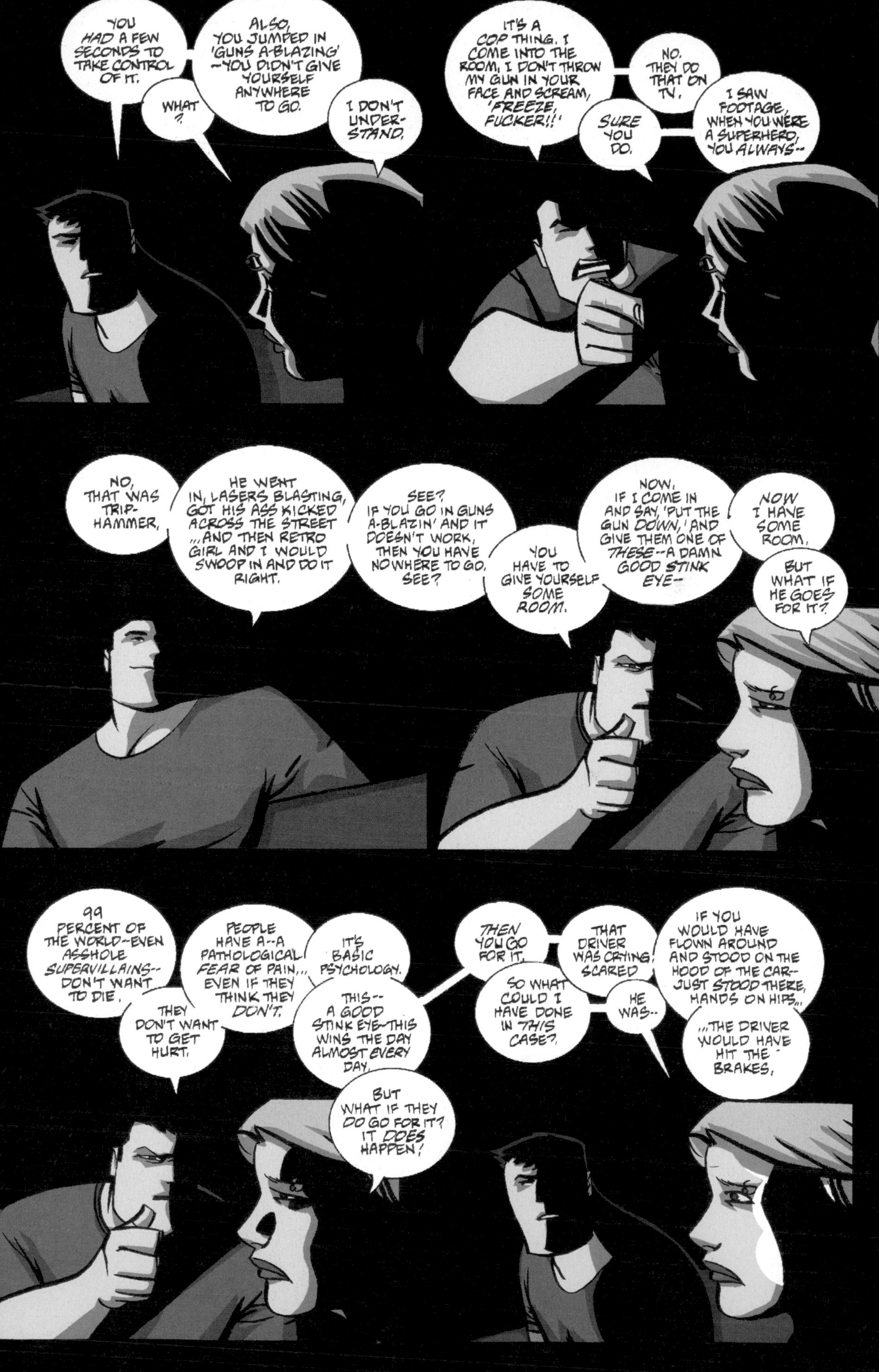
YOU HAD A FEW SECONDS TO TAKE CONTROL OF IT.
WHAT?
ALSO, YOU JUMPED IN 'GUNS A-BLAZING' --YOU DIDN'T GIVE YOURSELF ANYWHERE TO GO.
I DON'T UNDER-STAND.
IT'S A COP THING. I COME INTO THE ROOM, I DON'T THROW MY GUN IN YOUR FACE AND SCREAM, 'FREEZE, FUCKER!!'
NO. THEY DO THAT ON TV.
SURE YOU DO.
I SAW FOOTAGE. WHEN YOU WERE A SUPERHERO, YOU ALWAYS--
NO, THAT WAS TRIP-HAMMER.
HE WENT IN, LASERS BLASTING, GOT HIS ASS KICKED ACROSS THE STREET ...AND THEN RETRO GIRL AND I WOULD SWOOP IN AND DO IT RIGHT.
SEE? IF YOU GO IN GUNS A-BLAZIN' AND IT DOESN'T WORK, THEN YOU HAVE NOWHERE TO GO. SEE?
YOU HAVE TO GIVE YOURSELF SOME ROOM.
NOW, IF I COME IN AND SAY, 'PUT THE GUN DOWN,' AND GIVE THEM ONE OF THESE--A DAMN GOOD STINK EYE--
NOW I HAVE SOME ROOM.
BUT WHAT IF HE GOES FOR IT?
99 PERCENT OF THE WORLD--EVEN ASSHOLE SUPERVILLAINS--DON'T WANT TO DIE.
THEY DON'T WANT TO GET HURT.
PEOPLE HAVE A--A PATHOLOGICAL FEAR OF PAIN... EVEN IF THEY THINK THEY DON'T.
IT'S BASIC PSYCHOLOGY.
THIS--A GOOD STINK EYE--THIS WINS THE DAY ALMOST EVERY DAY.
BUT WHAT IF THEY DO GO FOR IT? IT DOES HAPPEN!
THEN YOU GO FOR IT.
THAT DRIVER WAS CRYING. SCARED
SO WHAT COULD I HAVE DONE IN THIS CASE?
HE WAS...
IF YOU WOULD HAVE FLOWN AROUND AND STOOD ON THE HOOD OF THE CAR--JUST STOOD THERE, HANDS ON HIPS...
...THE DRIVER WOULD HAVE HIT THE BRAKES.

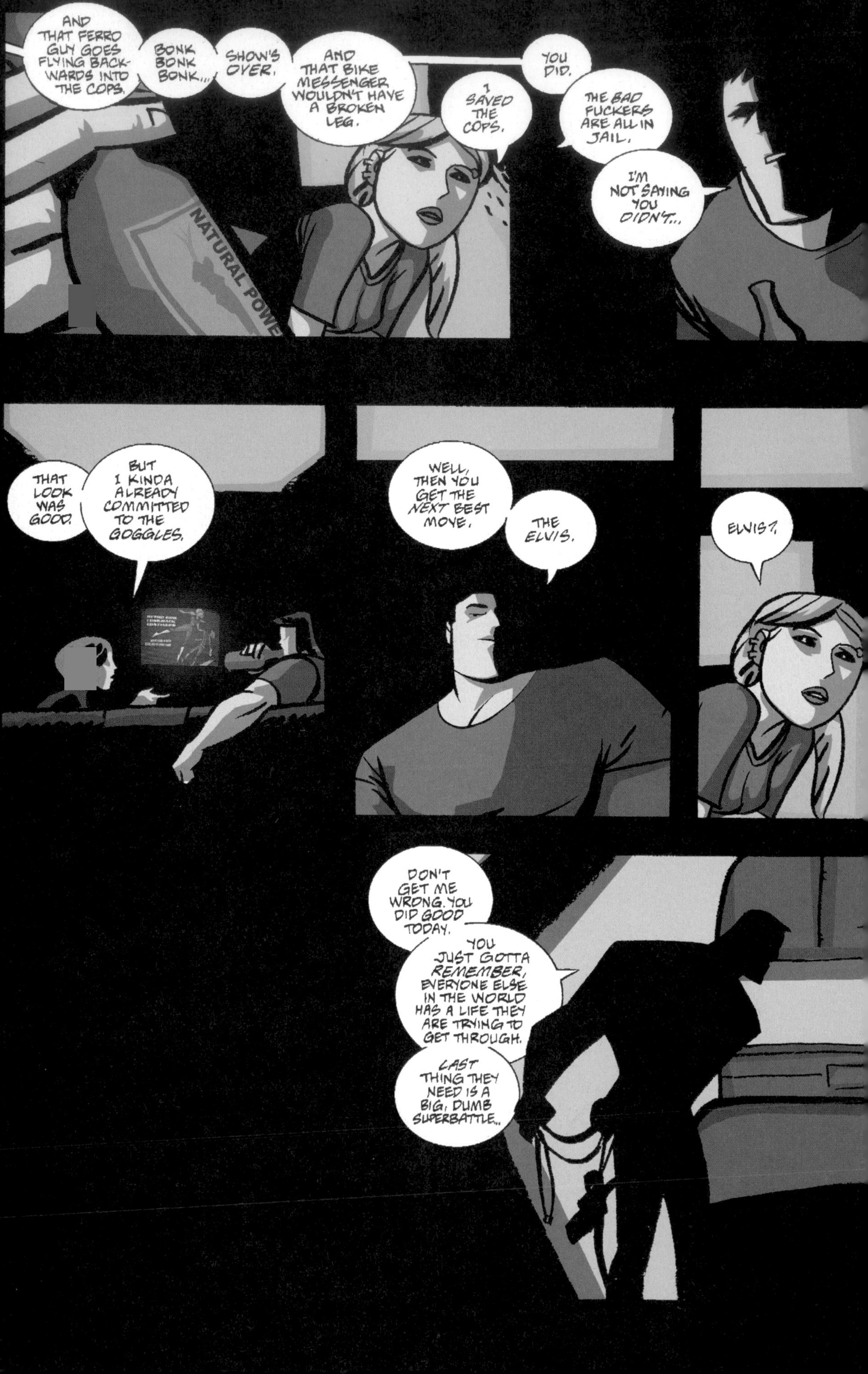
AND THAT FERRO GUY GOES FLYING BACK-WARDS INTO THE COPS.
BONK BONK BONK...
SHOW'S OVER.
AND THAT BIKE MESSENGER WOULDN'T HAVE A BROKEN LEG.
I SAVED THE COPS.
YOU DID.
THE BAD FUCKERS ARE ALL IN JAIL.
I'M NOT SAYING YOU DIDN'T...
NATURAL POWE
THAT LOOK WAS GOOD.
BUT I KINDA ALREADY COMMITTED TO THE GOGGLES.
WELL, THEN YOU GET THE NEXT BEST MOVE.
THE ELVIS.
ELVIS?
DON'T GET ME WRONG. YOU DID GOOD TODAY.
YOU JUST GOTTA REMEMBER, EVERYONE ELSE IN THE WORLD HAS A LIFE THEY ARE TRYING TO GET THROUGH.
LAST THING THEY NEED IS A BIG, DUMB SUPERBATTLE...

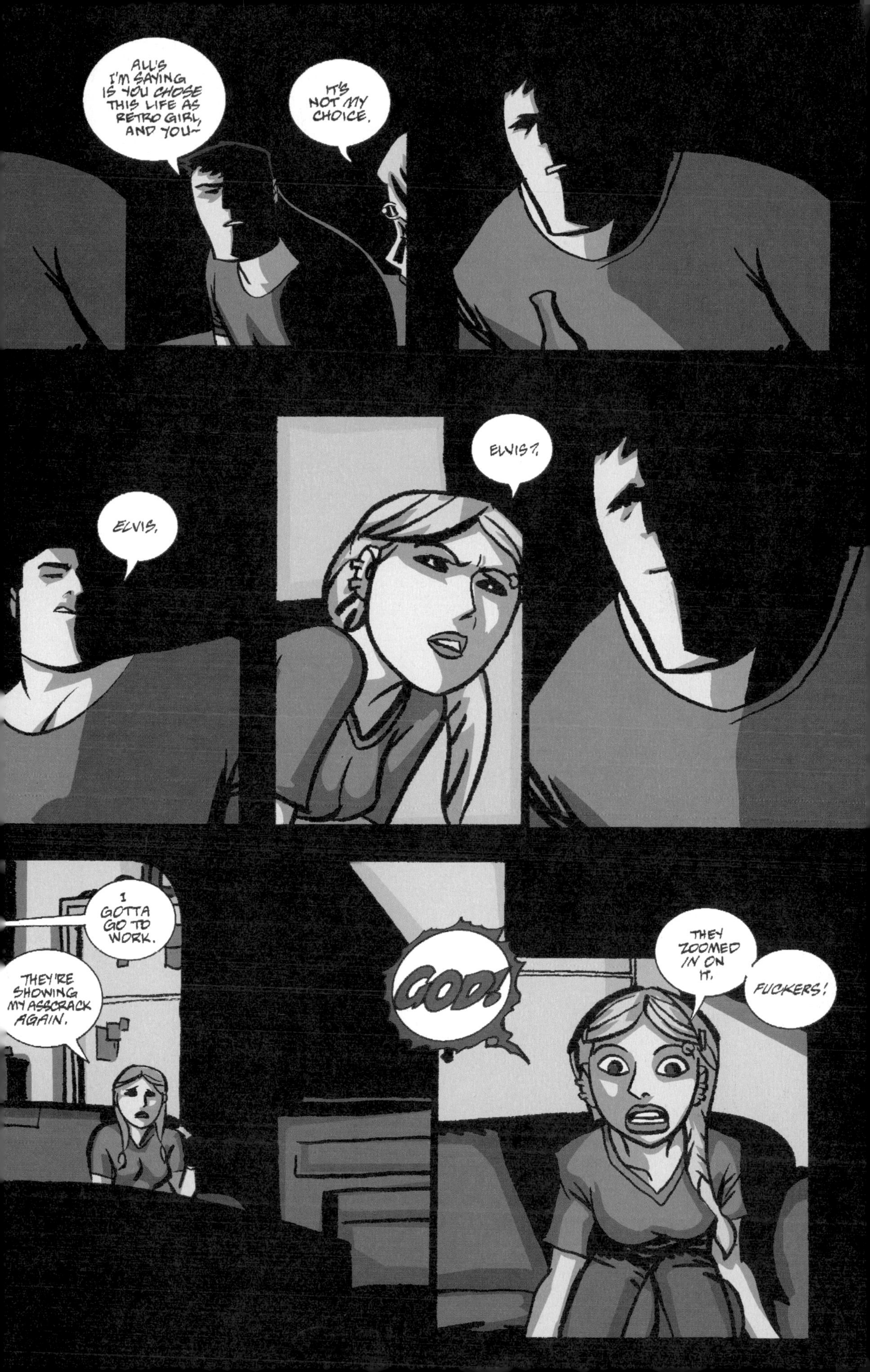
ALL'S I'M SAYING IS YOU CHOSE THIS LIFE AS RETRO GIRL, AND YOU--
IT'S NOT MY CHOICE.
ELVIS.
ELVIS?
I GOTTA GO TO WORK.
THEY'RE SHOWING MY ASSCRACK AGAIN.
GOD!
THEY ZOOMED IN ON IT.
FUCKERS!

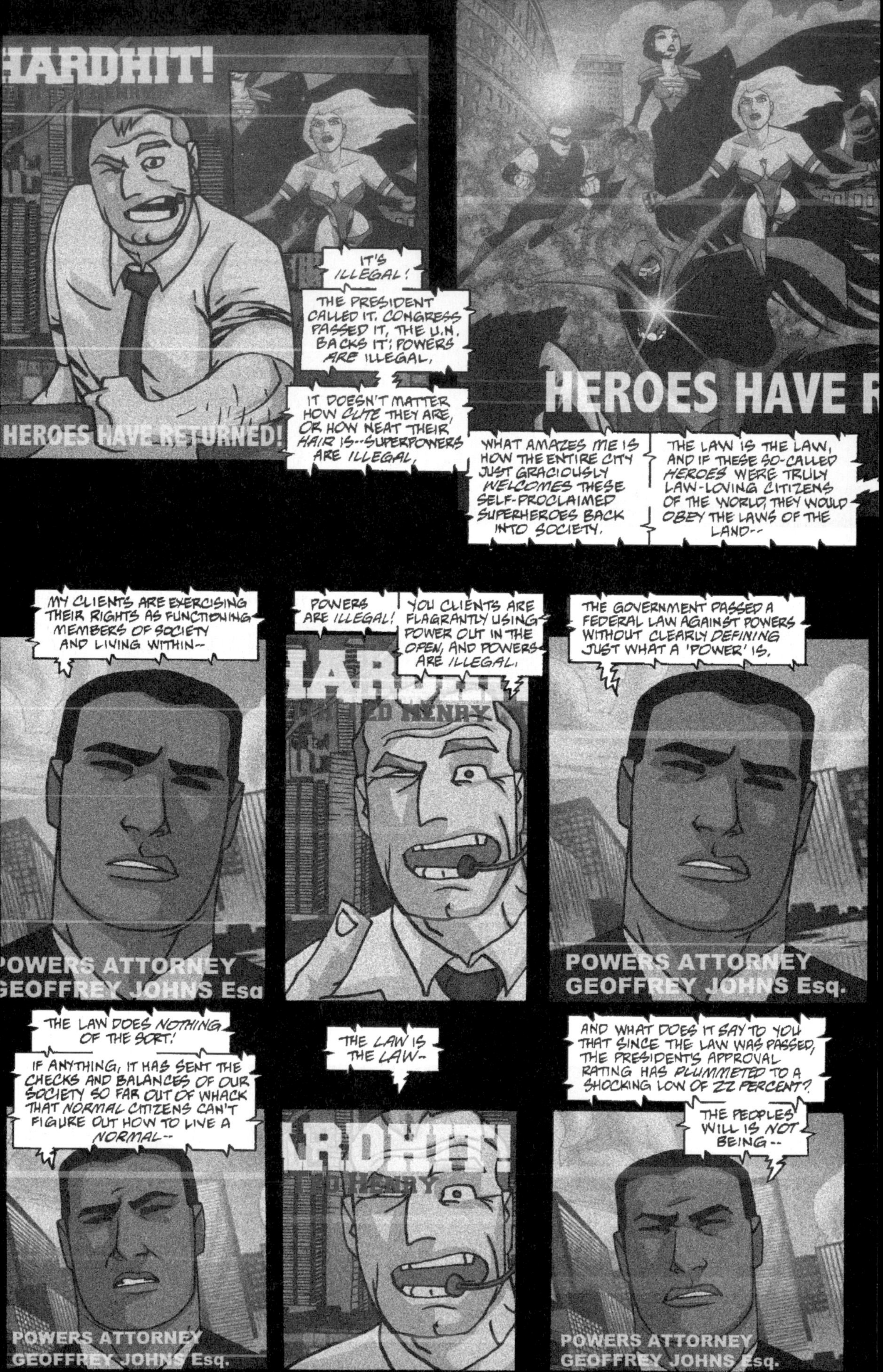
HARDHIT!
HEROES HAVE RETURNED!
IT'S ILLEGAL!
THE PRESIDENT CALLED IT, CONGRESS PASSED IT, THE U.N. BACKS IT: POWERS ARE ILLEGAL.
IT DOESN'T MATTER HOW CUTE THEY ARE, OR HOW NEAT THEIR HAIR IS--SUPERPOWERS ARE ILLEGAL.
HEROES HAVE R
WHAT AMAZES ME IS HOW THE ENTIRE CITY JUST GRACIOUSLY WELCOMES THESE SELF-PROCLAIMED SUPERHEROES BACK INTO SOCIETY.
THE LAW IS THE LAW, AND IF THESE SO-CALLED HEROES WERE TRULY LAW-LOVING CITIZENS OF THE WORLD, THEY WOULD OBEY THE LAWS OF THE LAND--
MY CLIENTS ARE EXERCISING THEIR RIGHTS AS FUNCTIONING MEMBERS OF SOCIETY AND LIVING WITHIN--
POWERS ATTORNEY
GEOFFREY JOHNS Esq
POWERS ARE ILLEGAL!
YOU CLIENTS ARE FLAGRANTLY USING POWER OUT IN THE OPEN, AND POWERS ARE ILLEGAL.
THE GOVERNMENT PASSED A FEDERAL LAW AGAINST POWERS WITHOUT CLEARLY DEFINING JUST WHAT A 'POWER' IS.
POWERS ATTORNEY
GEOFFREY JOHNS Esq.
THE LAW DOES NOTHING OF THE SORT!
IF ANYTHING, IT HAS SENT THE CHECKS AND BALANCES OF OUR SOCIETY SO FAR OUT OF WHACK THAT NORMAL CITIZENS CAN'T FIGURE OUT HOW TO LIVE A NORMAL--
POWERS ATTORNEY
GEOFFREY JOHNS Esq.
THE LAW IS THE LAW--
ARDHIT!
AND WHAT DOES IT SAY TO YOU THAT SINCE THE LAW WAS PASSED, THE PRESIDENT'S APPROVAL RATING HAS PLUMMETED TO A SHOCKING LOW OF 22 PERCENT?
THE PEOPLES' WILL IS NOT BEING--
POWERS ATTORNEY
GEOFFREY JOHNS Esq.

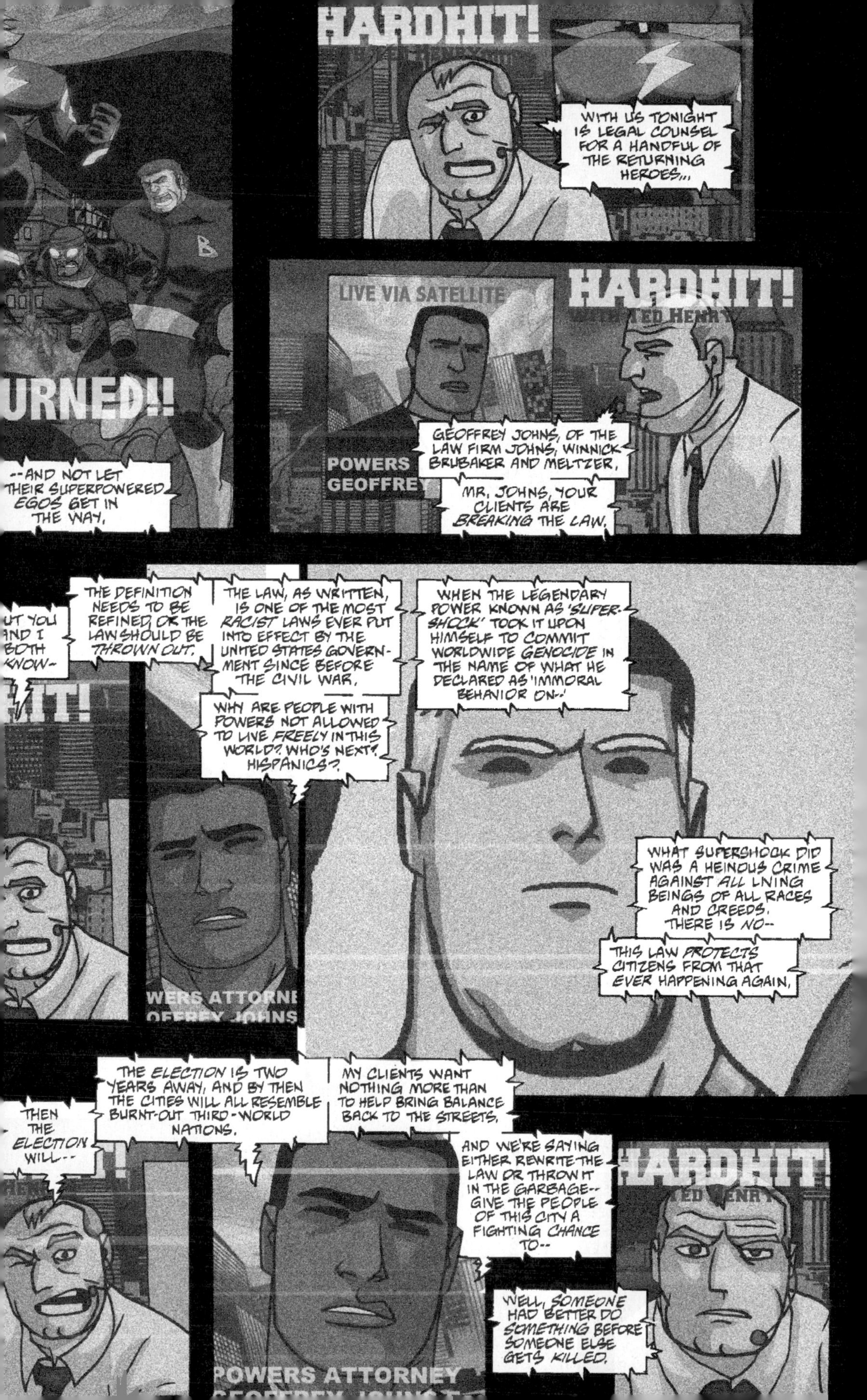
HARDHIT!
WITH US TONIGHT IS LEGAL COUNSEL FOR A HANDFUL OF THE RETURNING HEROES...
URNED!!
--AND NOT LET THEIR SUPERPOWERED EGOS GET IN THE WAY.
LIVE VIA SATELLITE
HARDHIT!
WITH TED HENRY
POWERS
GEOFFREY
GEOFFREY JOHNS, OF THE LAW FIRM JOHNS, WINNICK, BRUBAKER AND MELTZER.
MR. JOHNS, YOUR CLIENTS ARE BREAKING THE LAW.
UT YOU AND I BOTH KNOW--
THE DEFINITION NEEDS TO BE REFINED, OR THE LAW SHOULD BE THROWN OUT.
THE LAW, AS WRITTEN, IS ONE OF THE MOST RACIST LAWS EVER PUT INTO EFFECT BY THE UNITED STATES GOVERNMENT SINCE BEFORE THE CIVIL WAR.
WHY ARE PEOPLE WITH POWERS NOT ALLOWED TO LIVE FREELY IN THIS WORLD? WHO'S NEXT? HISPANICS?
WHEN THE LEGENDARY POWER KNOWN AS 'SUPERSHOCK' TOOK IT UPON HIMSELF TO COMMIT WORLDWIDE GENOCIDE IN THE NAME OF WHAT HE DECLARED AS 'IMMORAL BEHAVIOR ON--'
WHAT SUPERSHOCK DID WAS A HEINOUS CRIME AGAINST ALL LIVING BEINGS OF ALL RACES AND CREEDS. THERE IS NO--
THIS LAW PROTECTS CITIZENS FROM THAT EVER HAPPENING AGAIN.
WERS ATTORNE
OFFREY JOHNS
THEN THE ELECTION WILL--
THE ELECTION IS TWO YEARS AWAY, AND BY THEN THE CITIES WILL ALL RESEMBLE BURNT-OUT THIRD-WORLD NATIONS.
MY CLIENTS WANT NOTHING MORE THAN TO HELP BRING BALANCE BACK TO THE STREETS.
AND WE'RE SAYING EITHER REWRITE THE LAW OR THROW IT IN THE GARBAGE--GIVE THE PEOPLE OF THIS CITY A FIGHTING CHANCE TO--
HARDHIT!
WELL, SOMEONE HAD BETTER DO SOMETHING BEFORE SOMEONE ELSE GETS KILLED.
POWERS ATTORNEY

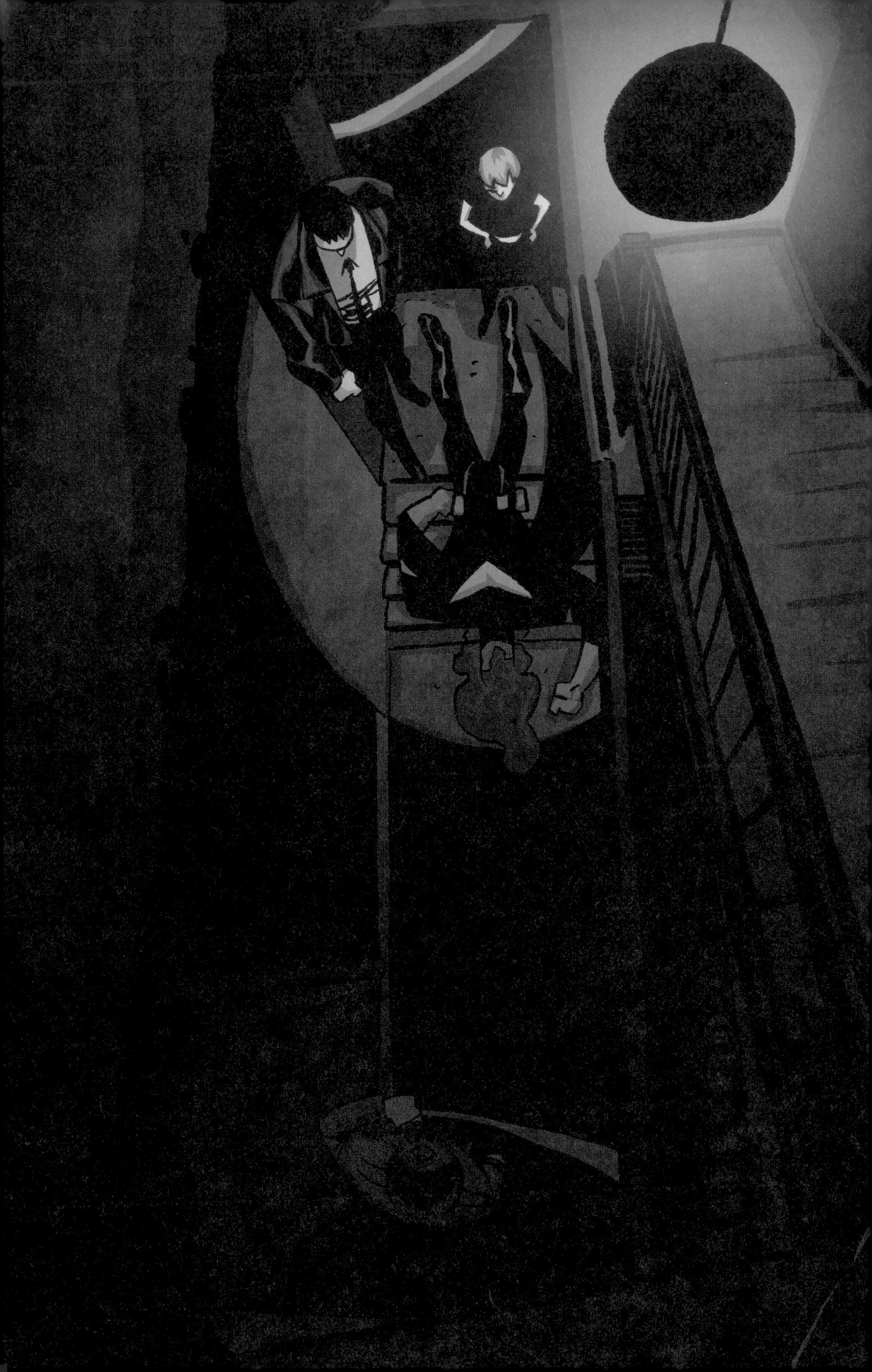

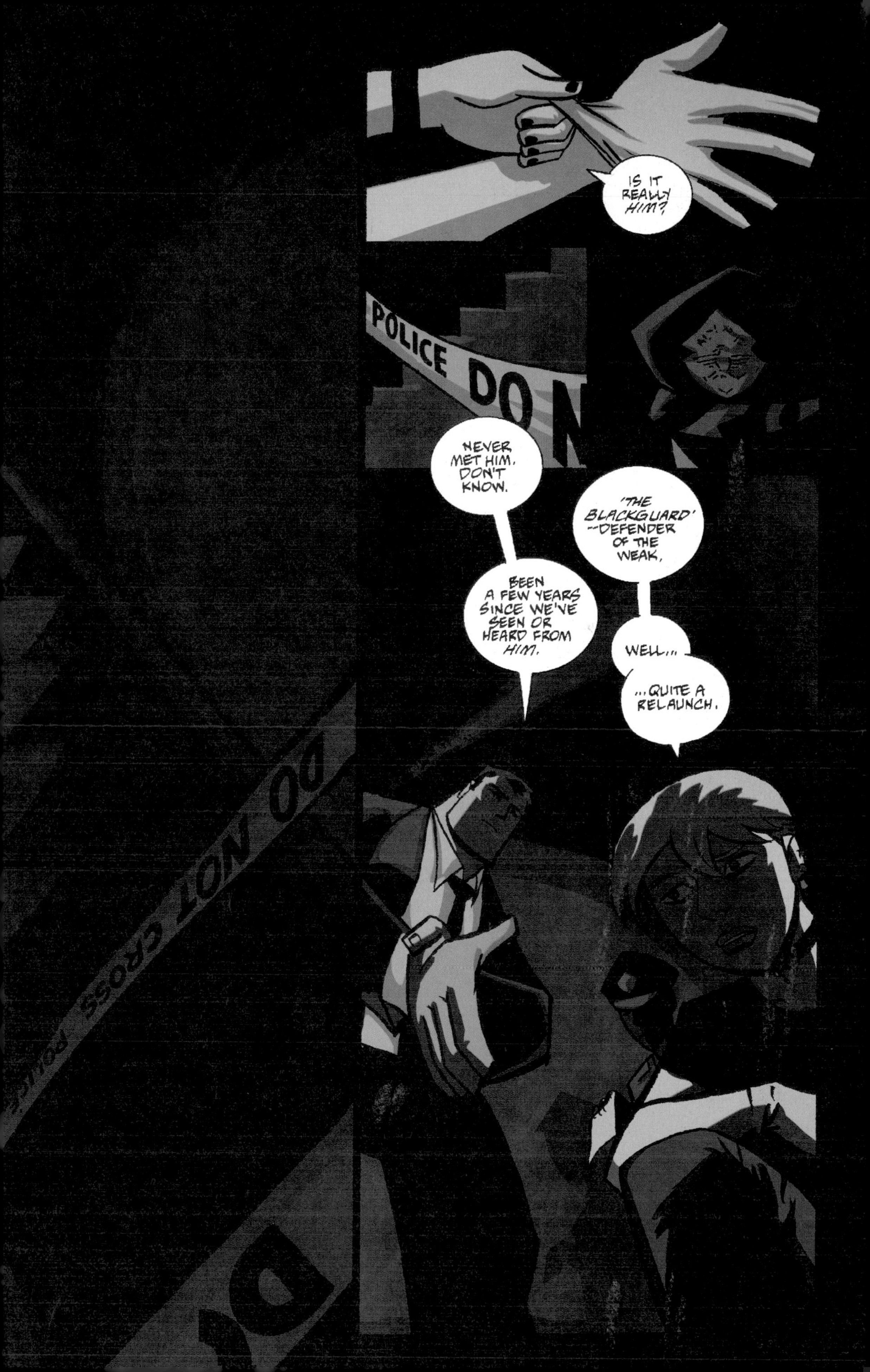
IS IT REALLY *HIM*?
NEVER MET HIM. DON'T KNOW.
BEEN A FEW YEARS SINCE WE'VE SEEN OR HEARD FROM *HIM*.
'THE BLACKGUARD' --DEFENDER OF THE WEAK.
WELL...
...QUITE A RELAUNCH.

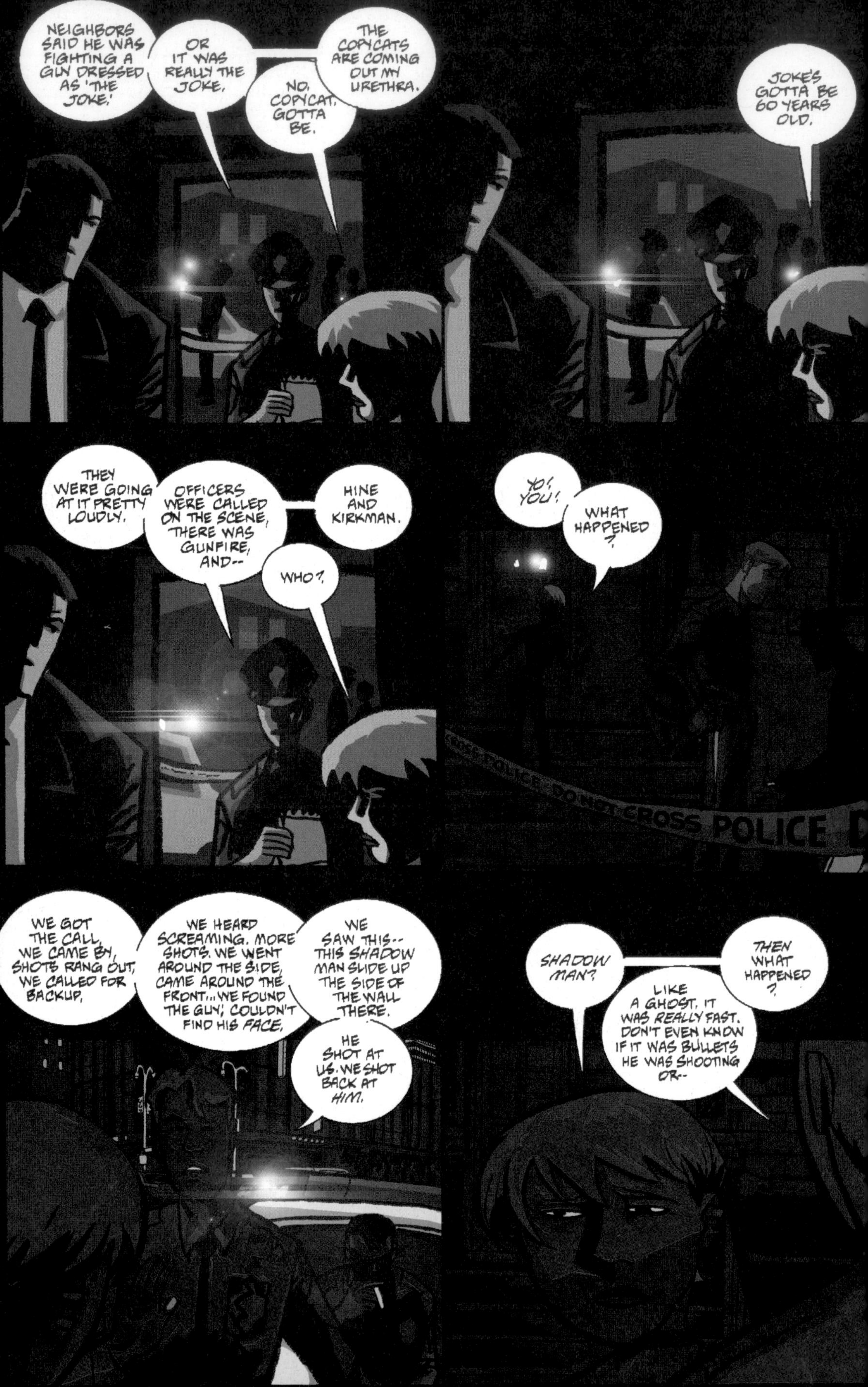
NEIGHBORS SAID HE WAS FIGHTING A GUY DRESSED AS 'THE JOKE.'
OR IT WAS REALLY THE JOKE.
THE COPYCATS ARE COMING OUT MY URETHRA.
NO, COPYCAT, GOTTA BE.
JOKE'S GOTTA BE 60 YEARS OLD.
THEY WERE GOING AT IT PRETTY LOUDLY.
OFFICERS WERE CALLED ON THE SCENE, THERE WAS GUNFIRE, AND--
HINE AND KIRKMAN.
WHO?
YO! YOU!
WHAT HAPPENED?
POLICE DO NOT CROSS POLICE
WE GOT THE CALL, WE CAME BY, SHOTS RANG OUT, WE CALLED FOR BACKUP.
WE HEARD SCREAMING. MORE SHOTS. WE WENT AROUND THE SIDE, CAME AROUND THE FRONT... WE FOUND THE GUY; COULDN'T FIND HIS FACE.
WE SAW THIS-- THIS SHADOW MAN SLIDE UP THE SIDE OF THE WALL THERE.
HE SHOT AT US. WE SHOT BACK AT HIM.
SHADOW MAN?
THEN WHAT HAPPENED?
LIKE A GHOST. IT WAS REALLY FAST. DON'T EVEN KNOW IF IT WAS BULLETS HE WAS SHOOTING OR--

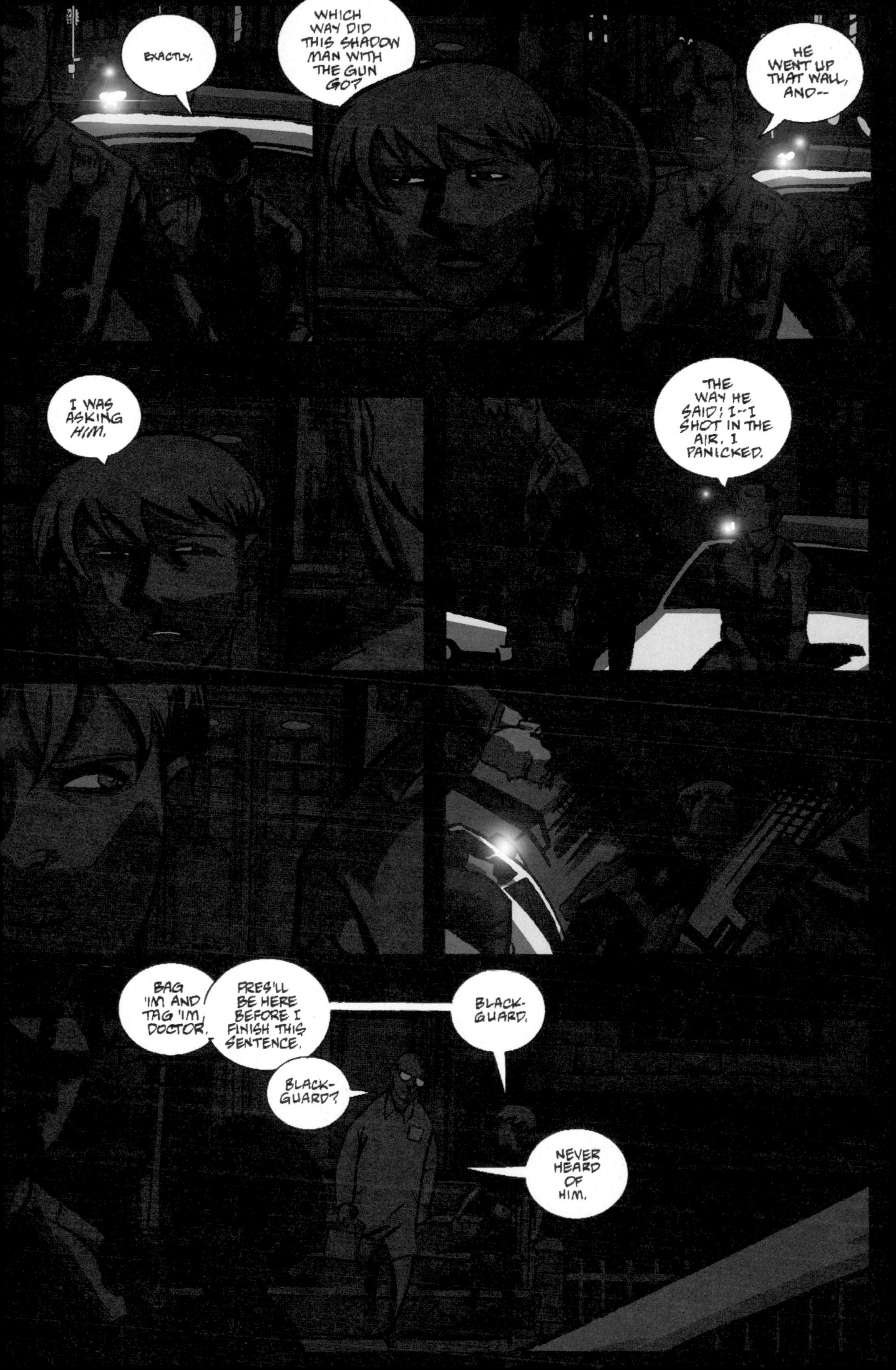
EXACTLY.
WHICH WAY DID THIS SHADOW MAN WITH THE GUN GO?
HE WENT UP THAT WALL, AND--
I WAS ASKING HIM.
THE WAY HE SAID; I--I SHOT IN THE AIR. I PANICKED.
BAG 'IM AND TAG 'IM, DOCTOR.
PRES'LL BE HERE BEFORE I FINISH THIS SENTENCE.
BLACK-GUARD.
BLACK-GUARD?
NEVER HEARD OF HIM.

# Blackguard

**Real name**
Matthew Michaels

**Occupation**
Social worker

**Identity**
Secret

**Legal status**
Citizen of the United States
with no criminal record

**Place of birth**
New York City

**Group affiliation**
None

**Base of operations**
New York City

**First appearance**
Lone Wolves #4

**Height**   6 ft.
**Weight**   200 lbs.
**Eyes**   Blue
**Hair**   Red

## History
Young Matt Michaels, while on a hunting trip with his father and three brothers, found an unmarked tomb in the foothills of upstate New York.

Not knowing it was a tomb, the men entered, but only young Matt came out. Young Matt was found wandering about the countryside holding a small black jewel in the palm of his hand. Matt doesn't remember what happened that day and was nevee able to find the tomb again.

The black jewel gave Matt heightened senses and mastery over his entire physical form. He becme a martial arts master without ever training.

As the Blackguard, Matt uses his heightened powers to forever seek justice, whenever law fails.

## Known powers
Blackguard possesses slightly better than normal human strength for a man of his age, height and build who engages in intensive regular exercise. Blackguard's five senses ar heightened to beyond even a superhumanly enhanced range.

Blackguard is an Olympic-level athlete and gymnast, possessing extraordinary agility, endurance, skill and balance.

Blackguard's unique fighting style is a blend of many trainings, among them ninjitsu judo and traditional kung fu.

How the mysterious black jewel grants Matt these abilities is unknown and protected under the Simonson act.

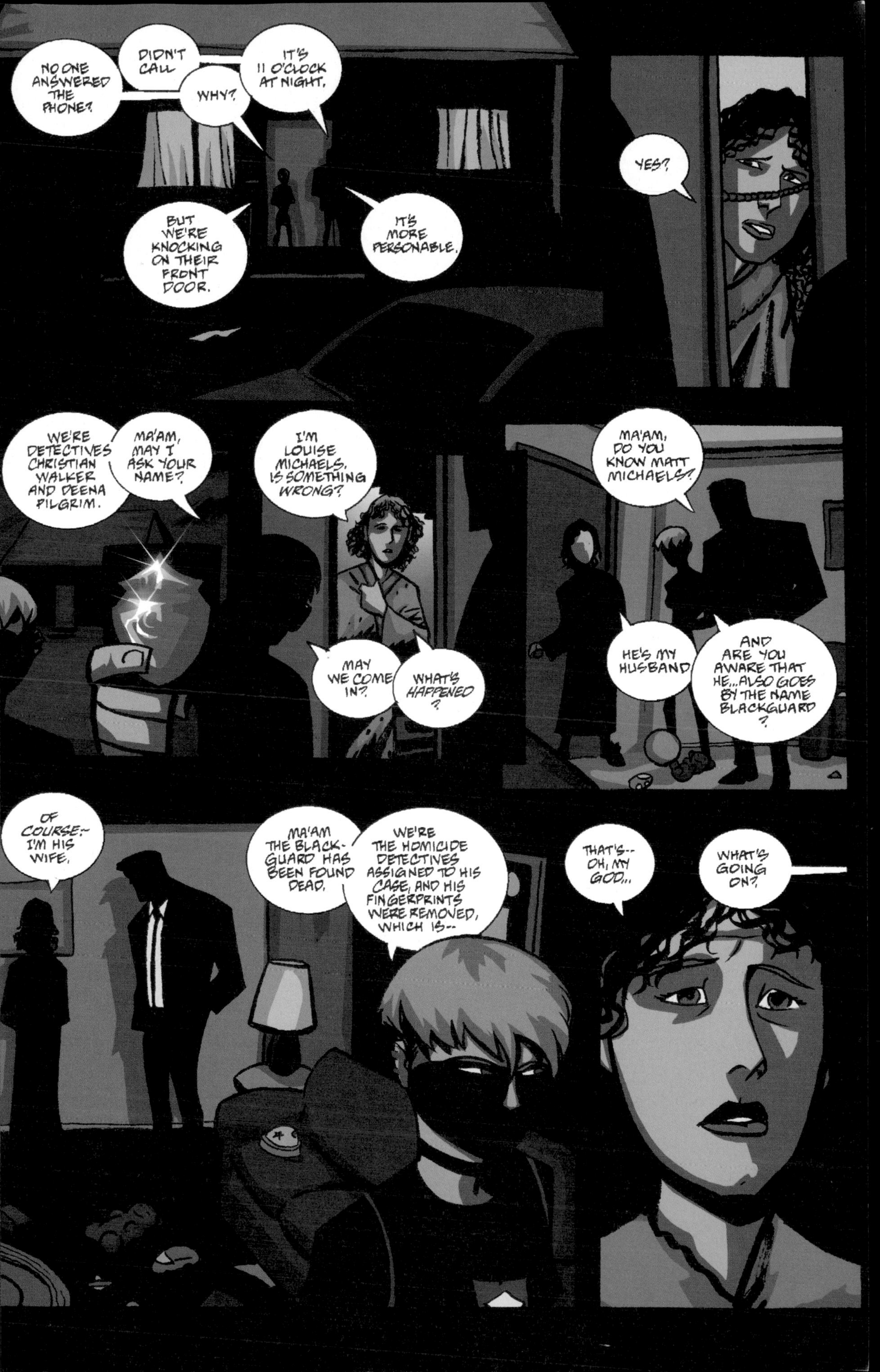
NO ONE ANSWERED THE PHONE?
DIDN'T CALL
WHY?
IT'S 11 O'CLOCK AT NIGHT.
BUT WE'RE KNOCKING ON THEIR FRONT DOOR.
IT'S MORE PERSONABLE.
YES?
WE'RE DETECTIVES CHRISTIAN WALKER AND DEENA PILGRIM.
MA'AM, MAY I ASK YOUR NAME?
I'M LOUISE MICHAELS. IS SOMETHING WRONG?
MAY WE COME IN?
WHAT'S HAPPENED?
MA'AM, DO YOU KNOW MATT MICHAELS?
HE'S MY HUSBAND
AND ARE YOU AWARE THAT HE...ALSO GOES BY THE NAME BLACKGUARD?
OF COURSE:-- I'M HIS WIFE.
MA'AM THE BLACK-GUARD HAS BEEN FOUND DEAD.
WE'RE THE HOMICIDE DETECTIVES ASSIGNED TO HIS CASE, AND HIS FINGERPRINTS WERE REMOVED, WHICH IS--
THAT'S-- OH, MY GOD...
WHAT'S GOING ON?

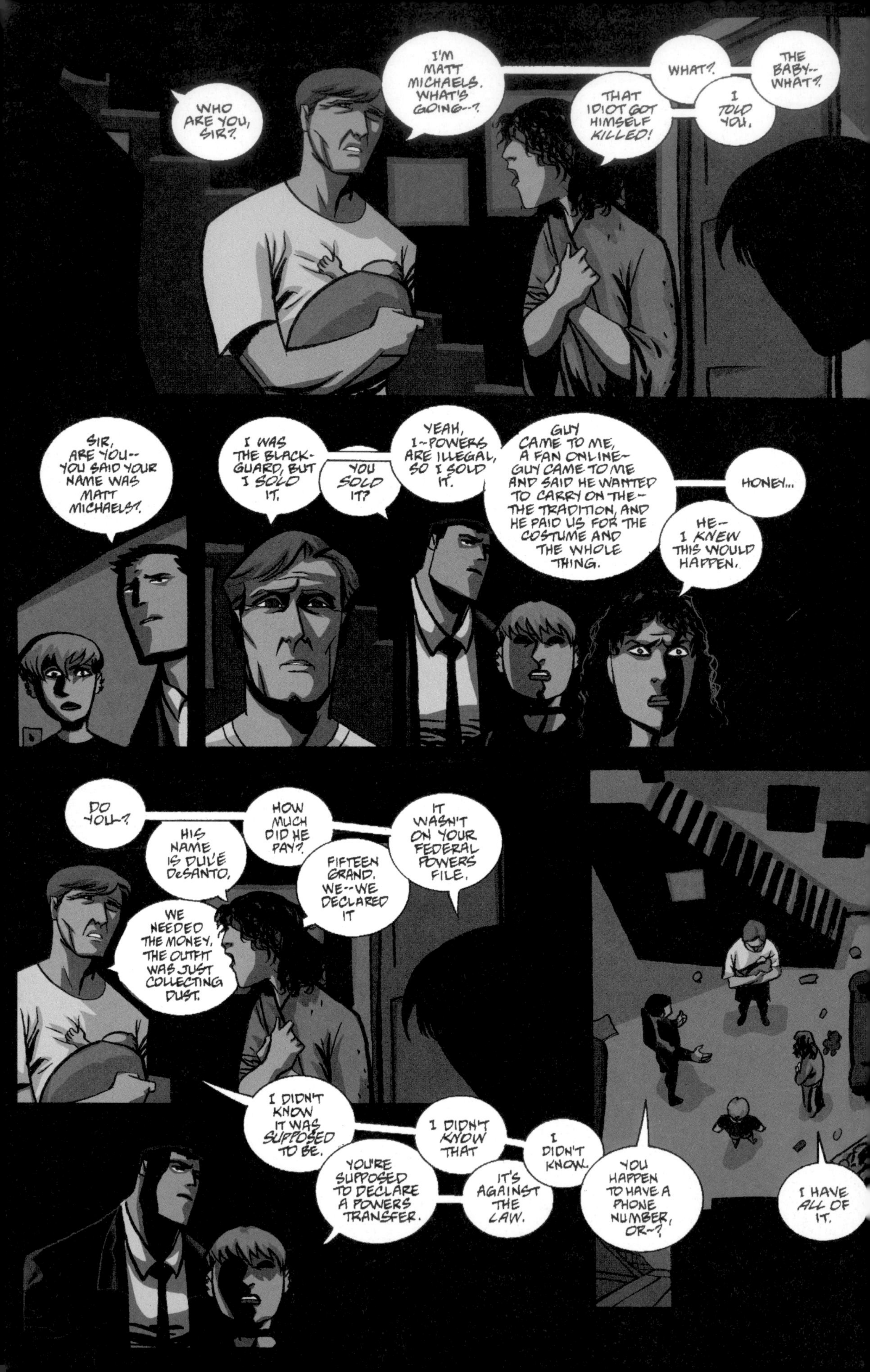
WHO ARE YOU, SIR?
I'M MATT MICHAELS. WHAT'S GOING--?
WHAT?
THAT IDIOT GOT HIMSELF KILLED!
THE BABY-- WHAT?
I TOLD YOU.
SIR, ARE YOU-- YOU SAID YOUR NAME WAS MATT MICHAELS?
I WAS THE BLACK-GUARD, BUT I SOLD IT.
YOU SOLD IT?
YEAH, I--POWERS ARE ILLEGAL, SO I SOLD IT.
GUY CAME TO ME, A FAN ONLINE-- GUY CAME TO ME AND SAID HE WANTED TO CARRY ON THE-- THE TRADITION, AND HE PAID US FOR THE COSTUME AND THE WHOLE THING.
HONEY...
HE-- I KNEW THIS WOULD HAPPEN.
DO YOU--?
HIS NAME IS DULÉ DeSANTO.
HOW MUCH DID HE PAY?
FIFTEEN GRAND. WE--WE DECLARED IT
IT WASN'T ON YOUR FEDERAL POWERS FILE.
WE NEEDED THE MONEY. THE OUTFIT WAS JUST COLLECTING DUST.
I DIDN'T KNOW IT WAS SUPPOSED TO BE.
YOU'RE SUPPOSED TO DECLARE A POWERS TRANSFER.
I DIDN'T KNOW THAT
IT'S AGAINST THE LAW.
I DIDN'T KNOW.
YOU HAPPEN TO HAVE A PHONE NUMBER, OR--?
I HAVE ALL OF IT.

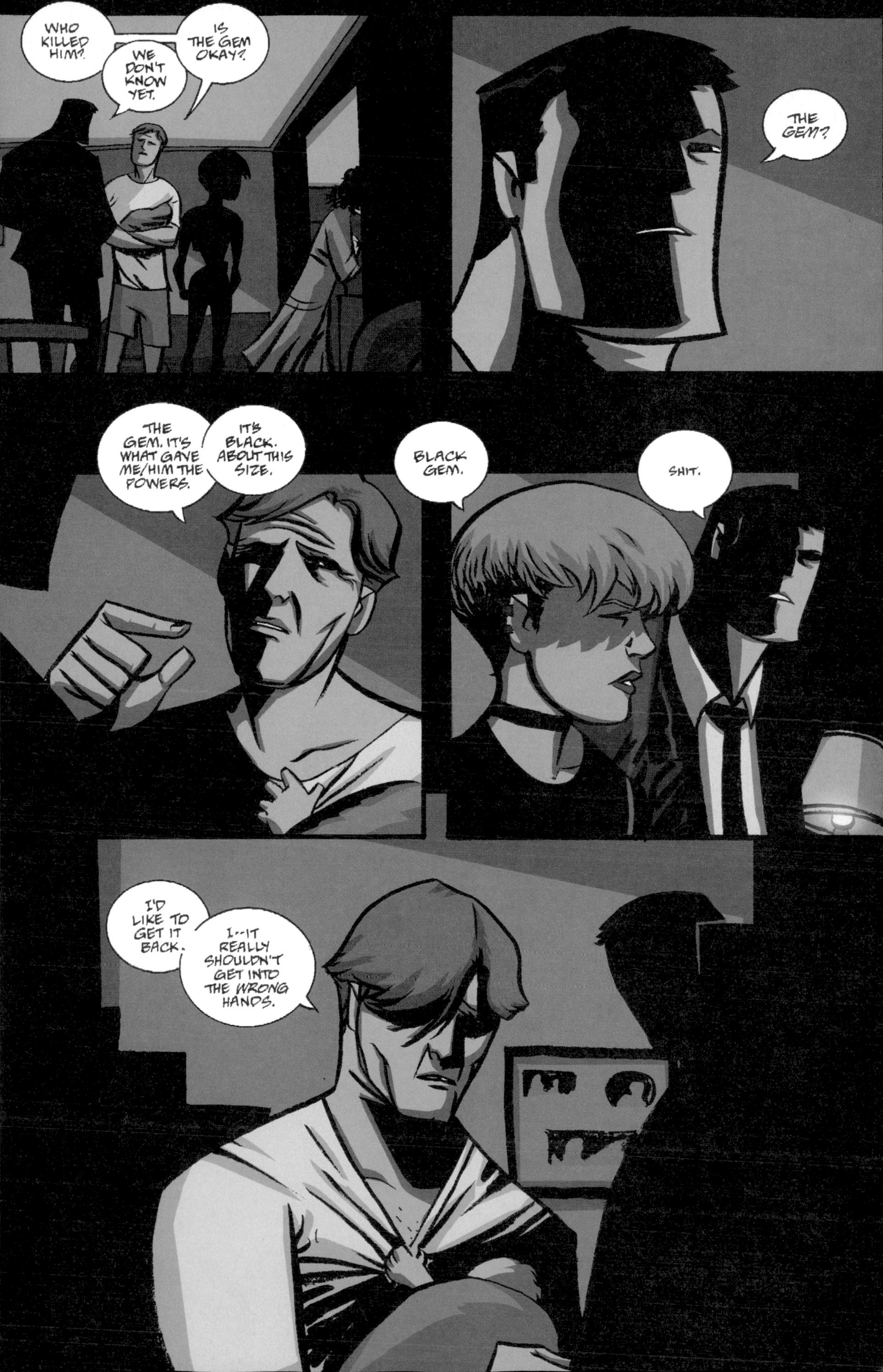
WHO KILLED HIM?
WE DON'T KNOW YET.
IS THE GEM OKAY?
THE GEM?
THE GEM. IT'S WHAT GAVE ME/HIM THE POWERS.
IT'S BLACK. ABOUT THIS SIZE.
BLACK GEM.
SHIT.
I'D LIKE TO GET IT BACK.
I--IT REALLY SHOULDN'T GET INTO THE WRONG HANDS.

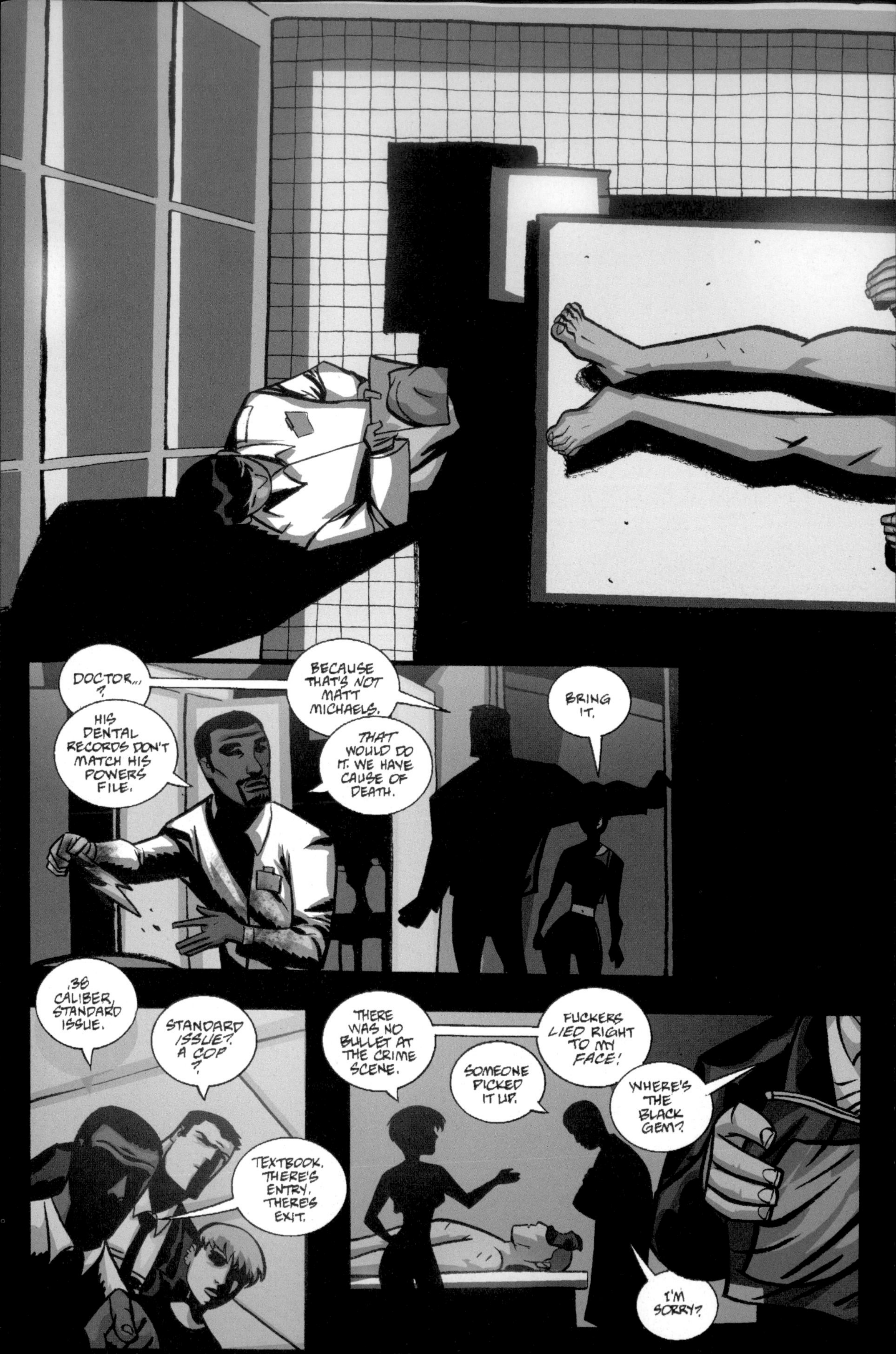
DOCTOR... ?
HIS DENTAL RECORDS DON'T MATCH HIS POWERS FILE.
BECAUSE THAT'S NOT MATT MICHAELS.
THAT WOULD DO IT. WE HAVE CAUSE OF DEATH.
BRING IT.
.38 CALIBER, STANDARD ISSUE.
STANDARD ISSUE? A COP ?
TEXTBOOK. THERE'S ENTRY, THERE'S EXIT.
THERE WAS NO BULLET AT THE CRIME SCENE.
FUCKERS LIED RIGHT TO MY FACE!
SOMEONE PICKED IT UP.
WHERE'S THE BLACK GEM?
I'M SORRY?

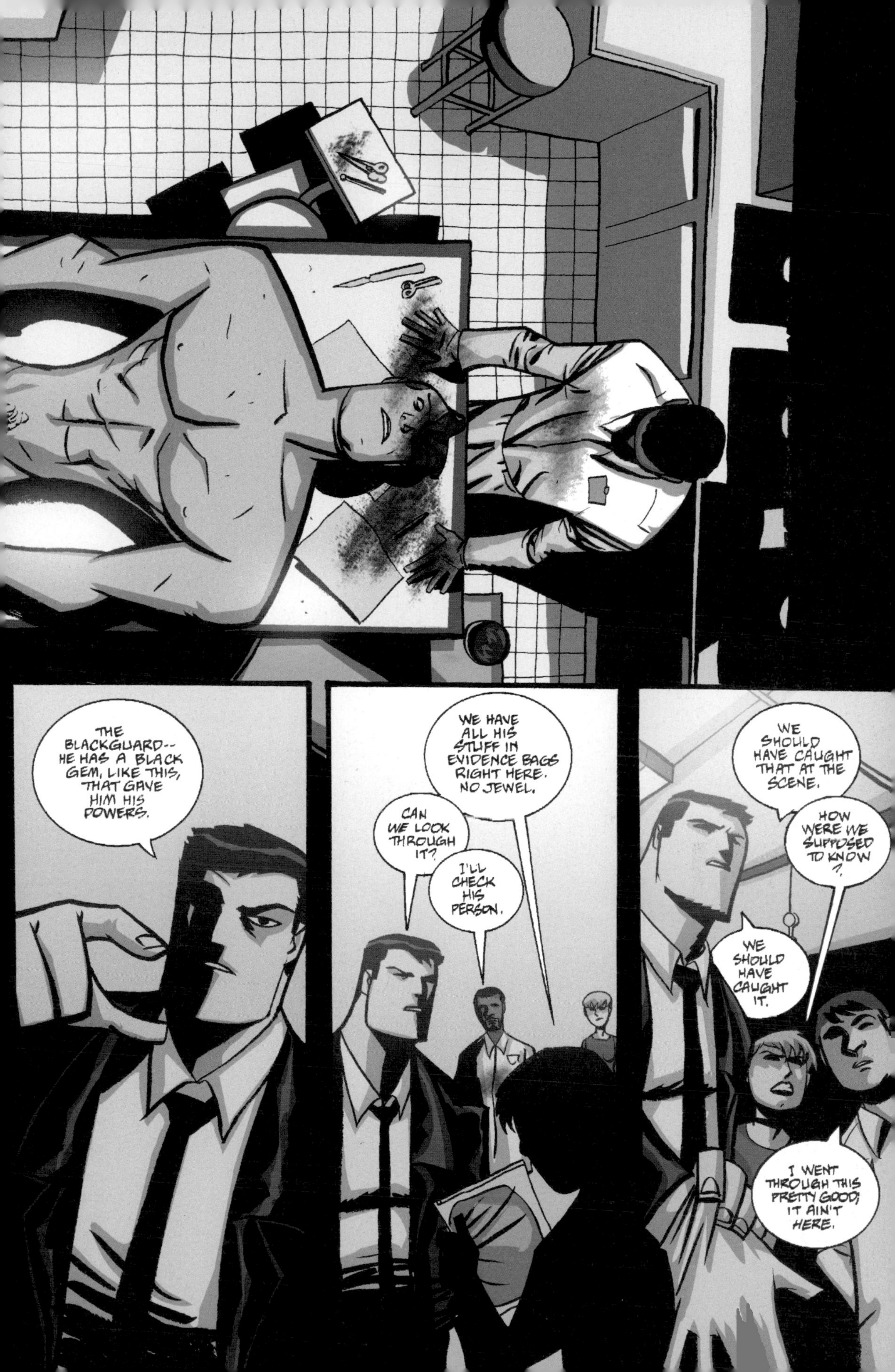
THE BLACKGUARD-- HE HAS A BLACK GEM, LIKE THIS, THAT GAVE HIM HIS POWERS.
WE HAVE ALL HIS STUFF IN EVIDENCE BAGS RIGHT HERE. NO JEWEL.
CAN WE LOOK THROUGH IT?
I'LL CHECK HIS PERSON.
WE SHOULD HAVE CAUGHT THAT AT THE SCENE.
HOW WERE WE SUPPOSED TO KNOW?
WE SHOULD HAVE CAUGHT IT.
I WENT THROUGH THIS PRETTY GOOD; IT AIN'T HERE.

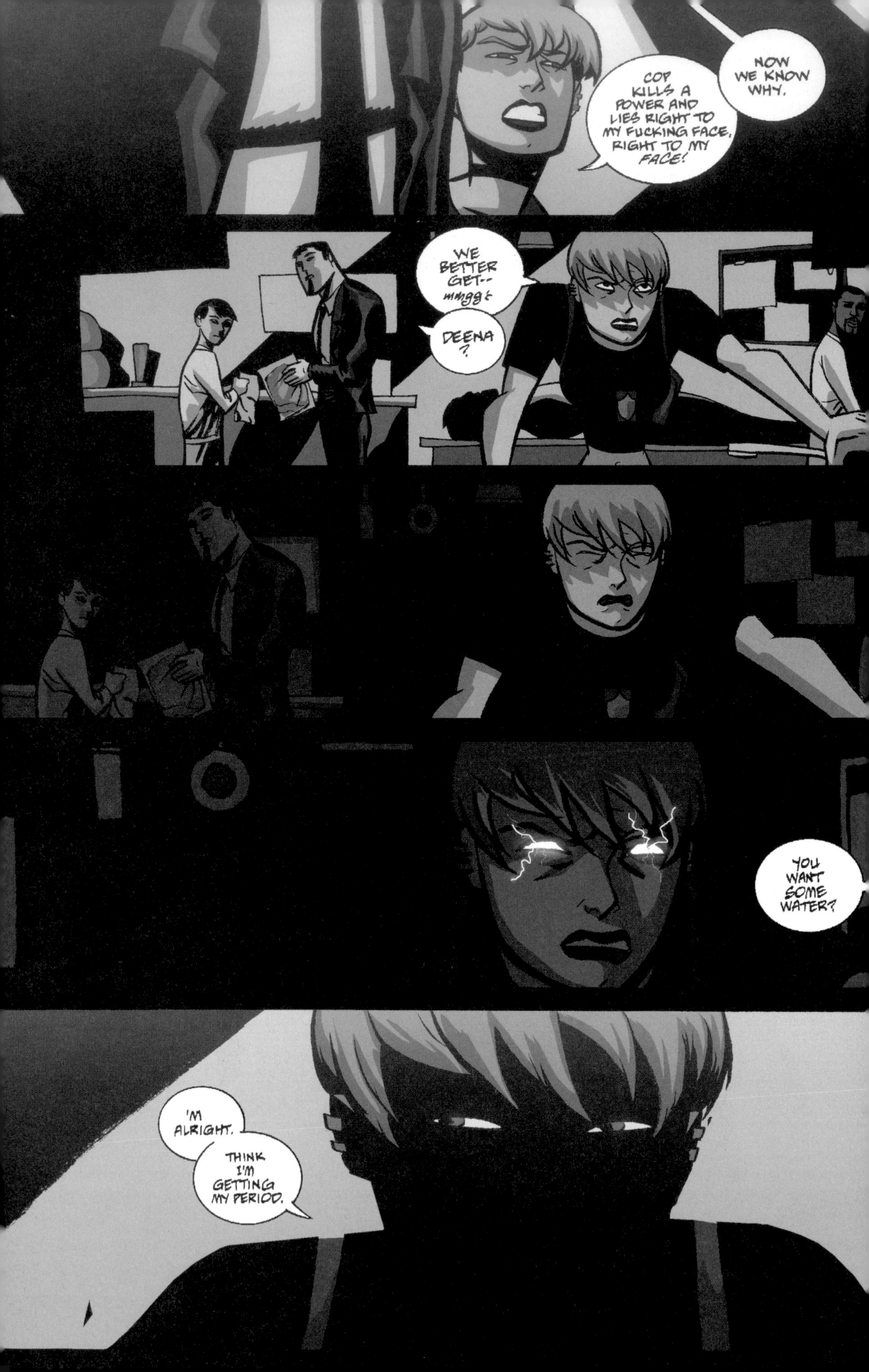
COP KILLS A POWER AND LIES RIGHT TO MY FUCKING FACE. RIGHT TO MY FACE!
NOW WE KNOW WHY.
WE BETTER GET-- mmgg:
DEENA?
YOU WANT SOME WATER?
'M ALRIGHT.
THINK I'M GETTING MY PERIOD.

IBrowseBMB (1)    Index

Address: http://www.powersforever.org/members/forum6969.htm    Go

# POWERS ONLINE

- POWERS NEWS
- PHOTOS
- VIDEOS
- MEMBERS
- NEWSLETTER
- MESSAGEBOARD
- INTERVIEWS
- FAN FICTION
- SEWING TIPS
- RECIPES
- STORE
- LINKS
- PERSONALS
- FAN CLUB
- CONTACT

## 217666
#ofthebeast.com

site design by
MonsterToolDiddy

---

**POWERS COMICS COMMUNITY**

# BLACKGUARD IS DEAD

Go to Page 1 2 3 4 5 Next                    Previous topic :: Next topic

| Author | Message |
|---|---|
| **Agent Desmond** <br> Joined: 11 Aug 2005 <br> Posts: 11965 <br> Location: Ess Ee Ay Tee Tee Ell Ee <br> Posted: Wed Jul 28, 2005 5:41 am <br><br> Back to top | Posted: Jul 28, 2005 5:41 am    Subject: Blackguard is Dead <br><br> by Frank D'armata (07/27/2005) RUETERS -- <br><br> A man wearing the infamous costume of the legendary vigilante BLACKGUARD was found dead from a wound to the head in an apartment stairwell on the east side of the city. <br><br> Police were called to a city apartment building by resident Mahalla Johnson, 66. Johnson reported that she witnessed a rooftop fist-fight between The Blackguard and the criminal known as THE JOKE. Another resident, also witnessed the fight but did not see the actual shooting. <br><br> The Blackguard was found in the apartment stairway with a head wound, possibly caused by a bullet discharged when the two grappled. He was declared dead on the scene. A police spokesman quoted neighbors as saying that they had seen The Blackguard around the neighborhood all month- ever since other known heroes had publicly broken the federal law banning powers. <br><br> The identity of The Blackguard is a public secret as the case is still under investigation. The Joke made his first appearance in the 1950's. It is not known if this is the same person donning the identify currently. <br><br> Homicide detectives were not available for comment. |
| **THWIP!** <br> Addict <br> Joined: 12 Dec 2003 <br> Posts: 6408 <br> Location: Hogwarts School of Witchcraft and Wizardry <br><br> Back to top | Posted: Jul 28, 2005 6:19 am    Subject: Re: Blackguard is Dead <br><br> I don't get it. Is he really dead? <br><br>  |
| **JonnyZ** <br> Addict <br> Joined: 11 Aug 2003 <br> Posts: 8343 <br> Location: Long Island, New York <br><br> Back to top | Posted: Jul 28, 2004 6:19 am    Subject: Re: Blackguard is Dead <br><br> **THWIP! Wrote:** <br> I don't get it. Is he really dead? <br><br> Well, a gun shot to the face tends to do that, ass! |
| **RangerChic** <br> Veteran <br> Joined: 12 Aug 2003 <br> Posts: 3525 <br> Location: FL, USA <br><br> Back to top | Posted: Jul 28, 2005 6:24 am    Subject: Re: Blackguard is Dead <br><br> I'm confused. Who? <br> RC <br><br> :-) |
| **Matt Higgins** <br> Enthusiast <br> Joined: 28 Jun 2004 Posts: 597 <br> Location: Asteroid | Posted: Jul 28, 2004 6:40 am    Subject: Re: Blackguard is Dead <br><br> AW, THIS SUCKS DONKEY ASS! <br> THE BLACKGUARD RULED!! FUCK!  ●●●●● |

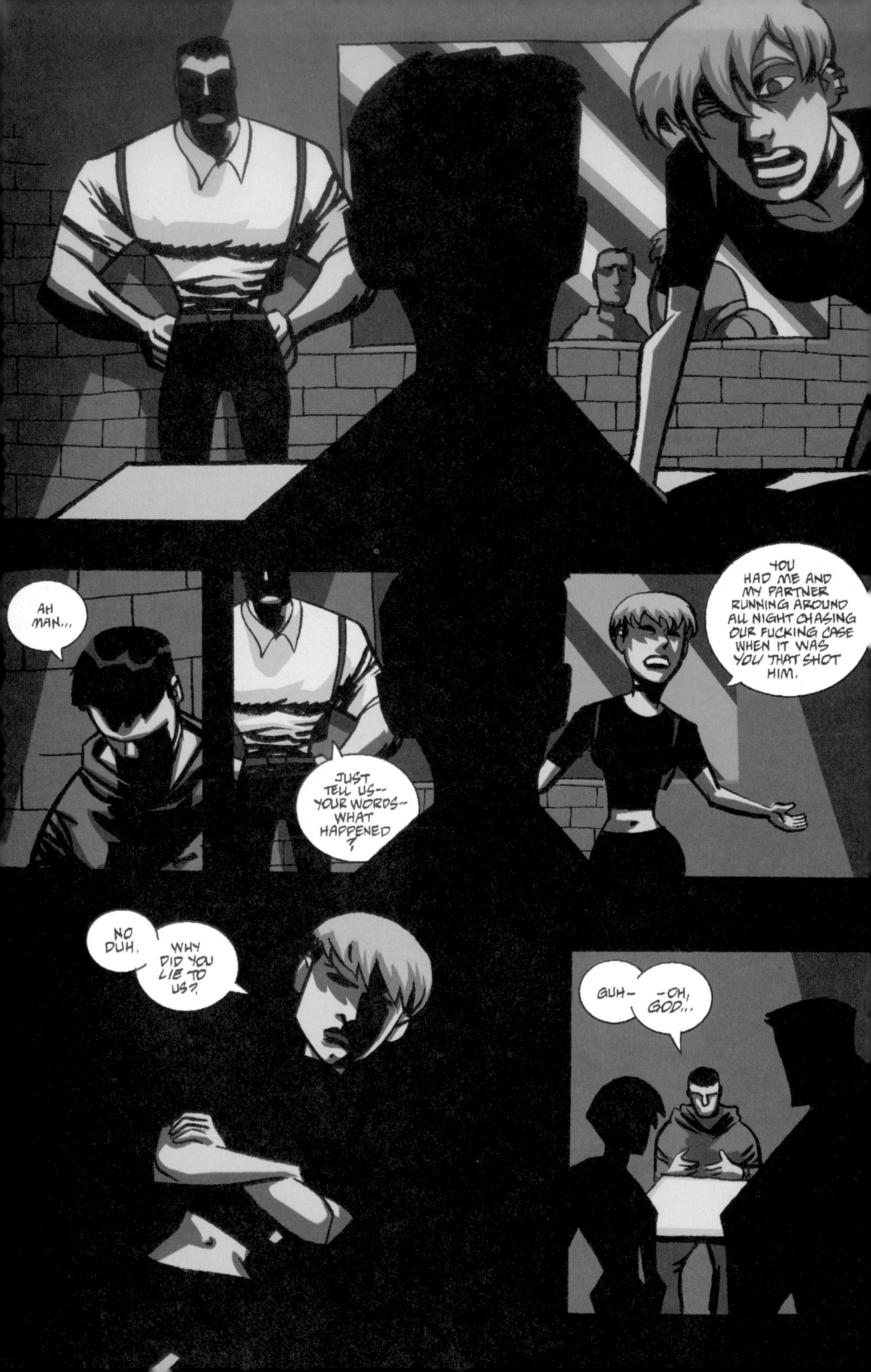
AH MAN...
JUST TELL US-- YOUR WORDS-- WHAT HAPPENED?
YOU HAD ME AND MY PARTNER RUNNING AROUND ALL NIGHT CHASING OUR FUCKING CASE WHEN IT WAS YOU THAT SHOT HIM.
NO DUH.
WHY DID YOU LIE TO US?
GUH--
--OH, GOD...

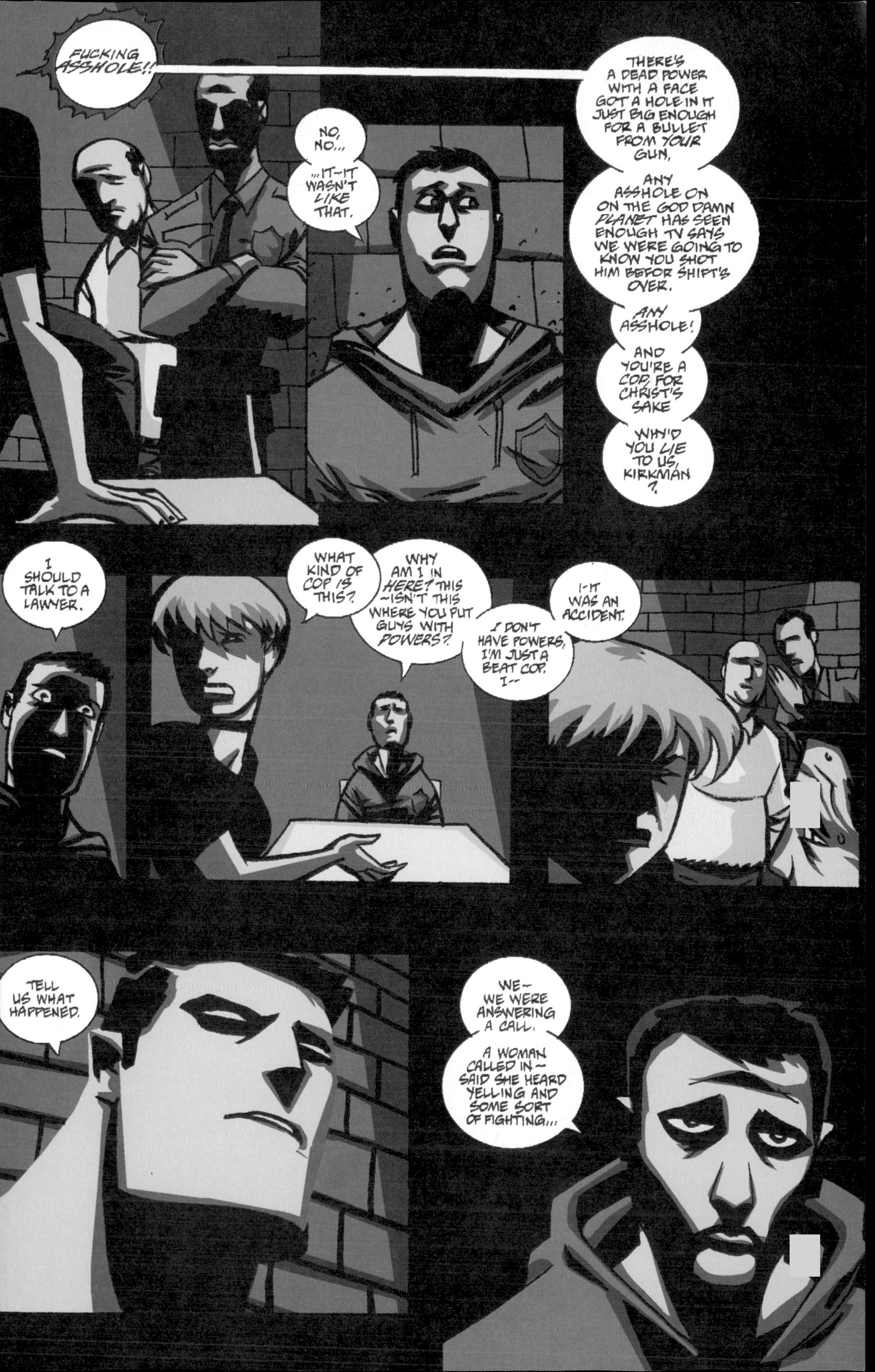
FUCKING ASSHOLE!!
THERE'S A DEAD POWER WITH A FACE GOT A HOLE IN IT JUST BIG ENOUGH FOR A BULLET FROM YOUR GUN.
ANY ASSHOLE ON ON THE GOD DAMN PLANET HAS SEEN ENOUGH TV SAYS WE WERE GOING TO KNOW YOU SHOT HIM BEFOR SHIFT'S OVER.
ANY ASSHOLE!
AND YOU'RE A COP, FOR CHRIST'S SAKE
WHY'D YOU LIE TO US, KIRKMAN ?
NO, NO...
...IT-IT WASN'T LIKE THAT.
I SHOULD TALK TO A LAWYER.
WHAT KIND OF COP IS THIS?
WHY AM I IN HERE? THIS --ISN'T THIS WHERE YOU PUT GUYS WITH POWERS?
I DON'T HAVE POWERS, I'M JUST A BEAT COP. I--
I-IT WAS AN ACCIDENT.
TELL US WHAT HAPPENED.
WE-- WE WERE ANSWERING A CALL.
A WOMAN CALLED IN-- SAID SHE HEARD YELLING AND SOME SORT OF FIGHTING...

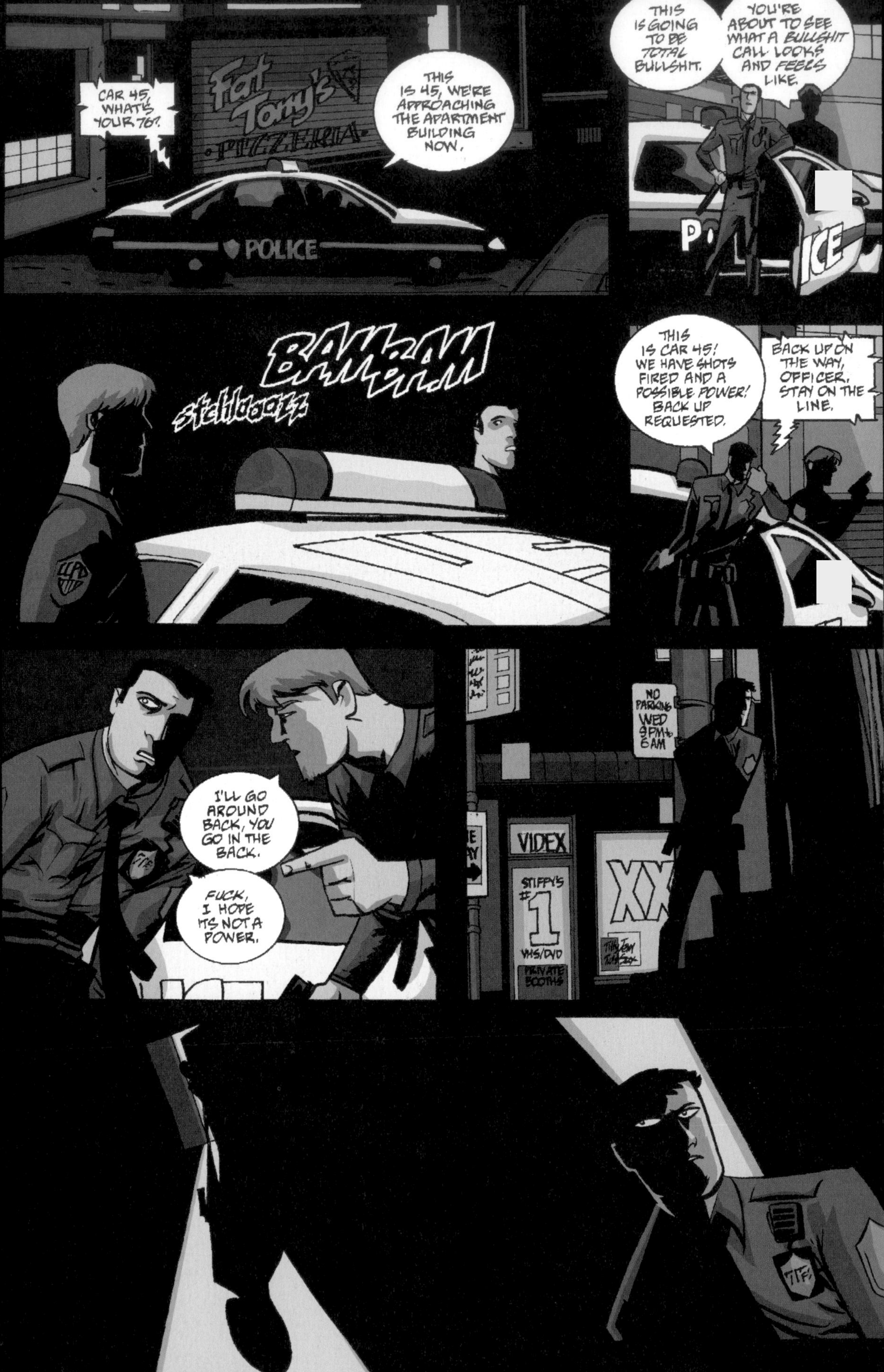
CAR 45, WHAT'S YOUR 76?
THIS IS 45, WE'RE APPROACHING THE APARTMENT BUILDING NOW.
Fat Tony's PIZZERIA
POLICE
THIS IS GOING TO BE TOTAL BULLSHIT.
YOU'RE ABOUT TO SEE WHAT A BULLSHIT CALL LOOKS AND FEELS LIKE.
BAM BAM
THIS IS CAR 45! WE HAVE SHOTS FIRED AND A POSSIBLE POWER! BACK UP REQUESTED.
BACK UP ON THE WAY, OFFICER. STAY ON THE LINE.
I'LL GO AROUND BACK, YOU GO IN THE BACK.
FUCK, I HOPE ITS NOT A POWER.
NO PARKING WED 9PM to 6AM
VIDEX
STIFFY'S #1 VHS/DVD PRIVATE BOOTHS

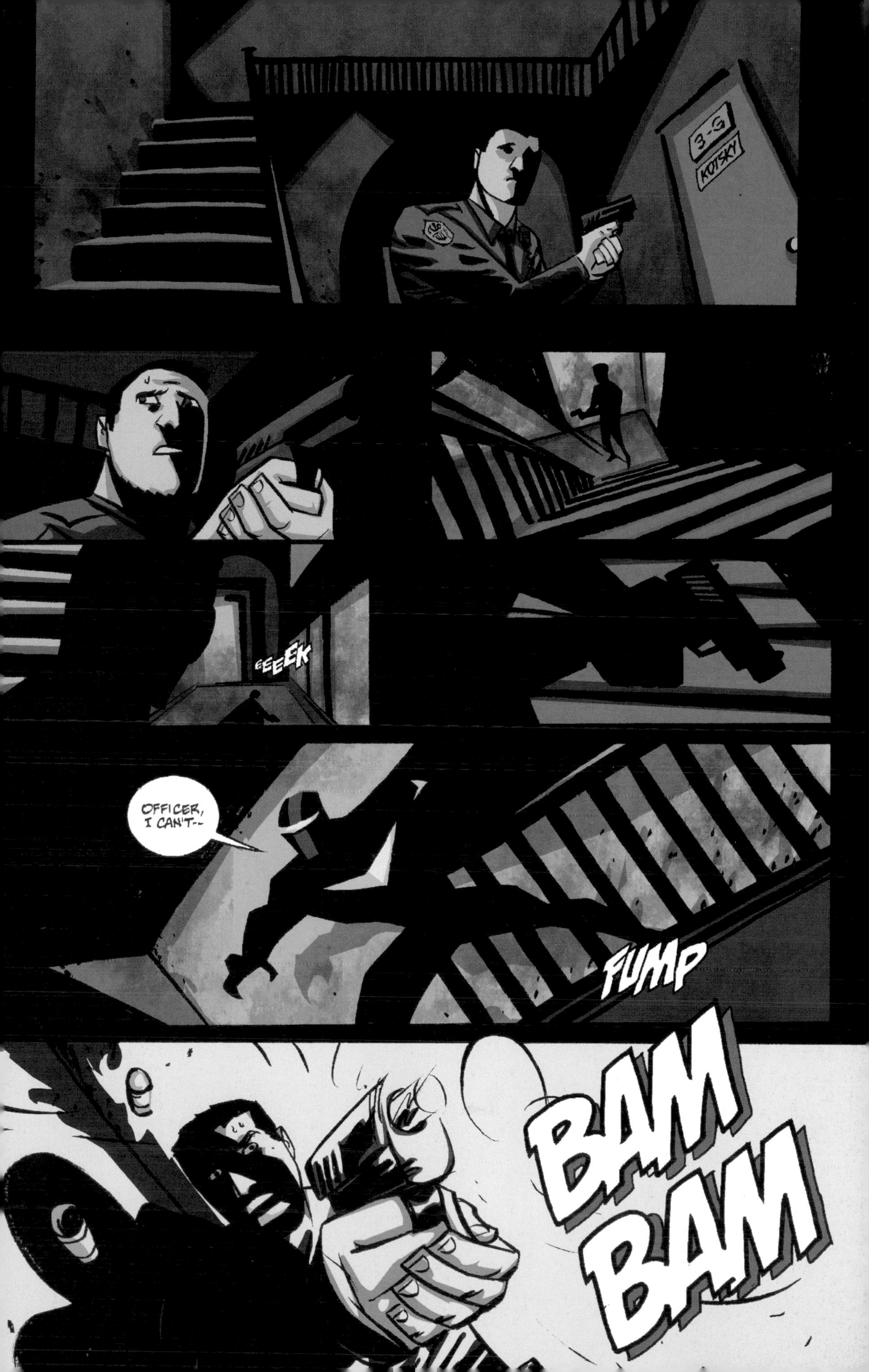
3-G
KOTSKY
EEEEK
OFFICER, I CAN'T--
FUMP
BAM
BAM

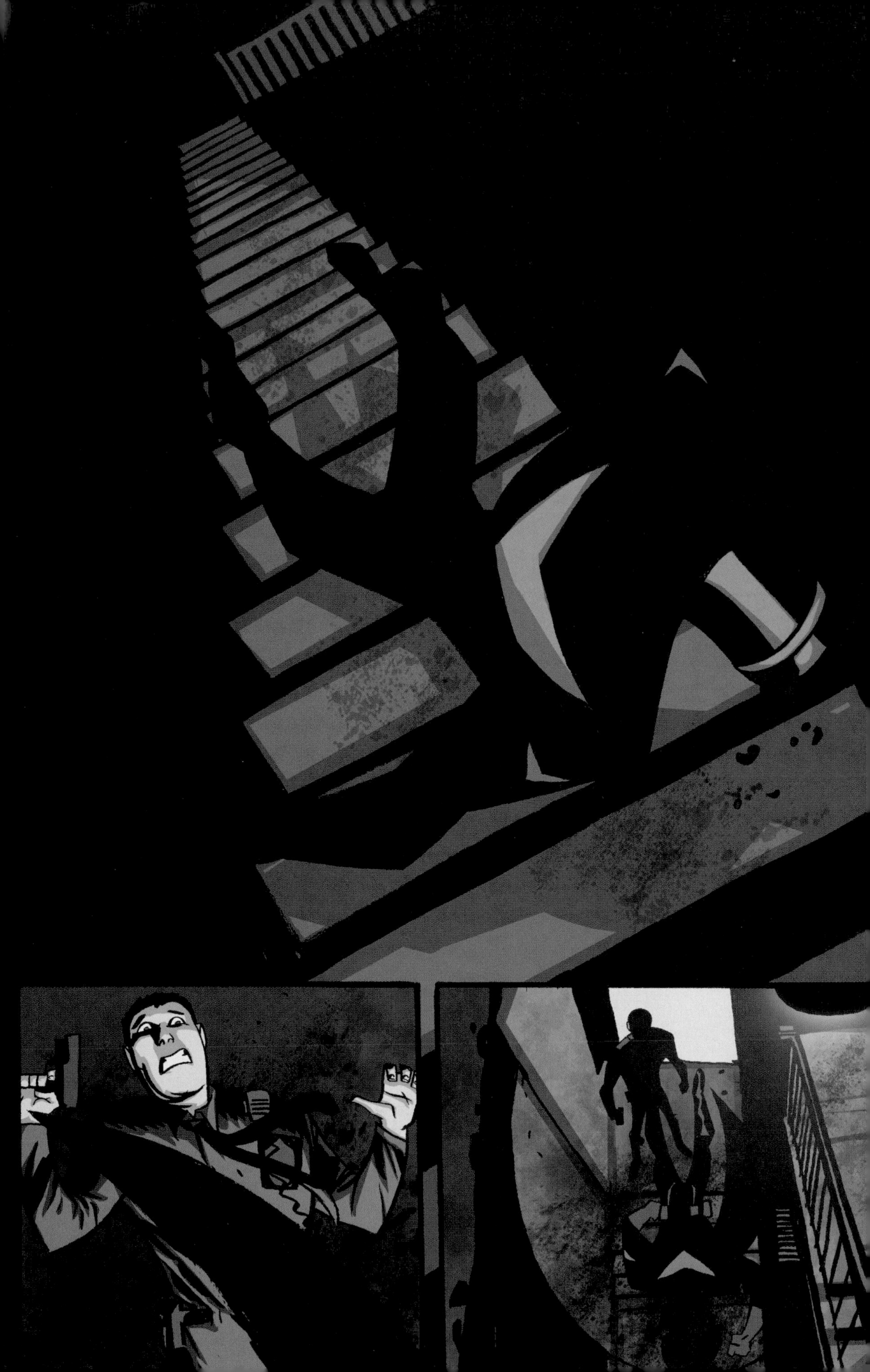

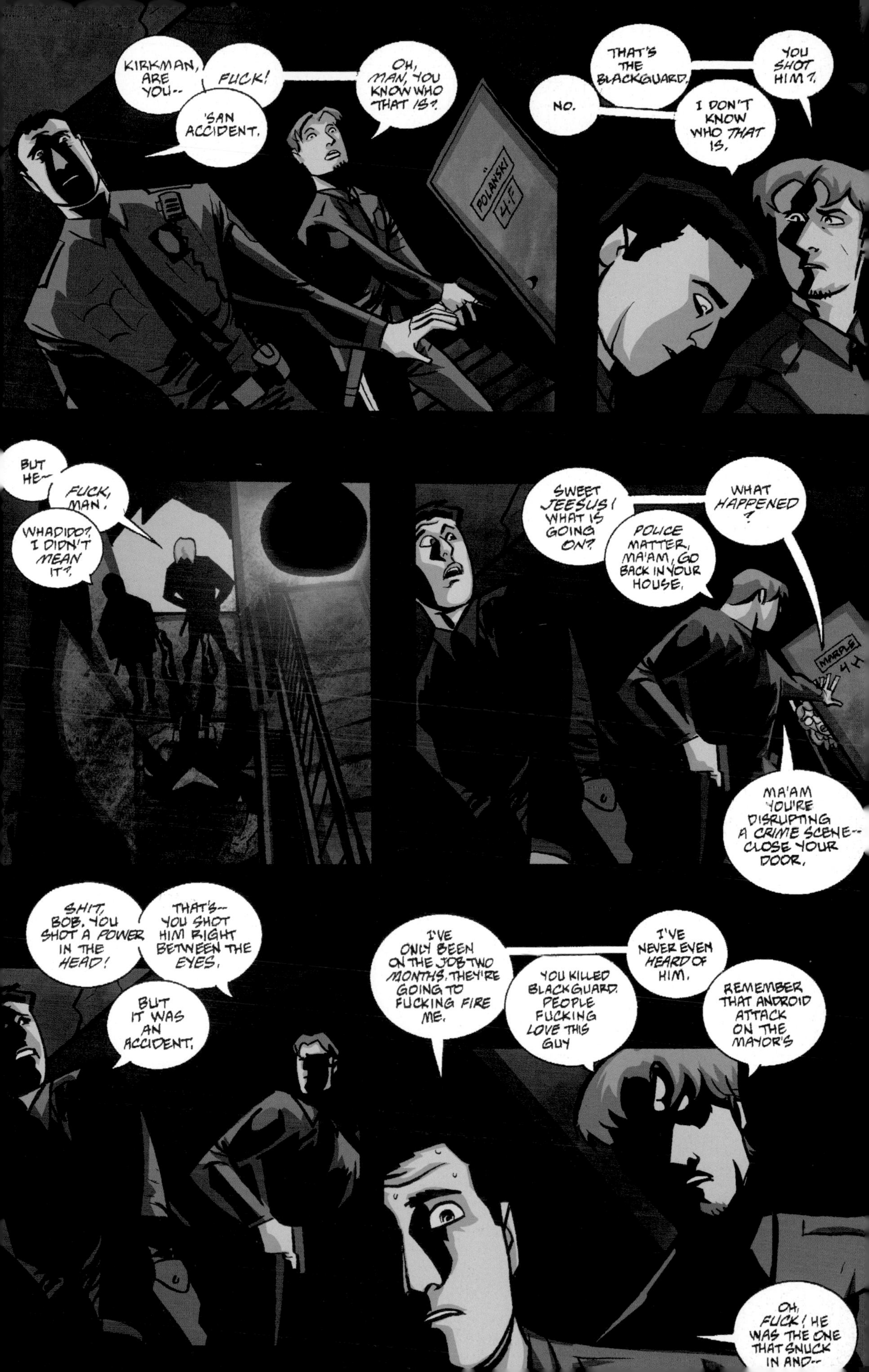
KIRKMAN, ARE YOU--
FUCK!
'SAN ACCIDENT.
OH, MAN, YOU KNOW WHO THAT IS?
POLANSKI 4-F
THAT'S THE BLACKGUARD.
YOU SHOT HIM?
NO.
I DON'T KNOW WHO THAT IS.
BUT HE--
FUCK, MAN.
WHADIDO? I DIDN'T MEAN IT?
SWEET JEESUS! WHAT IS GOING ON?
WHAT HAPPENED?
POLICE MATTER, MA'AM, GO BACK IN YOUR HOUSE.
MARPLE 4-H
MA'AM YOU'RE DISRUPTING A CRIME SCENE-- CLOSE YOUR DOOR.
SHIT, BOB. YOU SHOT A POWER IN THE HEAD!
THAT'S-- YOU SHOT HIM RIGHT BETWEEN THE EYES.
BUT IT WAS AN ACCIDENT.
I'VE ONLY BEEN ON THE JOB TWO MONTHS. THEY'RE GOING TO FUCKING FIRE ME.
I'VE NEVER EVEN HEARD OF HIM.
YOU KILLED BLACKGUARD. PEOPLE FUCKING LOVE THIS GUY
REMEMBER THAT ANDROID ATTACK ON THE MAYOR'S
OH, FUCK! HE WAS THE ONE THAT SNUCK IN AND--

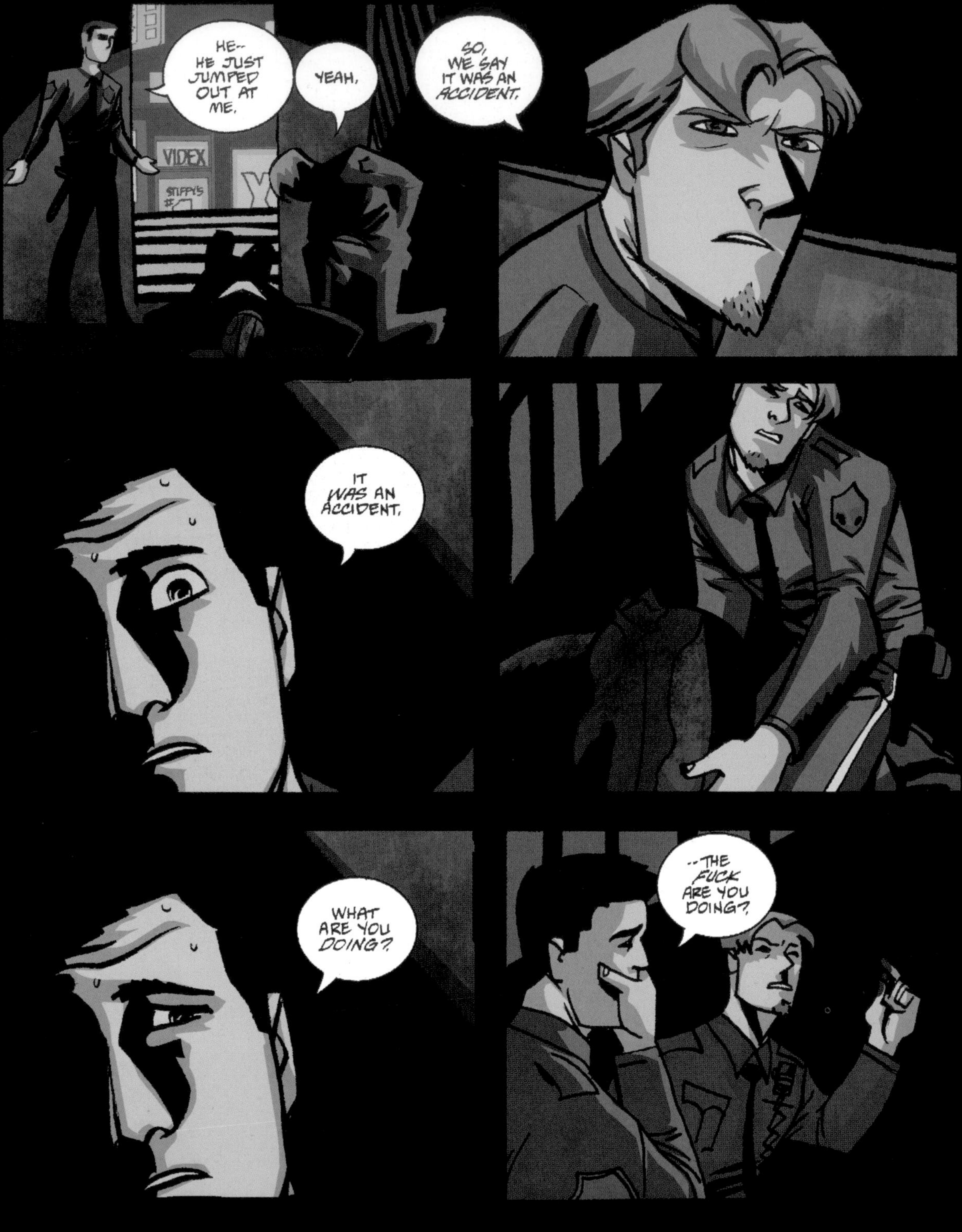
HE-- HE JUST JUMPED OUT AT ME.
YEAH.
SO, WE SAY IT WAS AN ACCIDENT.
VIDEX
STIFFY'S
IT WAS AN ACCIDENT.
WHAT ARE YOU DOING?
--THE FUCK ARE YOU DOING?

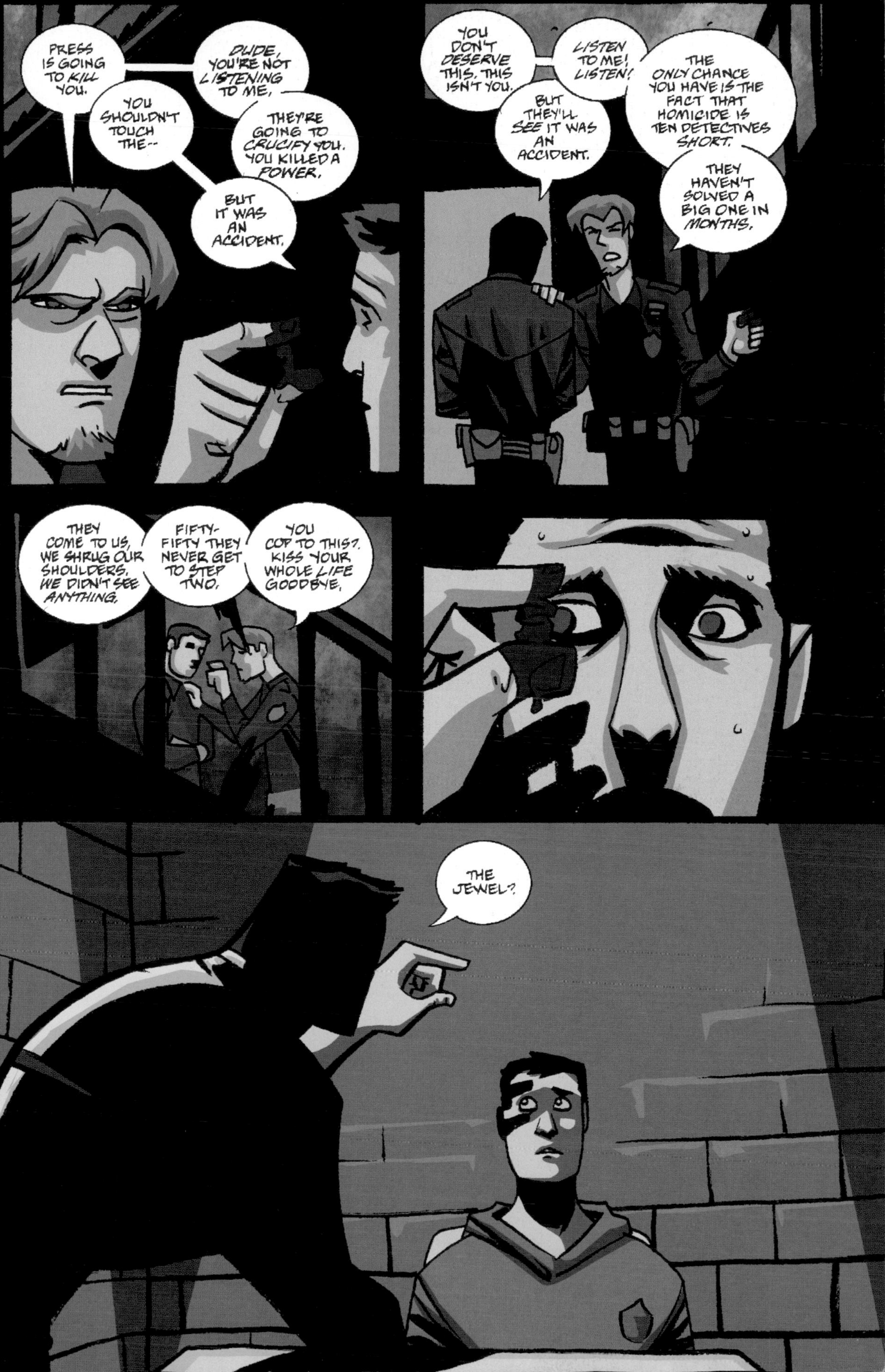
PRESS IS GOING TO KILL YOU.
DUDE, YOU'RE NOT LISTENING TO ME.
YOU SHOULDN'T TOUCH THE--
THEY'RE GOING TO CRUCIFY YOU. YOU KILLED A POWER.
BUT IT WAS AN ACCIDENT.
YOU DON'T DESERVE THIS. THIS ISN'T YOU.
LISTEN TO ME! LISTEN!
BUT THEY'LL SEE IT WAS AN ACCIDENT.
THE ONLY CHANCE YOU HAVE IS THE FACT THAT HOMICIDE IS TEN DETECTIVES SHORT.
THEY HAVEN'T SOLVED A BIG ONE IN MONTHS.
THEY COME TO US, WE SHRUG OUR SHOULDERS, WE DIDN'T SEE ANYTHING.
FIFTY-FIFTY THEY NEVER GET TO STEP TWO.
YOU COP TO THIS? KISS YOUR WHOLE LIFE GOODBYE.
THE JEWEL?

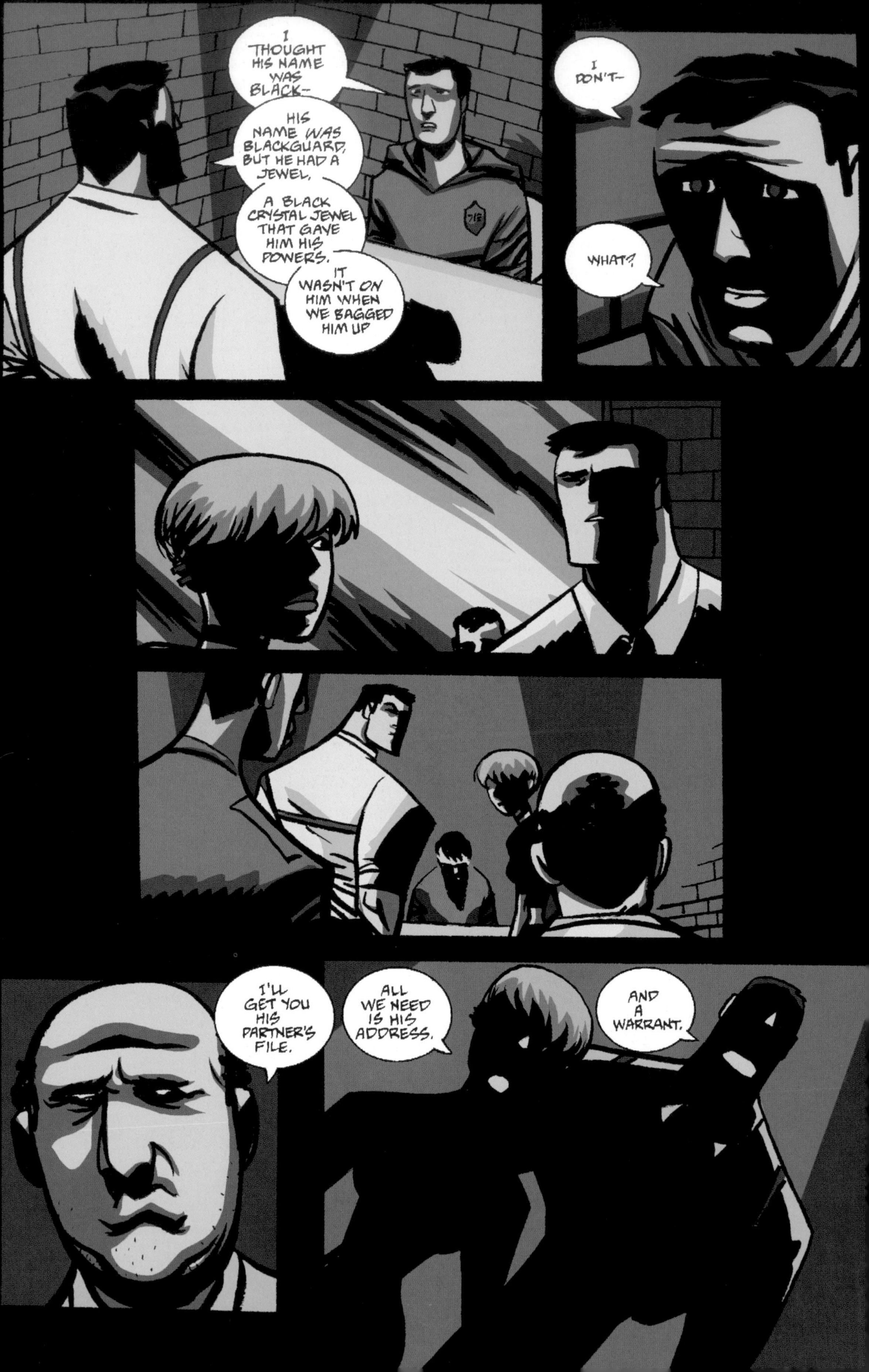
I THOUGHT HIS NAME WAS BLACK-
HIS NAME WAS BLACKGUARD, BUT HE HAD A JEWEL,
A BLACK CRYSTAL JEWEL THAT GAVE HIM HIS POWERS.
IT WASN'T ON HIM WHEN WE BAGGED HIM UP
I DON'T-
WHAT?
I'LL GET YOU HIS PARTNER'S FILE.
ALL WE NEED IS HIS ADDRESS.
AND A WARRANT.

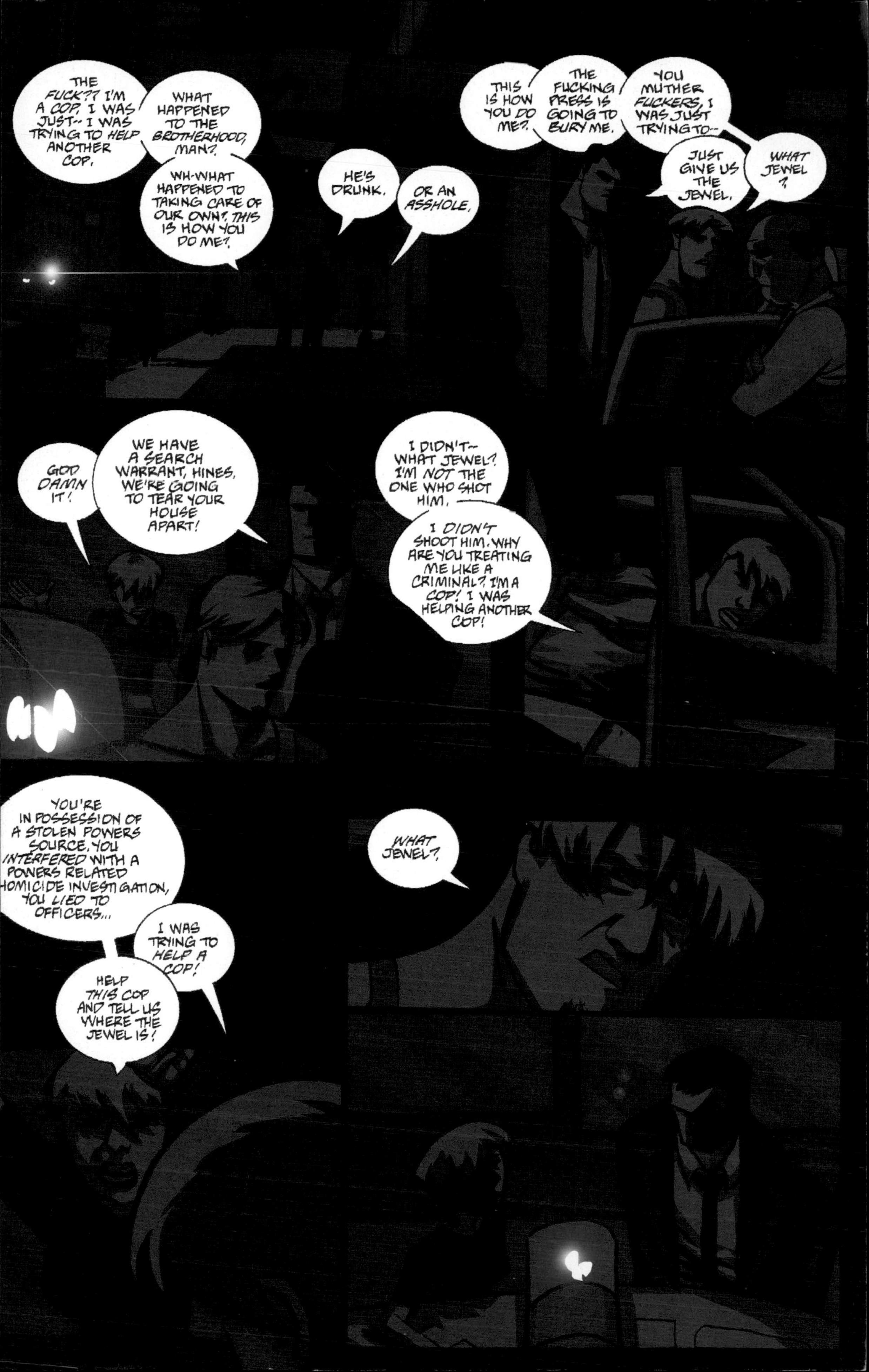
THE FUCK?? I'M A COP, I WAS JUST-- I WAS TRYING TO HELP ANOTHER COP.
WHAT HAPPENED TO THE BROTHERHOOD, MAN?
WH-WHAT HAPPENED TO TAKING CARE OF OUR OWN? THIS IS HOW YOU DO ME?
HE'S DRUNK.
OR AN ASSHOLE.
THIS IS HOW YOU DO ME?
THE FUCKING PRESS IS GOING TO BURY ME.
YOU MUTHER FUCKERS, I WAS JUST TRYING TO--
JUST GIVE US THE JEWEL.
WHAT JEWEL?
GOD DAMN IT!
WE HAVE A SEARCH WARRANT, HINES, WE'RE GOING TO TEAR YOUR HOUSE APART!
I DIDN'T-- WHAT JEWEL? I'M NOT THE ONE WHO SHOT HIM.
I DIDN'T SHOOT HIM. WHY ARE YOU TREATING ME LIKE A CRIMINAL? I'M A COP! I WAS HELPING ANOTHER COP!
YOU'RE IN POSSESSION OF A STOLEN POWERS SOURCE, YOU INTERFERED WITH A POWERS RELATED HOMICIDE INVESTIGATION, YOU LIED TO OFFICERS...
I WAS TRYING TO HELP A COP!
HELP THIS COP AND TELL US WHERE THE JEWEL IS!
WHAT JEWEL?

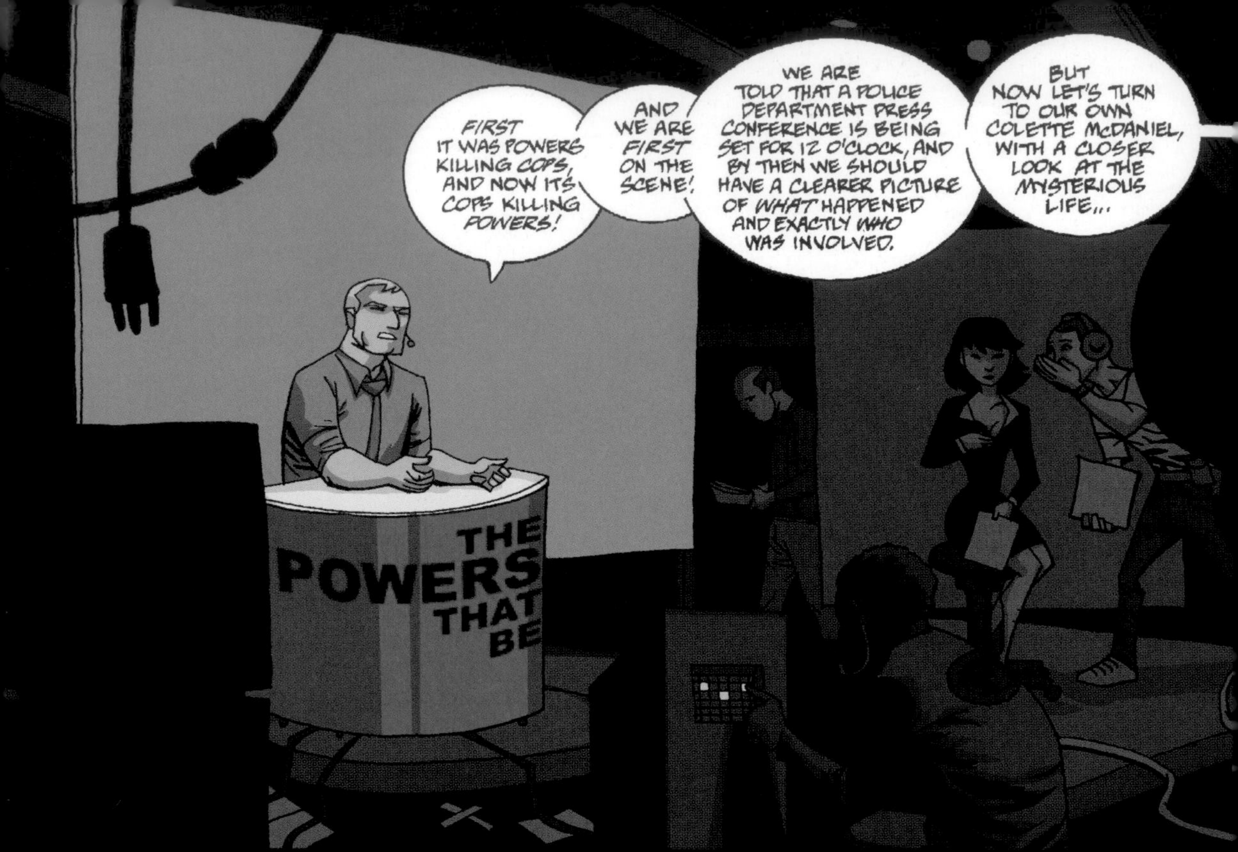
FIRST IT WAS POWERS KILLING COPS, AND NOW IT'S COPS KILLING POWERS!
AND WE ARE FIRST ON THE SCENE!
WE ARE TOLD THAT A POLICE DEPARTMENT PRESS CONFERENCE IS BEING SET FOR 12 O'CLOCK, AND BY THEN WE SHOULD HAVE A CLEARER PICTURE OF WHAT HAPPENED AND EXACTLY WHO WAS INVOLVED.
BUT NOW LET'S TURN TO OUR OWN COLETTE McDANIEL, WITH A CLOSER LOOK AT THE MYSTERIOUS LIFE...
THE POWERS THAT BE

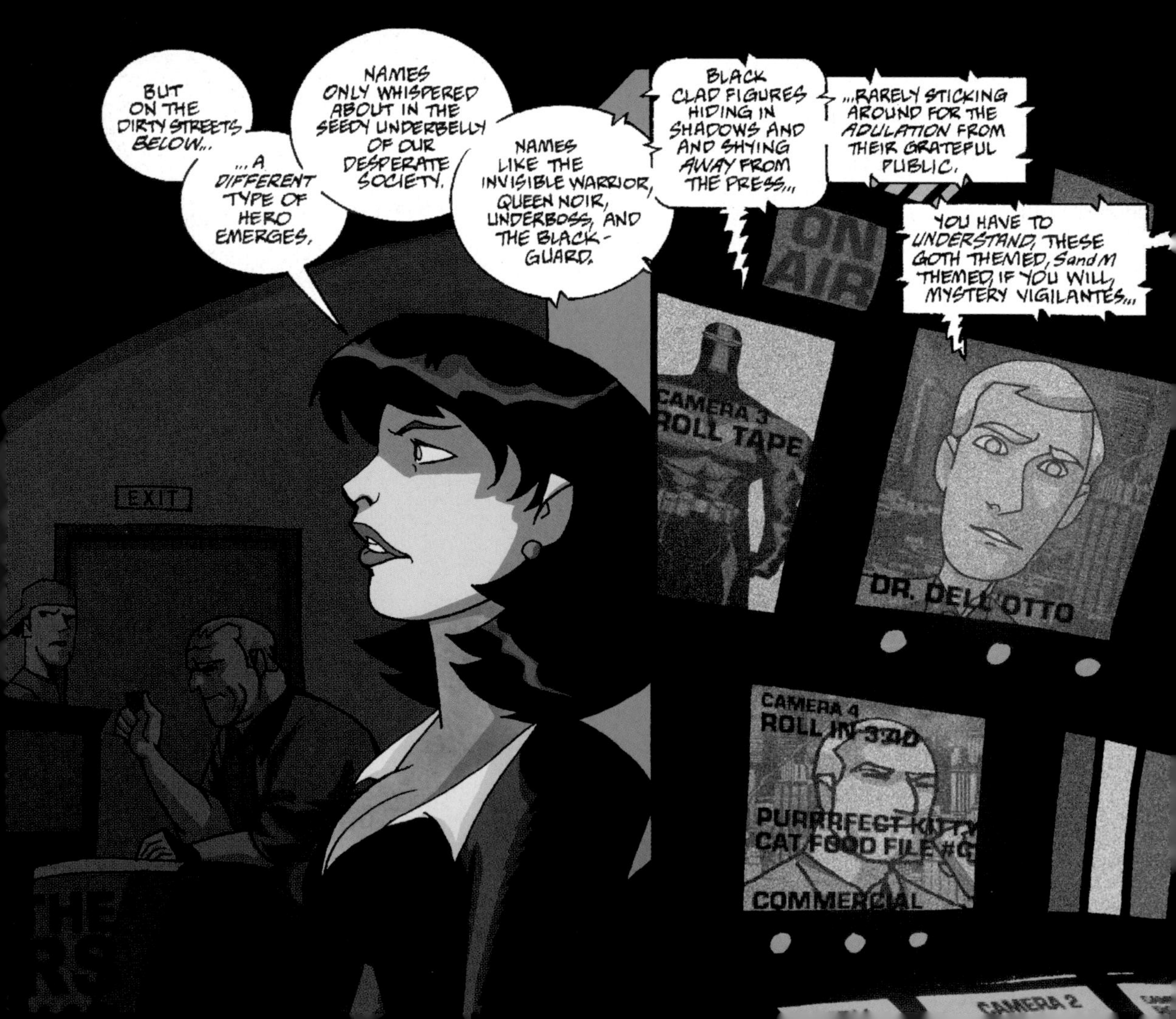
BUT ON THE DIRTY STREETS BELOW...
...A DIFFERENT TYPE OF HERO EMERGES.
NAMES ONLY WHISPERED ABOUT IN THE SEEDY UNDERBELLY OF OUR DESPERATE SOCIETY.
NAMES LIKE THE INVISIBLE WARRIOR, QUEEN NOIR, UNDERBOSS, AND THE BLACK-GUARD.
BLACK CLAD FIGURES HIDING IN SHADOWS AND AND SHYING AWAY FROM THE PRESS...
...RARELY STICKING AROUND FOR THE ADULATION FROM THEIR GRATEFUL PUBLIC.
YOU HAVE TO UNDERSTAND, THESE GOTH THEMED, S and M THEMED, IF YOU WILL, MYSTERY VIGILANTES...
ON AIR
CAMERA 3
ROLL TAPE
DR. DELL'OTTO
EXIT
COMMERCIAL
CAMERA 2

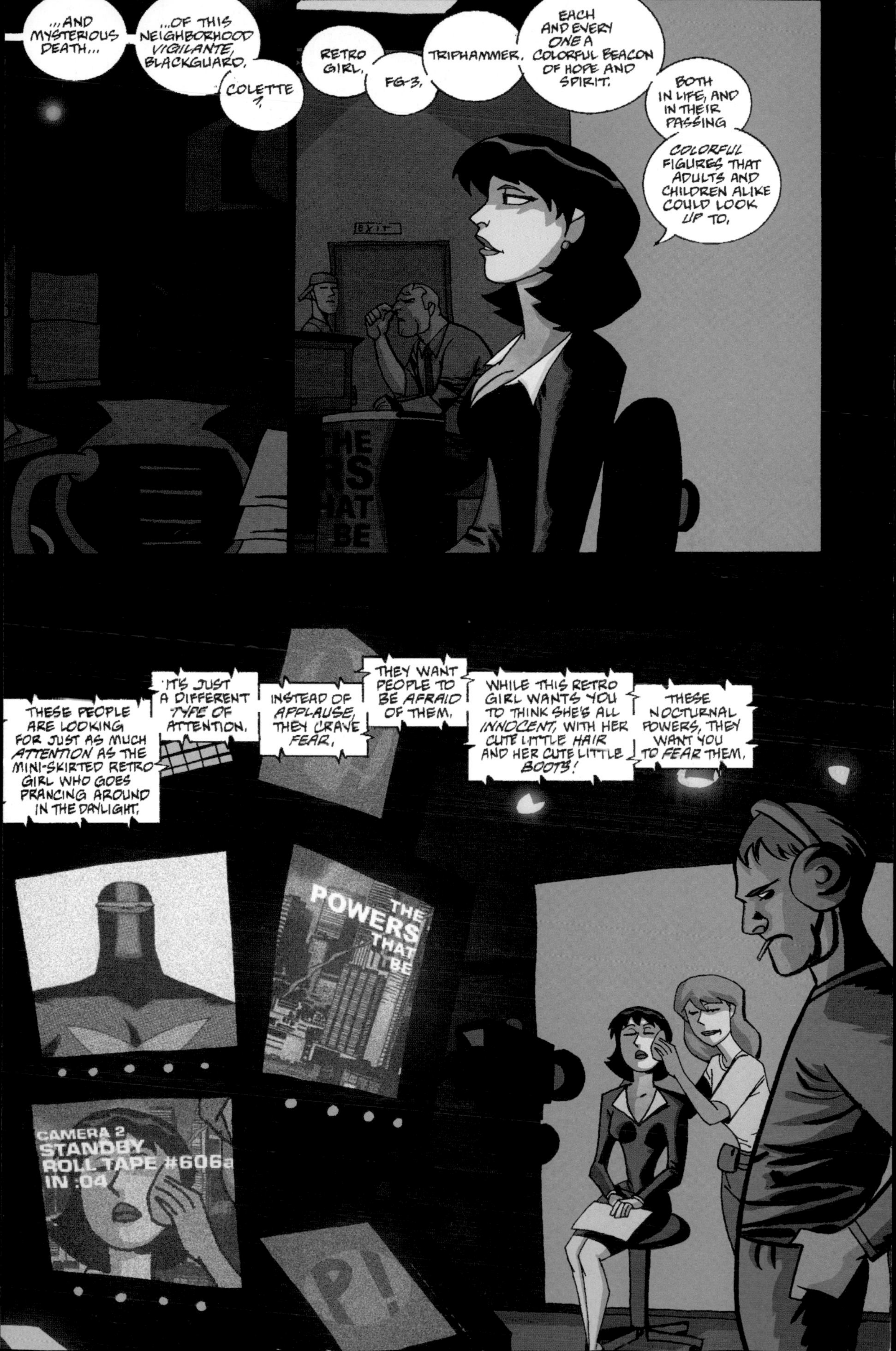
...AND MYSTERIOUS DEATH...
...OF THIS NEIGHBORHOOD *VIGILANTE*, BLACKGUARD,
COLETTE ?
RETRO GIRL,
FG-3,
TRIPHAMMER,
EACH AND EVERY *ONE* A COLORFUL BEACON OF HOPE AND SPIRIT.
BOTH IN LIFE, AND IN THEIR PASSING
*COLORFUL* FIGURES THAT ADULTS AND CHILDREN ALIKE COULD LOOK *UP* TO,
EXIT
THESE PEOPLE ARE LOOKING FOR JUST AS MUCH *ATTENTION* AS THE MINI-SKIRTED RETRO GIRL WHO GOES PRANCING AROUND IN THE DAYLIGHT,
IT'S JUST A DIFFERENT *TYPE* OF ATTENTION.
INSTEAD OF *APPLAUSE*, THEY CRAVE *FEAR*,
THEY WANT PEOPLE TO BE *AFRAID* OF THEM.
WHILE THIS RETRO GIRL WANTS YOU TO THINK SHE'S ALL *INNOCENT*, WITH HER CUTE LITTLE *HAIR* AND HER CUTE LITTLE *BOOTS*!
THESE NOCTURNAL POWERS, THEY WANT YOU TO *FEAR* THEM.
THE POWERS THAT BE
CAMERA 2
STANDBY
ROLL TAPE #606a
IN :04

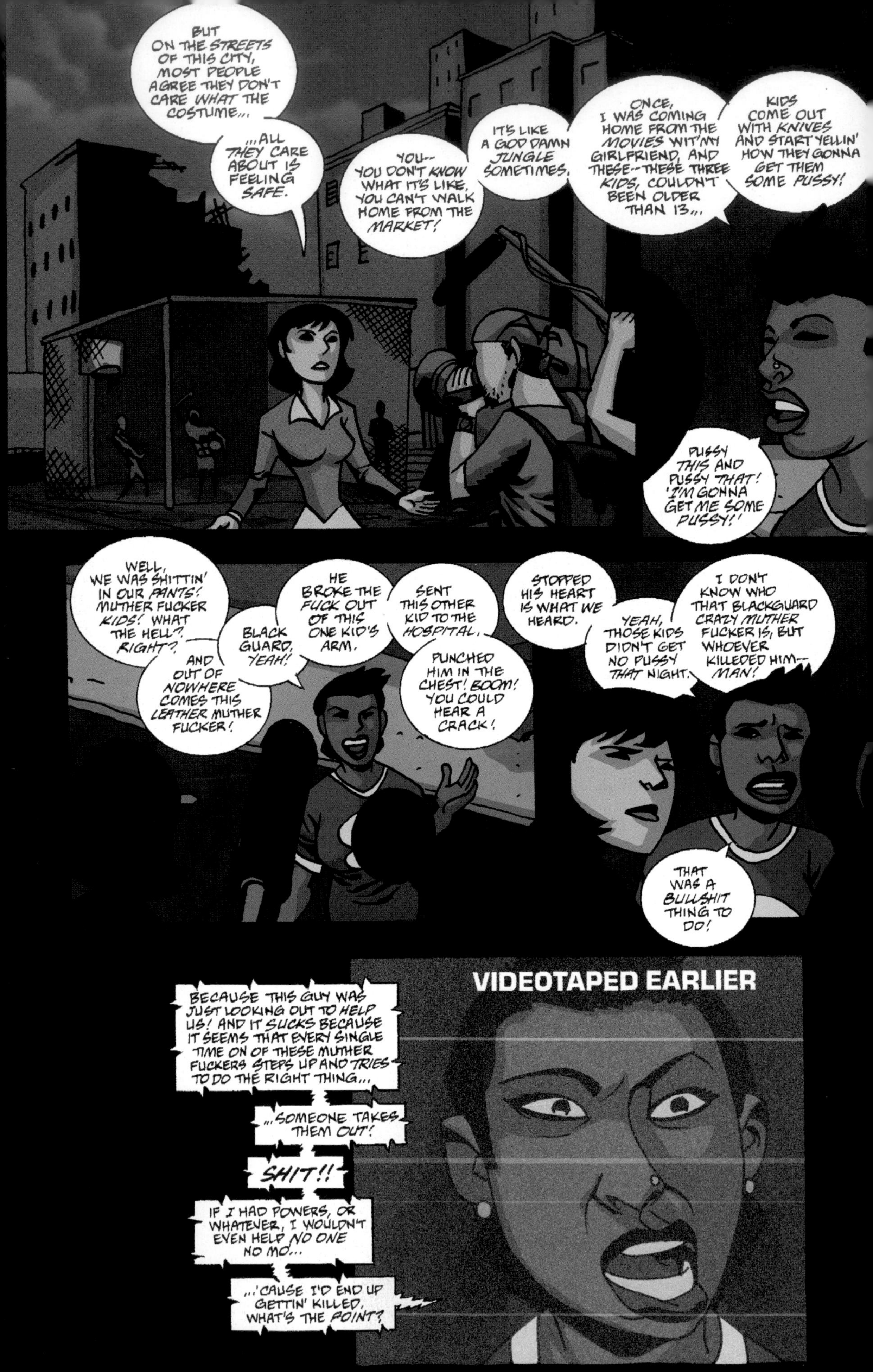

BUT ON THE STREETS OF THIS CITY, MOST PEOPLE AGREE THEY DON'T CARE WHAT THE COSTUME...
...ALL THEY CARE ABOUT IS FEELING SAFE.
YOU-- YOU DON'T KNOW WHAT IT'S LIKE, YOU CAN'T WALK HOME FROM THE MARKET!
IT'S LIKE A GOD DAMN JUNGLE SOMETIMES.
ONCE, I WAS COMING HOME FROM THE MOVIES WIT' MY GIRLFRIEND, AND THESE-- THESE THREE KIDS, COULDN'T BEEN OLDER THAN 13...
KIDS COME OUT WITH KNIVES AND START YELLIN' HOW THEY GONNA GET THEM SOME PUSSY!
PUSSY THIS AND PUSSY THAT! 'I'M GONNA GET ME SOME PUSSY!'
WELL, WE WAS SHITTIN' IN OUR PANTS! MUTHER FUCKER KIDS! WHAT THE HELL? RIGHT?
AND OUT OF NOWHERE COMES THIS LEATHER MUTHER FUCKER!
BLACK GUARD, YEAH!
HE BROKE THE FUCK OUT OF THIS ONE KID'S ARM.
SENT THIS OTHER KID TO THE HOSPITAL.
PUNCHED HIM IN THE CHEST! BOOM! YOU COULD HEAR A CRACK!
STOPPED HIS HEART IS WHAT WE HEARD.
YEAH, THOSE KIDS DIDN'T GET NO PUSSY THAT NIGHT.
I DON'T KNOW WHO THAT BLACKGUARD CRAZY MUTHER FUCKER IS, BUT WHOEVER KILLEDED HIM-- MAN!
THAT WAS A BULLSHIT THING TO DO!
VIDEOTAPED EARLIER
BECAUSE THIS GUY WAS JUST LOOKING OUT TO HELP US! AND IT SUCKS BECAUSE IT SEEMS THAT EVERY SINGLE TIME ON OF THESE MUTHER FUCKERS STEPS UP AND TRIES TO DO THE RIGHT THING...
...SOMEONE TAKES THEM OUT!
SHIT!!
IF I HAD POWERS, OR WHATEVER, I WOULDN'T EVEN HELP NO ONE NO MO...
...'CAUSE I'D END UP GETTIN' KILLED, WHAT'S THE POINT?

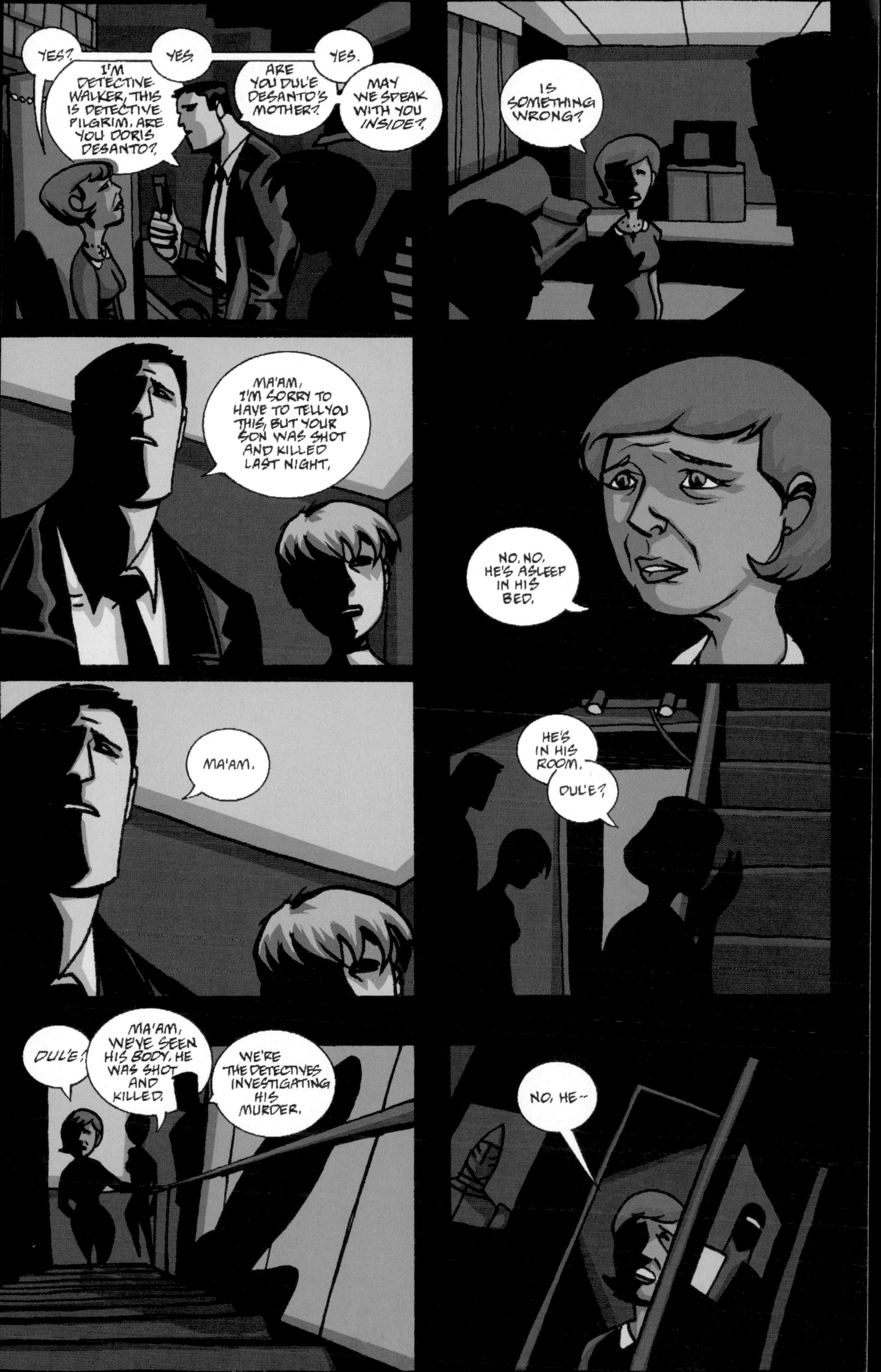
YES?
I'M DETECTIVE WALKER, THIS IS DETECTIVE PILGRIM. ARE YOU DORIS DESANTO?
YES.
ARE YOU DUL'E DESANTO'S MOTHER?
YES.
MAY WE SPEAK WITH YOU INSIDE?
IS SOMETHING WRONG?
MA'AM, I'M SORRY TO HAVE TO TELL YOU THIS, BUT YOUR SON WAS SHOT AND KILLED LAST NIGHT.
NO, NO, HE'S ASLEEP IN HIS BED.
MA'AM.
HE'S IN HIS ROOM.
DUL'E?
DUL'E!
MA'AM, WE'VE SEEN HIS BODY. HE WAS SHOT AND KILLED.
WE'RE THE DETECTIVES INVESTIGATING HIS MURDER.
NO, HE--

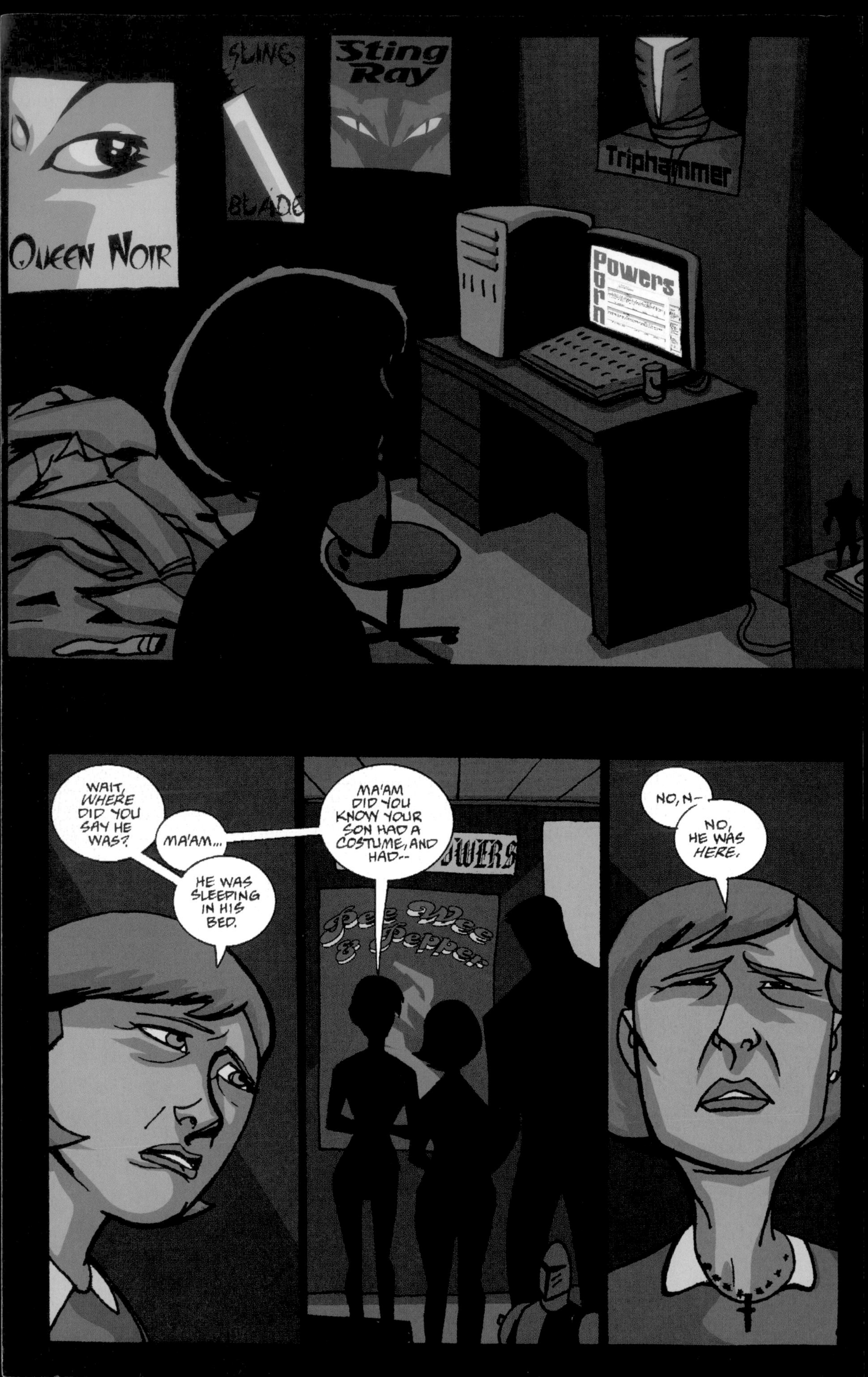

QUEEN NOIR
SLING BLADE
Sting Ray
Triphammer
Powers Porn
WAIT, WHERE DID YOU SAY HE WAS?
HE WAS SLEEPING IN HIS BED.
MA'AM...
MA'AM DID YOU KNOW YOUR SON HAD A COSTUME, AND HAD--
Pee Wee & Pepper
NO, N--
NO, HE WAS HERE.

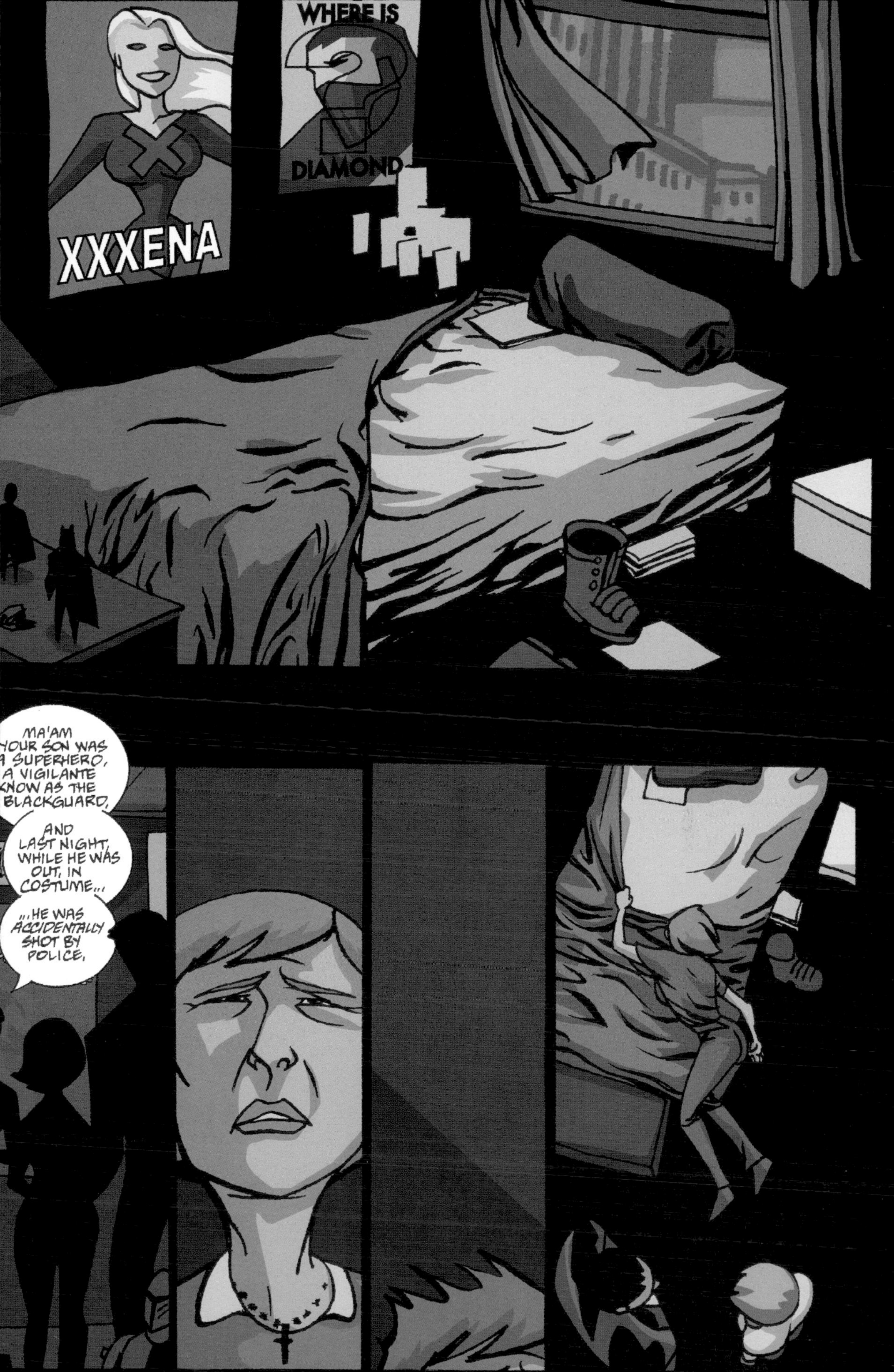
WHERE IS
DIAMOND
XXXENA
MA'AM YOUR SON WAS A SUPERHERO, A VIGILANTE KNOW AS THE BLACKGUARD,
AND LAST NIGHT, WHILE HE WAS OUT, IN COSTUME...
...HE WAS ACCIDENTALLY SHOT BY POLICE.

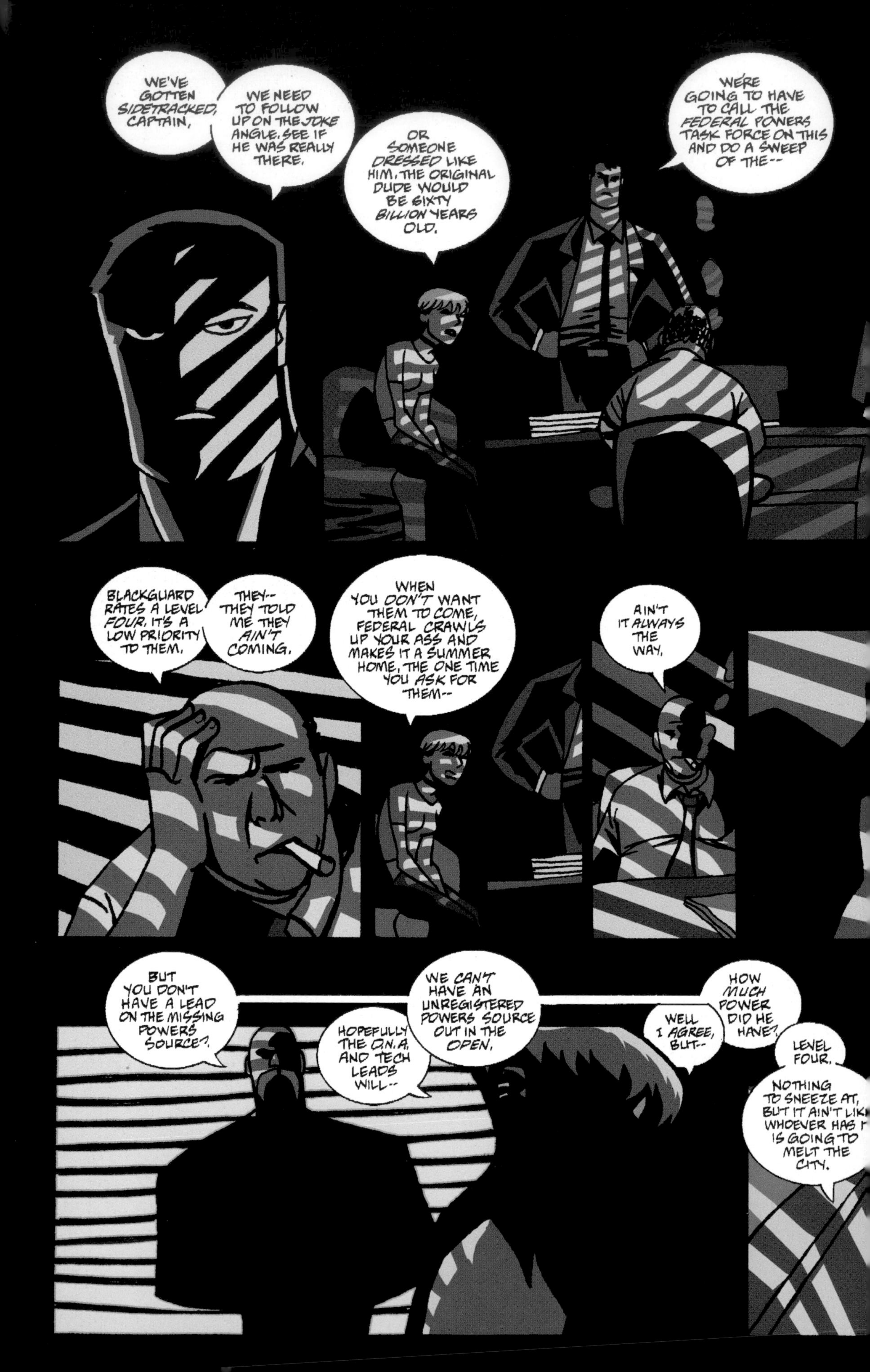
WE'VE GOTTEN SIDETRACKED, CAPTAIN.
WE NEED TO FOLLOW UP ON THE JOKE ANGLE. SEE IF HE WAS REALLY THERE.
OR SOMEONE DRESSED LIKE HIM. THE ORIGINAL DUDE WOULD BE SIXTY BILLION YEARS OLD.
WE'RE GOING TO HAVE TO CALL THE FEDERAL POWERS TASK FORCE ON THIS AND DO A SWEEP OF THE--
BLACKGUARD RATES A LEVEL FOUR. IT'S A LOW PRIORITY TO THEM.
THEY-- THEY TOLD ME THEY AIN'T COMING.
WHEN YOU DON'T WANT THEM TO COME, FEDERAL CRAWLS UP YOUR ASS AND MAKES IT A SUMMER HOME. THE ONE TIME YOU ASK FOR THEM--
AIN'T IT ALWAYS THE WAY.
BUT YOU DON'T HAVE A LEAD ON THE MISSING POWERS SOURCE?
HOPEFULLY THE D.N.A. AND TECH LEADS WILL--
WE CAN'T HAVE AN UNREGISTERED POWERS SOURCE OUT IN THE OPEN.
WELL I AGREE, BUT--
HOW MUCH POWER DID HE HAVE?
LEVEL FOUR.
NOTHING TO SNEEZE AT, BUT IT AIN'T LIKE WHOEVER HAS IT IS GOING TO MELT THE CITY.

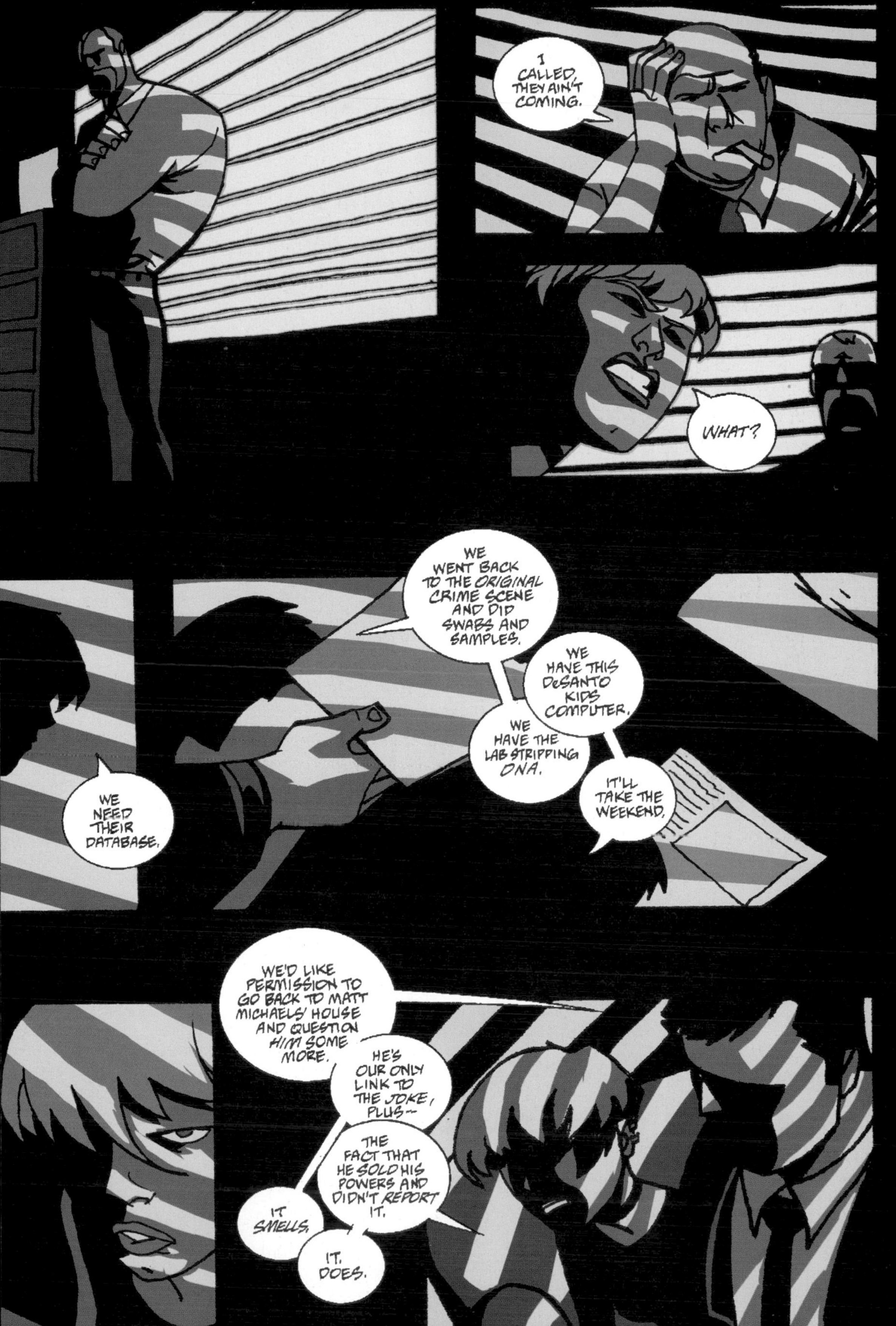
I CALLED. THEY AIN'T COMING.
WHAT?
WE WENT BACK TO THE ORIGINAL CRIME SCENE AND DID SWABS AND SAMPLES.
WE HAVE THIS DeSANTO KIDS COMPUTER.
WE HAVE THE LAB STRIPPING DNA.
IT'LL TAKE THE WEEKEND.
WE NEED THEIR DATABASE.
WE'D LIKE PERMISSION TO GO BACK TO MATT MICHAELS' HOUSE AND QUESTION HIM SOME MORE.
HE'S OUR ONLY LINK TO THE JOKE, PLUS--
THE FACT THAT HE SOLD HIS POWERS AND DIDN'T REPORT IT.
IT SMELLS.
IT. DOES.

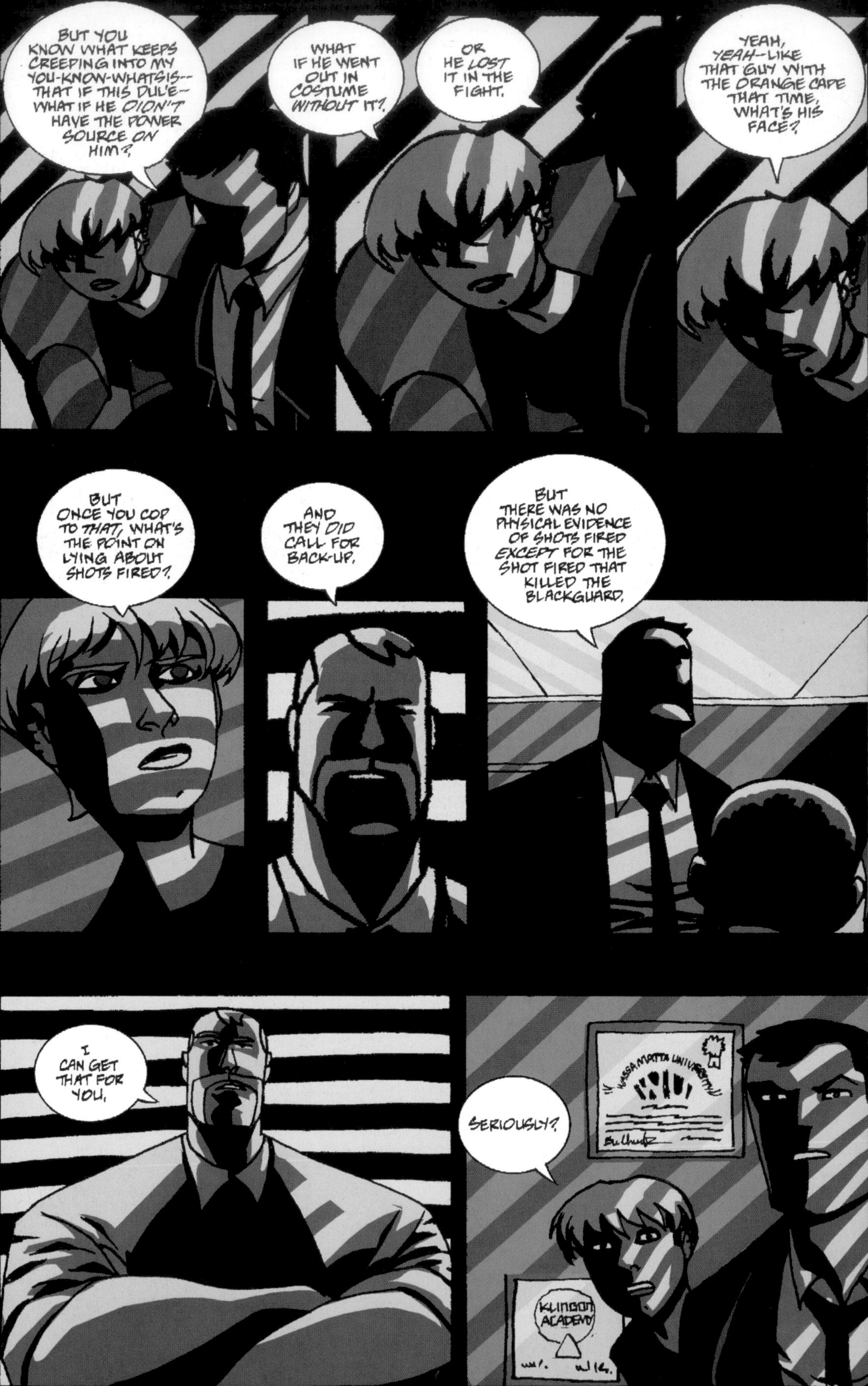
BUT YOU KNOW WHAT KEEPS CREEPING INTO MY YOU-KNOW-WHATSIS-- THAT IF THIS DUDE-- WHAT IF HE DIDN'T HAVE THE POWER SOURCE ON HIM?
WHAT IF HE WENT OUT IN COSTUME WITHOUT IT?
OR HE LOST IT IN THE FIGHT.
YEAH, YEAH--LIKE THAT GUY WITH THE ORANGE CAPE THAT TIME, WHAT'S HIS FACE?
BUT ONCE YOU COP TO THAT, WHAT'S THE POINT ON LYING ABOUT SHOTS FIRED?
AND THEY DID CALL FOR BACK-UP.
BUT THERE WAS NO PHYSICAL EVIDENCE OF SHOTS FIRED EXCEPT FOR THE SHOT FIRED THAT KILLED THE BLACKGUARD.
I CAN GET THAT FOR YOU.
SERIOUSLY?
WASSA MATTA UNIVERSITY
KLINGON ACADEMY

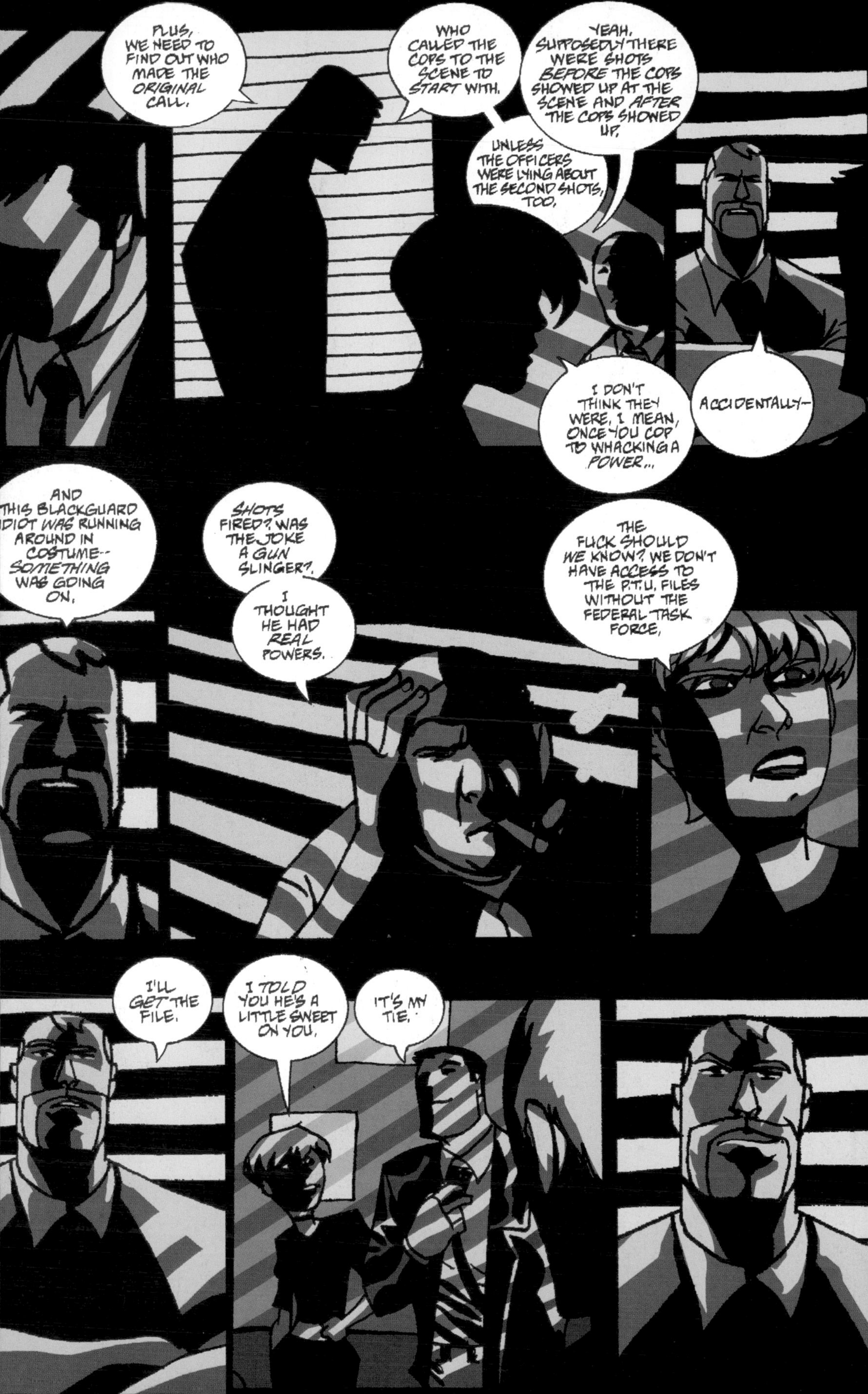
PLUS, WE NEED TO FIND OUT WHO MADE THE ORIGINAL CALL.
WHO CALLED THE COPS TO THE SCENE TO START WITH.
YEAH, SUPPOSEDLY THERE WERE SHOTS BEFORE THE COPS SHOWED UP AT THE SCENE AND AFTER THE COPS SHOWED UP.
UNLESS THE OFFICERS WERE LYING ABOUT THE SECOND SHOTS, TOO.
I DON'T THINK THEY WERE, I MEAN, ONCE YOU COP TO WHACKING A POWER...
ACCIDENTALLY--
AND THIS BLACKGUARD IDIOT WAS RUNNING AROUND IN COSTUME-- SOMETHING WAS GOING ON.
SHOTS FIRED? WAS THE JOKE A GUN SLINGER?
I THOUGHT HE HAD REAL POWERS.
THE FUCK SHOULD WE KNOW? WE DON'T HAVE ACCESS TO THE P.T.U. FILES WITHOUT THE FEDERAL TASK FORCE.
I'LL GET THE FILE.
I TOLD YOU HE'S A LITTLE SWEET ON YOU.
IT'S MY TIE.

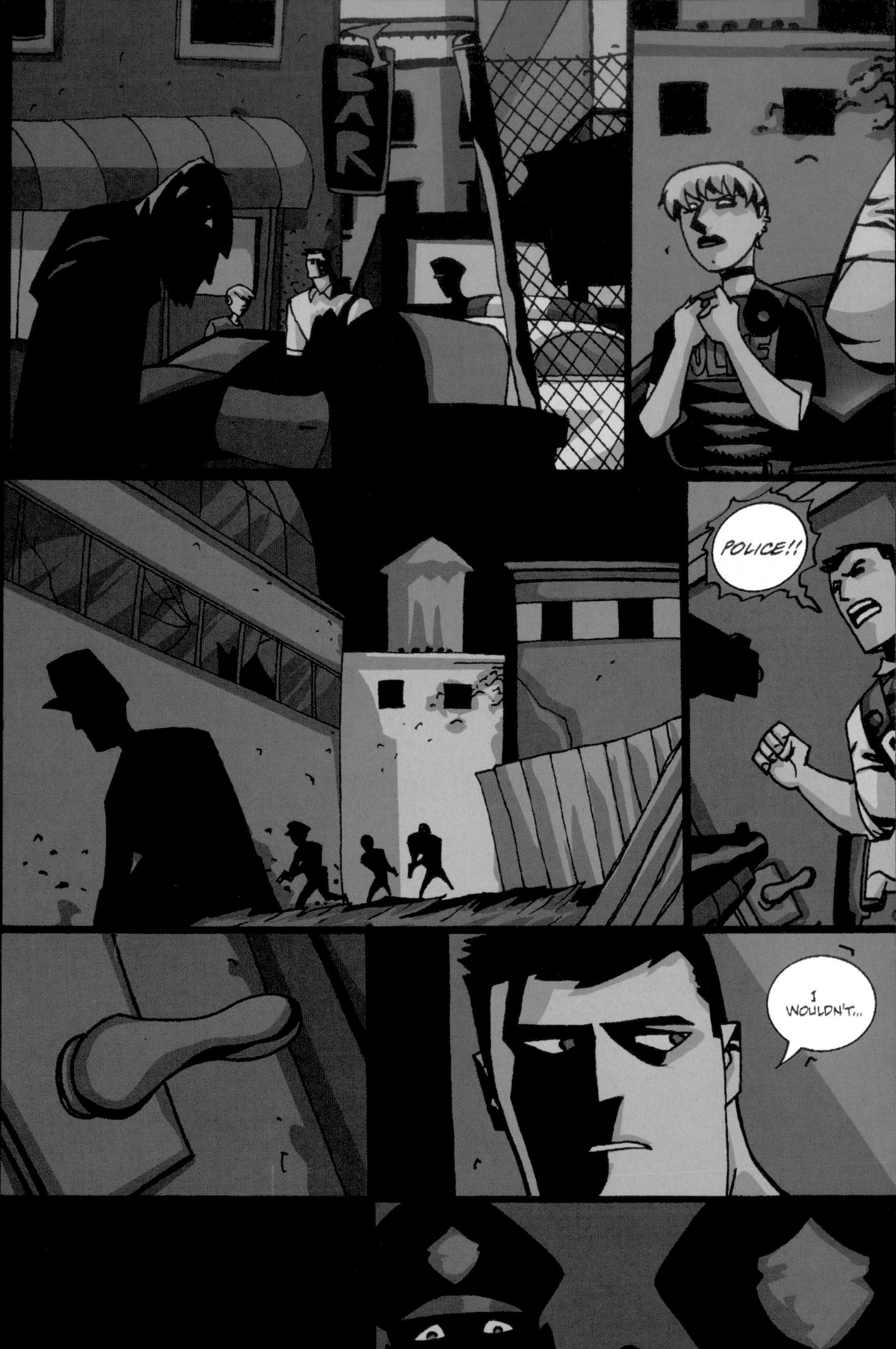
BAR
POLICE!!
I WOULDN'T...

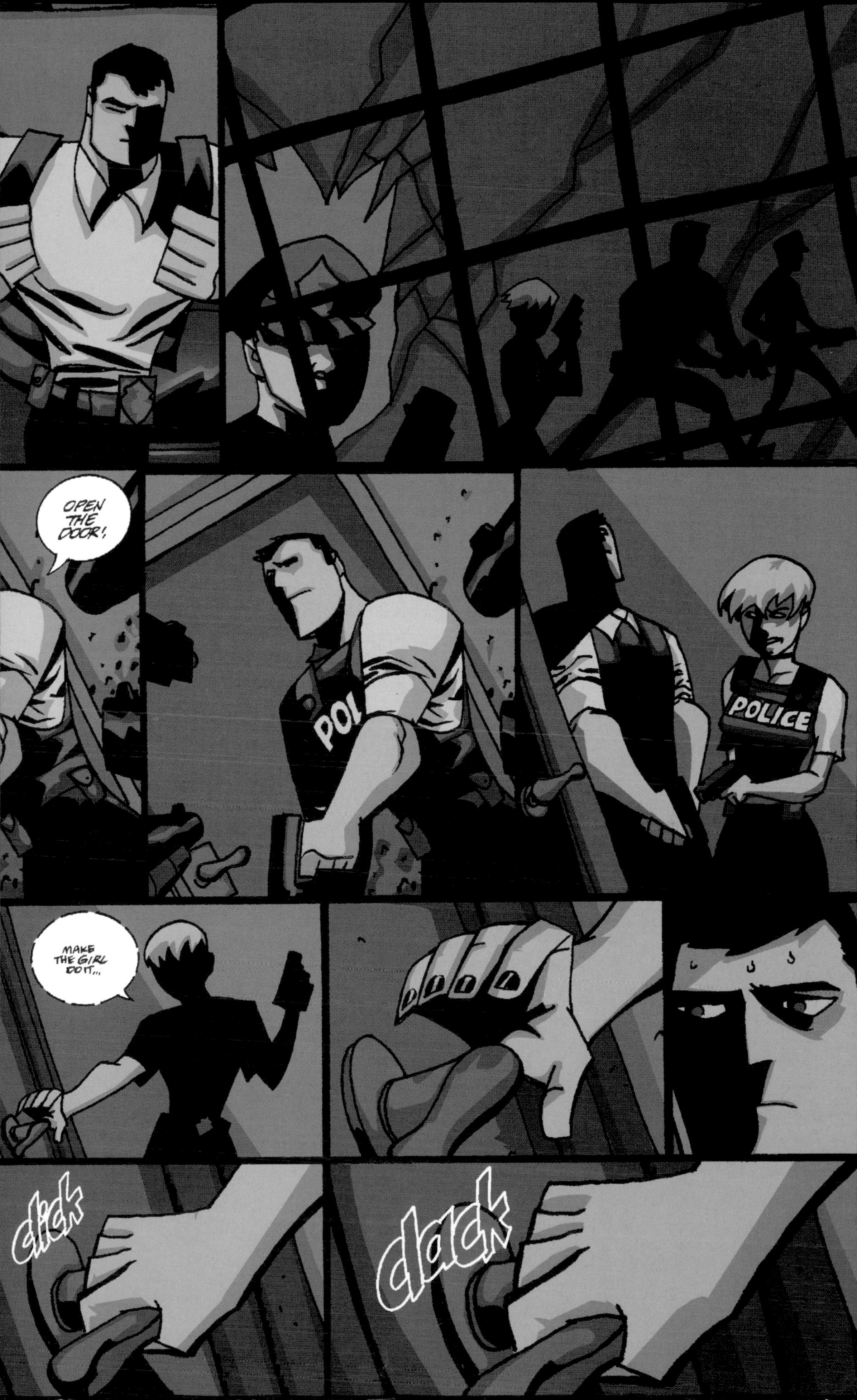
OPEN THE DOOR!
POLICE
MAKE THE GIRL DO IT...
click
clack

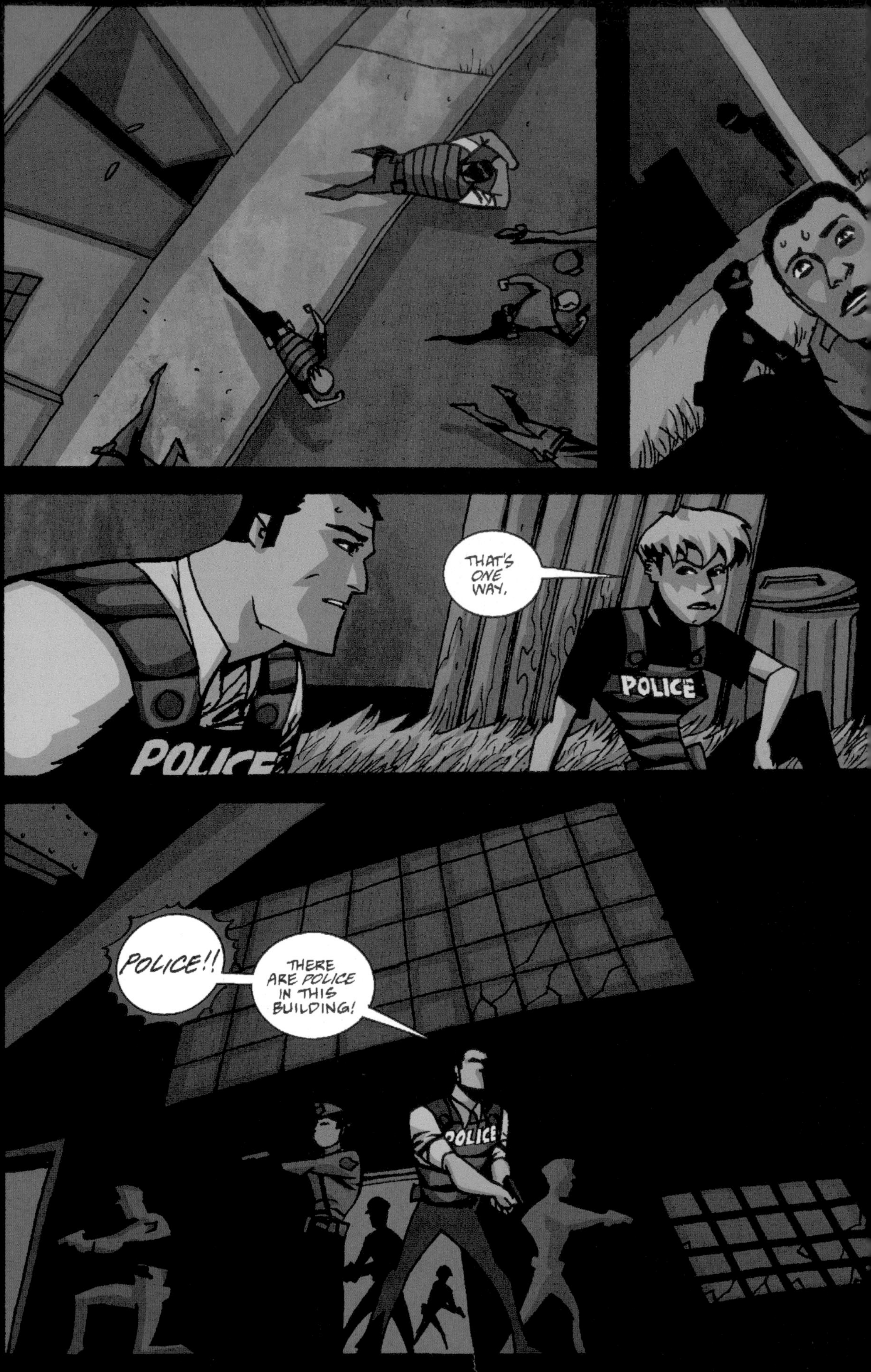
THAT'S ONE WAY.
POLICE
POLICE
POLICE!!
THERE ARE POLICE IN THIS BUILDING!
POLICE

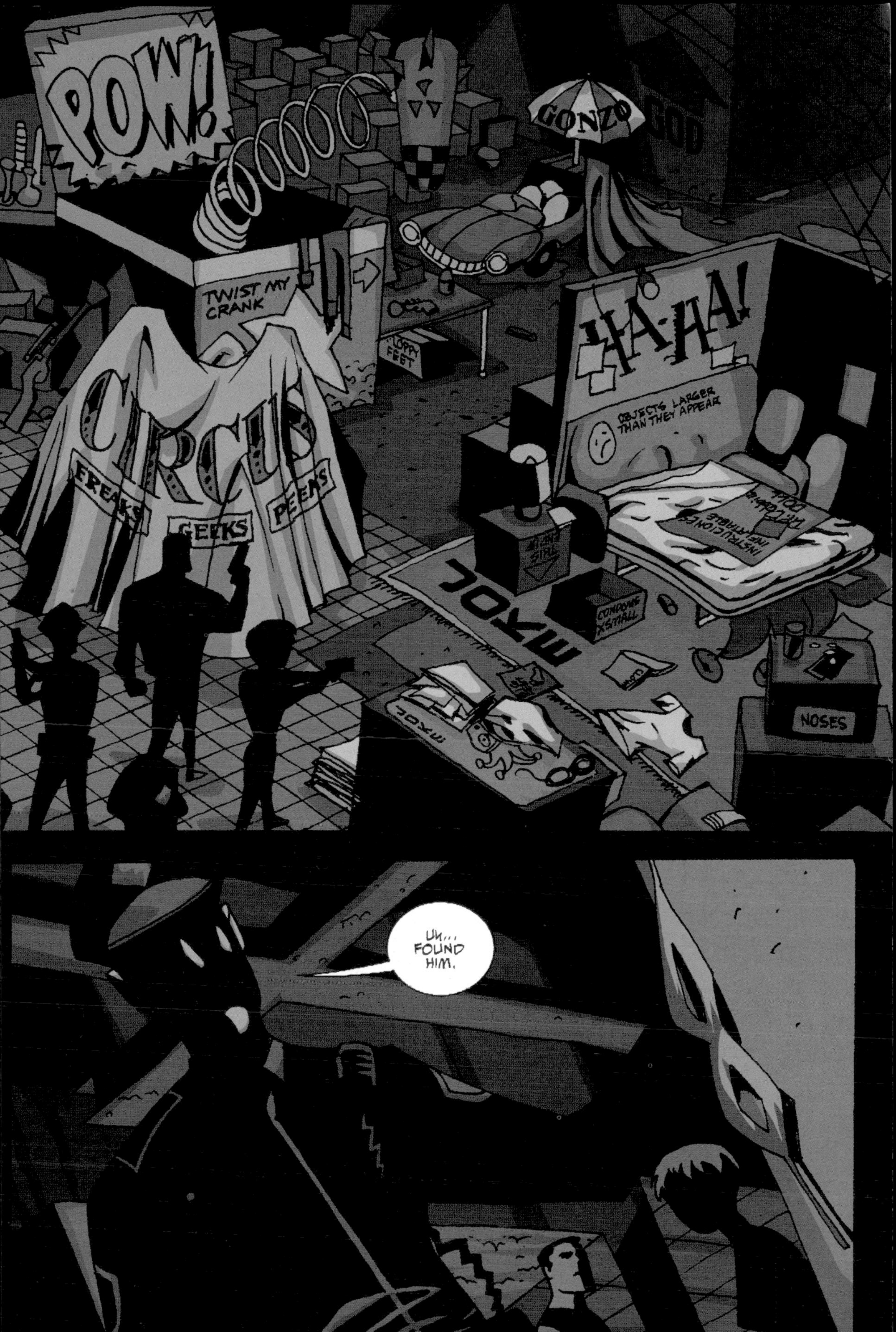
POW!
TWIST MY CRANK
GONZO
HA-HA!
OBJECTS LARGER THAN THEY APPEAR
CIRCUS
FREAKS
GEEKS
NOSES
UH... FOUND HIM.

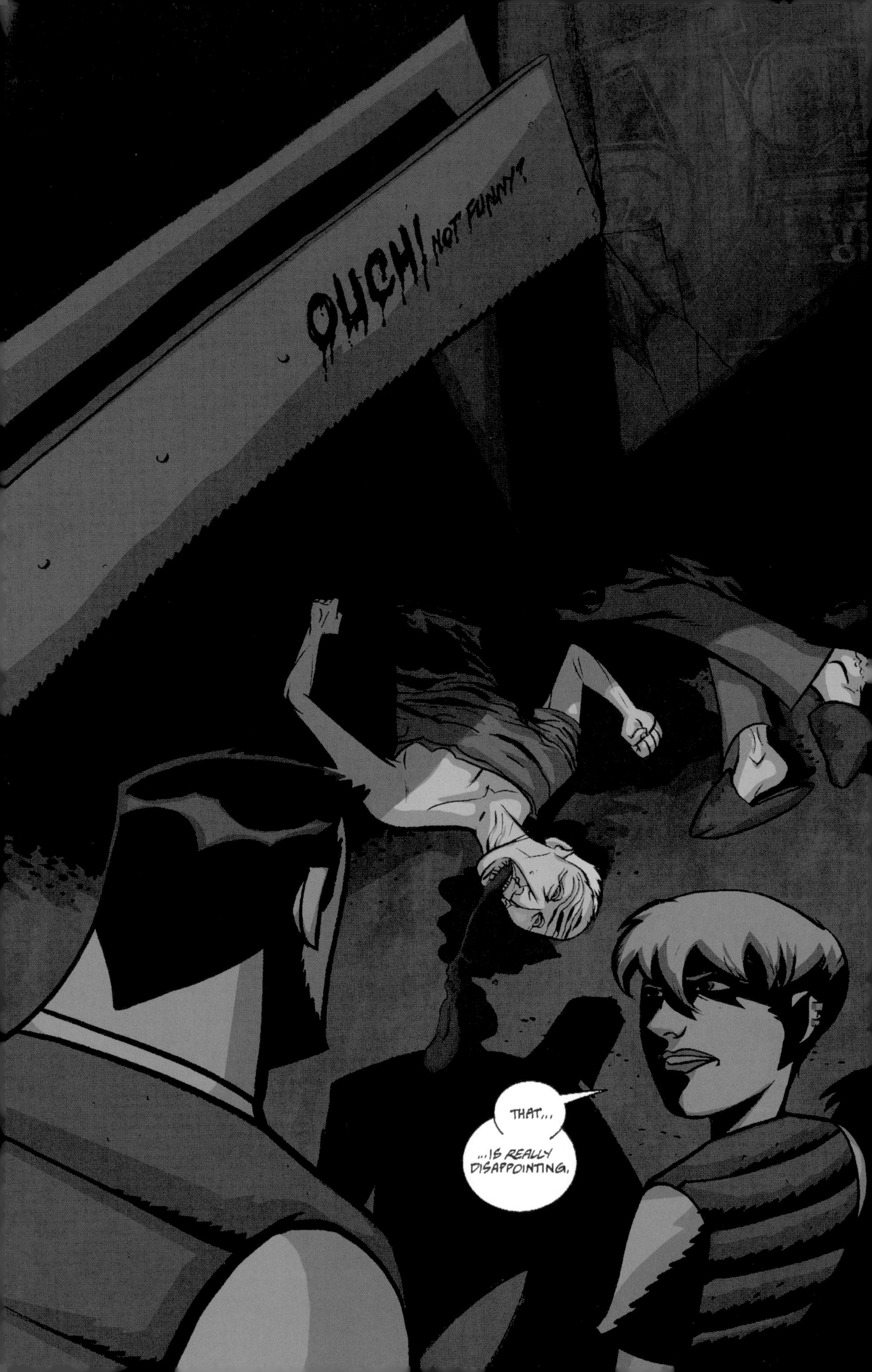
OUCH! NOT FUNNY?
THAT...
...IS REALLY DISAPPOINTING.

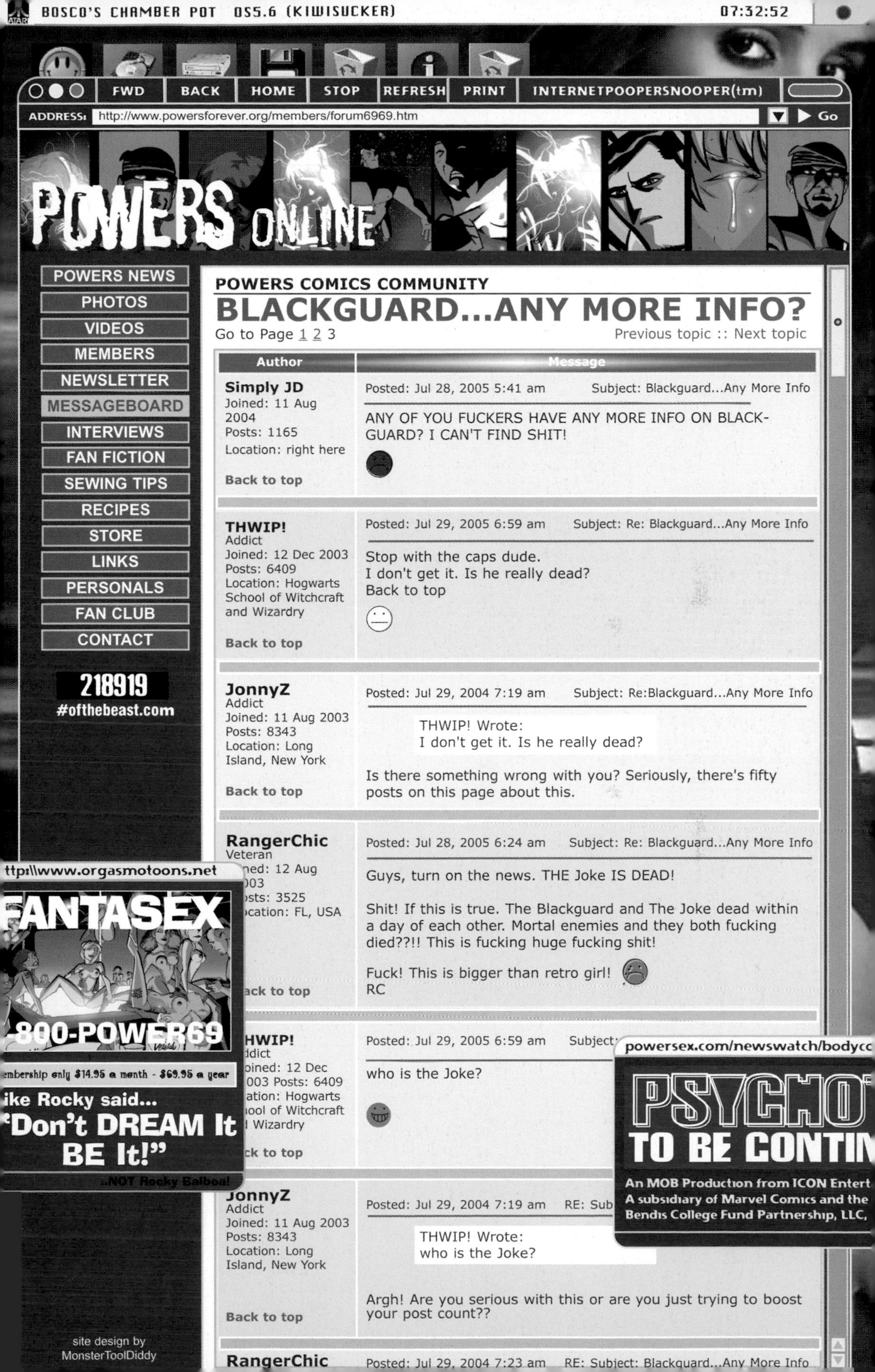

POWERS ONLINE

POWERS NEWS
PHOTOS
VIDEOS
MEMBERS
NEWSLETTER
MESSAGEBOARD
INTERVIEWS
FAN FICTION
SEWING TIPS
RECIPES
STORE
LINKS
PERSONALS
FAN CLUB
CONTACT

218919
#ofthebeast.com

## POWERS COMICS COMMUNITY
# BLACKGUARD...ANY MORE INFO?

Go to Page 1 2 3                                Previous topic :: Next topic

| Author | Message |
|---|---|
| **Simply JD** Joined: 11 Aug 2004 Posts: 1165 Location: right here Back to top | Posted: Jul 28, 2005 5:41 am    Subject: Blackguard...Any More Info ANY OF YOU FUCKERS HAVE ANY MORE INFO ON BLACK-GUARD? I CAN'T FIND SHIT! |
| **THWIP!** Addict Joined: 12 Dec 2003 Posts: 6409 Location: Hogwarts School of Witchcraft and Wizardry Back to top | Posted: Jul 29, 2005 6:59 am    Subject: Re: Blackguard...Any More Info Stop with the caps dude. I don't get it. Is he really dead? Back to top |
| **JonnyZ** Addict Joined: 11 Aug 2003 Posts: 8343 Location: Long Island, New York Back to top | Posted: Jul 29, 2004 7:19 am    Subject: Re:Blackguard...Any More Info   THWIP! Wrote:   I don't get it. Is he really dead? Is there something wrong with you? Seriously, there's fifty posts on this page about this. |
| **RangerChic** Veteran Joined: 12 Aug 2003 Posts: 3525 Location: FL, USA ack to top | Posted: Jul 28, 2005 6:24 am    Subject: Re: Blackguard...Any More Info Guys, turn on the news. THE Joke IS DEAD! Shit! If this is true. The Blackguard and The Joke dead within a day of each other. Mortal enemies and they both fucking died??!! This is fucking huge fucking shit! Fuck! This is bigger than retro girl! RC |
| **THWIP!** ddict oined: 12 Dec 003 Posts: 6409 ation: Hogwarts hool of Witchcraft Wizardry ck to top | Posted: Jul 29, 2005 6:59 am    Subject who is the Joke? |
| **JonnyZ** Addict Joined: 11 Aug 2003 Posts: 8343 Location: Long Island, New York Back to top | Posted: Jul 29, 2004 7:19 am    RE: Sub   THWIP! Wrote:   who is the Joke? Argh! Are you serious with this or are you just trying to boost your post count?? |
| **RangerChic** | Posted: Jul 29, 2004 7:23 am    RE: Subject: Blackguard...Any More Info |

site design by
MonsterToolDiddy

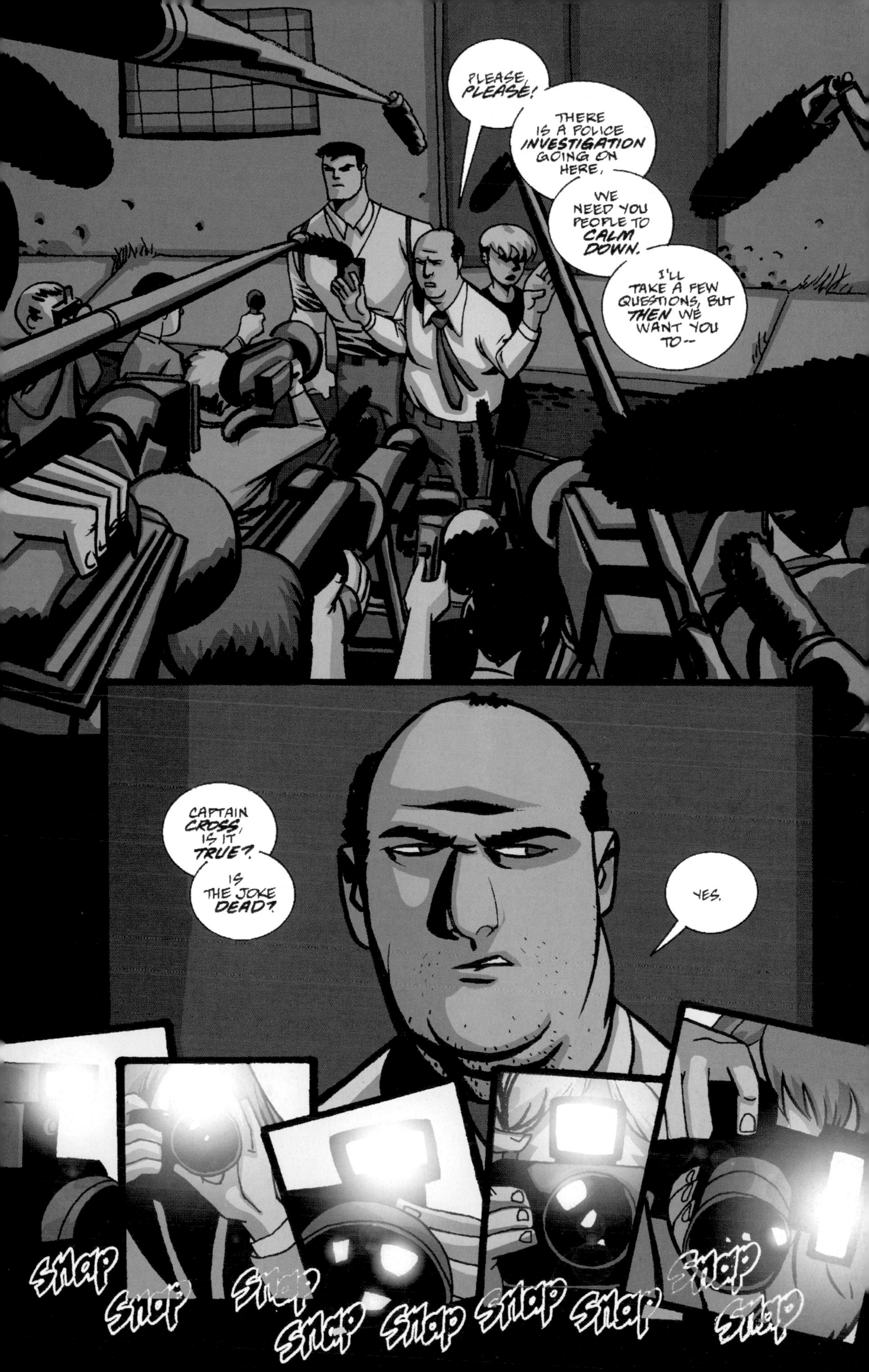
PLEASE, PLEASE!
THERE IS A POLICE INVESTIGATION GOING ON HERE.
WE NEED YOU PEOPLE TO CALM DOWN.
I'LL TAKE A FEW QUESTIONS, BUT THEN WE WANT YOU TO--
CAPTAIN CROSS, IS IT TRUE?
IS THE JOKE DEAD?
YES.
SNAP SNAP SNAP SNAP SNAP SNAP SNAP SNAP SNAP

# The Joke.

| | |
|---|---|
| **Real name** | Tyler Kimmel |
| **Occupation** | Professional criminal<br>Author |
| **Identity** | Publicly known |
| **Legal status** | Citizen of the United States with criminal record |
| **Former Alias** | None |
| **Place of birth** | Hoboken, New Jersey |
| **Marital status** | Single |
| **Relatives** | None |
| **Affiliation** | None |
| **Height** | 6 ft. |
| **Weight** | 190 lbs. |
| **Eyes** | Blue |
| **Hair** | Gray |

**History**  Tyler Kimmel was a struggling author who initially started his criminal career in the name of writer research.

After an unsuccessful start, Kimmel was approached by a mysterious figure known only as the benefactor. He offered Kimmel illegal genetic powers in return for a piece of whatever profit he turned as a criminal and an undisclosed portion of his book royalties.

As detailed in his national best sellers: THE JOKE, MIND POWERS, and THE LAST POWER, Kimmel's powers accentuated his already existing mental and physical gifts.

Committing a wave of crimes based on his theory that the world was a cosmic Joke, the Joke often left calling cards and word puzzles that were mostly incomprehensible to police and his Powers opponents.

The Joke was often confronted by the Blackguard, who eventually stopped his criminal activities and saw him put behind bars. The Joke escaped on numerous occasions to promote his books and to seek revenge on the Blackguard, but eventually retired.

**Strength**  The Joke possesses extra level strength of a man of his age, height, and build.

**Known Powers** Accentuated brain activity and metabolism.

**Abilities**  The Joke is a superb athlete with exceptional skills in gymnastics and unarmed combat.

**Weapons**  The Joke employs a variety of deadly weapons or special tools, some of which he constructed himself, and he also stole many of his weapons from other sources.

Besides various conventional guns and explosives, The Joke employed many highly advanced weapons. In his early battles with Blackguard he wore devices in his gloves and mask that projected concussive blasts of energy. The Joke had electronically-amplified nunchakas, a small but powerful hovering electro-magnets, and flying "razor-discs." The Joke also used stun-guns and custom made concussion bombs.The Joke constantly expanded and refined his arsenal of deadly weapons.

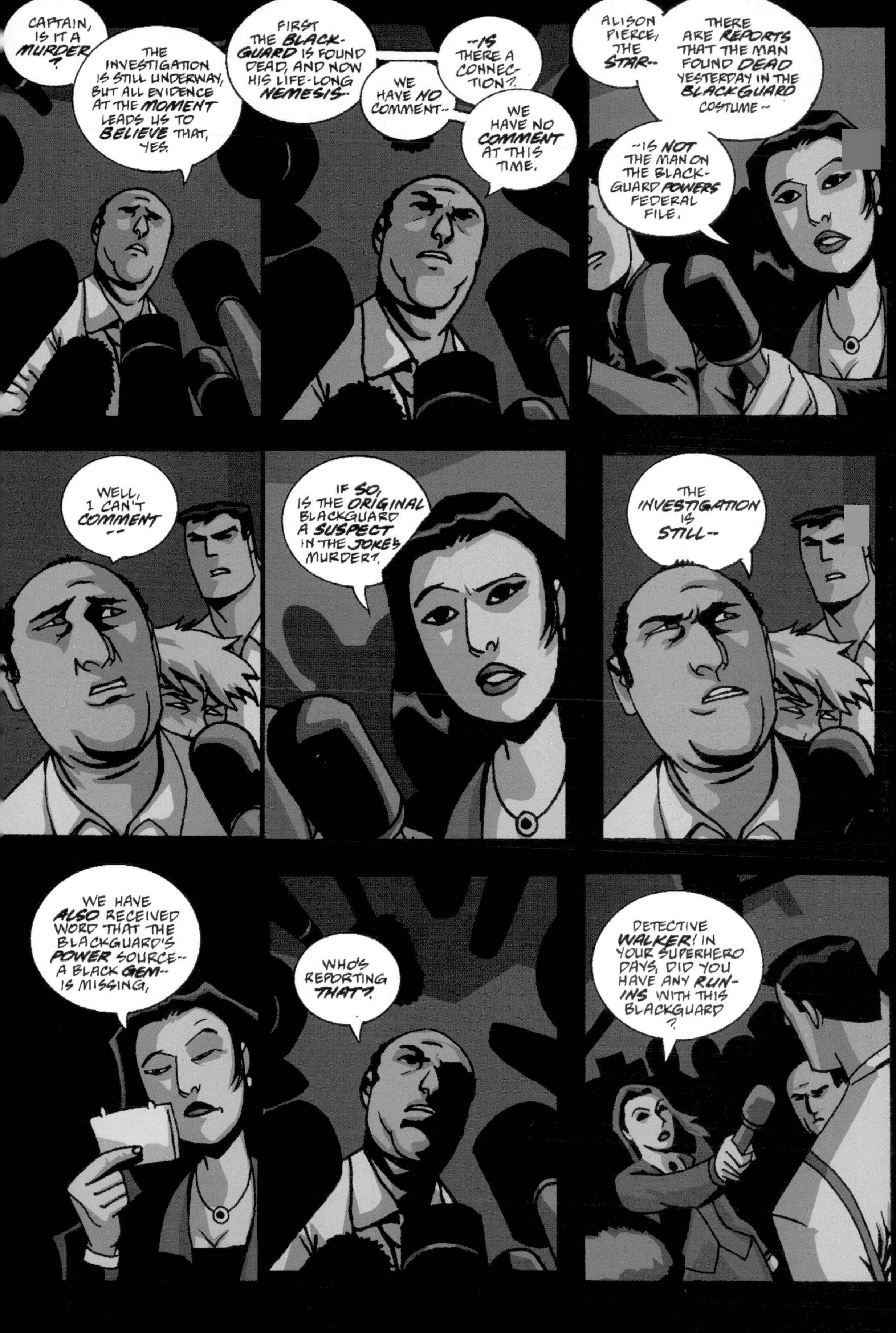
CAPTAIN, IS IT A MURDER?
THE INVESTIGATION IS STILL UNDERWAY, BUT ALL EVIDENCE AT THE MOMENT LEADS US TO BELIEVE THAT, YES.
FIRST THE BLACK-GUARD IS FOUND DEAD, AND NOW HIS LIFE-LONG NEMESIS--
--IS THERE A CONNEC-TION?
WE HAVE NO COMMENT--
WE HAVE NO COMMENT AT THIS TIME.
ALISON PIERCE, THE STAR--
THERE ARE REPORTS THAT THE MAN FOUND DEAD YESTERDAY IN THE BLACKGUARD COSTUME--
--IS NOT THE MAN ON THE BLACK-GUARD POWERS FEDERAL FILE.
WELL, I CAN'T COMMENT--
IF SO, IS THE ORIGINAL BLACKGUARD A SUSPECT IN THE JOKE'S MURDER?
THE INVESTIGATION IS STILL--
WE HAVE ALSO RECEIVED WORD THAT THE BLACKGUARD'S POWER SOURCE-- A BLACK GEM-- IS MISSING.
WHO'S REPORTING THAT?
DETECTIVE WALKER! IN YOUR SUPERHERO DAYS, DID YOU HAVE ANY RUN-INS WITH THIS BLACKGUARD?

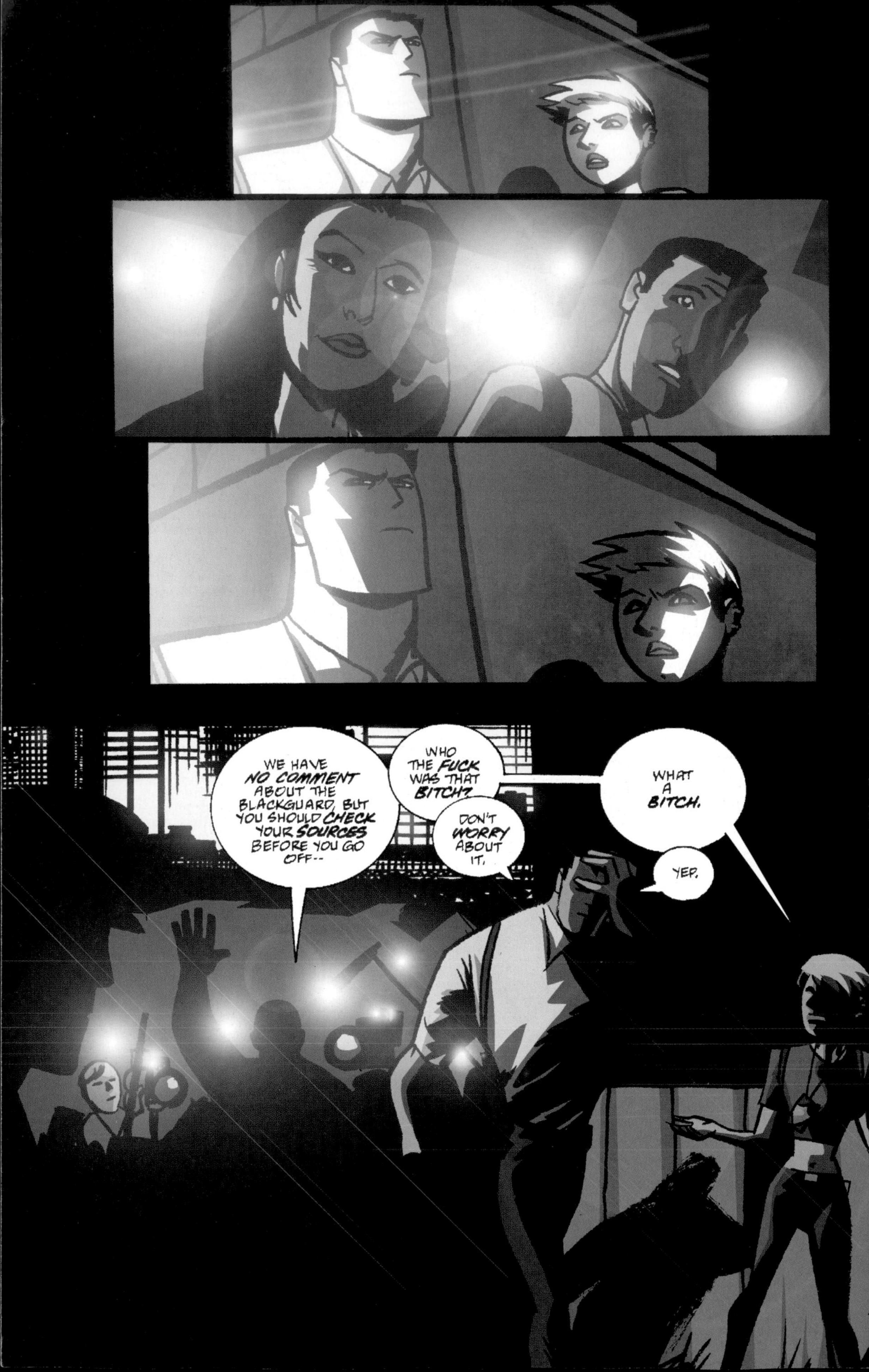

WE HAVE NO COMMENT ABOUT THE BLACKGUARD, BUT YOU SHOULD CHECK YOUR SOURCES BEFORE YOU GO OFF--
WHO THE FUCK WAS THAT BITCH?
DON'T WORRY ABOUT IT.
WHAT A BITCH.
YEP.

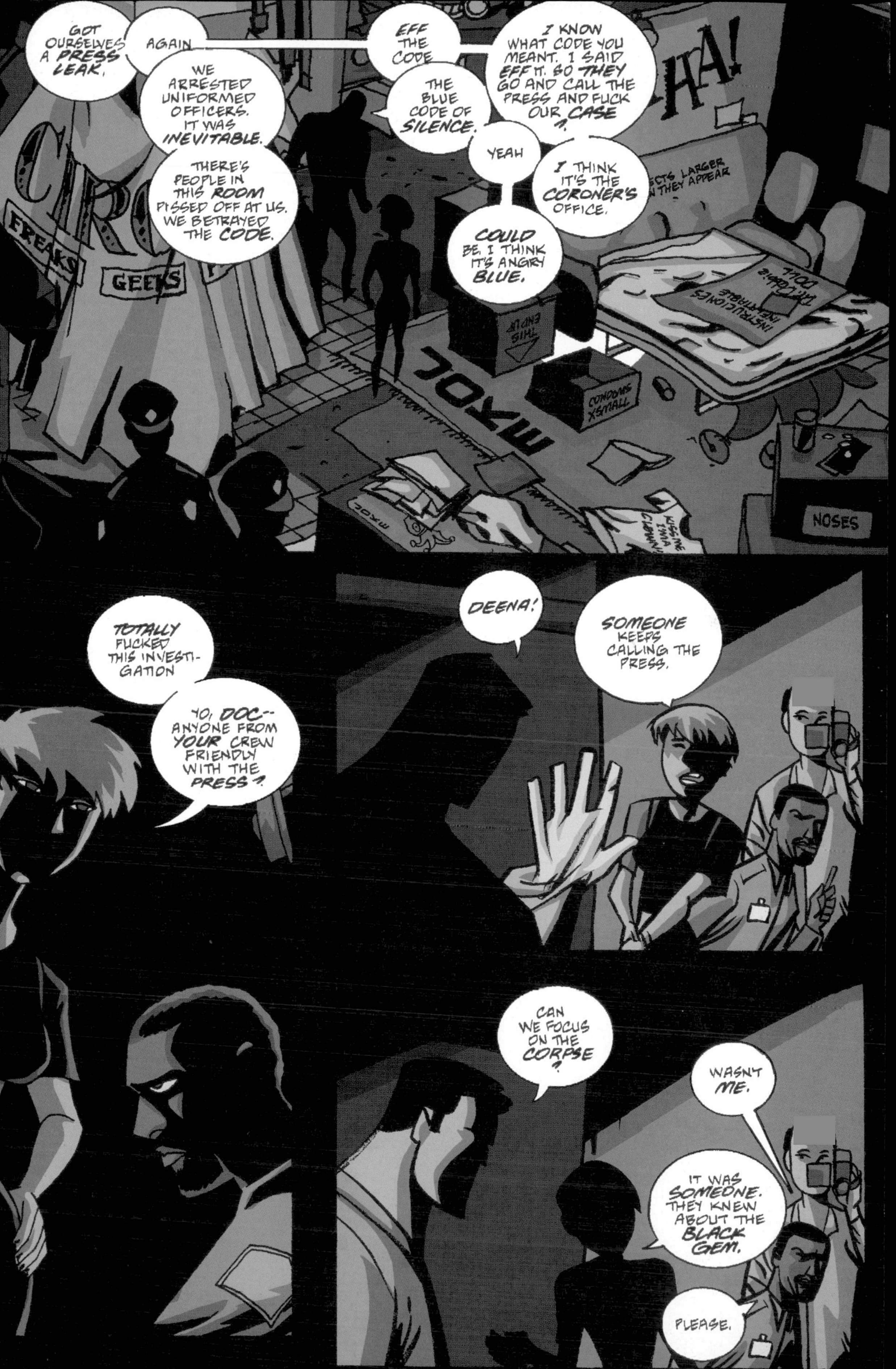

GOT OURSELVES A PRESS LEAK.
AGAIN
WE ARRESTED UNIFORMED OFFICERS. IT WAS INEVITABLE.
THERE'S PEOPLE IN THIS ROOM PISSED OFF AT US. WE BETRAYED THE CODE.
EFF THE CODE
THE BLUE CODE OF SILENCE.
I KNOW WHAT CODE YOU MEANT. I SAID EFF IT. SO THEY GO AND CALL THE PRESS AND FUCK OUR CASE ?
YEAH
I THINK IT'S THE CORONER'S OFFICE.
COULD BE. I THINK IT'S ANGRY BLUE.
HA!
FREAKS
GEEKS
NOSES
TOTALLY FUCKED THIS INVESTI-GATION
YO, DOC-- ANYONE FROM YOUR CREW FRIENDLY WITH THE PRESS ?
DEENA!
SOMEONE KEEPS CALLING THE PRESS.
CAN WE FOCUS ON THE CORPSE ?
WASN'T ME.
IT WAS SOMEONE. THEY KNEW ABOUT THE BLACK GEM.
PLEASE.

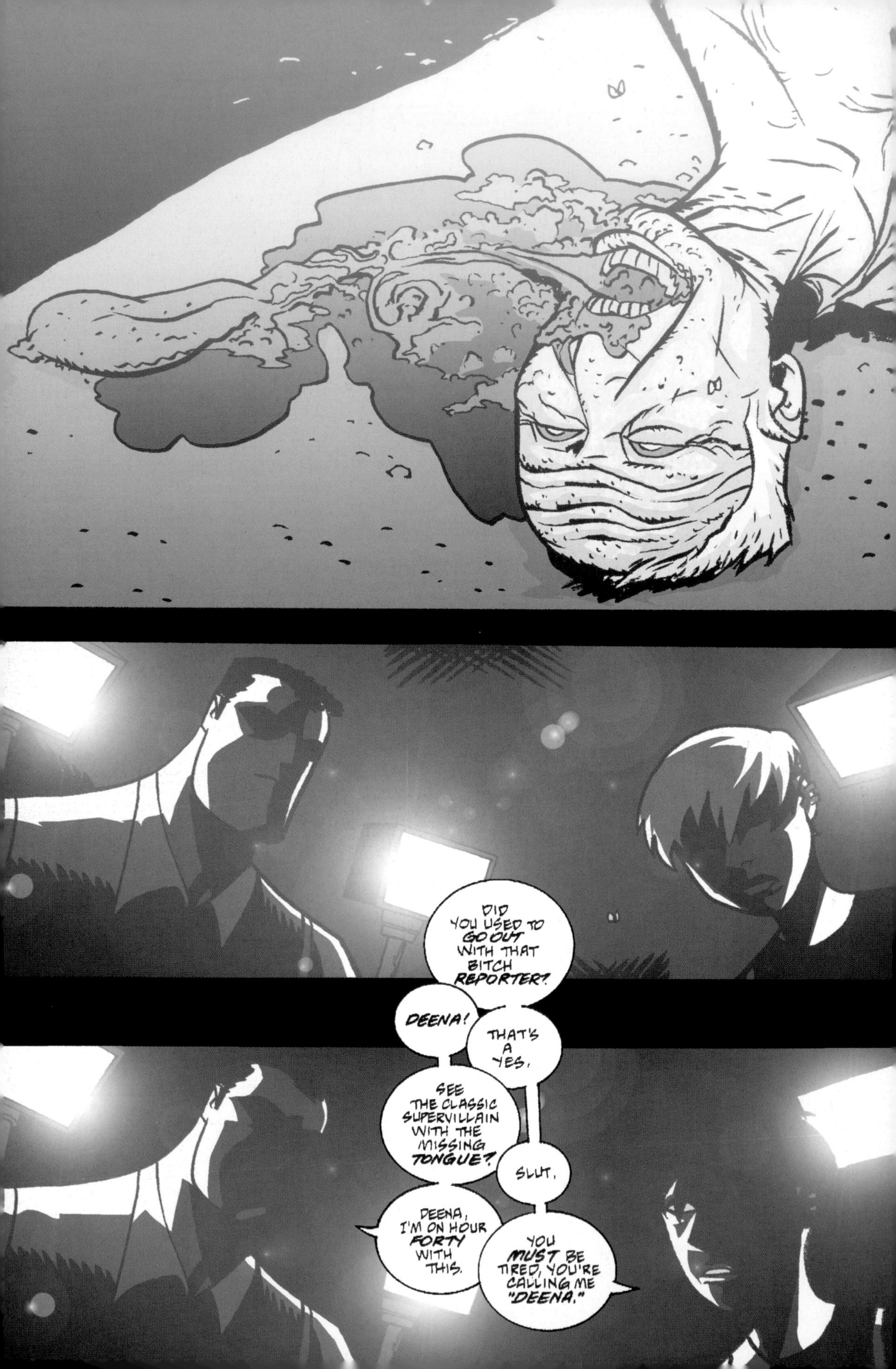
DID YOU USED TO GO OUT WITH THAT BITCH REPORTER?
DEENA!
THAT'S A YES.
SEE THE CLASSIC SUPERVILLAIN WITH THE MISSING TONGUE?
SLUT.
DEENA, I'M ON HOUR FORTY WITH THIS.
YOU MUST BE TIRED, YOU'RE CALLING ME "DEENA."

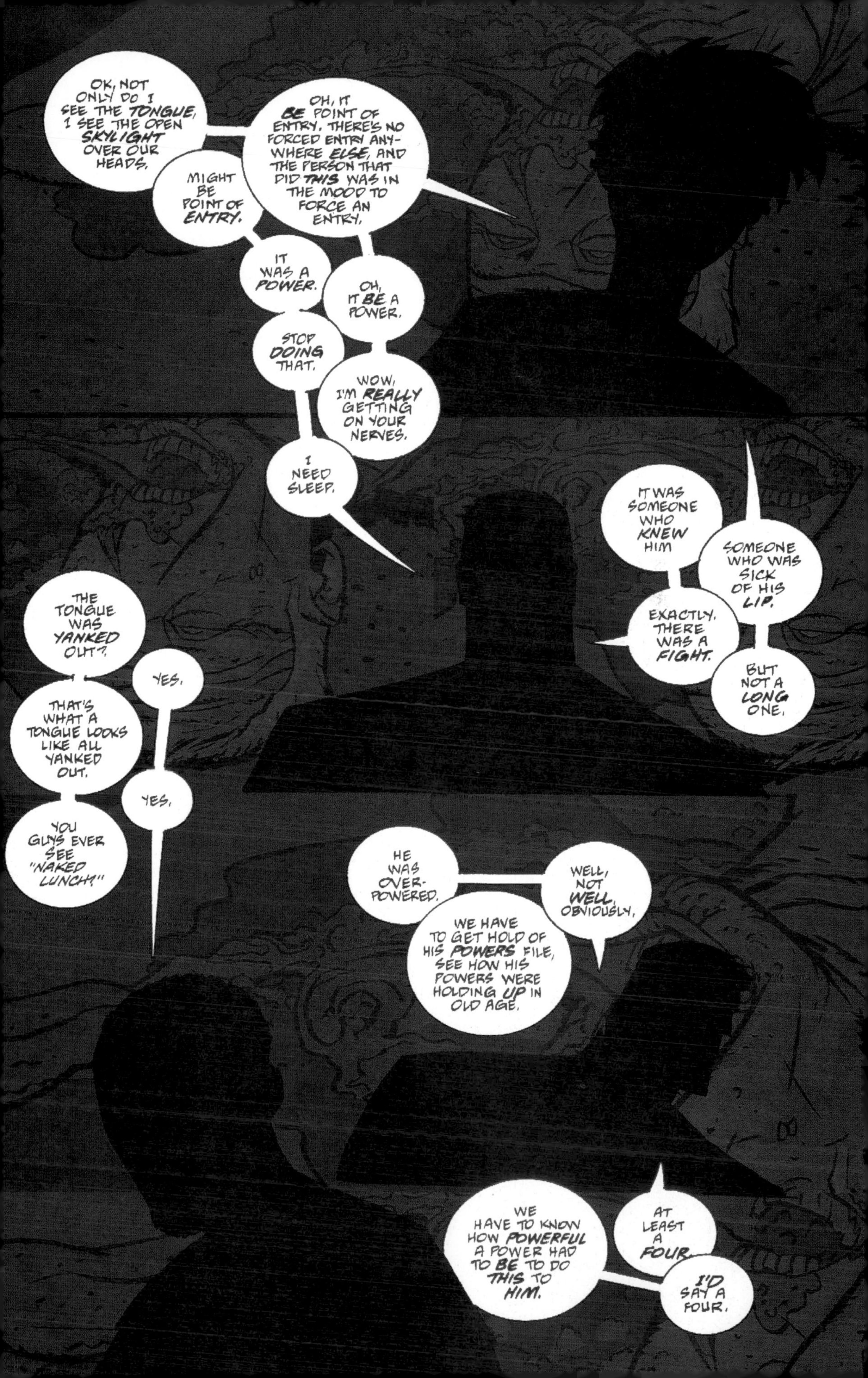

OK, NOT ONLY DO I SEE THE TONGUE, I SEE THE OPEN SKYLIGHT OVER OUR HEADS.
MIGHT BE POINT OF ENTRY.
OH, IT BE POINT OF ENTRY. THERE'S NO FORCED ENTRY ANYWHERE ELSE, AND THE PERSON THAT DID THIS WAS IN THE MOOD TO FORCE AN ENTRY.
IT WAS A POWER.
OH, IT BE A POWER.
STOP DOING THAT.
WOW, I'M REALLY GETTING ON YOUR NERVES.
I NEED SLEEP.
IT WAS SOMEONE WHO KNEW HIM
SOMEONE WHO WAS SICK OF HIS LIP.
EXACTLY. THERE WAS A FIGHT.
BUT NOT A LONG ONE.
THE TONGUE WAS YANKED OUT?
YES.
THAT'S WHAT A TONGUE LOOKS LIKE ALL YANKED OUT.
YES.
YOU GUYS EVER SEE "NAKED LUNCH?"
HE WAS OVER-POWERED.
WELL, NOT WELL, OBVIOUSLY.
WE HAVE TO GET HOLD OF HIS POWERS FILE, SEE HOW HIS POWERS WERE HOLDING UP IN OLD AGE.
WE HAVE TO KNOW HOW POWERFUL A POWER HAD TO BE TO DO THIS TO HIM.
AT LEAST A FOUR.
I'D SAY A FOUR.

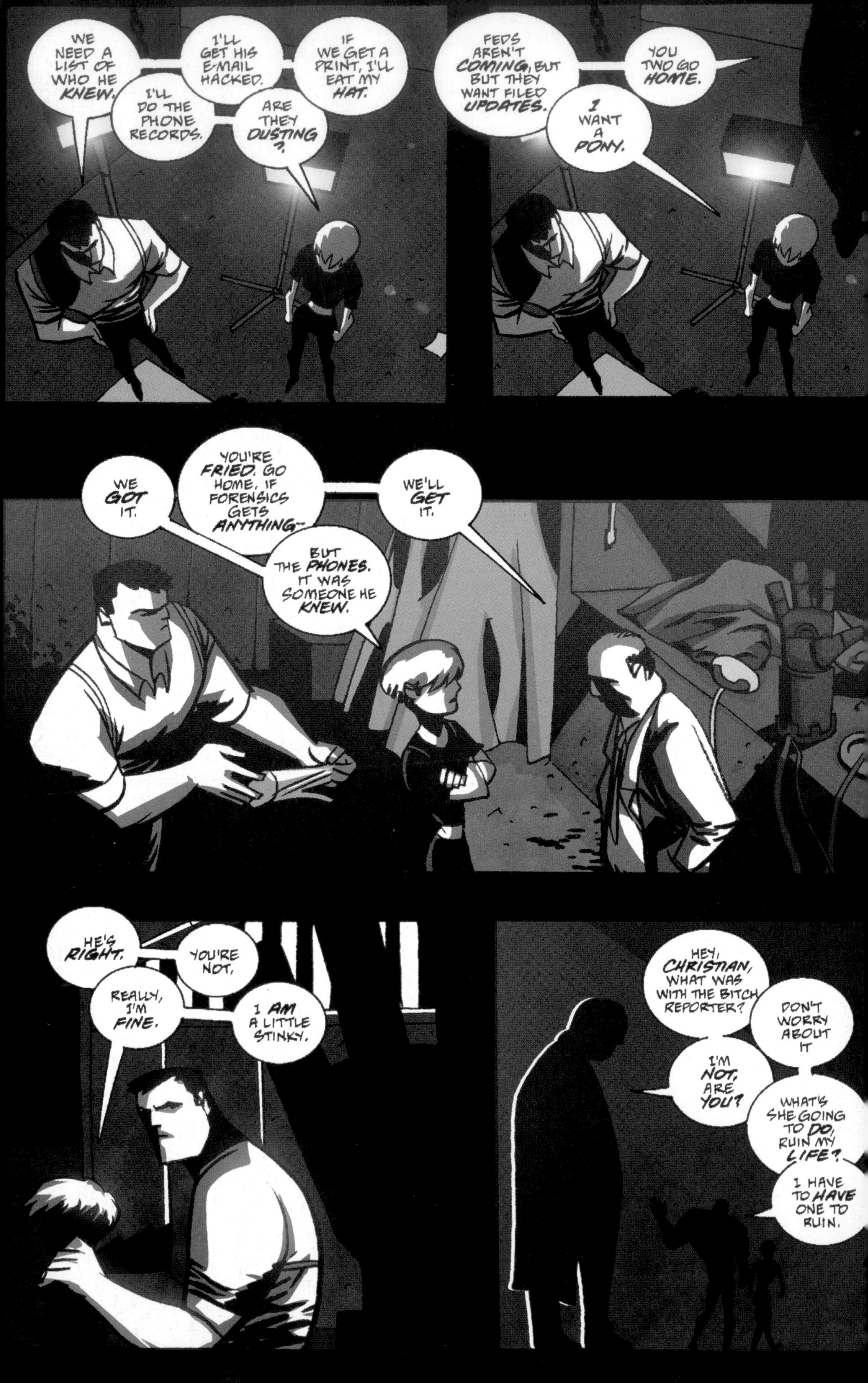
WE NEED A LIST OF WHO HE KNEW.
I'LL DO THE PHONE RECORDS.
I'LL GET HIS E-MAIL HACKED.
ARE THEY DUSTING?
IF WE GET A PRINT, I'LL EAT MY HAT.
FEDS AREN'T COMING, BUT BUT THEY WANT FILED UPDATES.
YOU TWO GO HOME.
I WANT A PONY.
WE GOT IT.
YOU'RE FRIED. GO HOME. IF FORENSICS GETS ANYTHING--
WE'LL GET IT.
BUT THE PHONES. IT WAS SOMEONE HE KNEW.
HE'S RIGHT.
YOU'RE NOT,
REALLY, I'M FINE.
I AM A LITTLE STINKY.
HEY, CHRISTIAN, WHAT WAS WITH THE BITCH REPORTER?
DON'T WORRY ABOUT IT
I'M NOT, ARE YOU?
WHAT'S SHE GOING TO DO, RUIN MY LIFE?
I HAVE TO HAVE ONE TO RUIN.

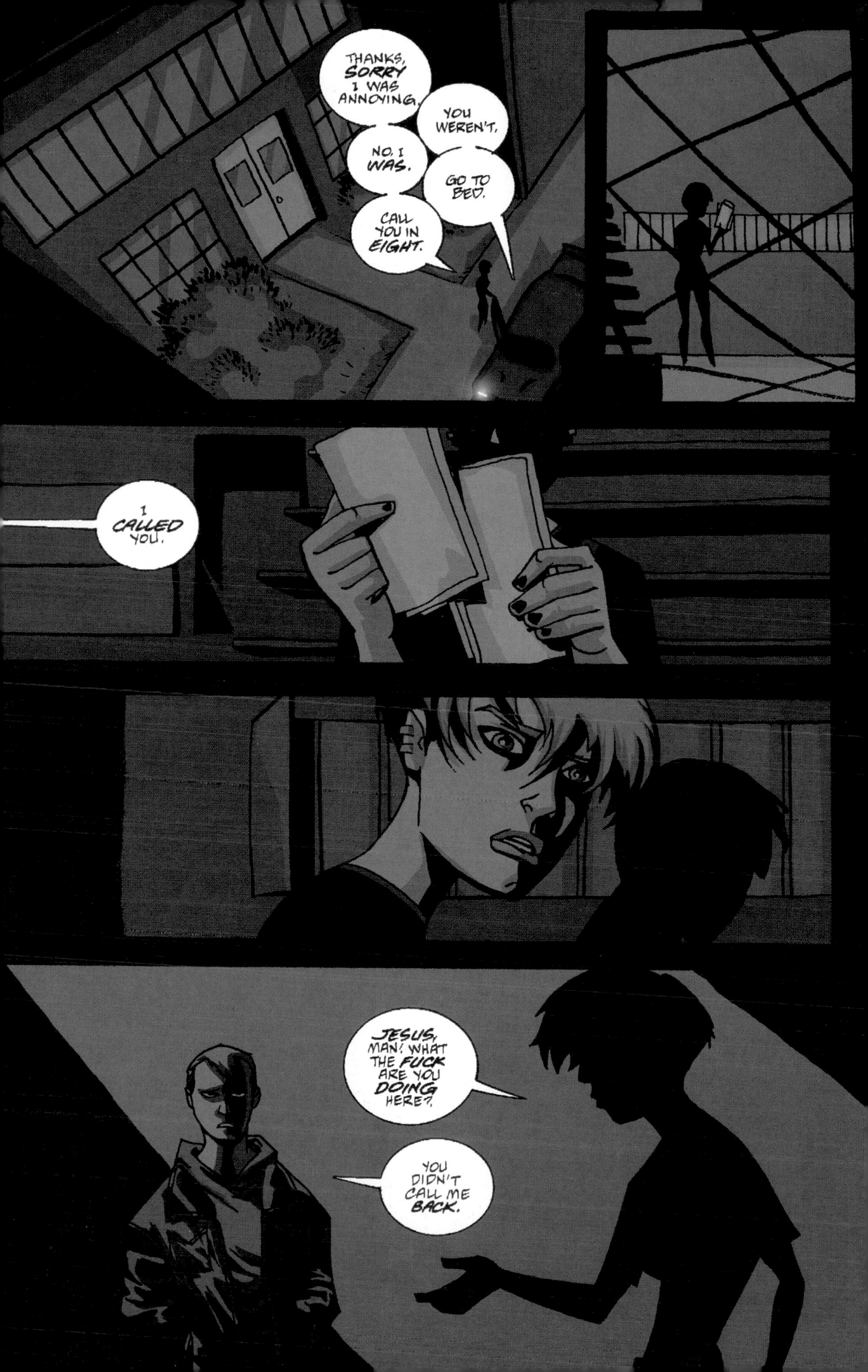
THANKS, SORRY I WAS ANNOYING.
YOU WEREN'T.
NO, I WAS.
GO TO BED.
CALL YOU IN EIGHT.
I CALLED YOU.
JESUS, MAN! WHAT THE FUCK ARE YOU DOING HERE?
YOU DIDN'T CALL ME BACK.

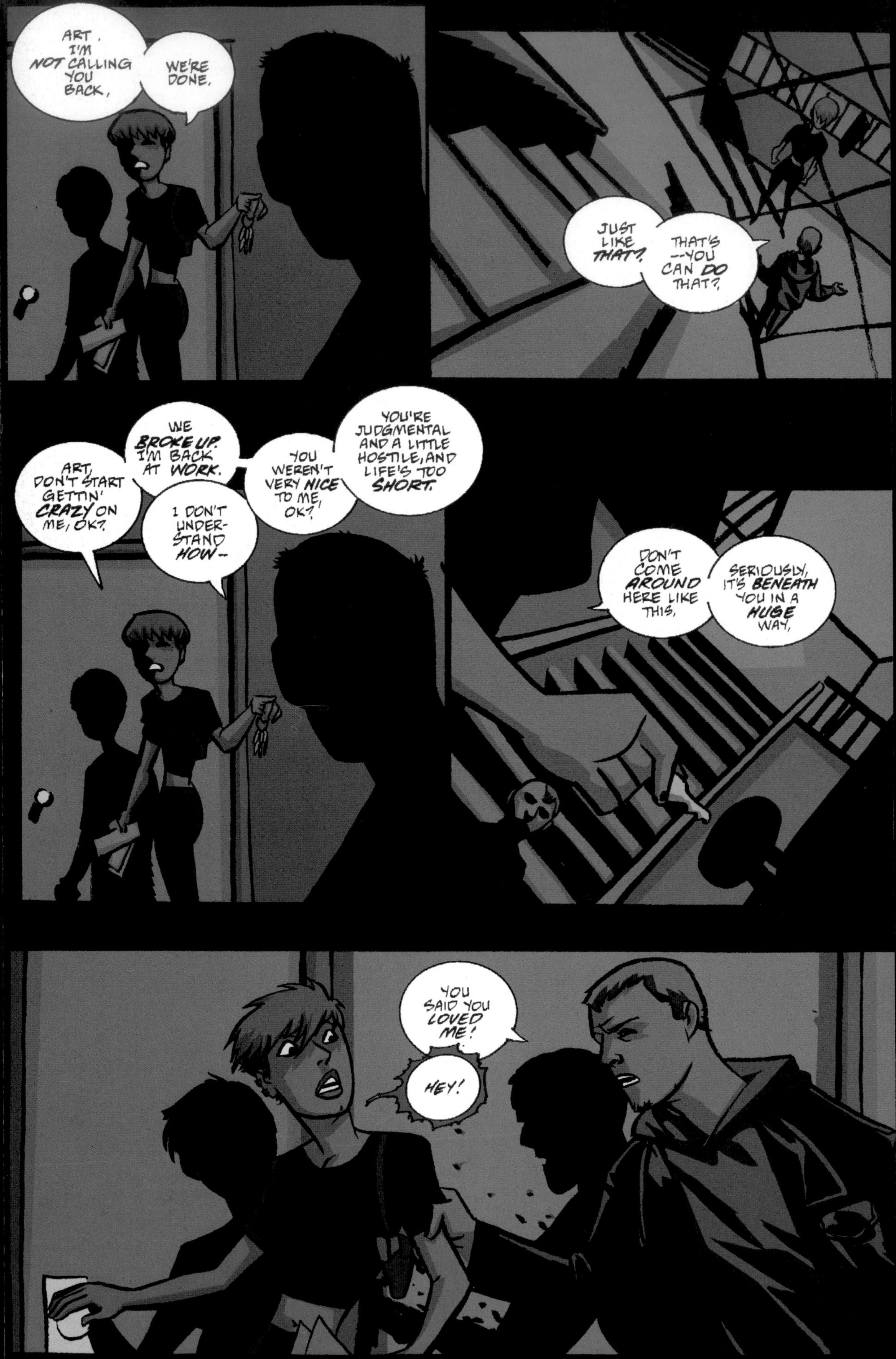
ART. I'M NOT CALLING YOU BACK.
WE'RE DONE.
JUST LIKE THAT?
THAT'S --YOU CAN DO THAT?
ART, DON'T START GETTIN' CRAZY ON ME, OK?
WE BROKE UP. I'M BACK AT WORK.
I DON'T UNDER-STAND HOW--
YOU WEREN'T VERY NICE TO ME, OK?
YOU'RE JUDGMENTAL AND A LITTLE HOSTILE, AND LIFE'S TOO SHORT.
DON'T COME AROUND HERE LIKE THIS.
SERIOUSLY, IT'S BENEATH YOU IN A HUGE WAY.
YOU SAID YOU LOVED ME!
HEY!

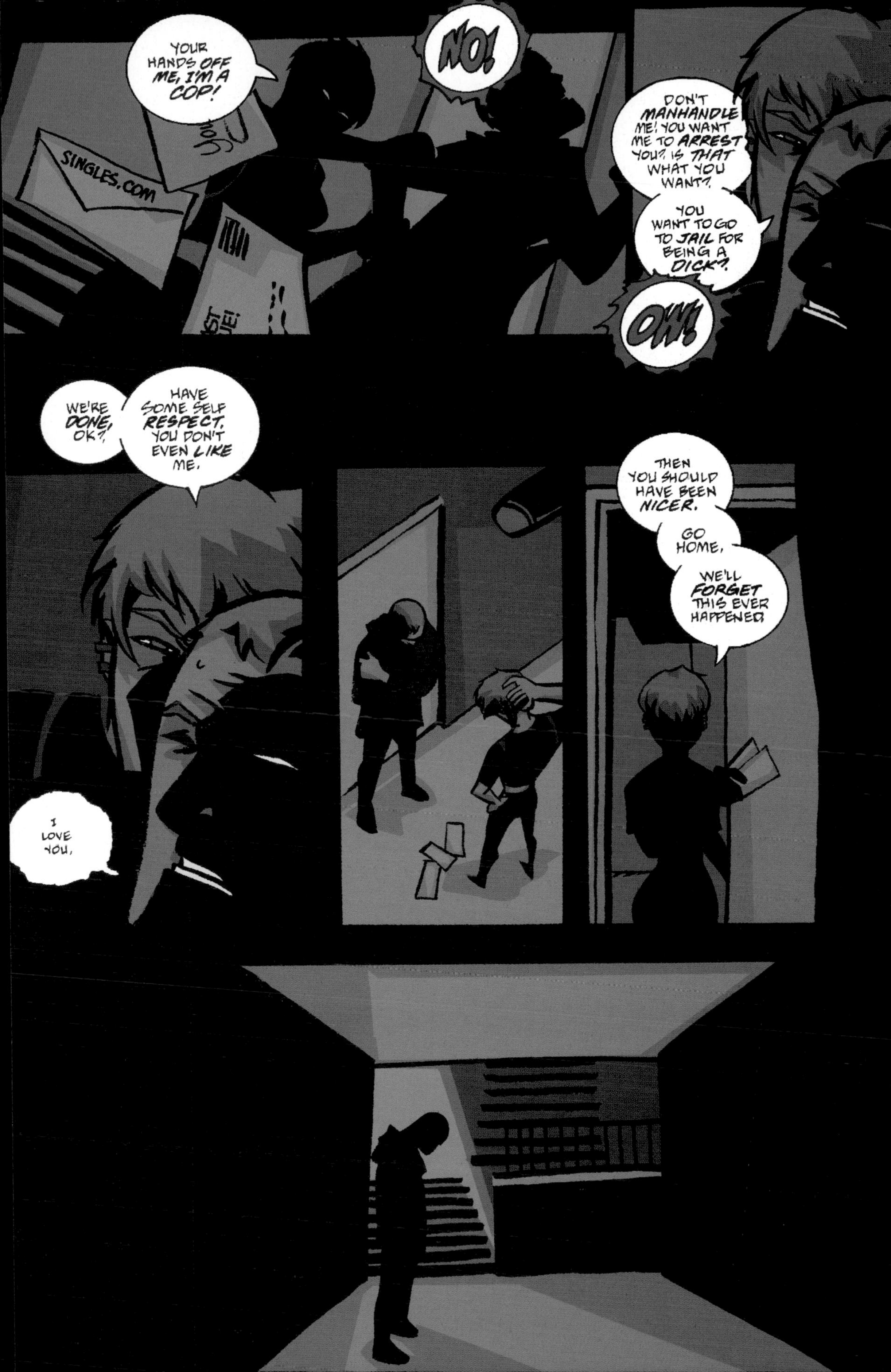

YOUR HANDS OFF ME, I'M A COP!
NO!
SINGLES.COM
DON'T MANHANDLE ME! YOU WANT ME TO ARREST YOU? IS THAT WHAT YOU WANT?
YOU WANT TO GO TO JAIL FOR BEING A DICK?
OW!
WE'RE DONE, OK?
HAVE SOME SELF RESPECT. YOU DON'T EVEN LIKE ME.
THEN YOU SHOULD HAVE BEEN NICER.
GO HOME.
WE'LL FORGET THIS EVER HAPPENED.
I LOVE YOU.

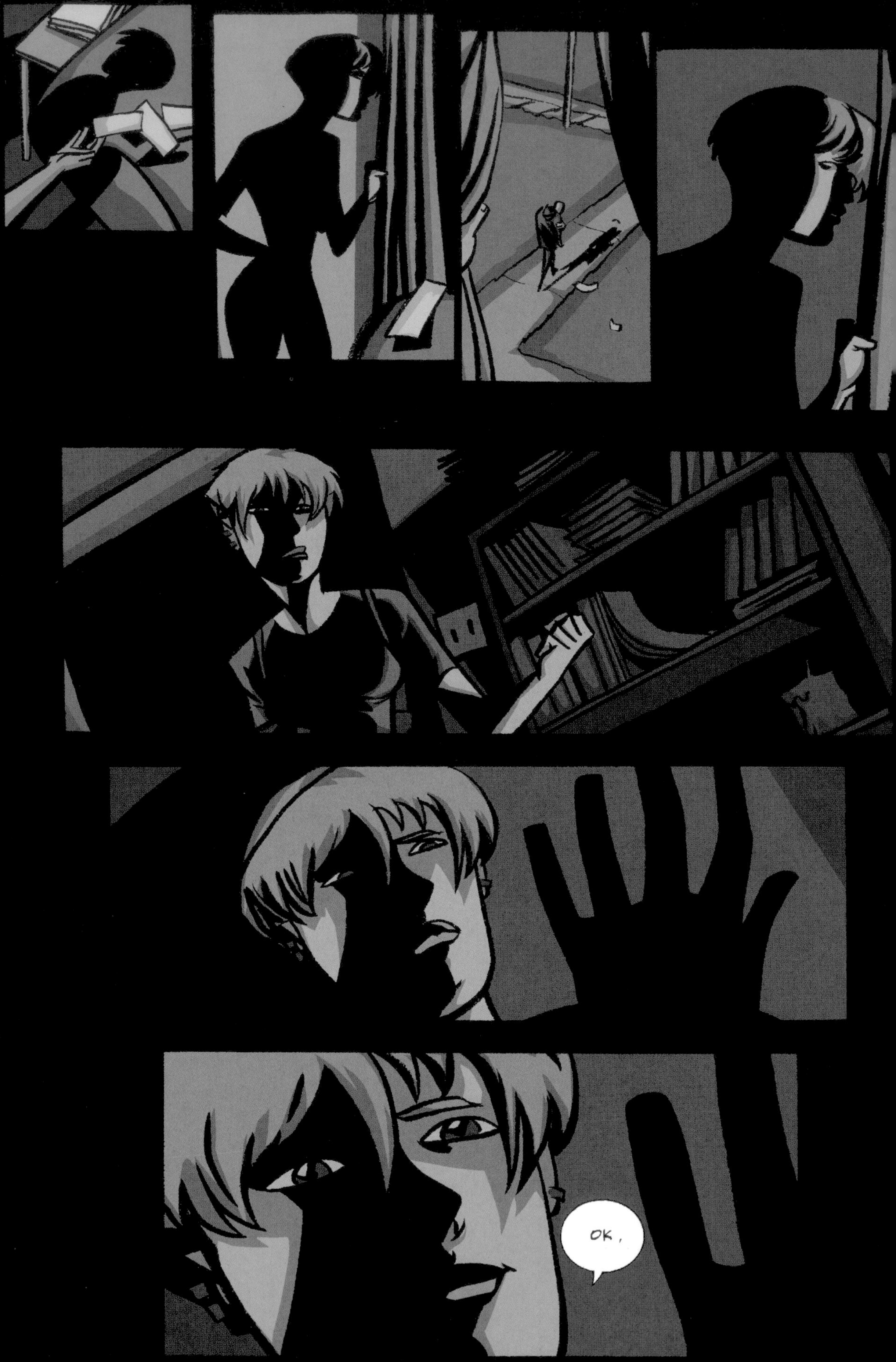
OK,

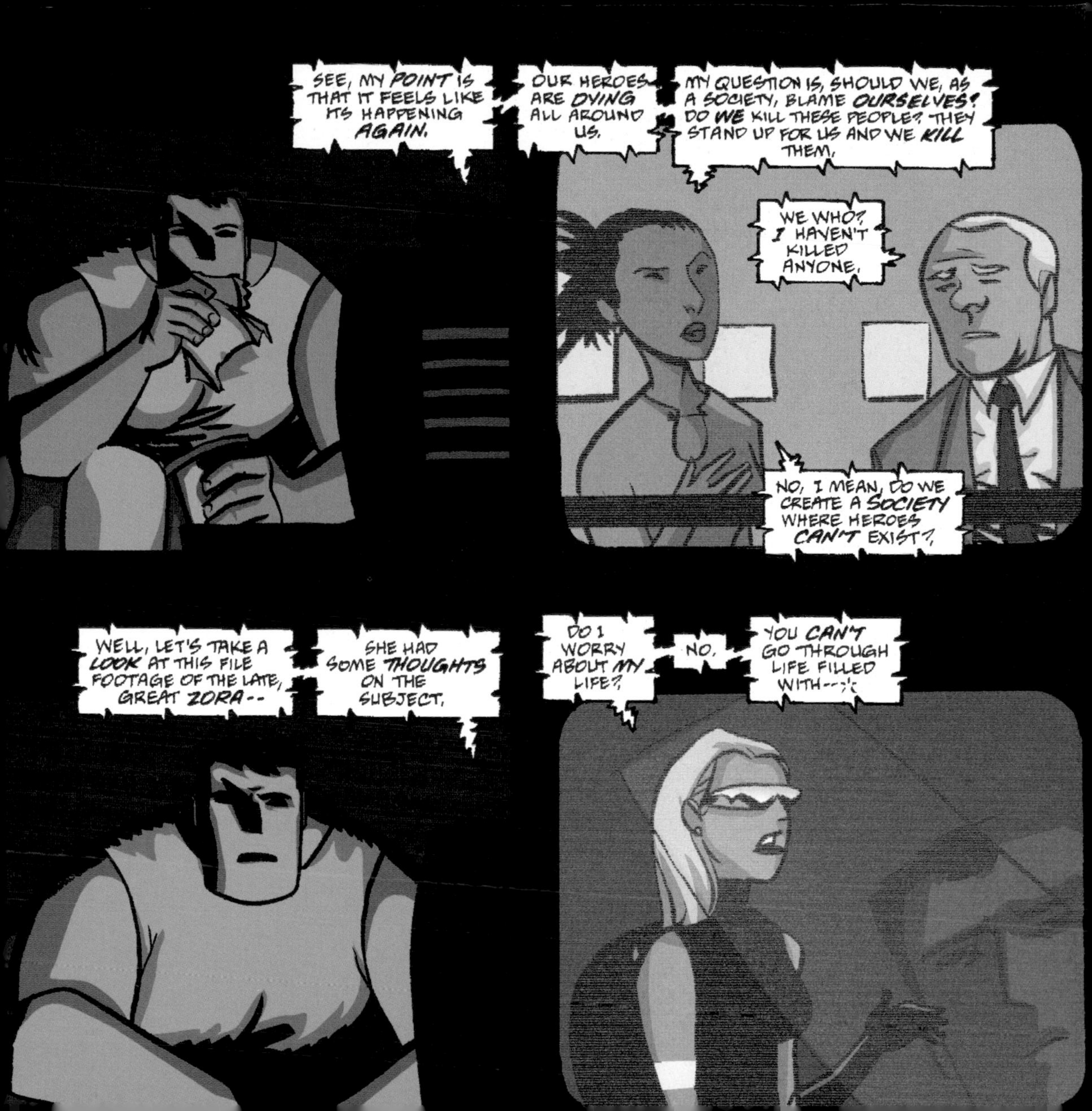
SEE, MY POINT IS THAT IT FEELS LIKE ITS HAPPENING AGAIN.
OUR HEROES ARE DYING ALL AROUND US.
MY QUESTION IS, SHOULD WE, AS A SOCIETY, BLAME OURSELVES? DO WE KILL THESE PEOPLE? THEY STAND UP FOR US AND WE KILL THEM.
WE WHO? I HAVEN'T KILLED ANYONE.
NO, I MEAN, DO WE CREATE A SOCIETY WHERE HEROES CAN'T EXIST?
WELL, LET'S TAKE A LOOK AT THIS FILE FOOTAGE OF THE LATE, GREAT ZORA--
SHE HAD SOME THOUGHTS ON THE SUBJECT.
DO I WORRY ABOUT MY LIFE?
NO.
YOU CAN'T GO THROUGH LIFE FILLED WITH--

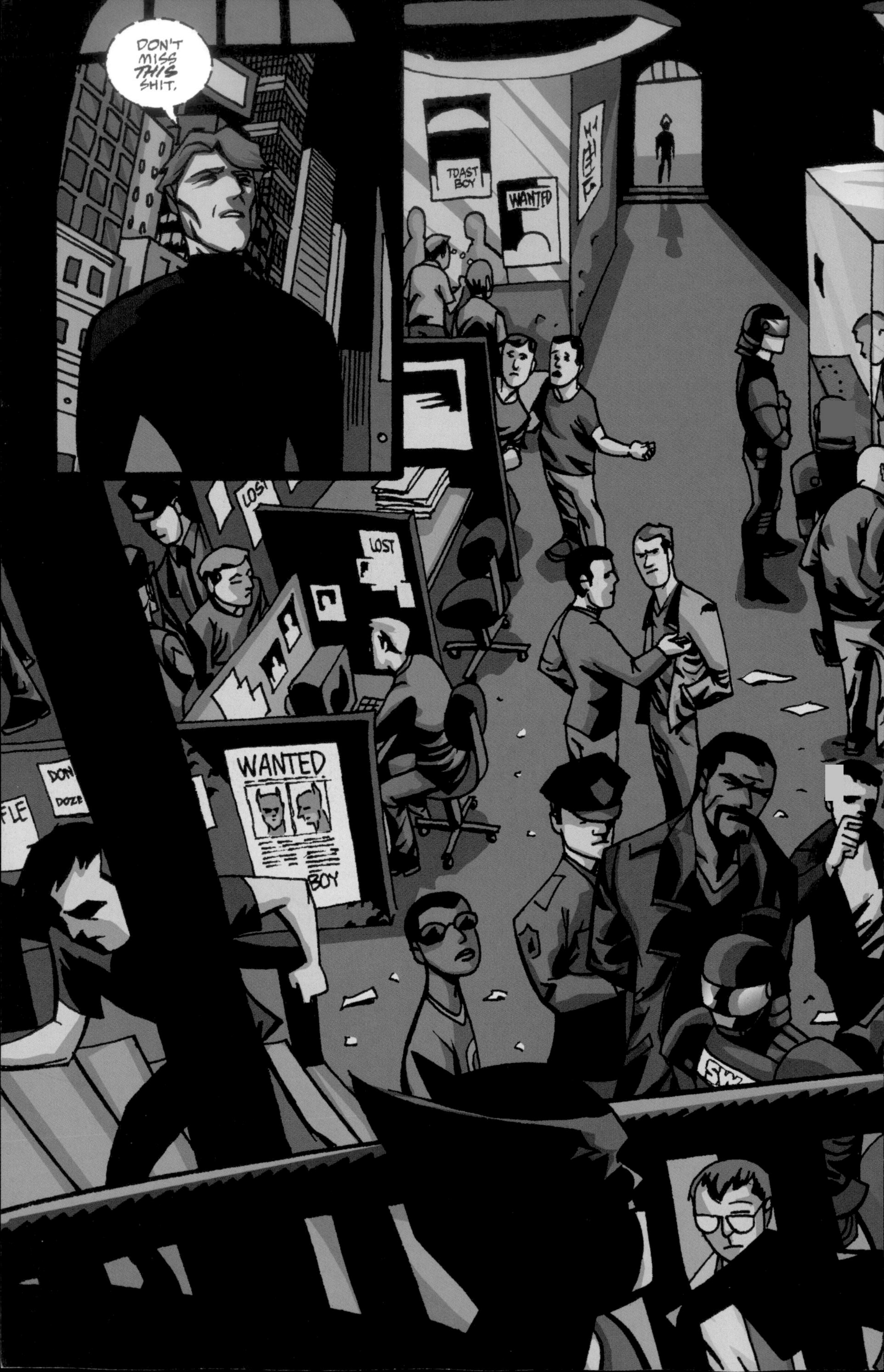
DON'T MISS THIS SHIT.
TOAST BOY
WANTED
LOST
LOST
WANTED
BOY

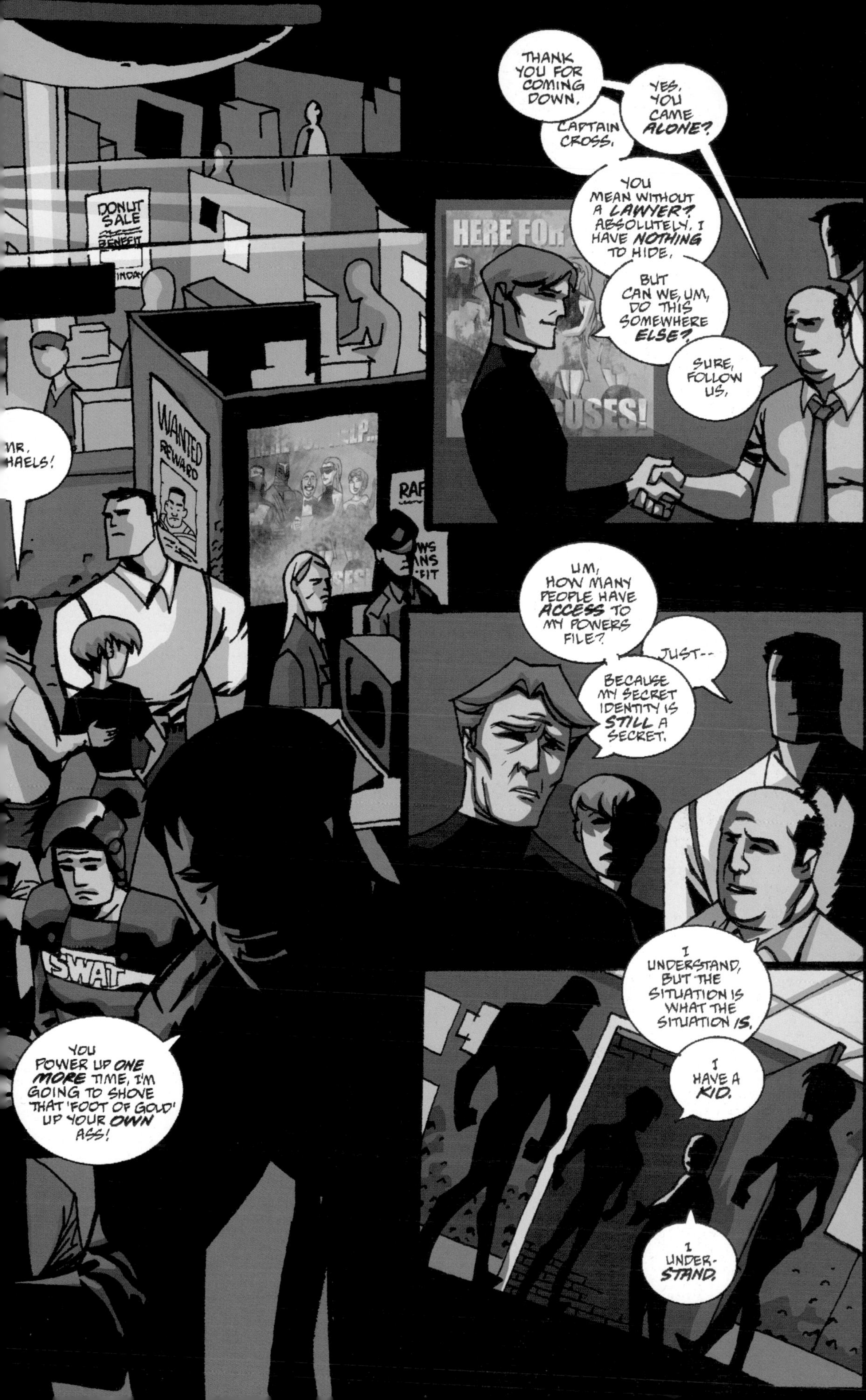
DONUT SALE
BENEFIT
WANTED
REWARD
MR. HAELS!
SWAT
YOU POWER UP ONE MORE TIME, I'M GOING TO SHOVE THAT 'FOOT OF GOLD' UP YOUR OWN ASS!
THANK YOU FOR COMING DOWN,
CAPTAIN CROSS.
YES. YOU CAME ALONE?
HERE FOR
YOU MEAN WITHOUT A LAWYER? ABSOLUTELY. I HAVE NOTHING TO HIDE.
BUT CAN WE, UM, DO THIS SOMEWHERE ELSE?
SURE, FOLLOW US.
UM, HOW MANY PEOPLE HAVE ACCESS TO MY POWERS FILE?
JUST--
BECAUSE MY SECRET IDENTITY IS STILL A SECRET.
I UNDERSTAND, BUT THE SITUATION IS WHAT THE SITUATION IS.
I HAVE A KID.
I UNDER-STAND.

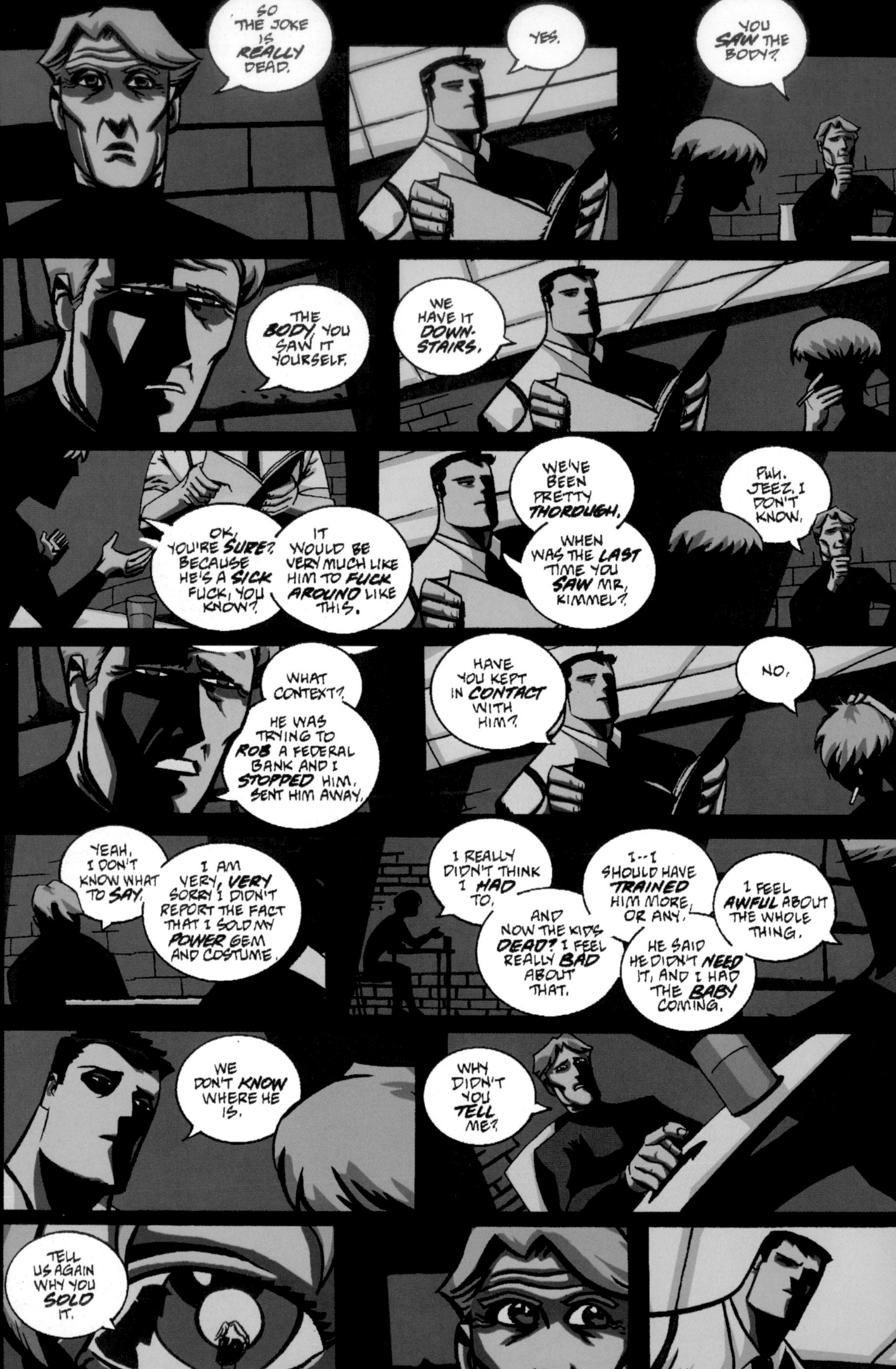
SO THE JOKE IS REALLY DEAD.
YES.
YOU SAW THE BODY?
THE BODY, YOU SAW IT YOURSELF.
WE HAVE IT DOWN-STAIRS.
OK, YOU'RE SURE? BECAUSE HE'S A SICK FUCK, YOU KNOW?
IT WOULD BE VERY MUCH LIKE HIM TO FUCK AROUND LIKE THIS.
WE'VE BEEN PRETTY THOROUGH.
WHEN WAS THE LAST TIME YOU SAW MR. KIMMEL?
PUH. JEEZ, I DON'T KNOW.
WHAT CONTEXT?
HE WAS TRYING TO ROB A FEDERAL BANK AND I STOPPED HIM. SENT HIM AWAY.
HAVE YOU KEPT IN CONTACT WITH HIM?
NO.
YEAH, I DON'T KNOW WHAT TO SAY.
I AM VERY, VERY SORRY I DIDN'T REPORT THE FACT THAT I SOLD MY POWER GEM AND COSTUME.
I REALLY DIDN'T THINK I HAD TO.
AND NOW THE KIDS DEAD? I FEEL REALLY BAD ABOUT THAT.
I--I SHOULD HAVE TRAINED HIM MORE, OR ANY.
HE SAID HE DIDN'T NEED IT, AND I HAD THE BABY COMING.
I FEEL AWFUL ABOUT THE WHOLE THING.
WE DON'T KNOW WHERE HE IS.
WHY DIDN'T YOU TELL ME?
TELL US AGAIN WHY YOU SOLD IT.

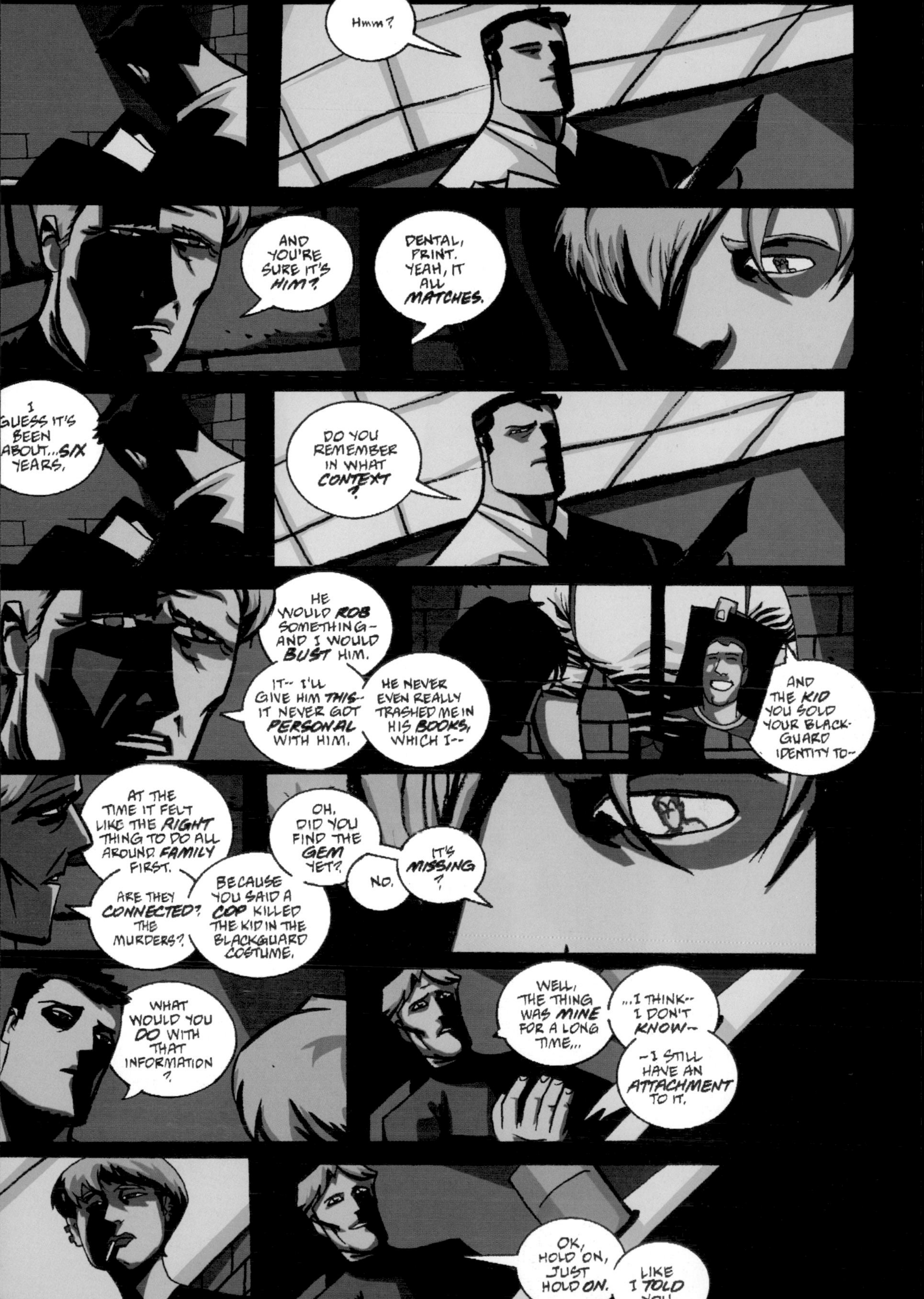
Hmm?
AND YOU'RE SURE IT'S HIM?
DENTAL, PRINT. YEAH, IT ALL MATCHES.
I GUESS IT'S BEEN ABOUT... SIX YEARS.
DO YOU REMEMBER IN WHAT CONTEXT?
HE WOULD ROB SOMETHING-- AND I WOULD BUST HIM.
IT-- I'LL GIVE HIM THIS-- IT NEVER GOT PERSONAL WITH HIM.
HE NEVER EVEN REALLY TRASHED ME IN HIS BOOKS, WHICH I--
AND THE KID YOU SOLD YOUR BLACK-GUARD IDENTITY TO--
AT THE TIME IT FELT LIKE THE RIGHT THING TO DO ALL AROUND. FAMILY FIRST.
ARE THEY CONNECTED? THE MURDERS?
BECAUSE YOU SAID A COP KILLED THE KID IN THE BLACKGUARD COSTUME.
OH, DID YOU FIND THE GEM YET?
NO.
IT'S MISSING?
WHAT WOULD YOU DO WITH THAT INFORMATION?
WELL, THE THING WAS MINE FOR A LONG TIME...
...I THINK-- I DON'T KNOW--
--I STILL HAVE AN ATTACHMENT TO IT.
OK, HOLD ON, JUST HOLD ON.
LIKE I TOLD YOU.

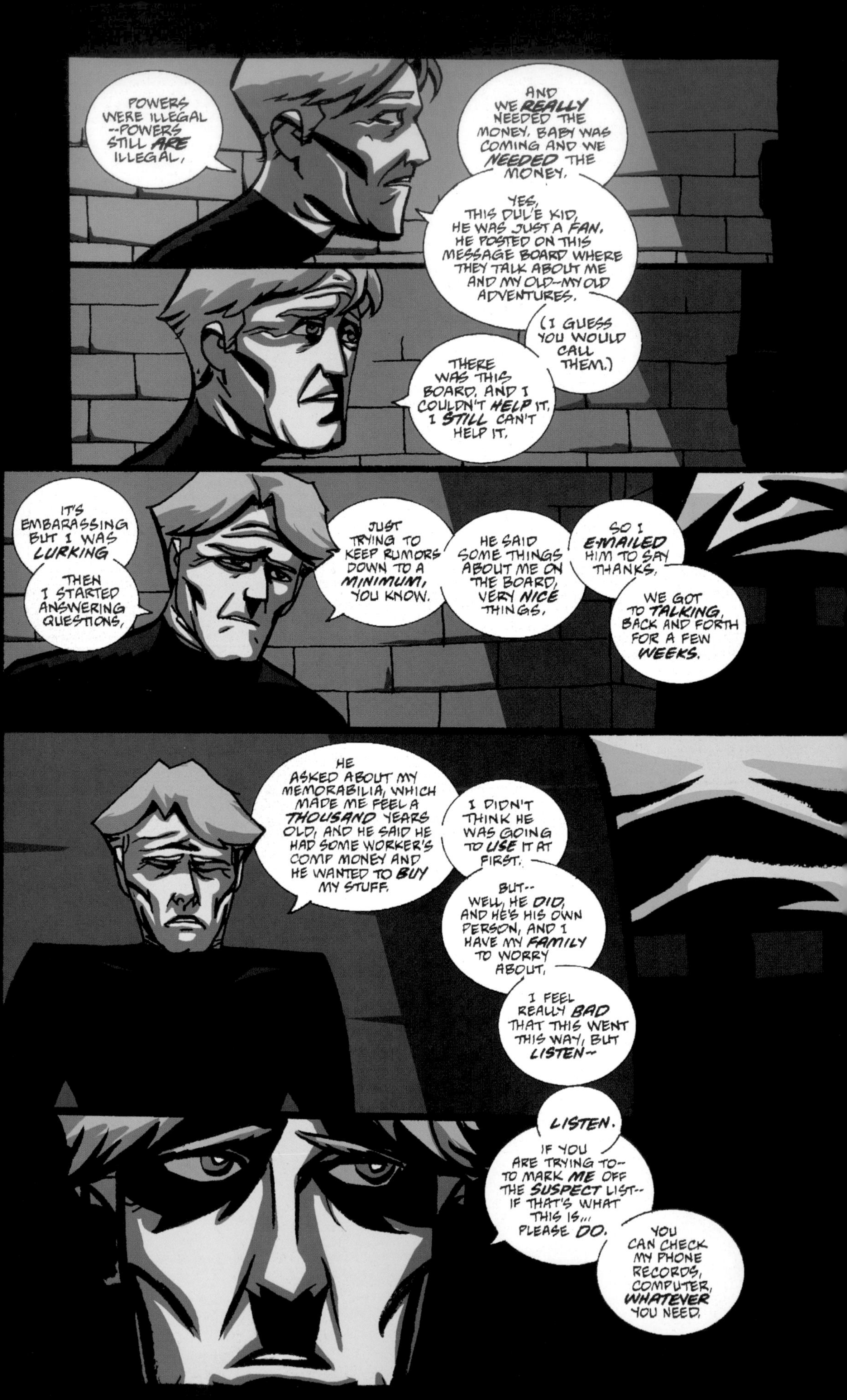
POWERS WERE ILLEGAL --POWERS STILL ARE ILLEGAL.
AND WE REALLY NEEDED THE MONEY. BABY WAS COMING AND WE NEEDED THE MONEY.
YES, THIS DULE KID, HE WAS JUST A FAN. HE POSTED ON THIS MESSAGE BOARD WHERE THEY TALK ABOUT ME AND MY OLD--MY OLD ADVENTURES.
(I GUESS YOU WOULD CALL THEM.)
THERE WAS THIS BOARD, AND I COULDN'T HELP IT. I STILL CAN'T HELP IT.
IT'S EMBARASSING BUT I WAS LURKING.
THEN I STARTED ANSWERING QUESTIONS.
JUST TRYING TO KEEP RUMORS DOWN TO A MINIMUM, YOU KNOW.
HE SAID SOME THINGS ABOUT ME ON THE BOARD, VERY NICE THINGS.
SO I E-MAILED HIM TO SAY THANKS.
WE GOT TO TALKING, BACK AND FORTH FOR A FEW WEEKS.
HE ASKED ABOUT MY MEMORABILIA, WHICH MADE ME FEEL A THOUSAND YEARS OLD, AND HE SAID HE HAD SOME WORKER'S COMP MONEY AND HE WANTED TO BUY MY STUFF.
I DIDN'T THINK HE WAS GOING TO USE IT AT FIRST.
BUT-- WELL, HE DID, AND HE'S HIS OWN PERSON, AND I HAVE MY FAMILY TO WORRY ABOUT.
I FEEL REALLY BAD THAT THIS WENT THIS WAY, BUT LISTEN--
LISTEN.
IF YOU ARE TRYING TO-- TO MARK ME OFF THE SUSPECT LIST-- IF THAT'S WHAT THIS IS... PLEASE DO.
YOU CAN CHECK MY PHONE RECORDS, COMPUTER, WHATEVER YOU NEED.

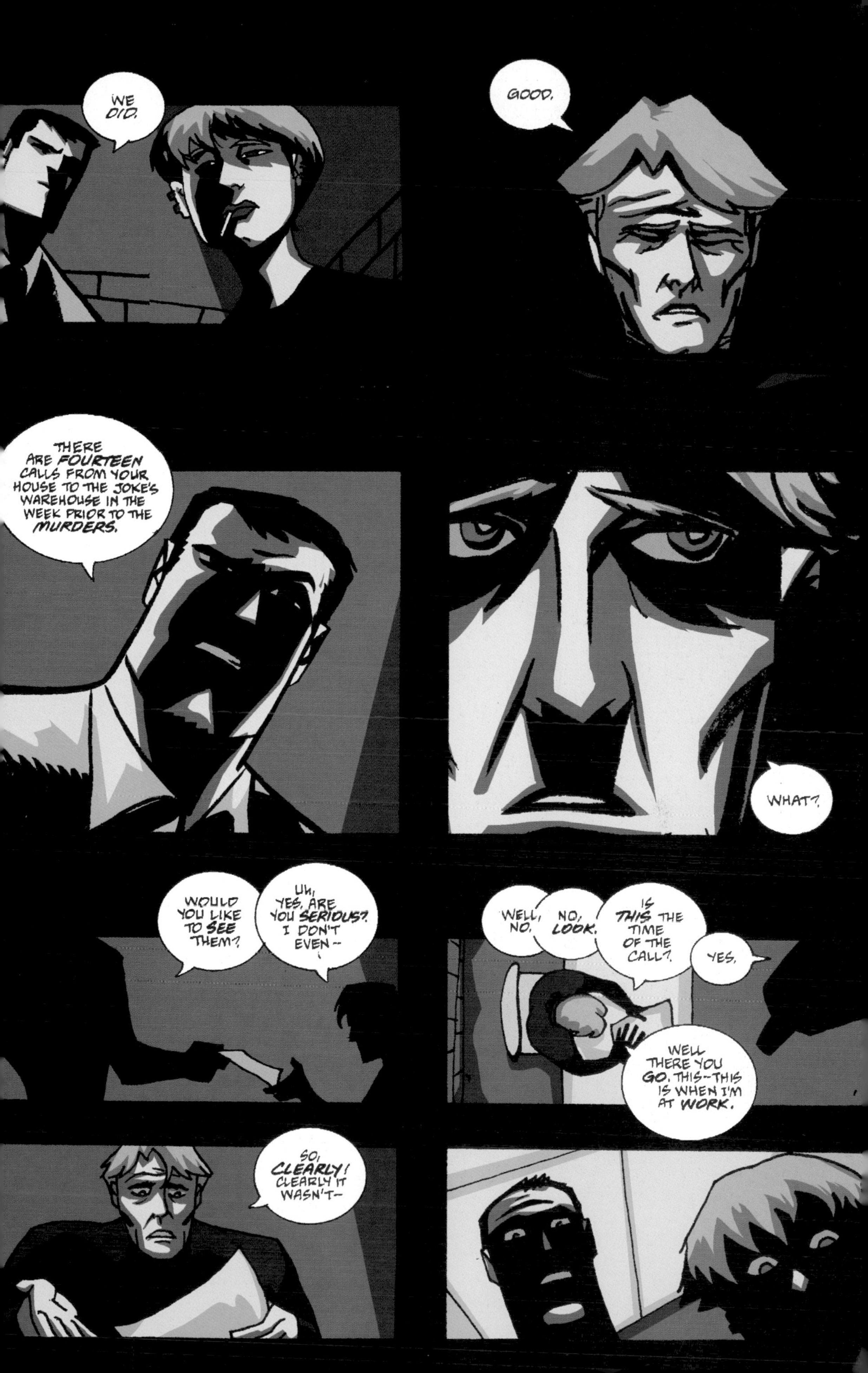

WE DID.
GOOD.
THERE ARE FOURTEEN CALLS FROM YOUR HOUSE TO THE JOKE'S WAREHOUSE IN THE WEEK PRIOR TO THE MURDERS.
WHAT?
WOULD YOU LIKE TO SEE THEM?
UH, YES. ARE YOU SERIOUS? I DON'T EVEN--
WELL, NO.
NO, LOOK.
IS THIS THE TIME OF THE CALL?
YES.
WELL THERE YOU GO. THIS--THIS IS WHEN I'M AT WORK.
SO, CLEARLY! CLEARLY IT WASN'T--

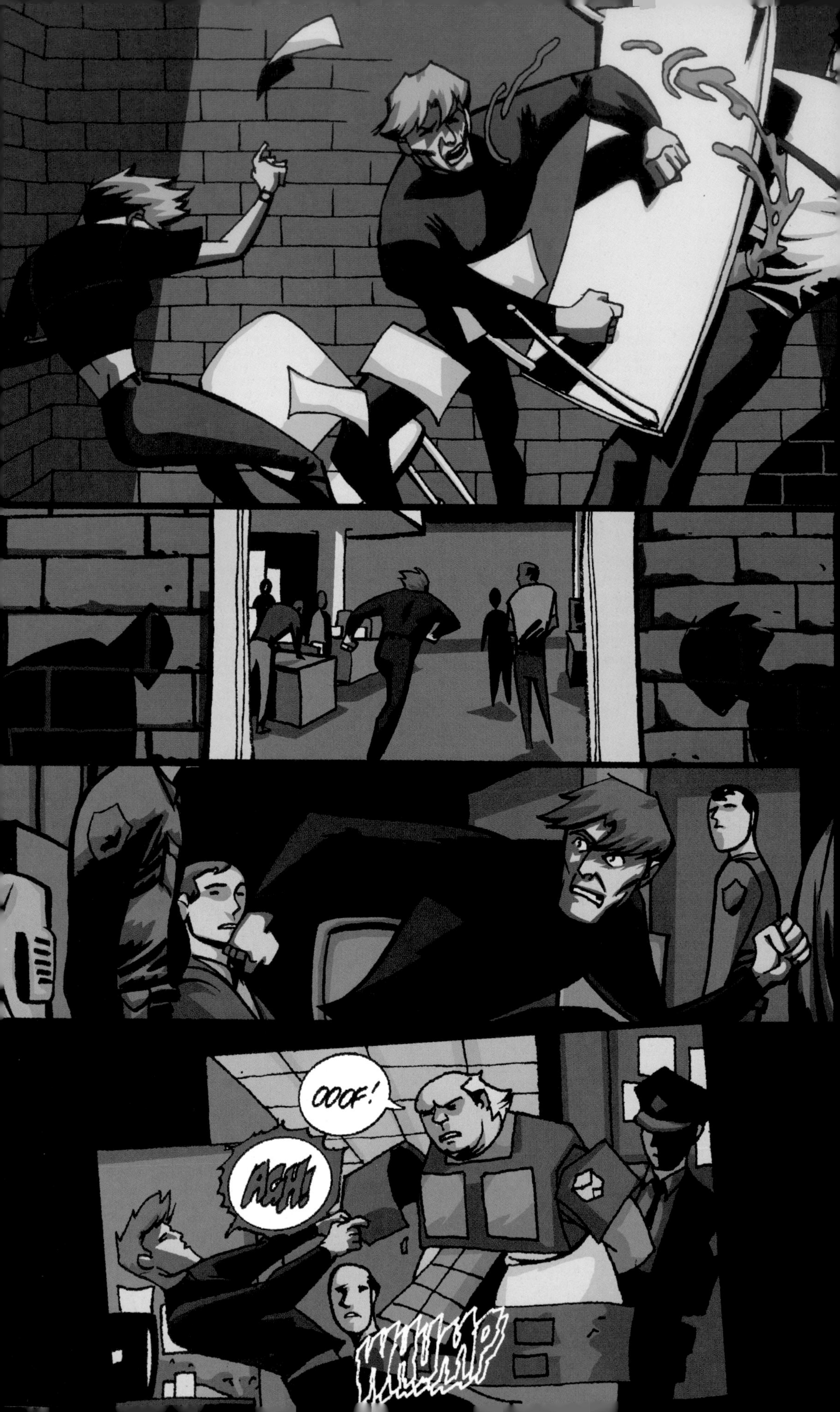
OOOF!
AGH!
WHUMP

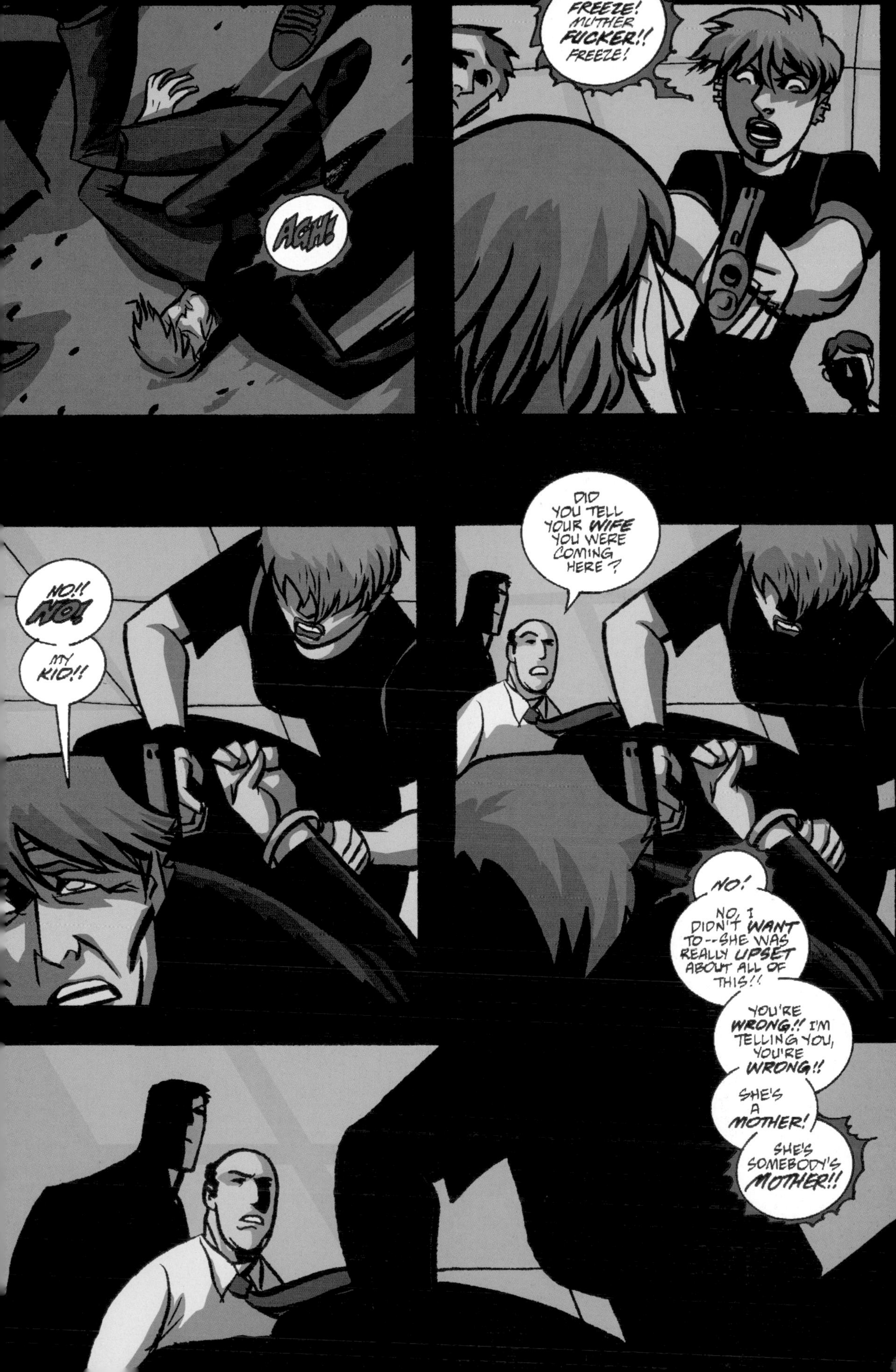
ACGH!
FREEZE! MUTHER FUCKER!! FREEZE!
NO!! NO!
MY KID!!
DID YOU TELL YOUR WIFE YOU WERE COMING HERE?
NO!
NO, I DIDN'T WANT TO--SHE WAS REALLY UPSET ABOUT ALL OF THIS!!
YOU'RE WRONG!! I'M TELLING YOU, YOU'RE WRONG!!
SHE'S A MOTHER!
SHE'S SOMEBODY'S MOTHER!!

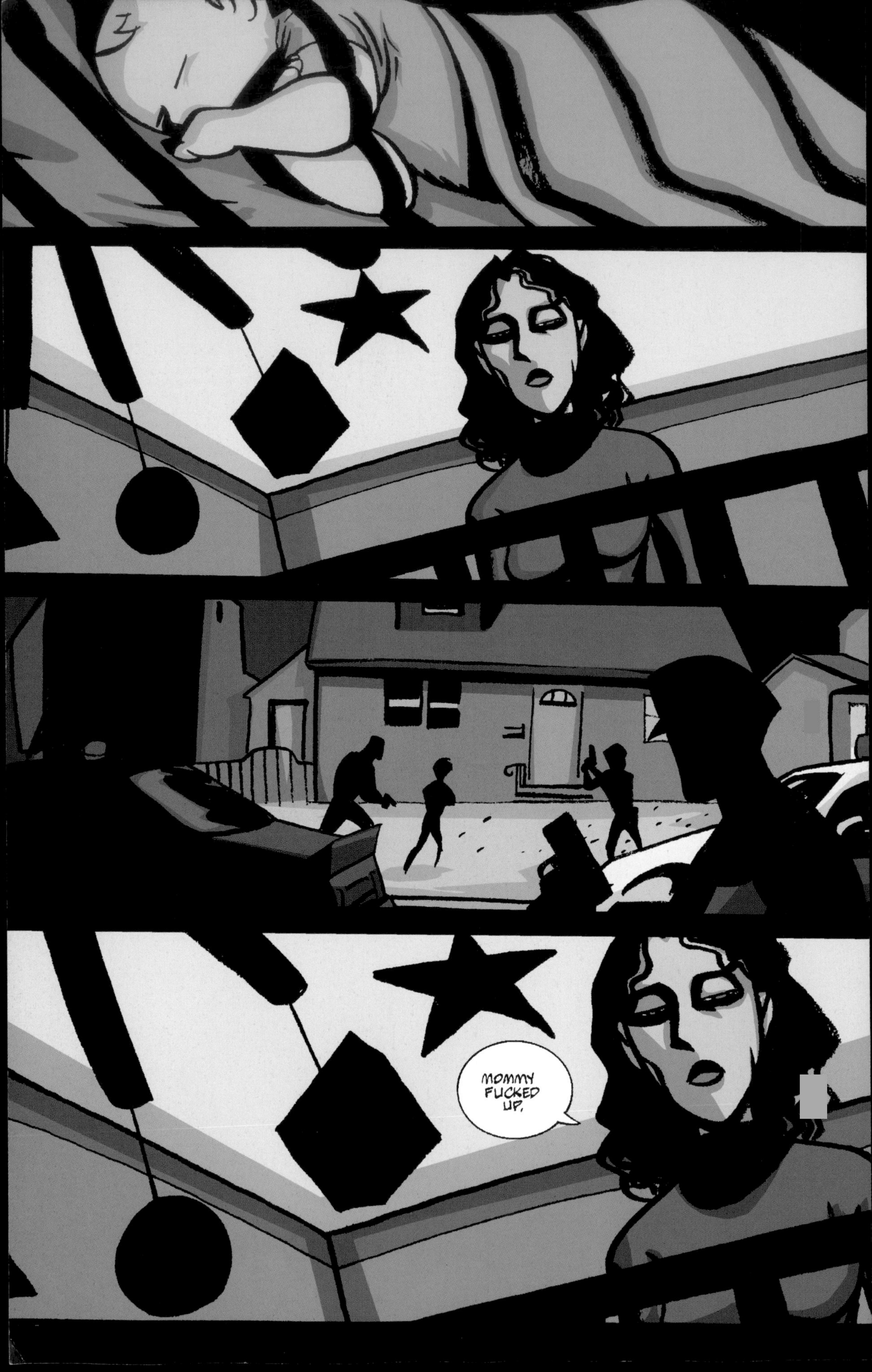
MOMMY FUCKED UP.

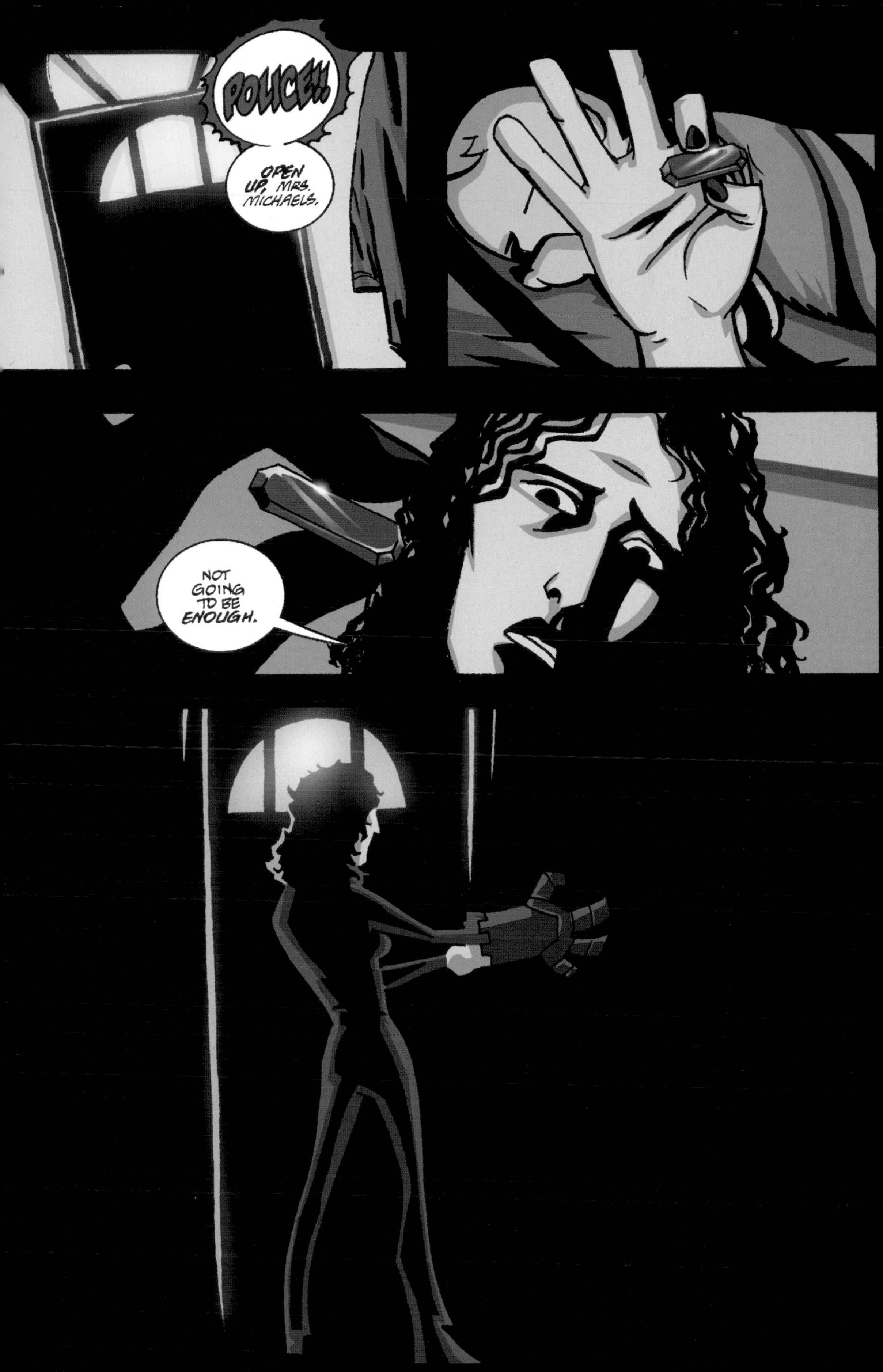
POLICE!!
OPEN UP, MRS. MICHAELS.
NOT GOING TO BE ENOUGH.

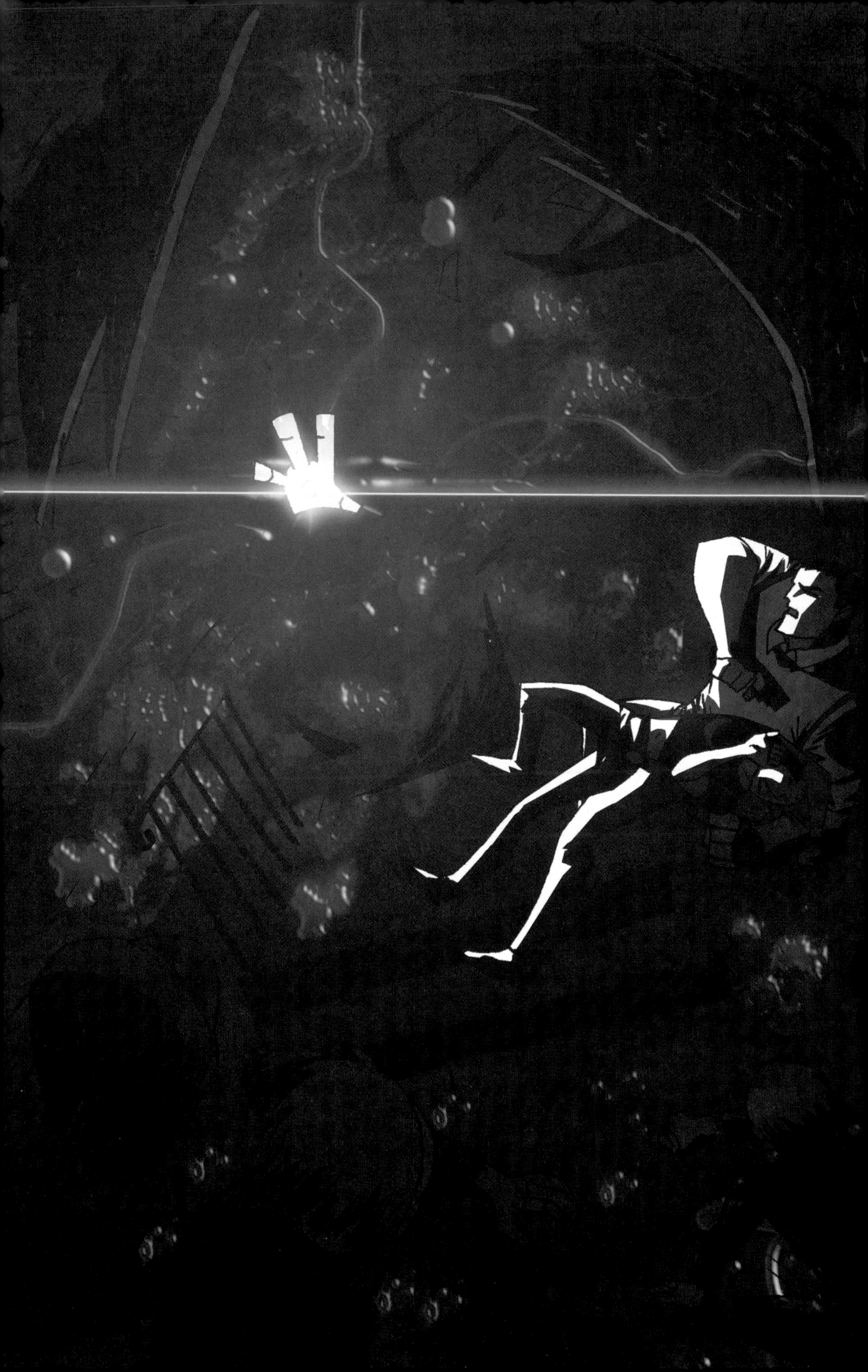

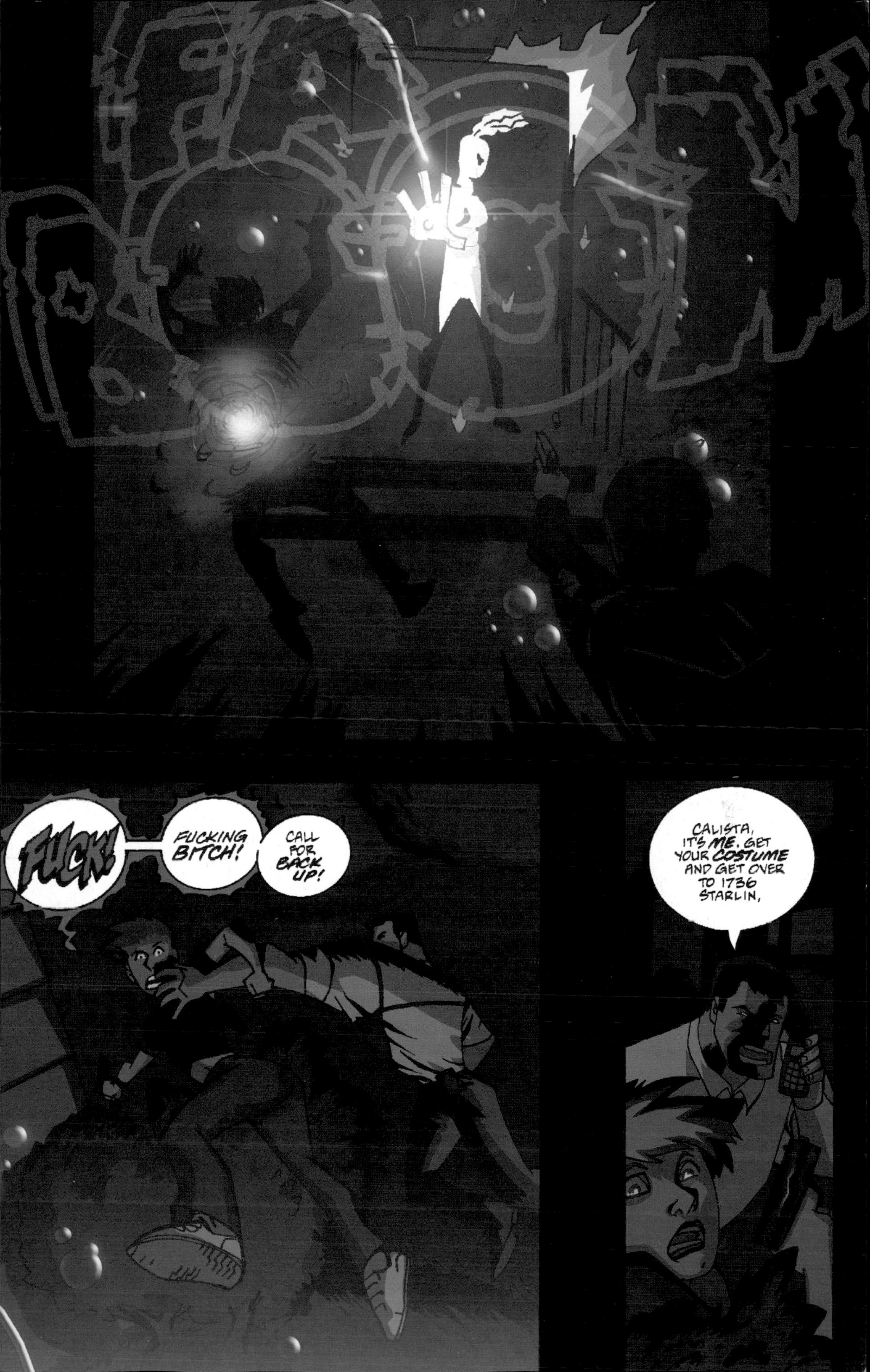
FUCK!
FUCKING BITCH!
CALL FOR BACK UP!
CALISTA, IT'S ME. GET YOUR COSTUME AND GET OVER TO 1736 STARLIN,

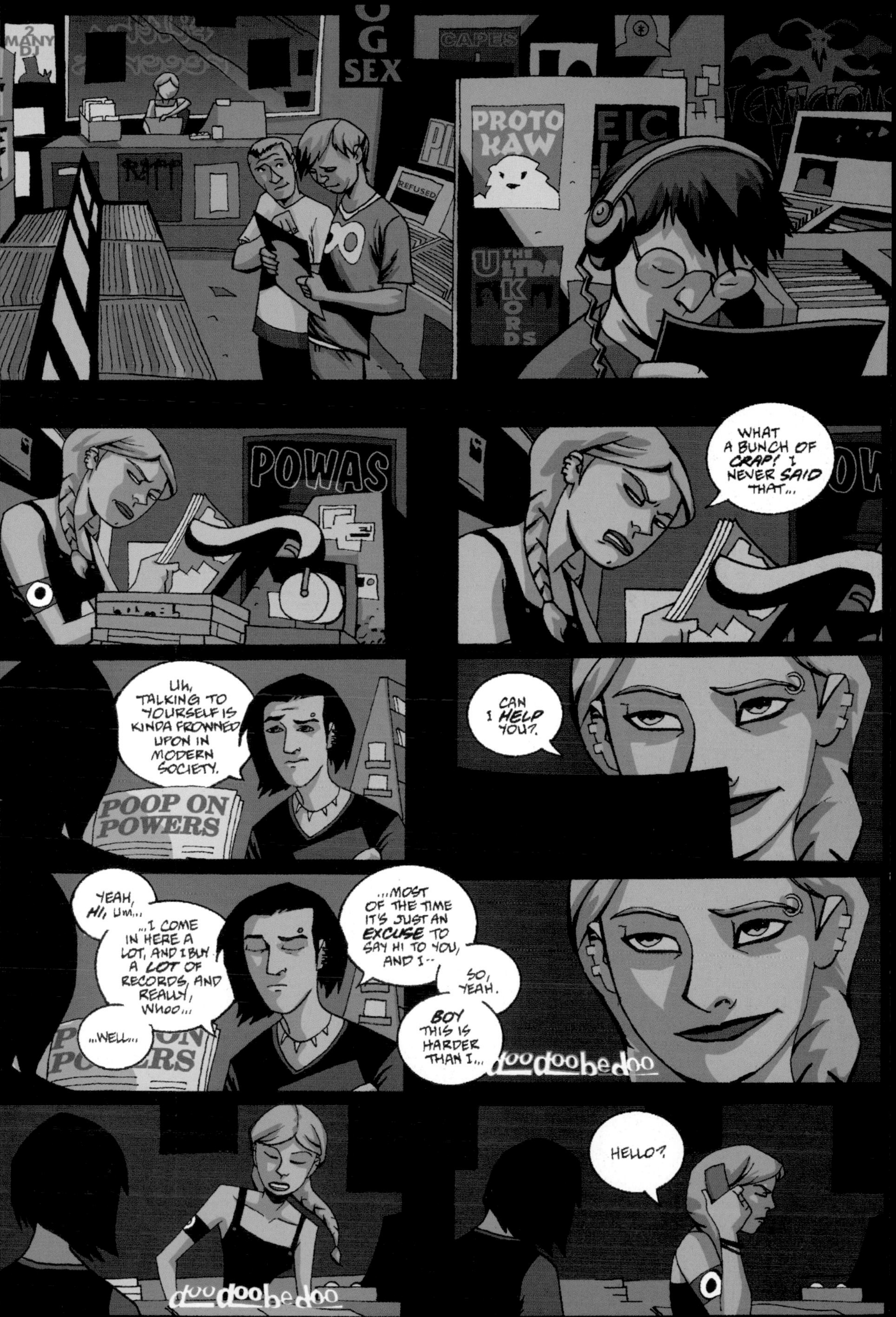

2 MANY DJ
UG SEX
CAPES
PROTO KAW
REFUSED
THE ULTRA KORDS
POWAS
WHAT A BUNCH OF CRAP! I NEVER SAID THAT...
UH, TALKING TO YOURSELF IS KINDA FROWNED UPON IN MODERN SOCIETY.
POOP ON POWERS
CAN I HELP YOU?
YEAH, HI, UM...
...I COME IN HERE A LOT, AND I BUY A LOT OF RECORDS, AND REALLY, WHOO...
...WELL...
...MOST OF THE TIME IT'S JUST AN EXCUSE TO SAY HI TO YOU, AND I--
SO, YEAH.
BOY THIS IS HARDER THAN I...
doodoobedoo
doodoobedoo
HELLO?

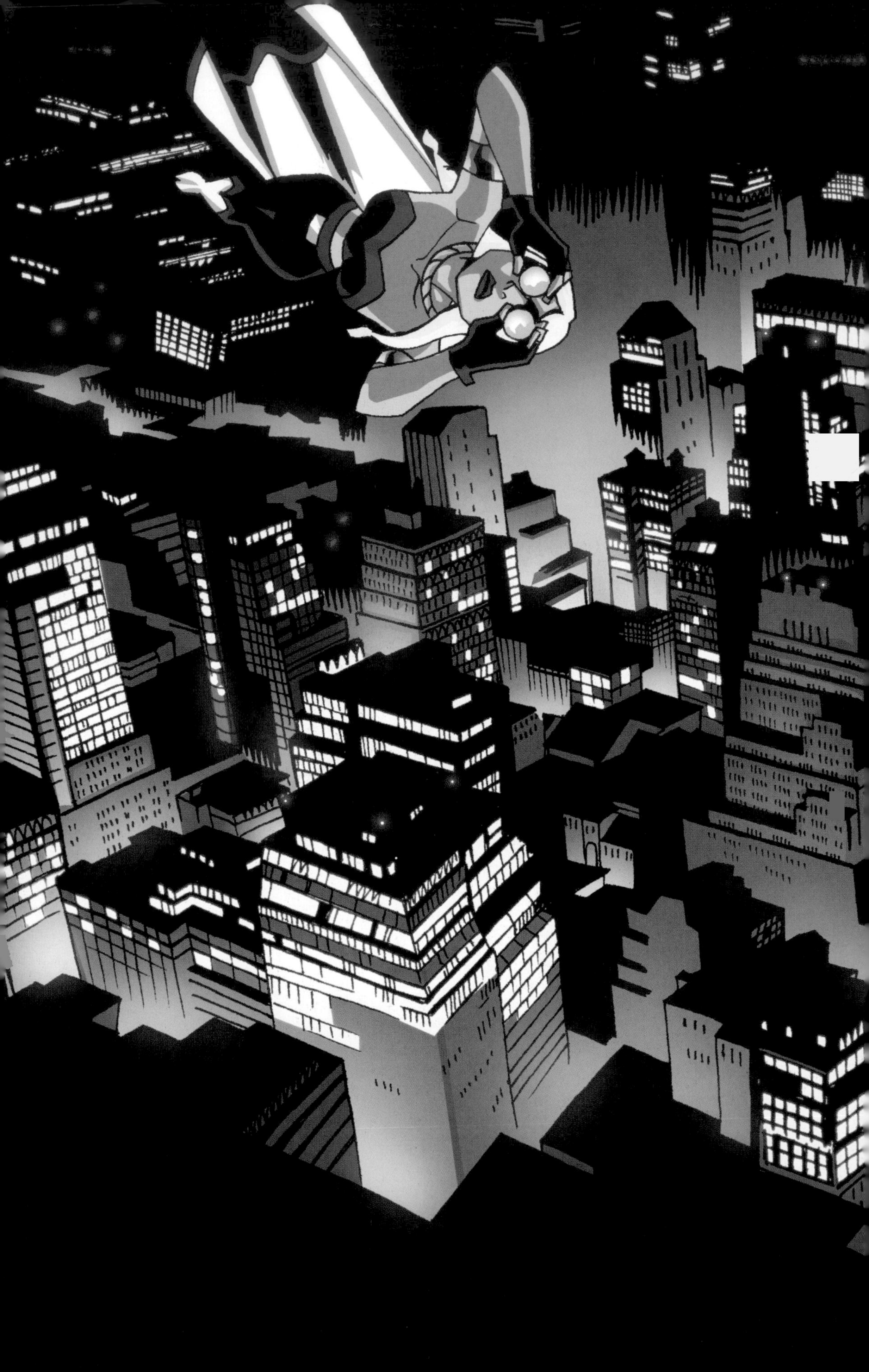

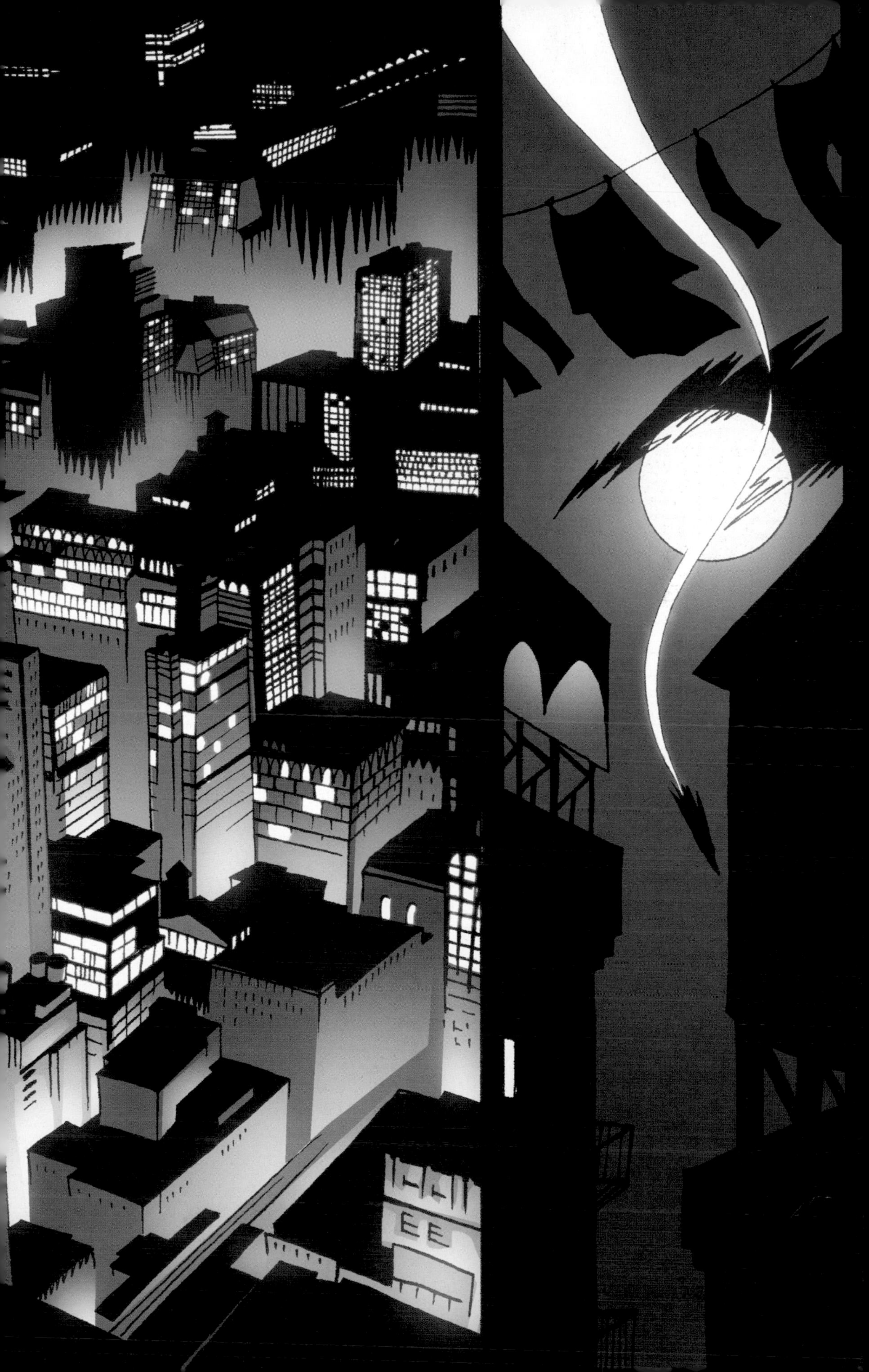

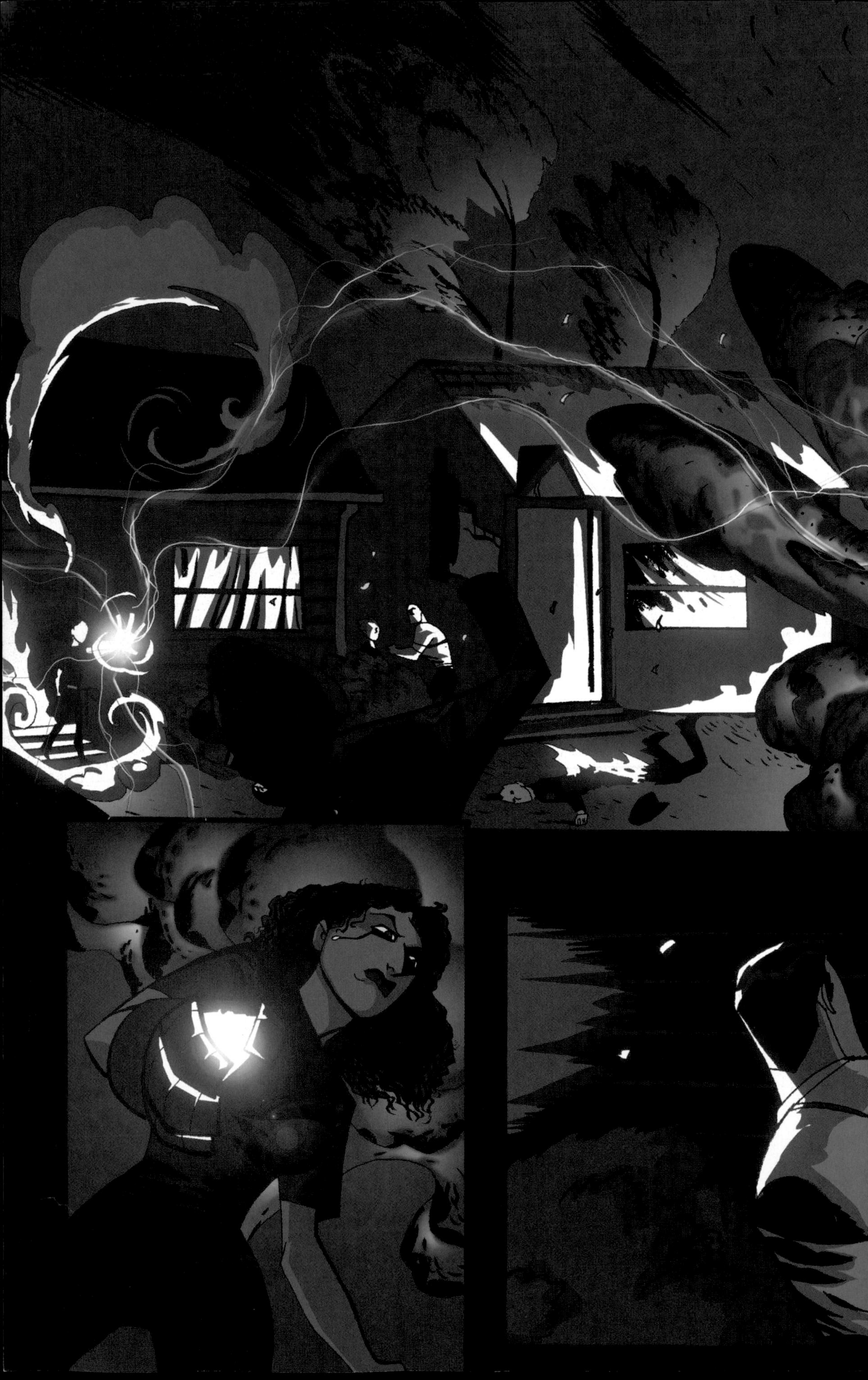

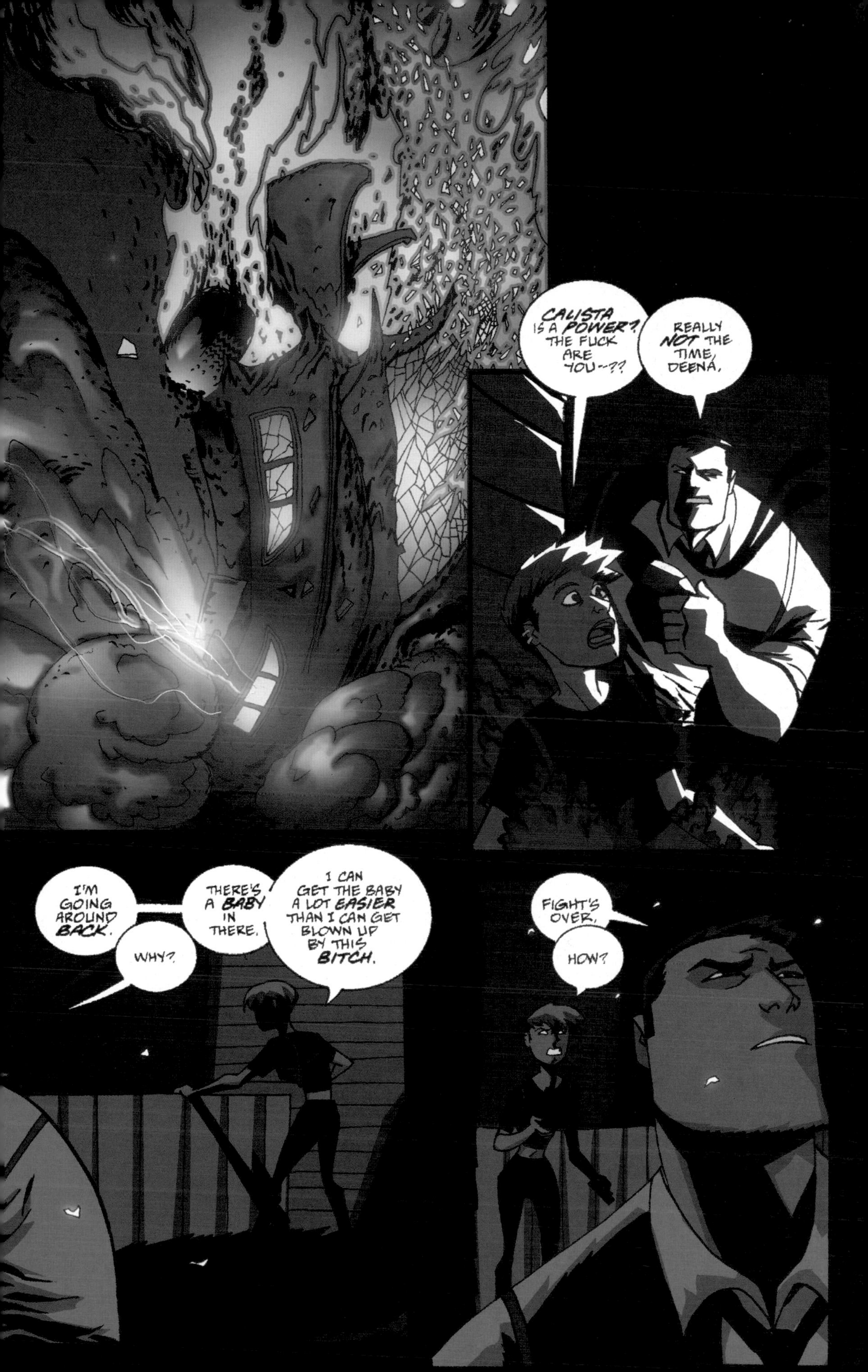
CALISTA IS A POWER? THE FUCK ARE YOU--??
REALLY NOT THE TIME, DEENA.
I'M GOING AROUND BACK.
WHY?
THERE'S A BABY IN THERE.
I CAN GET THE BABY A LOT EASIER THAN I CAN GET BLOWN UP BY THIS BITCH.
FIGHT'S OVER.
HOW?

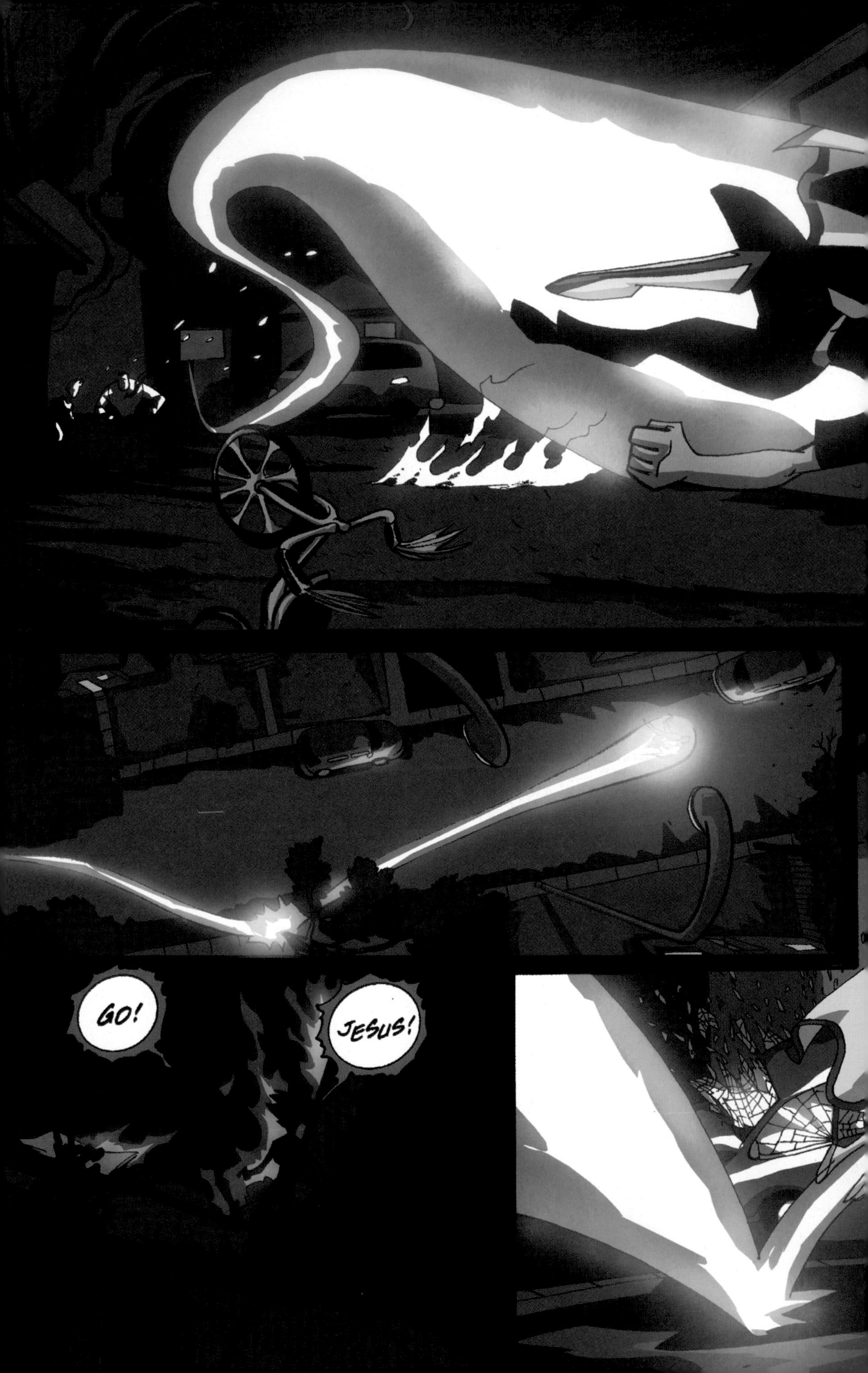
GO!
JESUS!

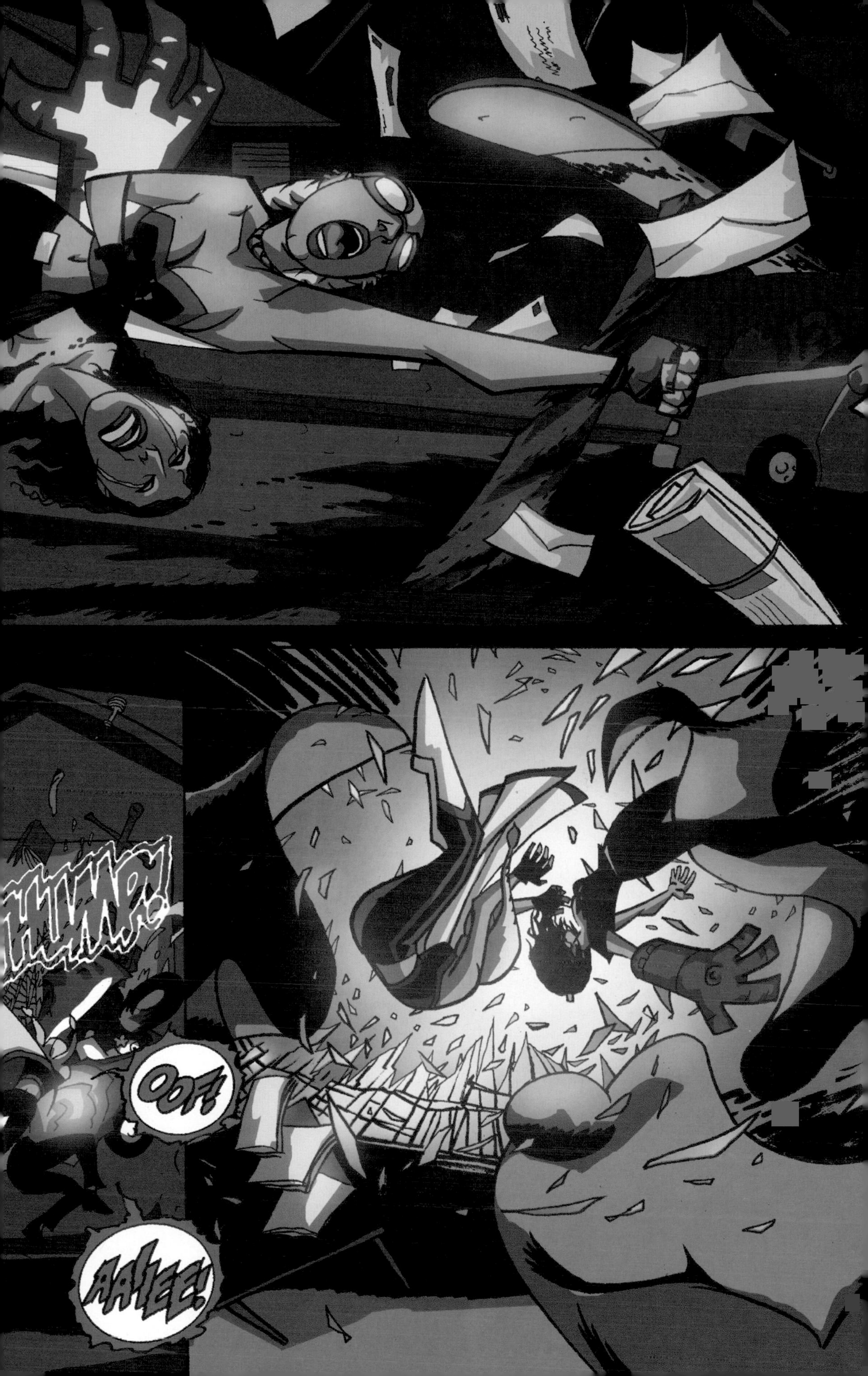
OOF!
AAIEE!

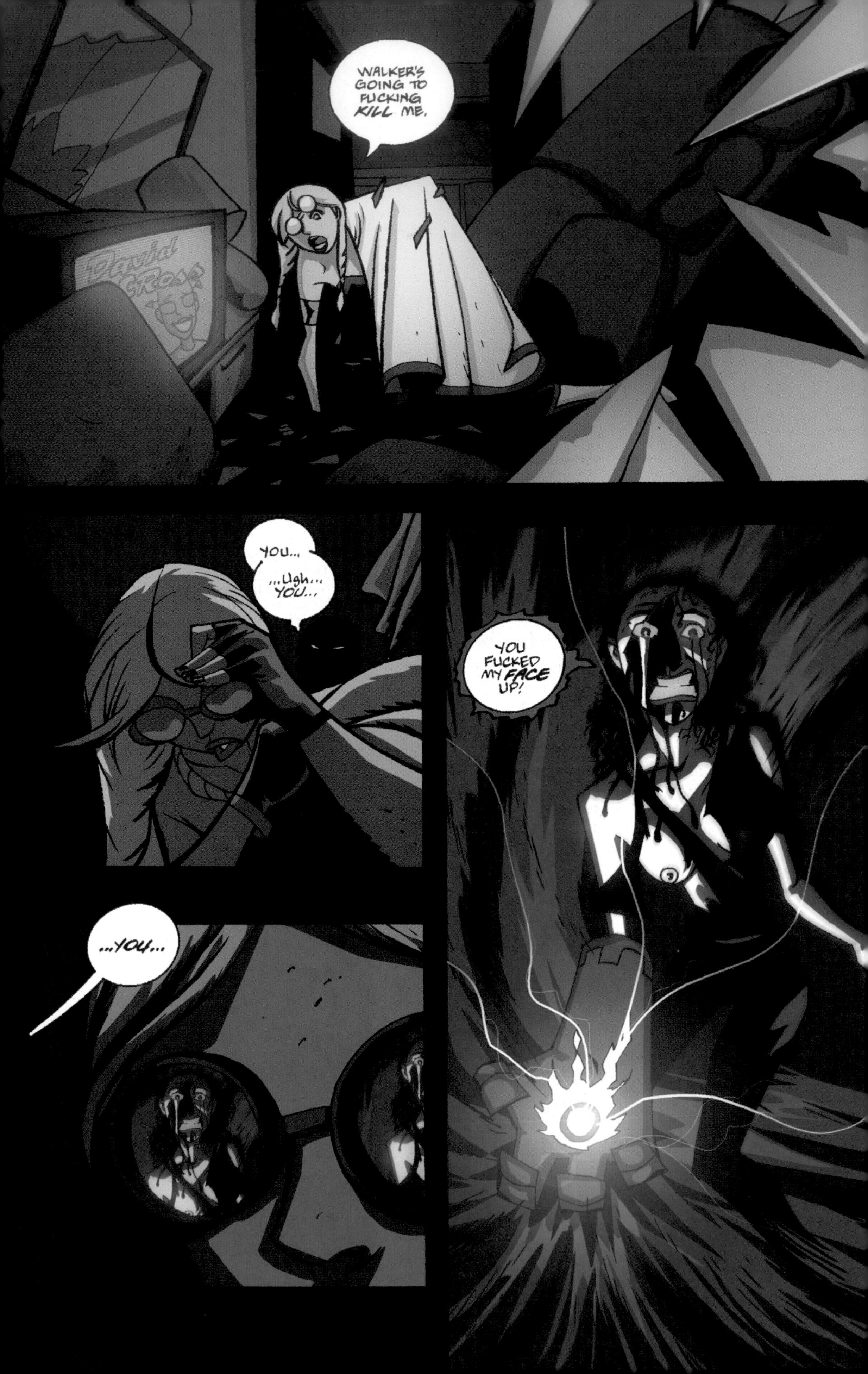
WALKER'S GOING TO FUCKING KILL ME.
YOU...
...Ugh... YOU...
YOU FUCKED MY FACE UP!
...YOU...

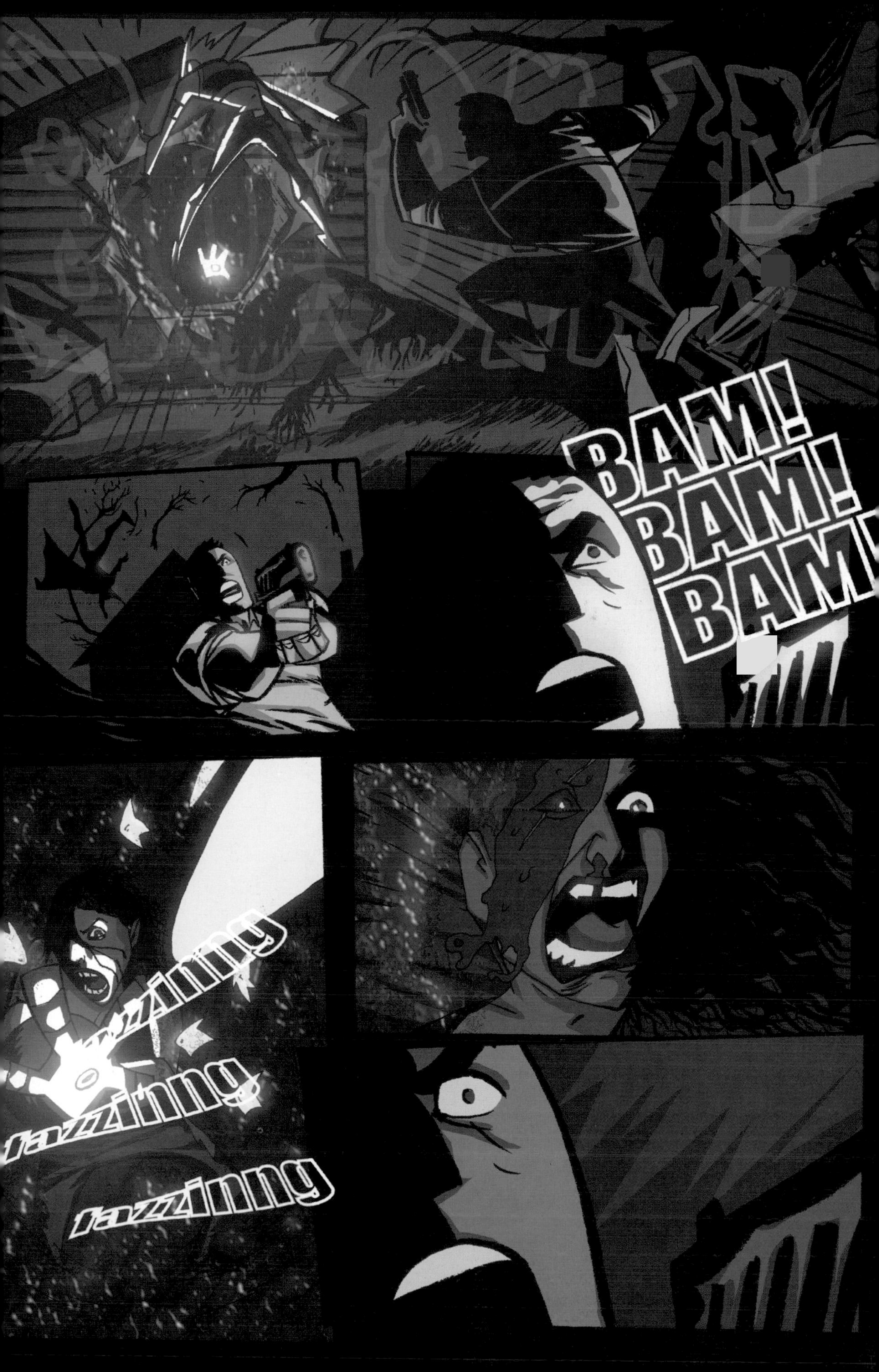
BAM!
BAM!
BAM!
tazzinng
tazzinng
tazzinng

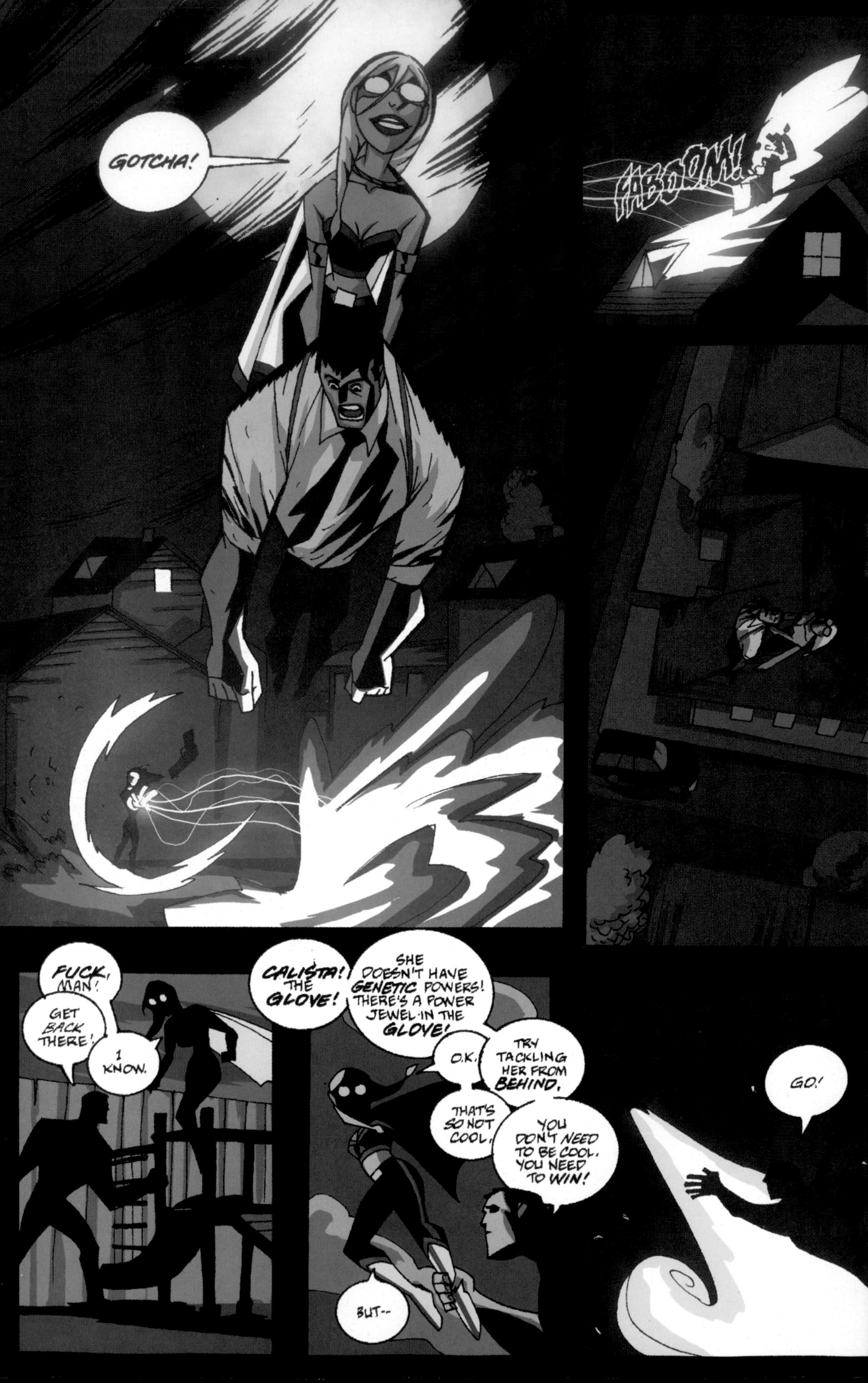
GOTCHA!
KABOOM!
FUCK, MAN!
GET BACK THERE!
I KNOW.
CALISTA! THE GLOVE!
SHE DOESN'T HAVE GENETIC POWERS! THERE'S A POWER JEWEL IN THE GLOVE!
O.K.
TRY TACKLING HER FROM BEHIND.
THAT'S SO NOT COOL.
YOU DON'T NEED TO BE COOL. YOU NEED TO WIN!
BUT--
GO!

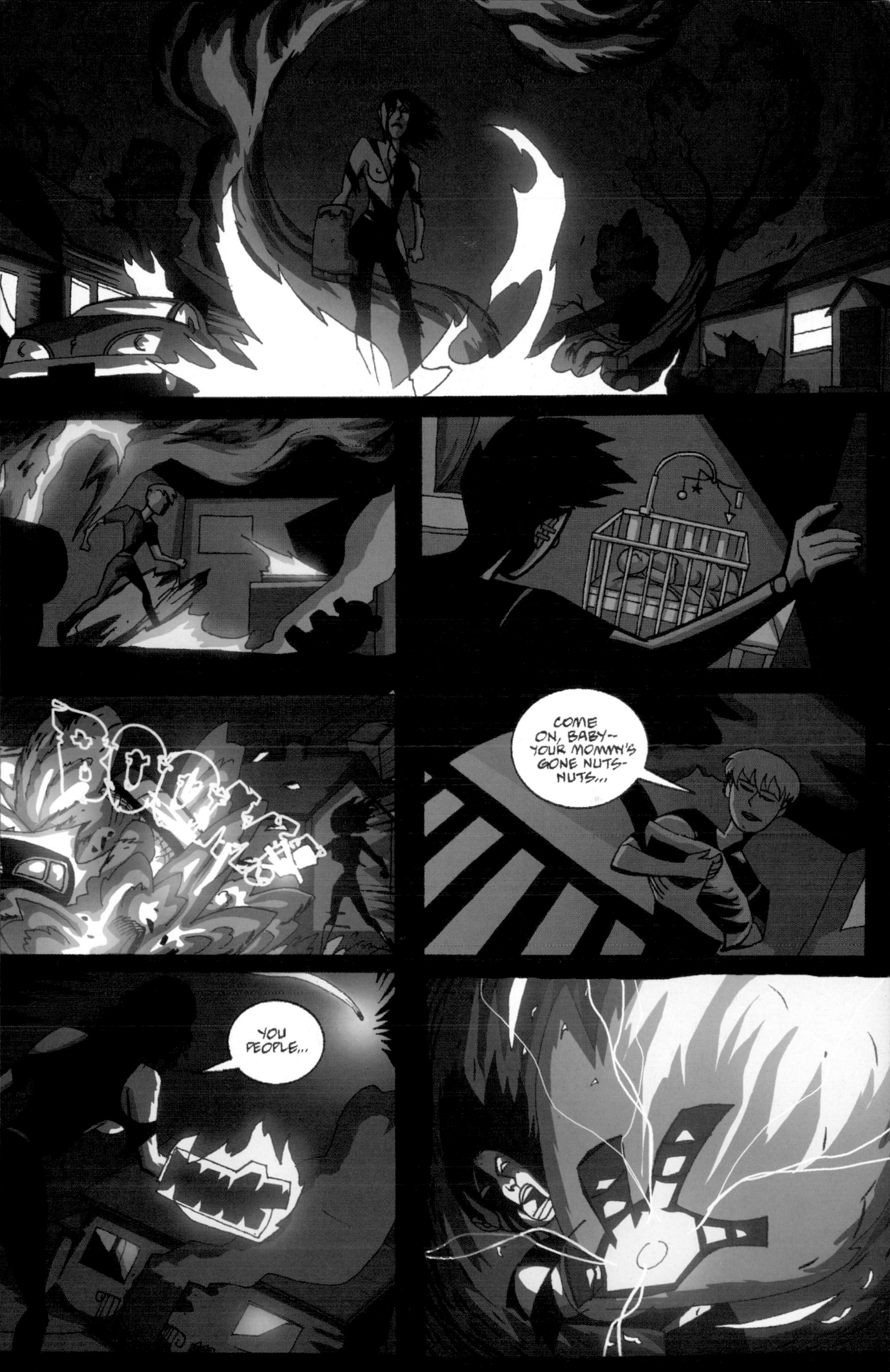
COME ON, BABY-- YOUR MOMMY'S GONE NUTS-NUTS...
YOU PEOPLE...

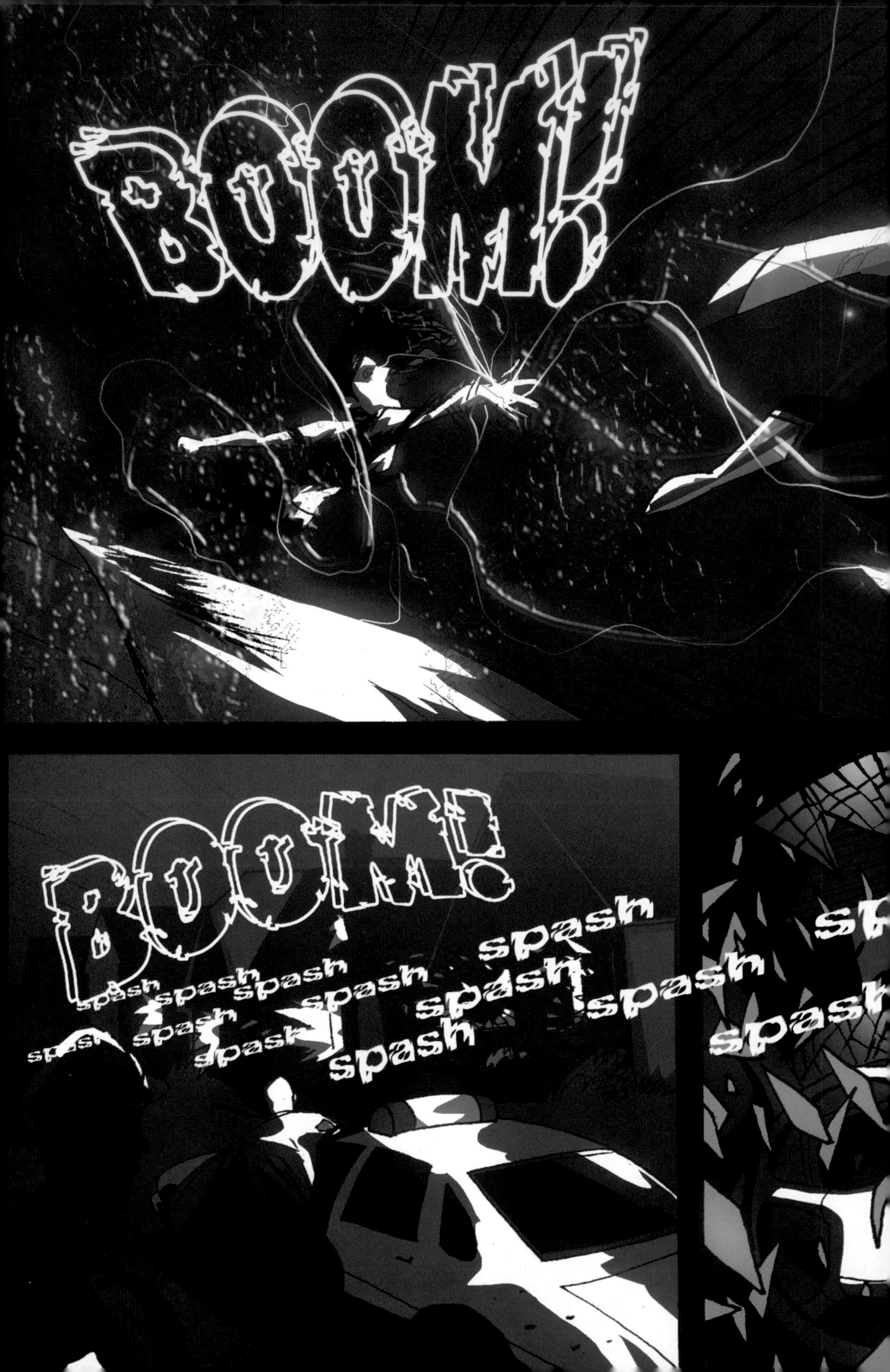
BOOM!!
BOOM!
spash
spash spash spash spash spash spash
spash spash spash
spash
spash

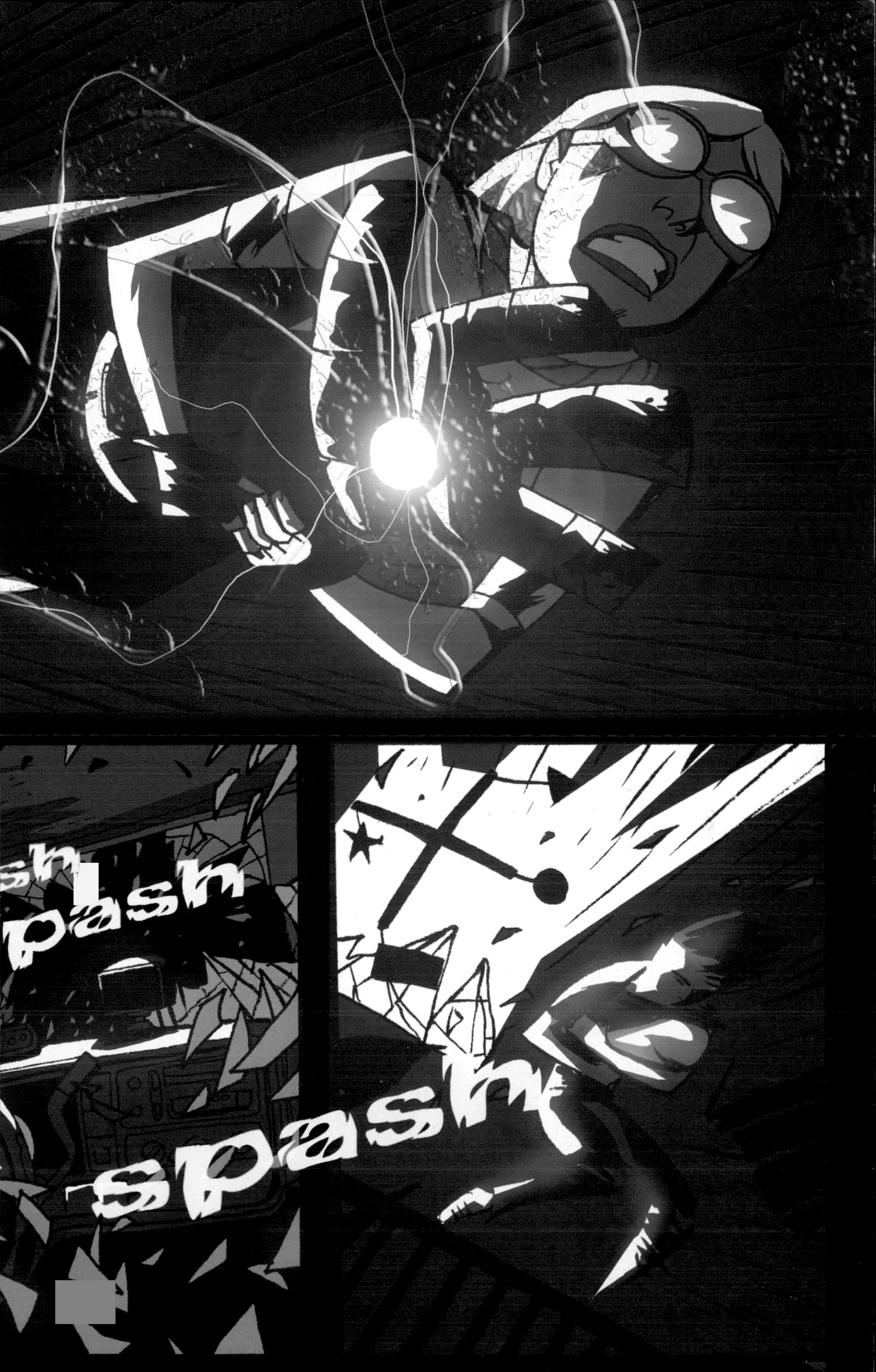
spash

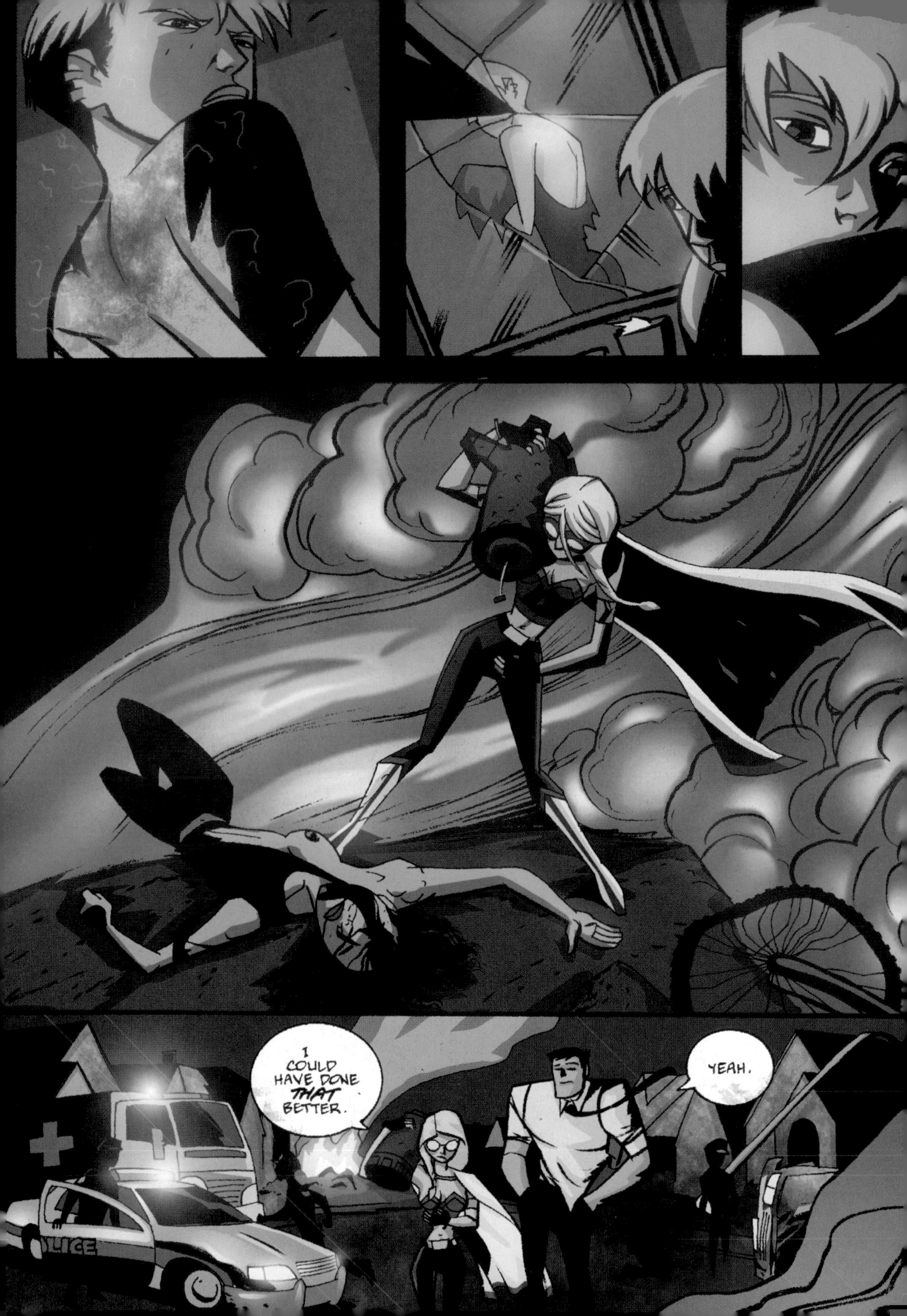
I COULD HAVE DONE THAT BETTER.
YEAH.
LICE

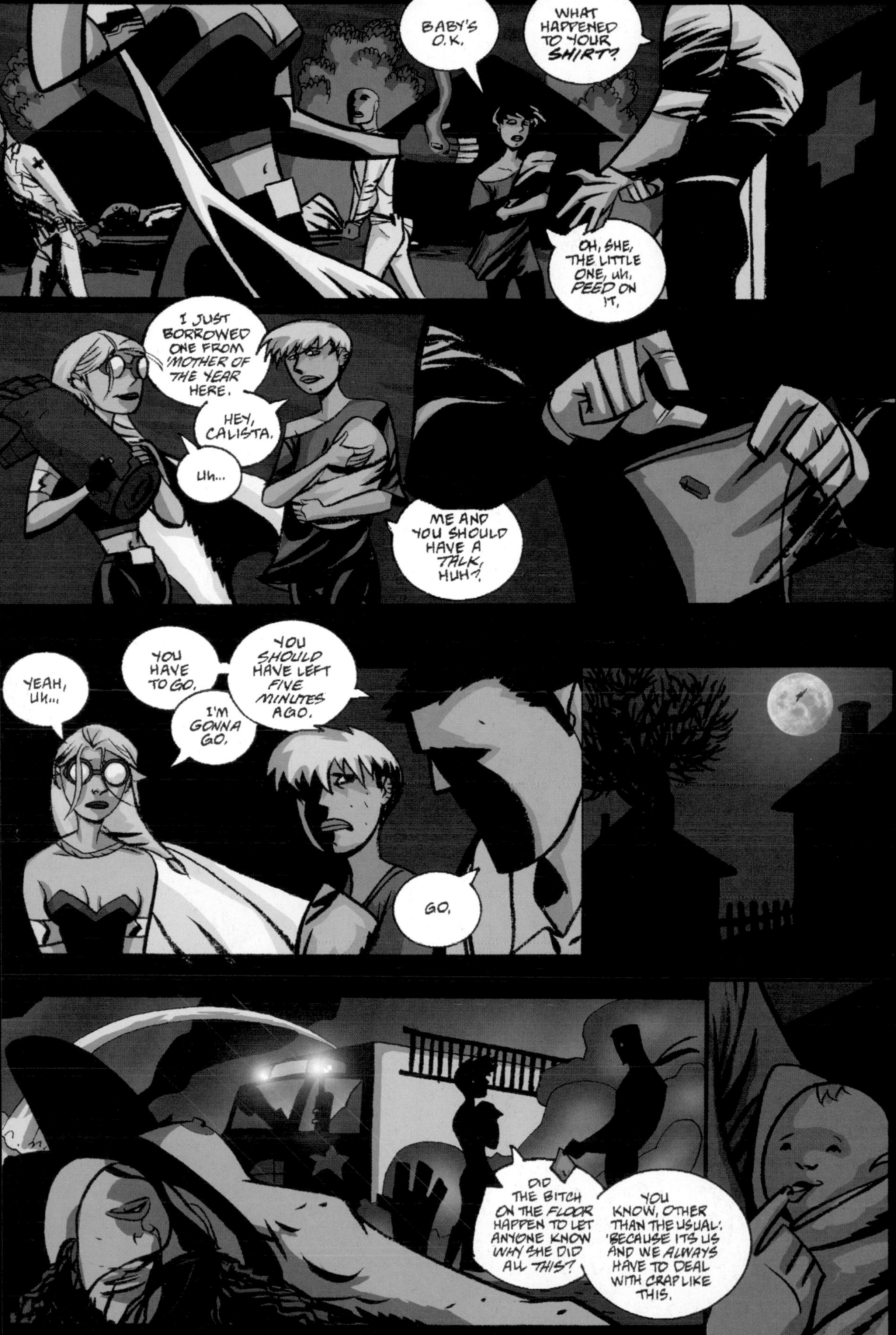
BABY'S O.K.
WHAT HAPPENED TO YOUR SHIRT?
OH, SHE, THE LITTLE ONE, uh, PEED ON IT,
I JUST BORROWED ONE FROM 'MOTHER OF THE YEAR HERE.
HEY, CALISTA.
uh...
ME AND YOU SHOULD HAVE A TALK, HUH?
YEAH, uh...
YOU HAVE TO GO.
YOU SHOULD HAVE LEFT FIVE MINUTES AGO.
I'M GONNA GO.
GO.
DID THE BITCH ON THE FLOOR HAPPEN TO LET ANYONE KNOW WHY SHE DID ALL THIS?
YOU KNOW, OTHER THAN THE USUAL: 'BECAUSE ITS US AND WE ALWAYS HAVE TO DEAL WITH CRAP LIKE THIS.

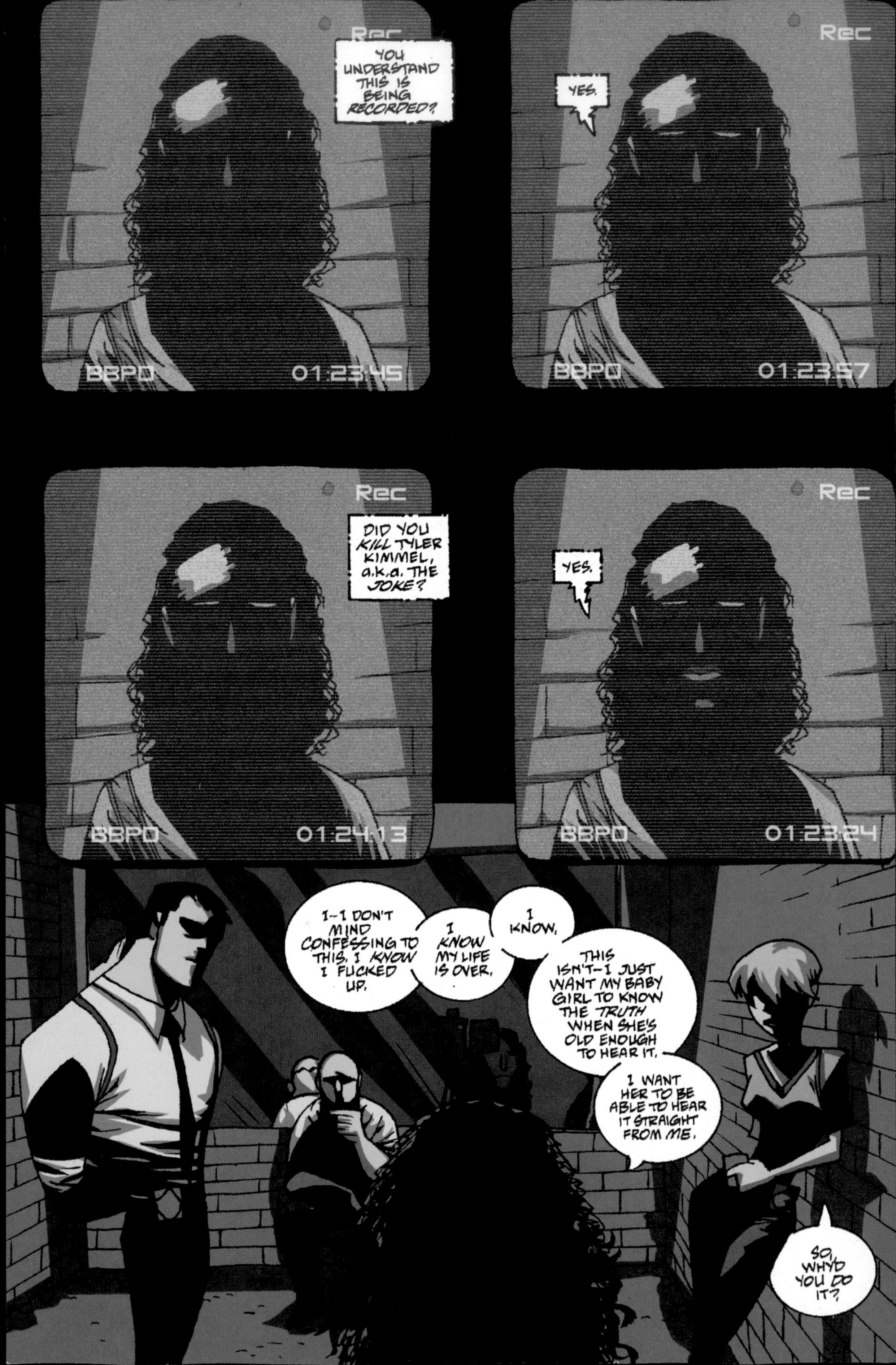
Rec
YOU UNDERSTAND THIS IS BEING RECORDED?
BBPD
01:23:45
Rec
YES.
BBPD
01:23:57
Rec
DID YOU KILL TYLER KIMMEL, a.k.a. THE JOKE?
BBPD
01:24:13
Rec
YES.
BBPD
01:23:24
I--I DON'T MIND CONFESSING TO THIS. I KNOW I FUCKED UP.
I KNOW MY LIFE IS OVER.
I KNOW.
THIS ISN'T--I JUST WANT MY BABY GIRL TO KNOW THE TRUTH WHEN SHE'S OLD ENOUGH TO HEAR IT.
I WANT HER TO BE ABLE TO HEAR IT STRAIGHT FROM ME.
SO, WHY'D YOU DO IT?

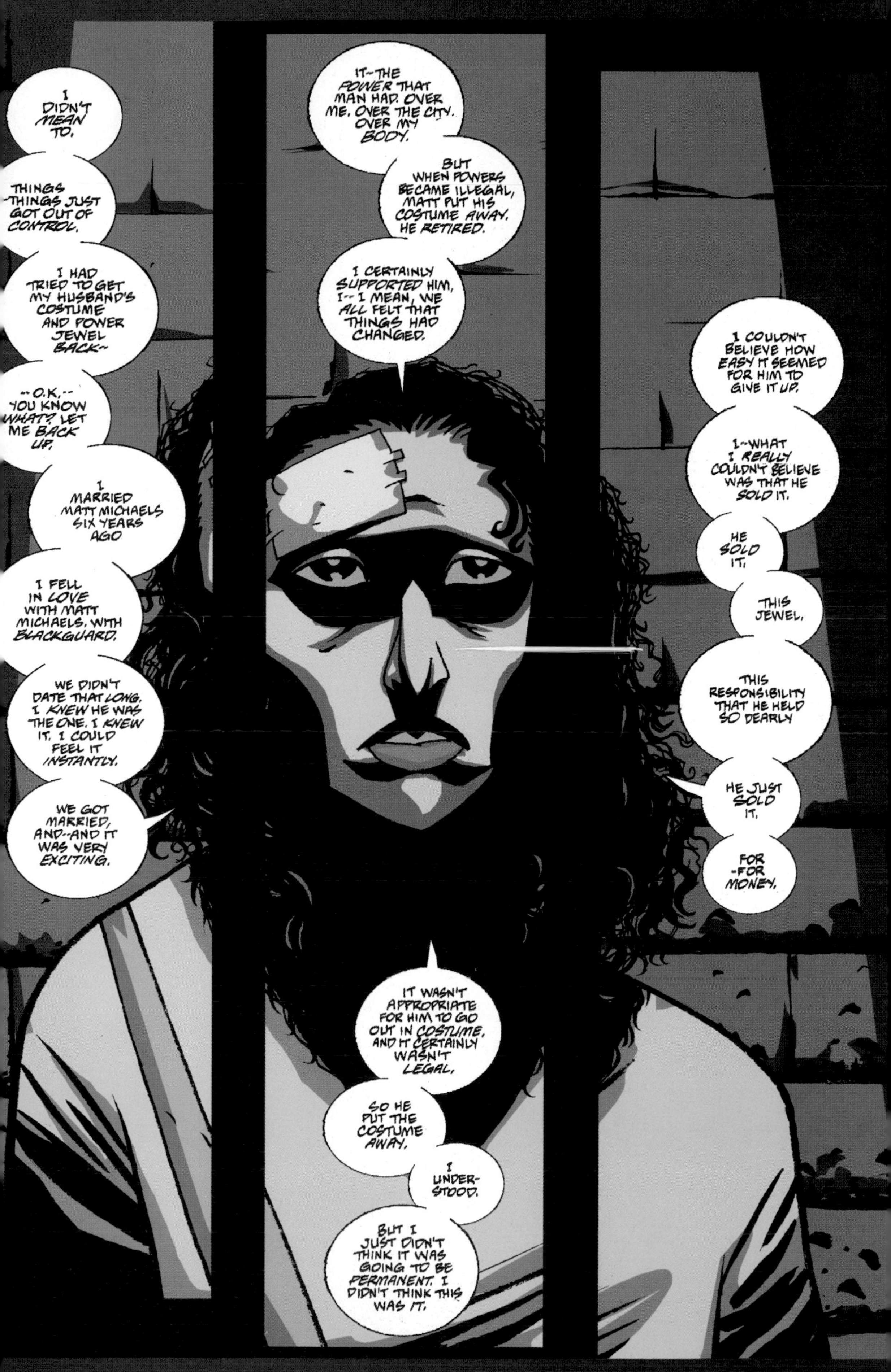
I DIDN'T MEAN TO.
THINGS -THINGS JUST GOT OUT OF CONTROL.
I HAD TRIED TO GET MY HUSBAND'S COSTUME AND POWER JEWEL BACK--
--O.K.-- YOU KNOW WHAT? LET ME BACK UP.
I MARRIED MATT MICHAELS SIX YEARS AGO
I FELL IN LOVE WITH MATT MICHAELS. WITH BLACKGUARD.
WE DIDN'T DATE THAT LONG. I KNEW HE WAS THE ONE. I KNEW IT. I COULD FEEL IT INSTANTLY.
WE GOT MARRIED, AND--AND IT WAS VERY EXCITING.
IT--THE POWER THAT MAN HAD. OVER ME. OVER THE CITY. OVER MY BODY.
BUT WHEN POWERS BECAME ILLEGAL, MATT PUT HIS COSTUME AWAY. HE RETIRED.
I CERTAINLY SUPPORTED HIM, I-- I MEAN, WE ALL FELT THAT THINGS HAD CHANGED.
I COULDN'T BELIEVE HOW EASY IT SEEMED FOR HIM TO GIVE IT UP.
I--WHAT I REALLY COULDN'T BELIEVE WAS THAT HE SOLD IT.
HE SOLD IT.
THIS JEWEL.
THIS RESPONSIBILITY THAT HE HELD SO DEARLY
HE JUST SOLD IT.
FOR -FOR MONEY.
IT WASN'T APPROPRIATE FOR HIM TO GO OUT IN COSTUME. AND IT CERTAINLY WASN'T LEGAL.
SO HE PUT THE COSTUME AWAY.
I UNDER-STOOD.
BUT I JUST DIDN'T THINK IT WAS GOING TO BE PERMANENT. I DIDN'T THINK THIS WAS IT.

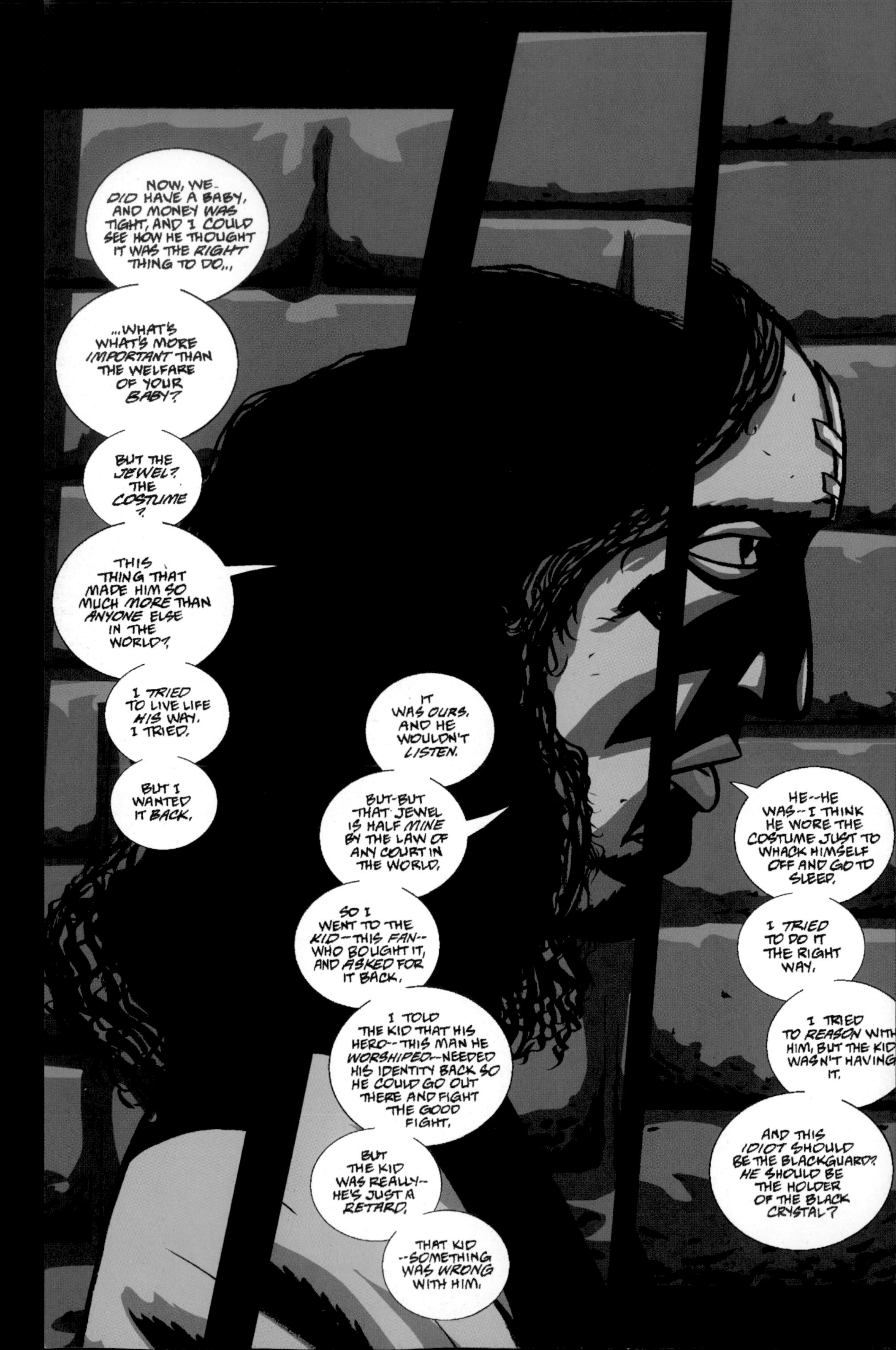
NOW, WE DID HAVE A BABY, AND MONEY WAS TIGHT, AND I COULD SEE HOW HE THOUGHT IT WAS THE RIGHT THING TO DO...
...WHAT'S WHAT'S MORE IMPORTANT THAN THE WELFARE OF YOUR BABY?
BUT THE JEWEL? THE COSTUME?
THIS THING THAT MADE HIM SO MUCH MORE THAN ANYONE ELSE IN THE WORLD?
I TRIED TO LIVE LIFE HIS WAY. I TRIED.
BUT I WANTED IT BACK.
IT WAS OURS. AND HE WOULDN'T LISTEN.
BUT-BUT THAT JEWEL IS HALF MINE BY THE LAW OF ANY COURT IN THE WORLD.
SO I WENT TO THE KID--THIS FAN--WHO BOUGHT IT, AND ASKED FOR IT BACK.
I TOLD THE KID THAT HIS HERO--THIS MAN HE WORSHIPED--NEEDED HIS IDENTITY BACK SO HE COULD GO OUT THERE AND FIGHT THE GOOD FIGHT.
BUT THE KID WAS REALLY--HE'S JUST A RETARD.
THAT KID--SOMETHING WAS WRONG WITH HIM.
HE--HE WAS--I THINK HE WORE THE COSTUME JUST TO WHACK HIMSELF OFF AND GO TO SLEEP.
I TRIED TO DO IT THE RIGHT WAY.
I TRIED TO REASON WITH HIM, BUT THE KID WASN'T HAVING IT.
AND THIS IDIOT SHOULD BE THE BLACKGUARD? HE SHOULD BE THE HOLDER OF THE BLACK CRYSTAL?

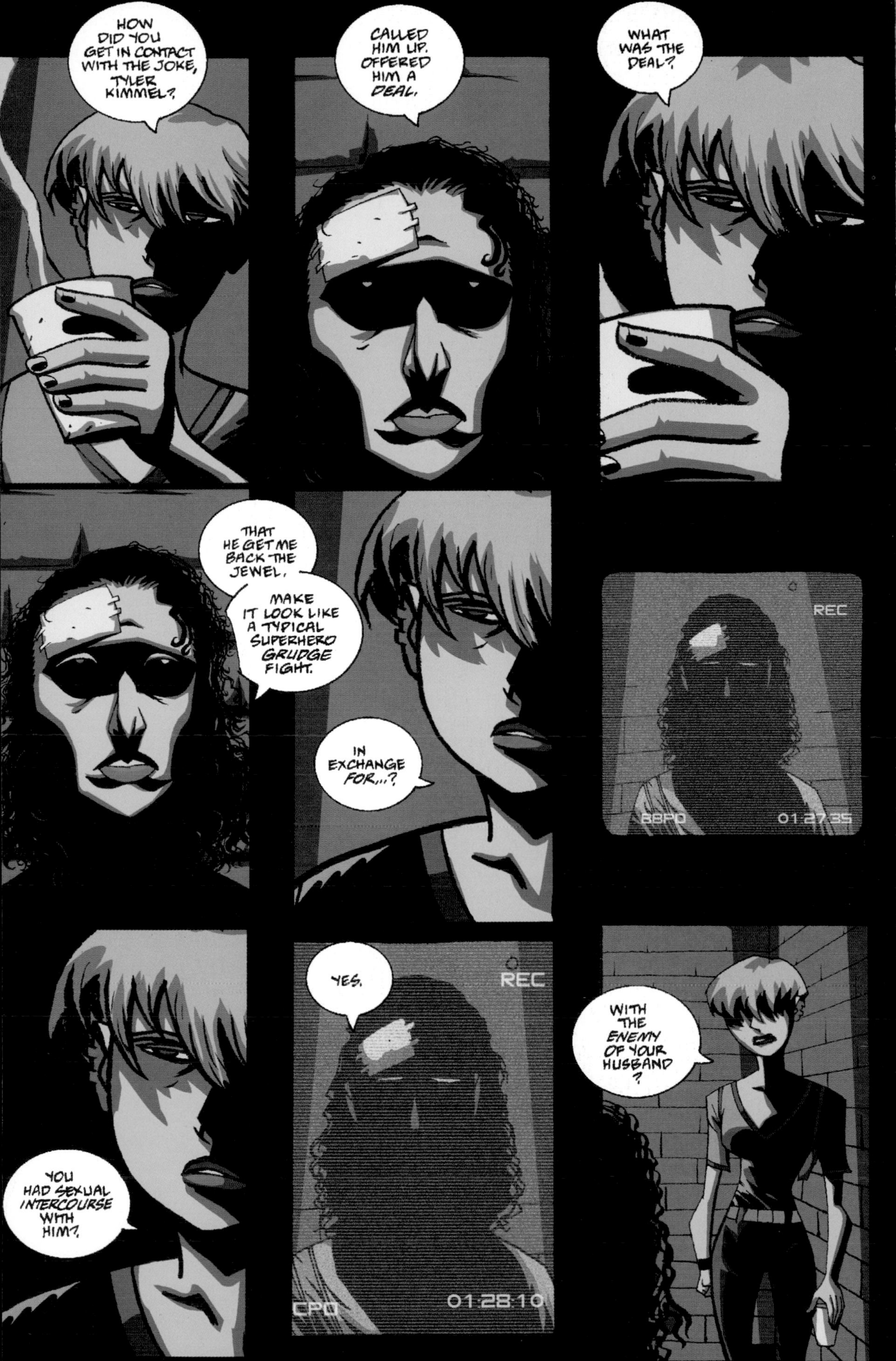
HOW DID YOU GET IN CONTACT WITH THE JOKE, TYLER KIMMEL?
CALLED HIM UP. OFFERED HIM A *DEAL*.
WHAT WAS THE DEAL?
THAT HE GET ME BACK THE JEWEL.
MAKE IT LOOK LIKE A TYPICAL SUPERHERO *GRUDGE* FIGHT.
IN EXCHANGE *FOR...?*
REC
BBPD
01:27:35
YOU HAD SEXUAL *INTERCOURSE* WITH HIM?
YES.
REC
CPD
01:28:10
WITH THE *ENEMY* OF YOUR HUSBAND?

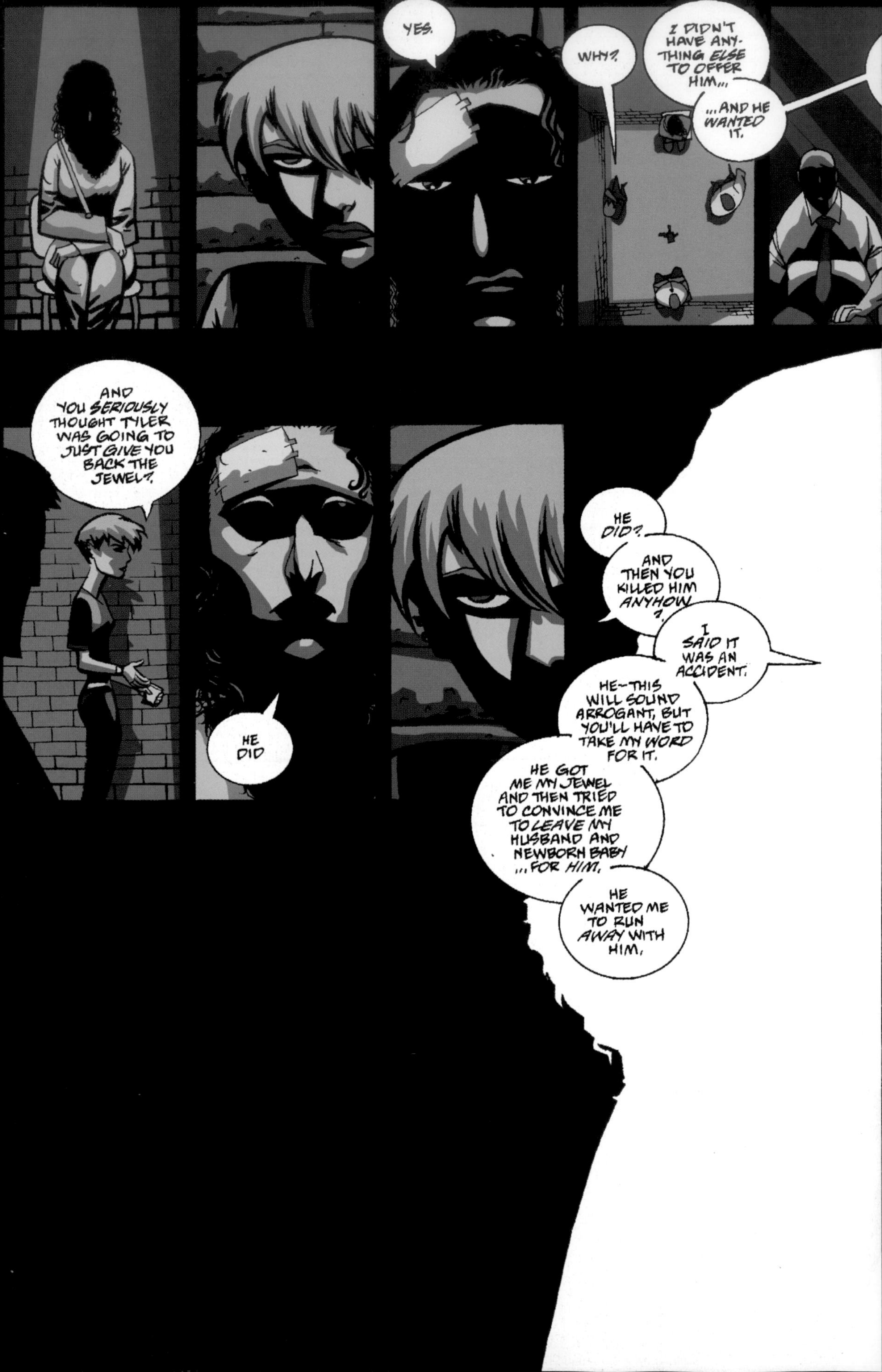
YES.
WHY?
I DIDN'T HAVE ANY-THING ELSE TO OFFER HIM...
...AND HE WANTED IT.
AND YOU SERIOUSLY THOUGHT TYLER WAS GOING TO JUST GIVE YOU BACK THE JEWEL?
HE DID
HE DID?
AND THEN YOU KILLED HIM ANYHOW?
I SAID IT WAS AN ACCIDENT.
HE--THIS WILL SOUND ARROGANT, BUT YOU'LL HAVE TO TAKE MY WORD FOR IT.
HE GOT ME MY JEWEL AND THEN TRIED TO CONVINCE ME TO LEAVE MY HUSBAND AND NEWBORN BABY ...FOR HIM.
HE WANTED ME TO RUN AWAY WITH HIM.

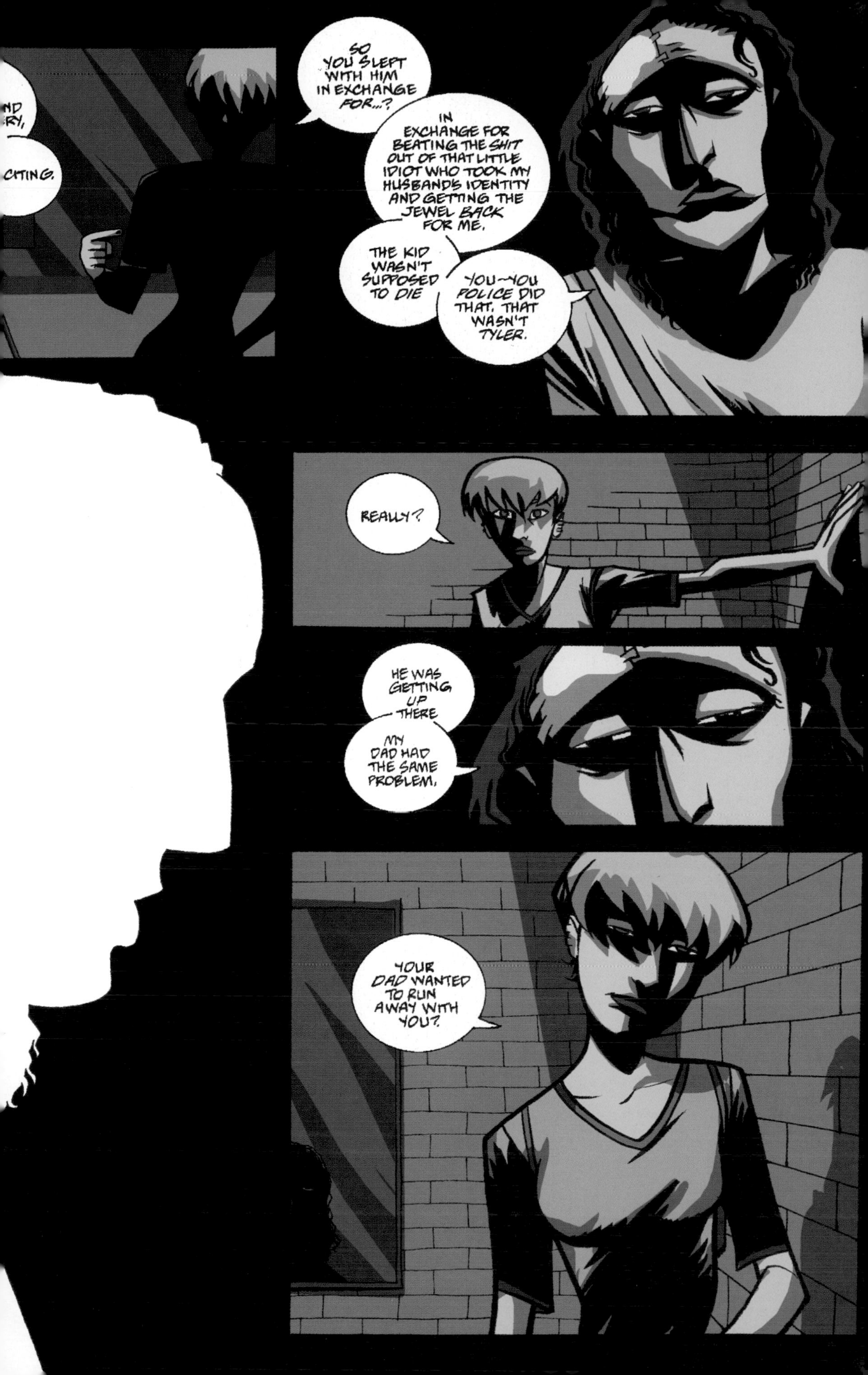
SO YOU SLEPT WITH HIM IN EXCHANGE FOR...?
IN EXCHANGE FOR BEATING THE SHIT OUT OF THAT LITTLE IDIOT WHO TOOK MY HUSBAND'S IDENTITY AND GETTING THE JEWEL BACK FOR ME.
THE KID WASN'T SUPPOSED TO DIE
YOU--YOU POLICE DID THAT. THAT WASN'T TYLER.
REALLY?
HE WAS GETTING UP THERE
MY DAD HAD THE SAME PROBLEM.
YOUR DAD WANTED TO RUN AWAY WITH YOU?

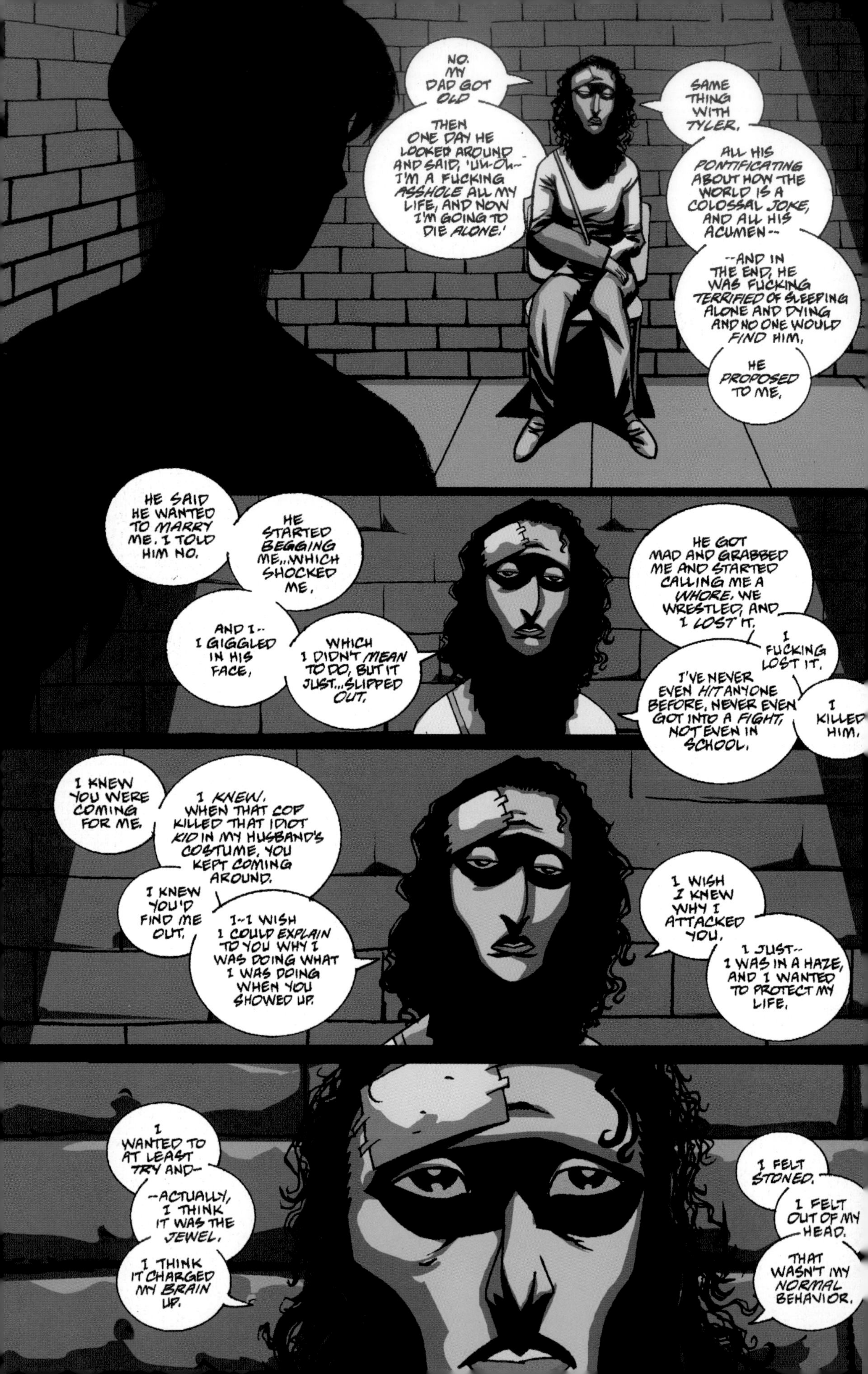
NO. MY DAD GOT *OLD*
THEN ONE DAY HE LOOKED AROUND AND SAID, 'UH-OH-- I'M A FUCKING *ASSHOLE* ALL MY LIFE, AND NOW I'M GOING TO DIE *ALONE*.'
SAME THING WITH *TYLER*.
ALL HIS *PONTIFICATING* ABOUT HOW THE WORLD IS A COLOSSAL JOKE, AND ALL HIS ACUMEN--
--AND IN THE END, HE WAS FUCKING *TERRIFIED* OF SLEEPING ALONE AND DYING AND NO ONE WOULD *FIND* HIM.
HE *PROPOSED* TO ME.
HE SAID HE WANTED TO *MARRY* ME. I TOLD HIM NO.
HE STARTED *BEGGING* ME... WHICH SHOCKED ME.
AND I-- I GIGGLED IN HIS FACE.
WHICH I DIDN'T *MEAN* TO DO, BUT IT JUST... SLIPPED OUT.
HE GOT MAD AND GRABBED ME AND STARTED CALLING ME A *WHORE*. WE WRESTLED, AND I *LOST* IT.
I FUCKING LOST IT.
I'VE NEVER EVEN *HIT* ANYONE BEFORE, NEVER EVEN GOT INTO A *FIGHT*, NOT EVEN IN SCHOOL.
I KILLED HIM.
I KNEW YOU WERE COMING FOR ME.
I *KNEW*. WHEN THAT COP KILLED THAT IDIOT *KID* IN MY HUSBAND'S COSTUME, YOU KEPT COMING AROUND.
I KNEW YOU'D FIND ME OUT.
I-- I WISH I COULD EXPLAIN TO YOU WHY I WAS DOING WHAT I WAS DOING WHEN YOU SHOWED UP.
I WISH I KNEW WHY I ATTACKED YOU.
I JUST-- I WAS IN A HAZE, AND I WANTED TO PROTECT MY LIFE.
I WANTED TO AT LEAST *TRY* AND--
--ACTUALLY, I THINK IT WAS THE *JEWEL*.
I THINK IT CHARGED MY *BRAIN* UP.
I FELT *STONED*.
I FELT OUT OF MY HEAD.
THAT WASN'T MY *NORMAL* BEHAVIOR.

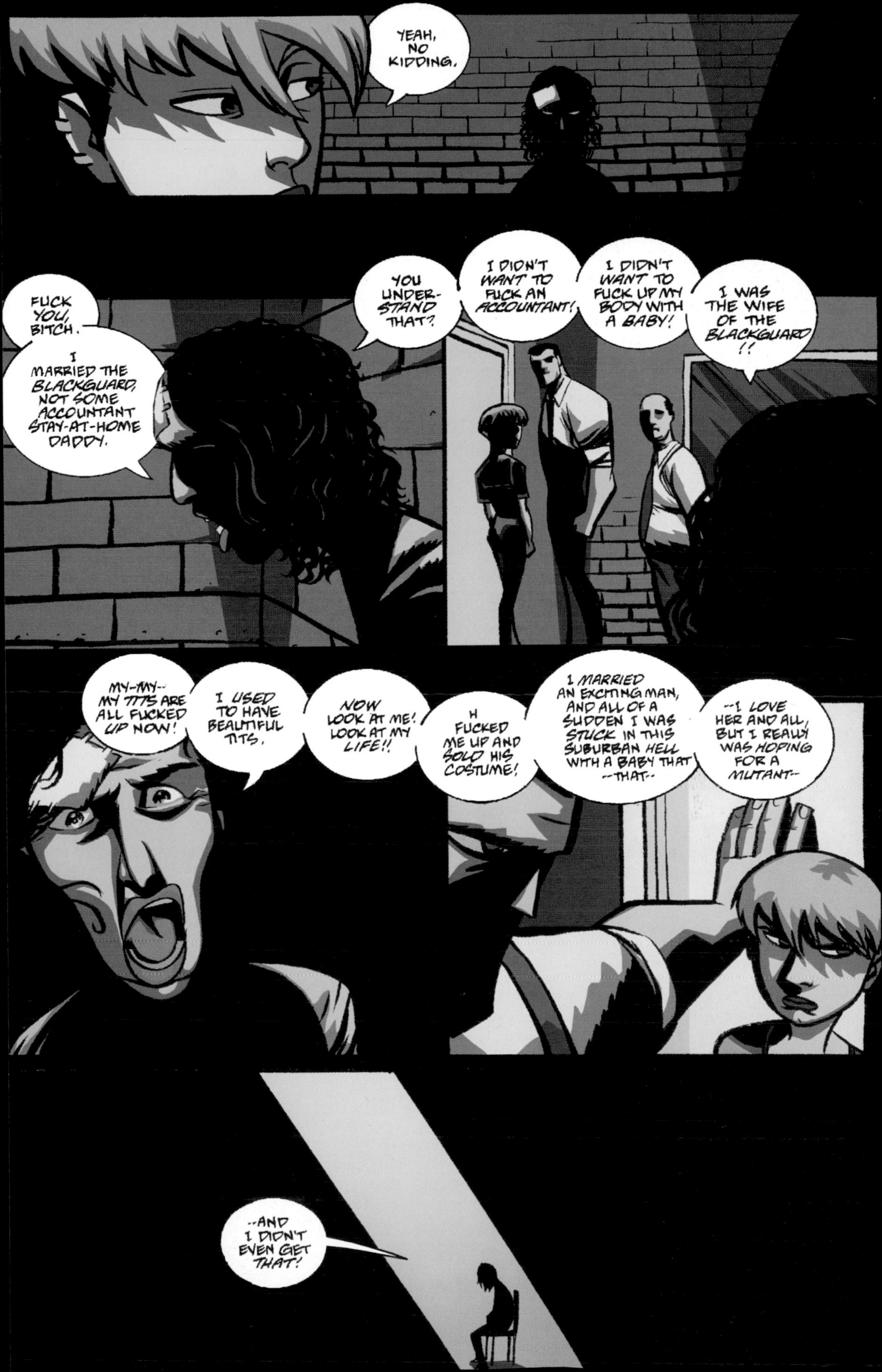
YEAH, NO KIDDING.
FUCK YOU, BITCH.
I MARRIED THE BLACKGUARD, NOT SOME ACCOUNTANT STAY-AT-HOME DADDY.
YOU UNDER-STAND THAT?
I DIDN'T WANT TO FUCK AN ACCOUNTANT!
I DIDN'T WANT TO FUCK UP MY BODY WITH A BABY!
I WAS THE WIFE OF THE BLACKGUARD!!
MY-MY-- MY TITS ARE ALL FUCKED UP NOW!
I USED TO HAVE BEAUTIFUL TITS.
NOW LOOK AT ME! LOOK AT MY LIFE!!
H FUCKED ME UP AND SOLD HIS COSTUME!
I MARRIED AN EXCITING MAN, AND ALL OF A SUDDEN I WAS STUCK IN THIS SUBURBAN HELL WITH A BABY THAT --THAT--
--I LOVE HER AND ALL, BUT I REALLY WAS HOPING FOR A MUTANT--
--AND I DIDN'T EVEN GET THAT!

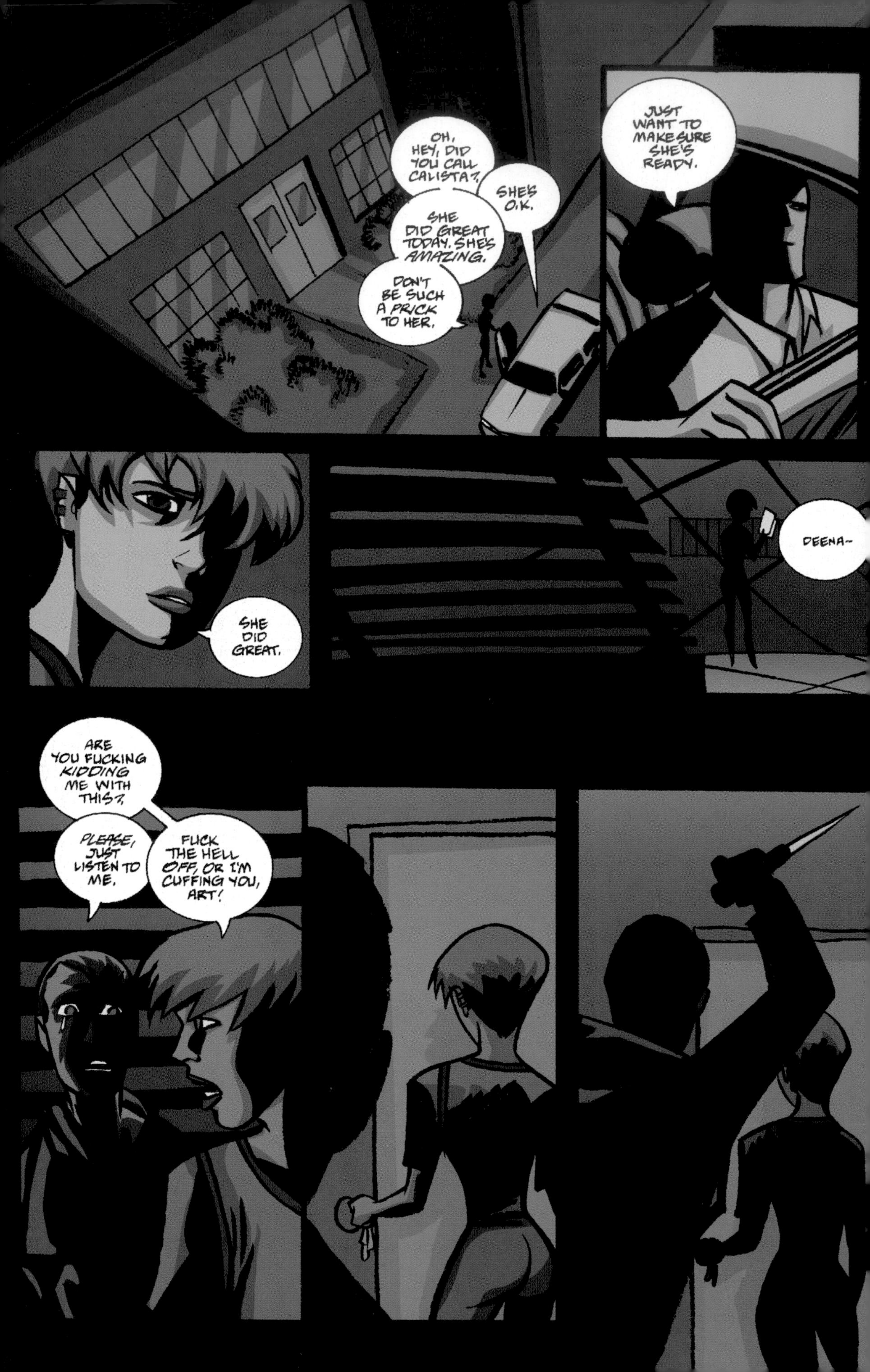
OH, HEY, DID YOU CALL CALISTA?
SHE'S O.K.
SHE DID GREAT TODAY. SHE'S AMAZING.
DON'T BE SUCH A PRICK TO HER.
JUST WANT TO MAKE SURE SHE'S READY.
SHE DID GREAT.
DEENA--
ARE YOU FUCKING KIDDING ME WITH THIS?
PLEASE, JUST LISTEN TO ME.
FUCK THE HELL OFF, OR I'M CUFFING YOU, ART!

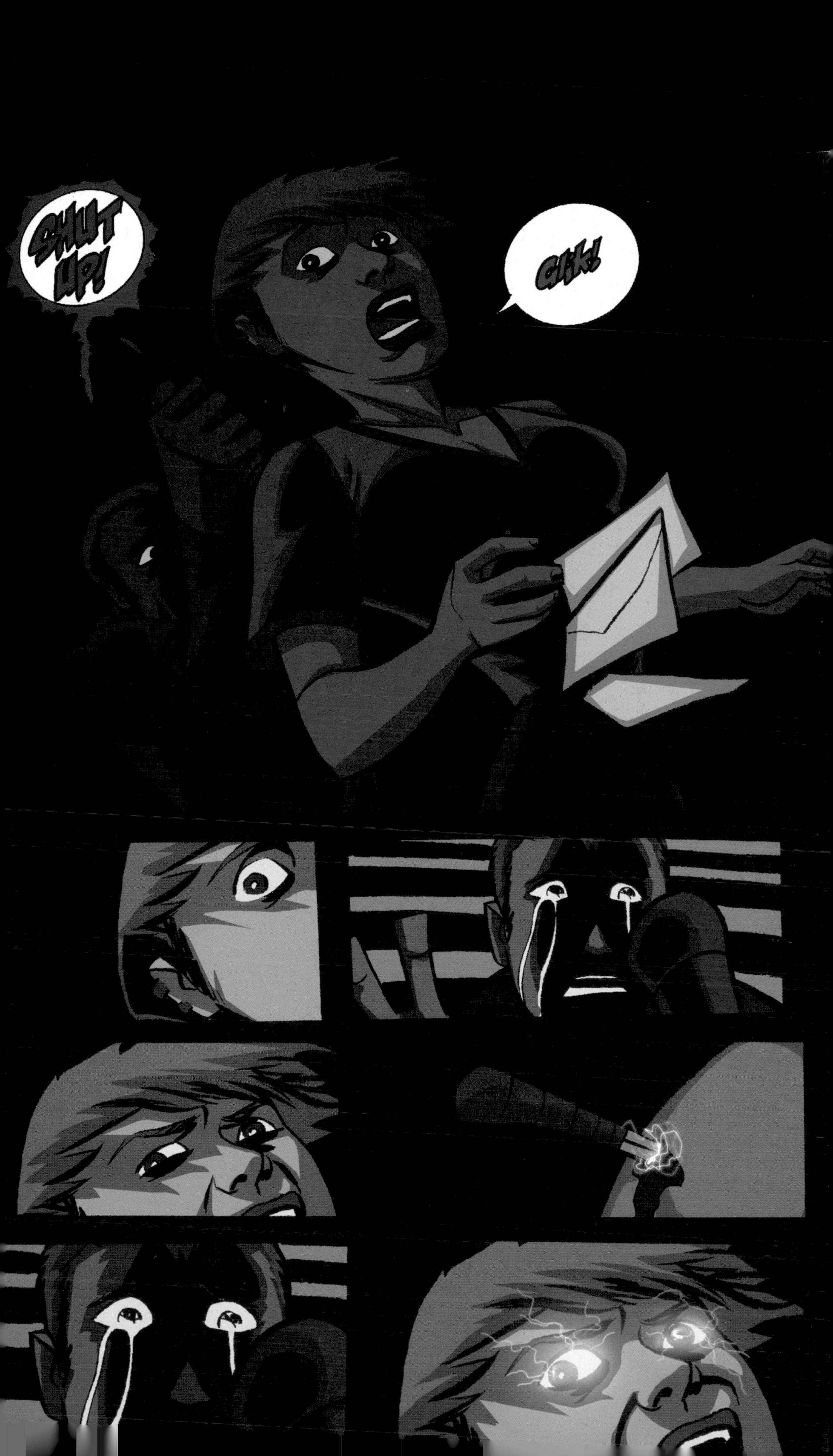
SHUT UP!
GLIK!

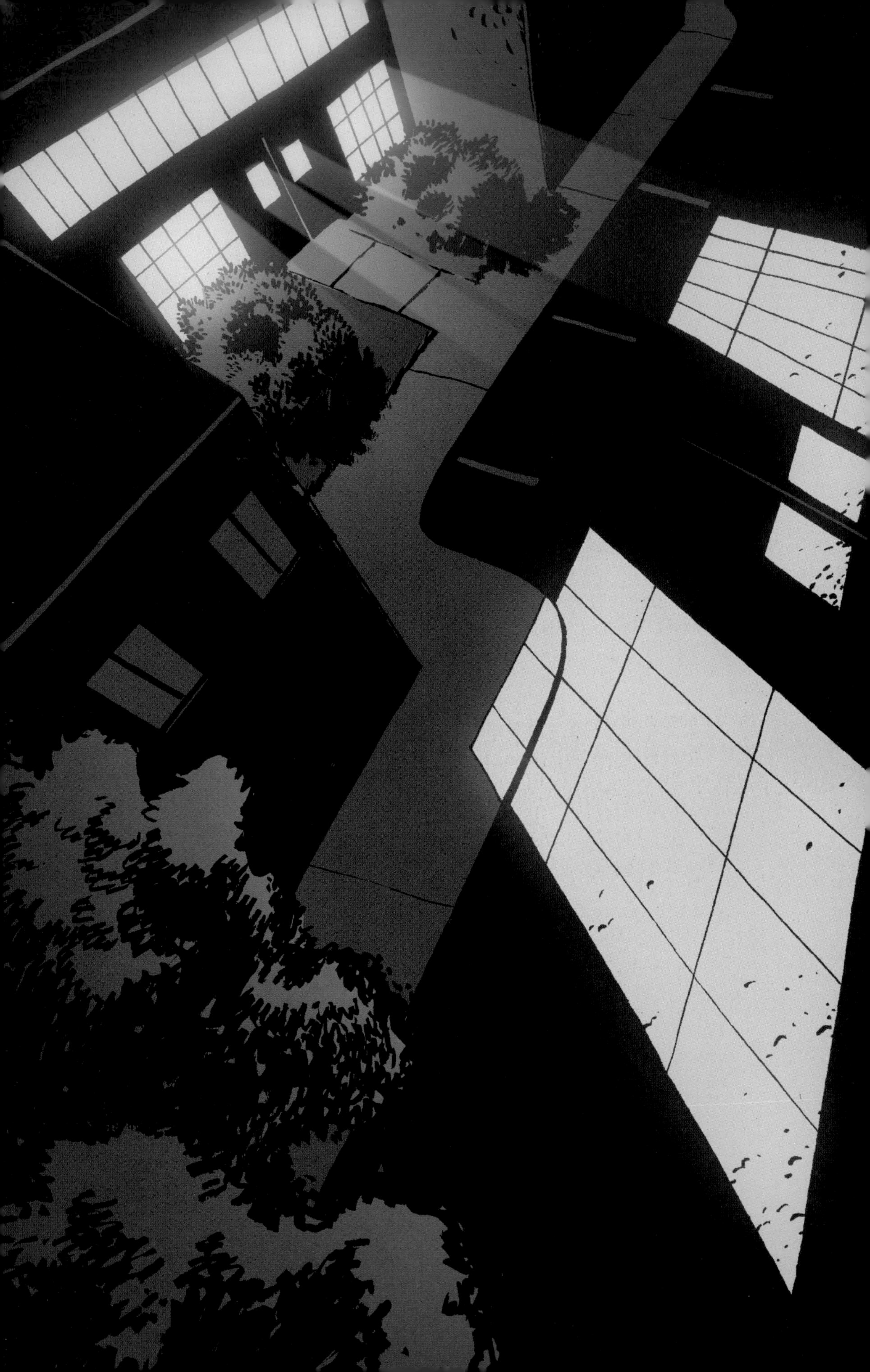

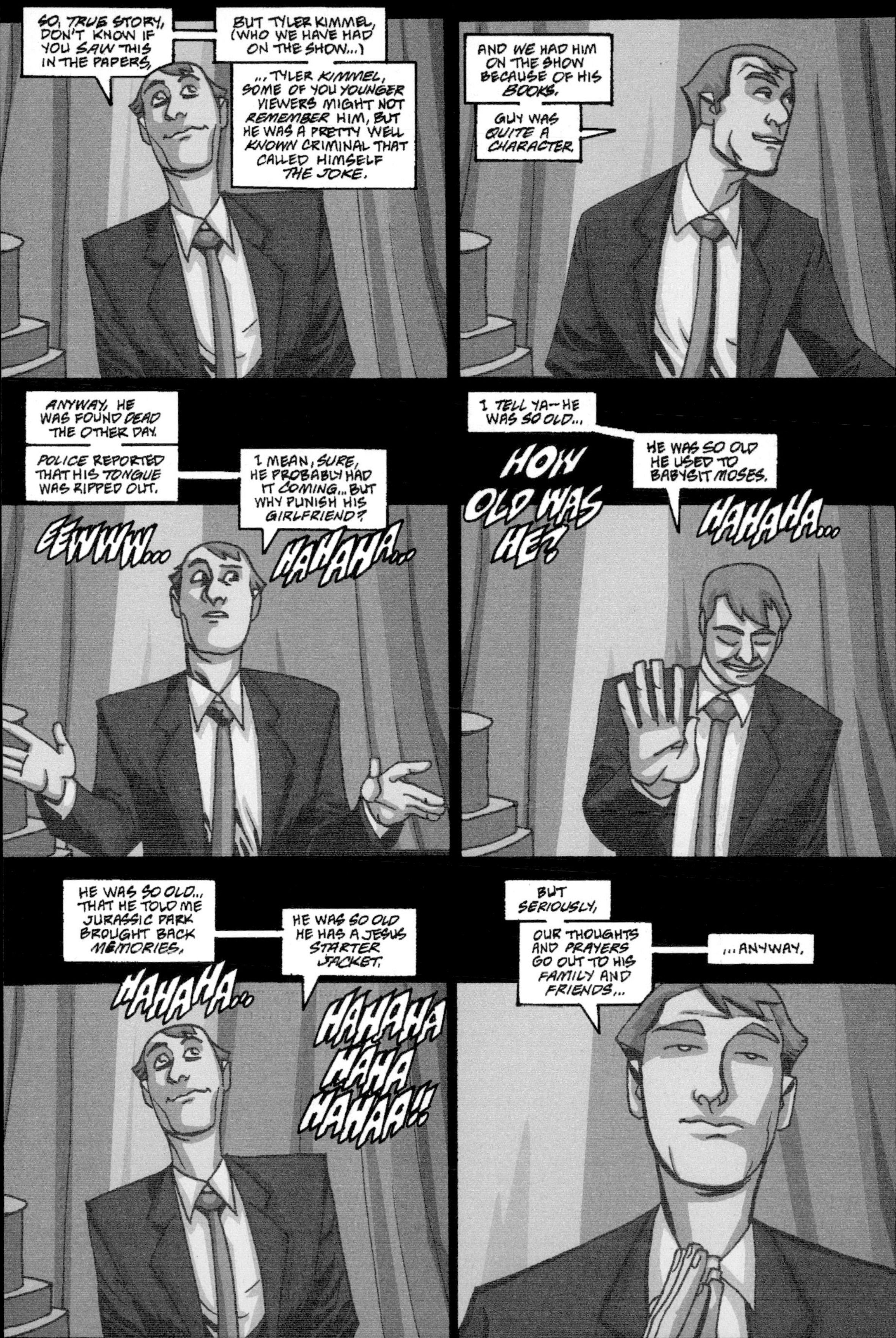
SO, TRUE STORY, DON'T KNOW IF YOU SAW THIS IN THE PAPERS,
BUT TYLER KIMMEL, (WHO WE HAVE HAD ON THE SHOW...)
...TYLER KIMMEL, SOME OF YOU YOUNGER VIEWERS MIGHT NOT REMEMBER HIM, BUT HE WAS A PRETTY WELL KNOWN CRIMINAL THAT CALLED HIMSELF THE JOKE.
AND WE HAD HIM ON THE SHOW BECAUSE OF HIS BOOKS.
GUY WAS QUITE A CHARACTER.
ANYWAY, HE WAS FOUND DEAD THE OTHER DAY.
POLICE REPORTED THAT HIS TONGUE WAS RIPPED OUT.
EEWWW...
I MEAN, SURE, HE PROBABLY HAD IT COMING... BUT WHY PUNISH HIS GIRLFRIEND?
HAHAHA...
I TELL YA--HE WAS SO OLD...
HOW OLD WAS HE?
HE WAS SO OLD HE USED TO BABYSIT MOSES.
HAHAHA...
HE WAS SO OLD... THAT HE TOLD ME JURASSIC PARK BROUGHT BACK MEMORIES.
HAHAHA...
HE WAS SO OLD HE HAS A JESUS STARTER JACKET.
HAHAHA HAHA HAHAA!!
BUT SERIOUSLY,
OUR THOUGHTS AND PRAYERS GO OUT TO HIS FAMILY AND FRIENDS...
...ANYWAY.

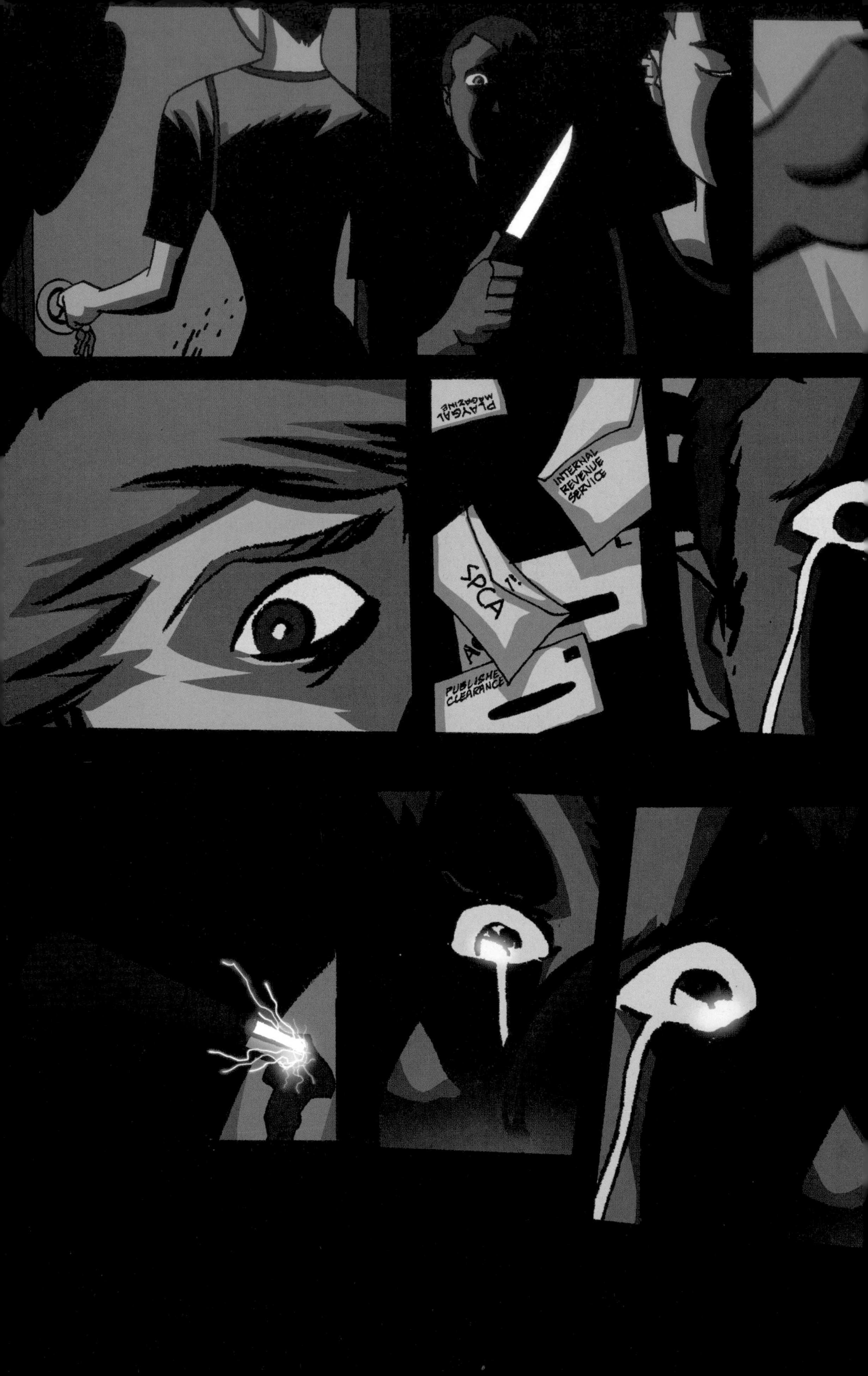
PLAYGAL MAGAZINE
INTERNAL REVENUE SERVICE
SPCA
PUBLISHE CLEARANCE

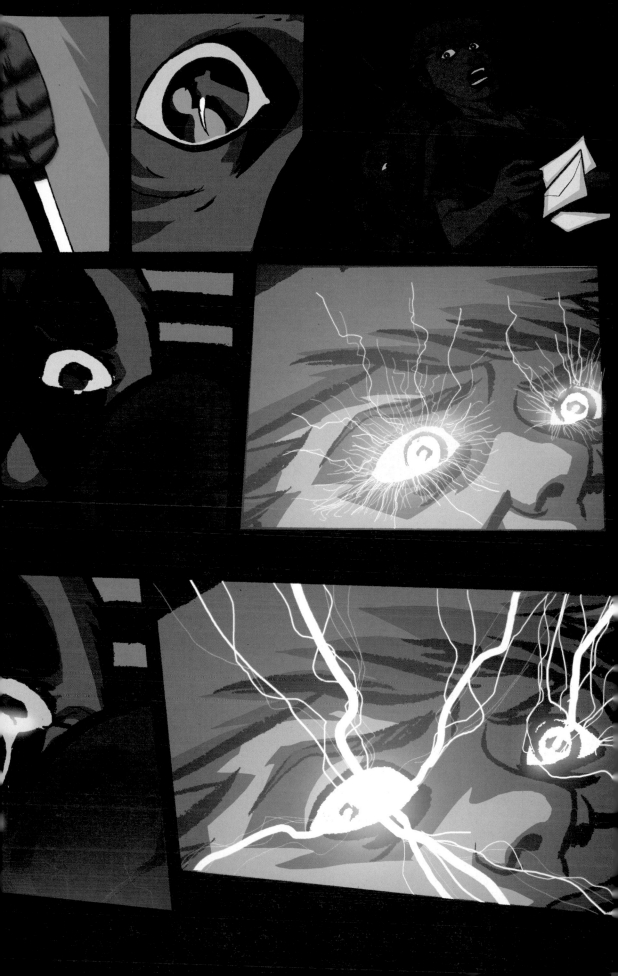

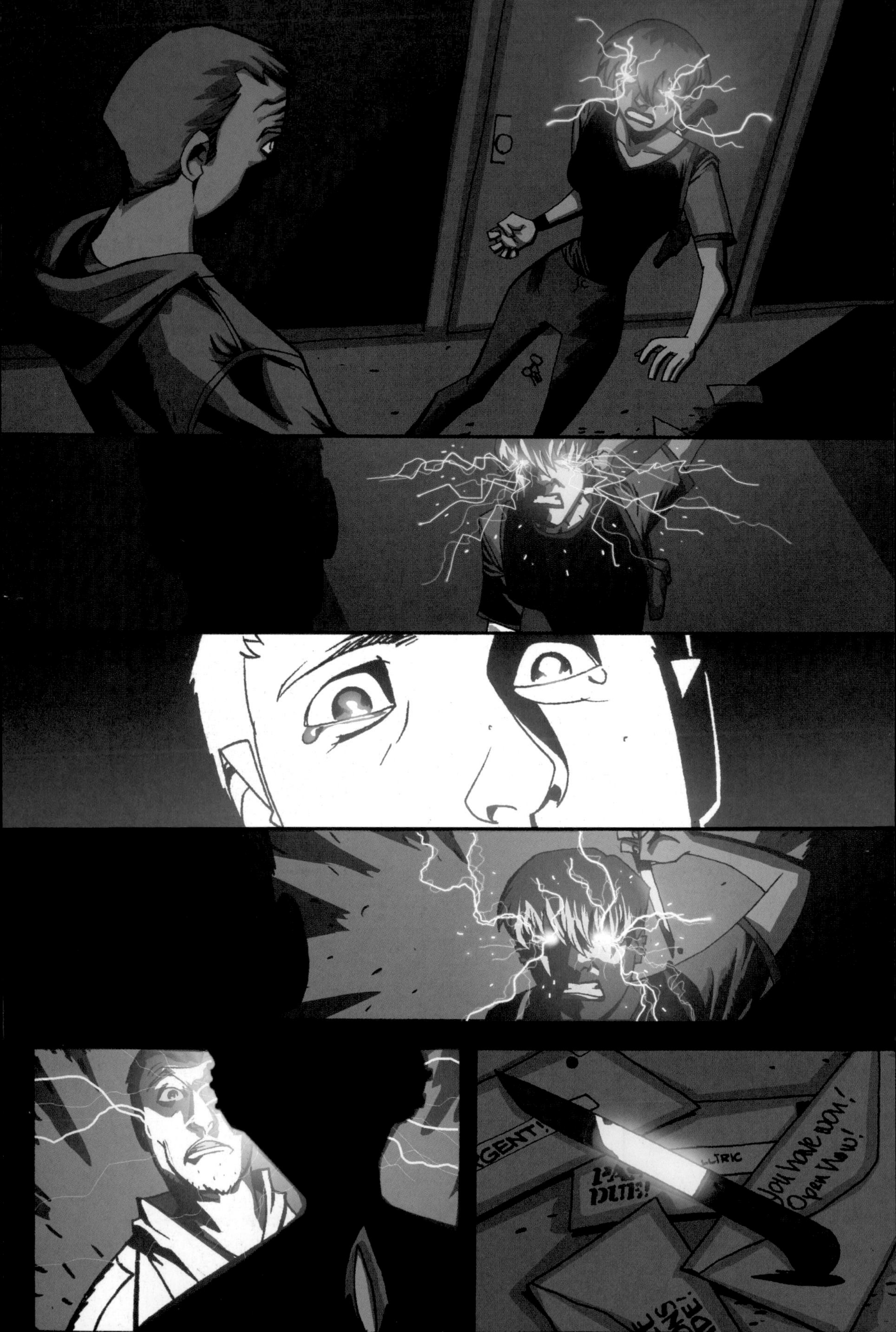
GENT!
You have won!
Open Now!

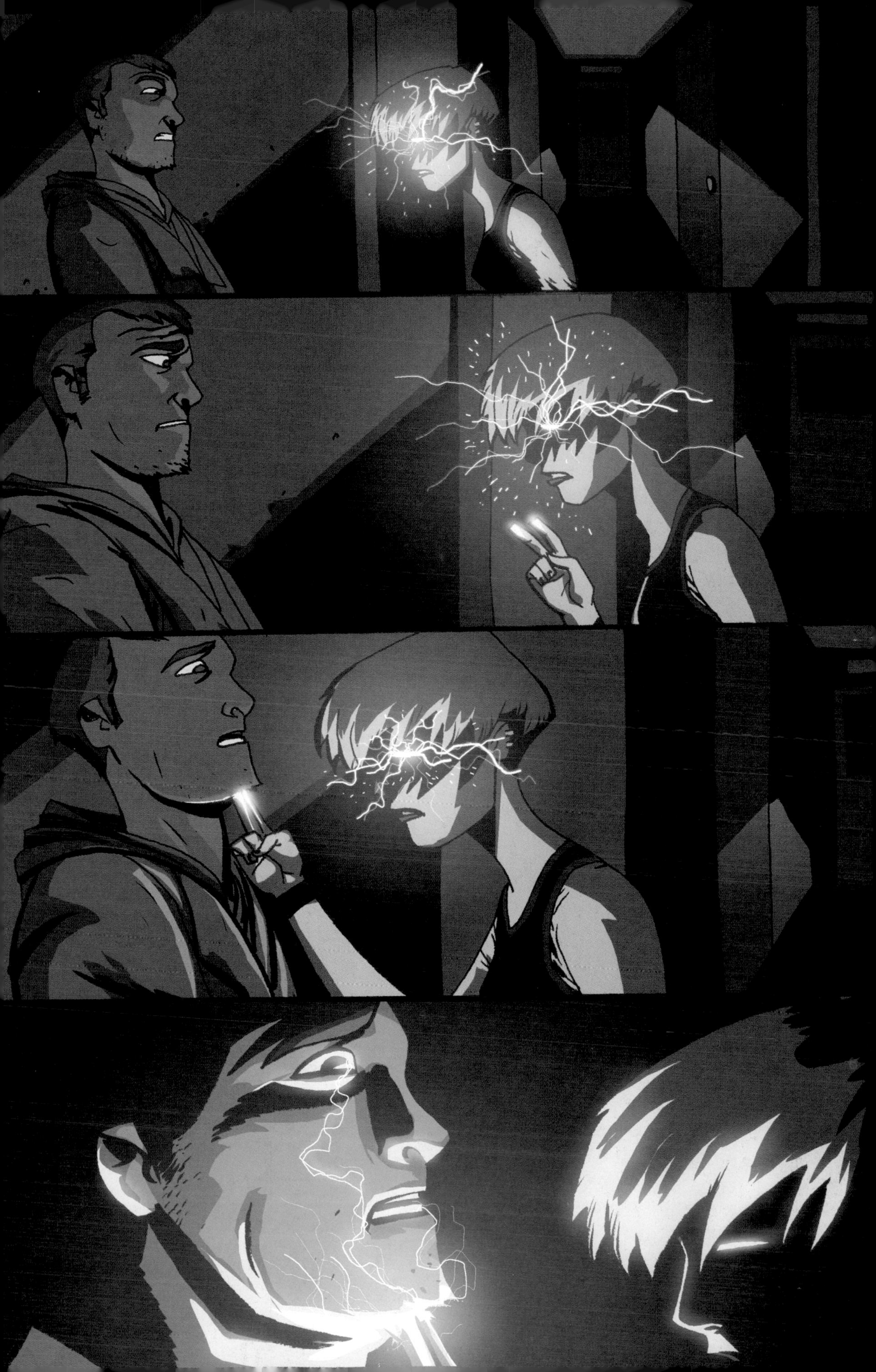

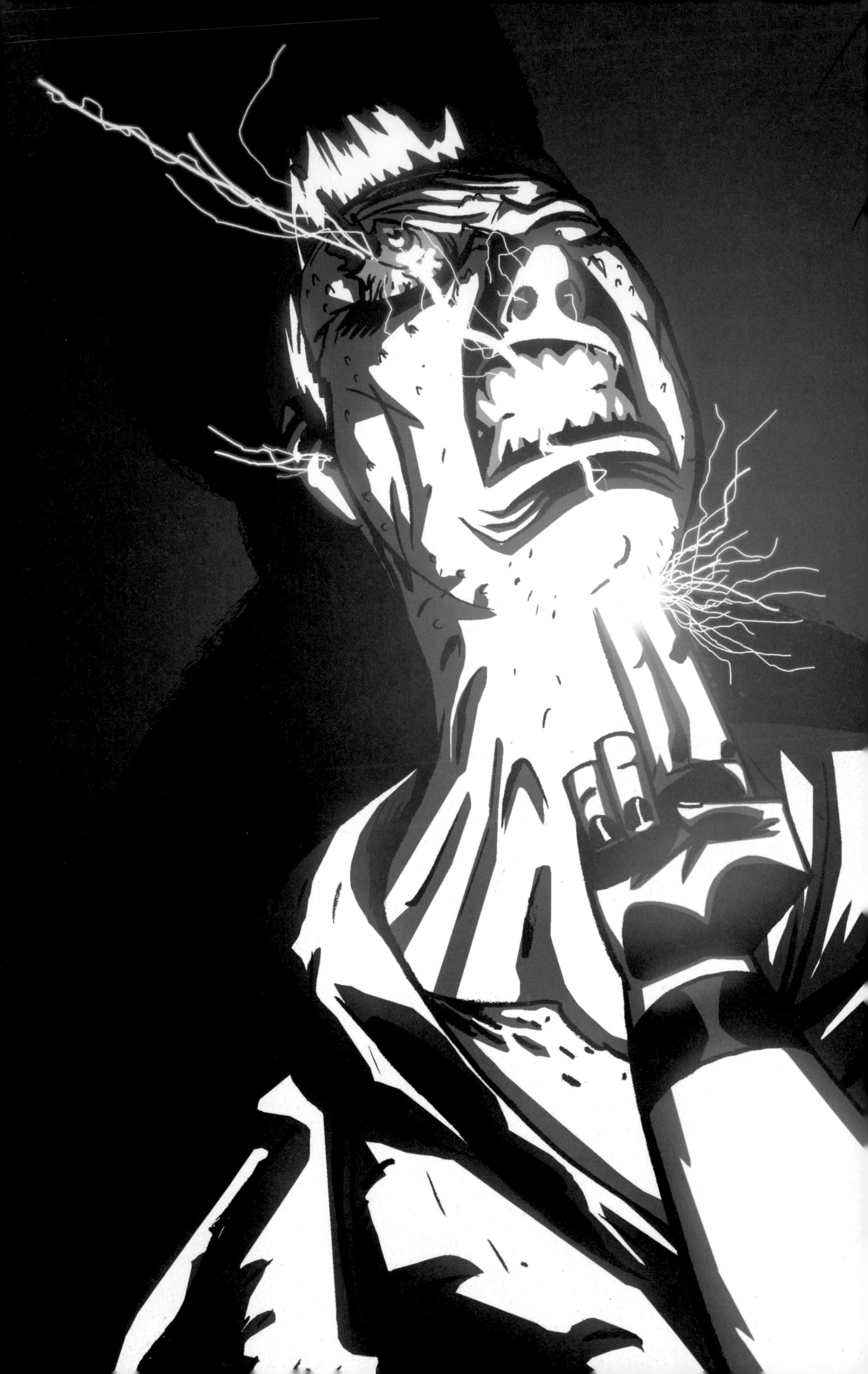

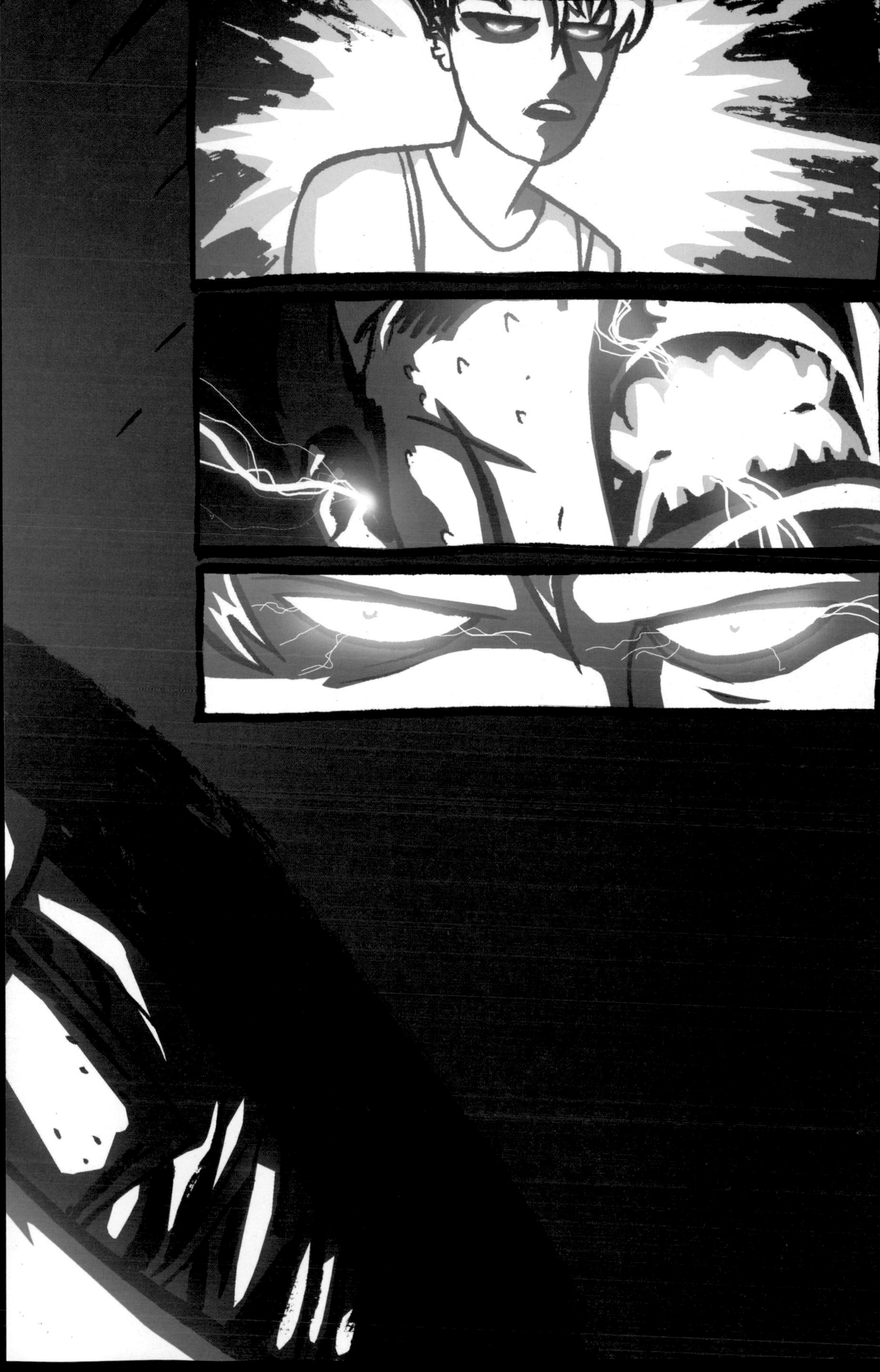

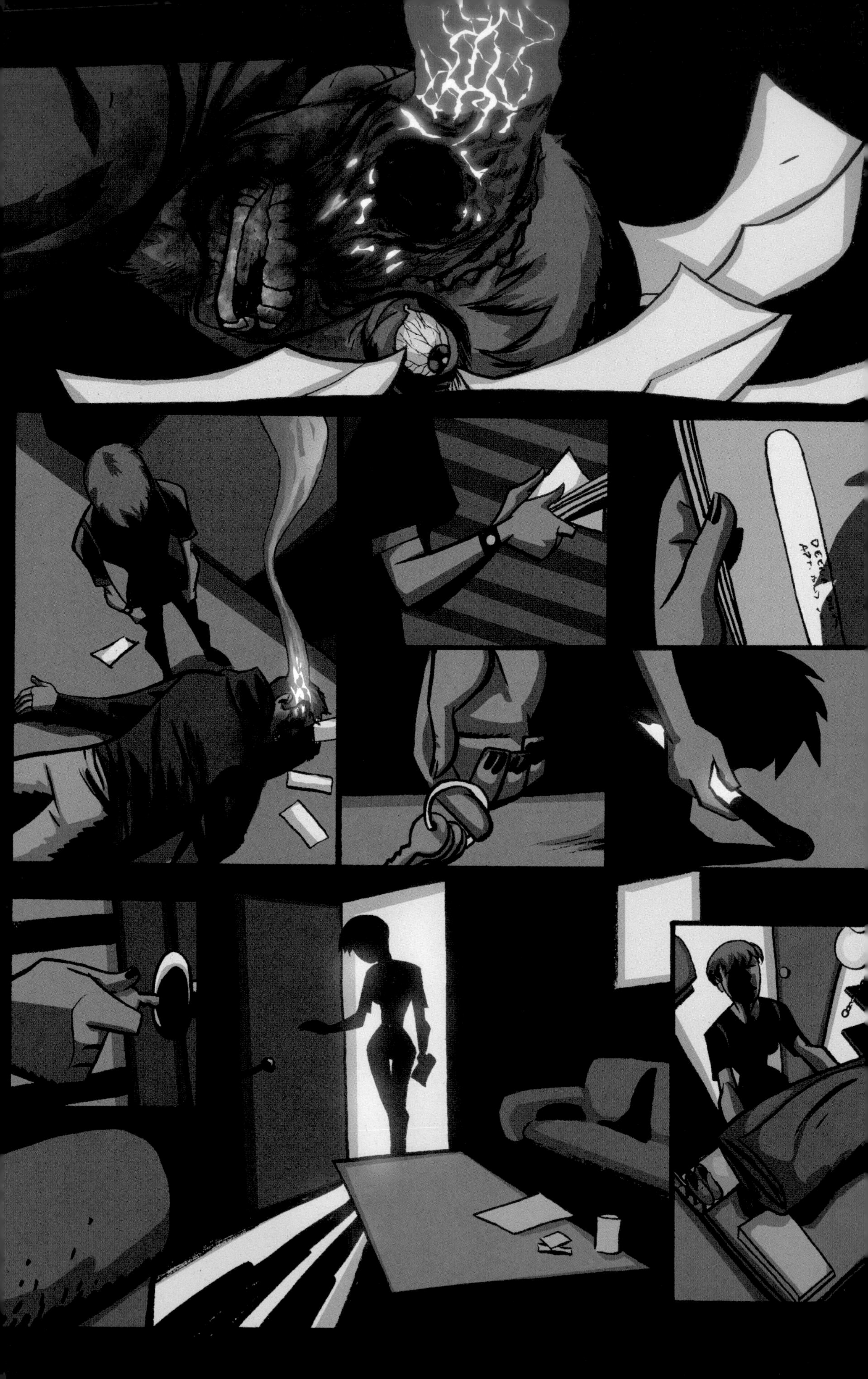

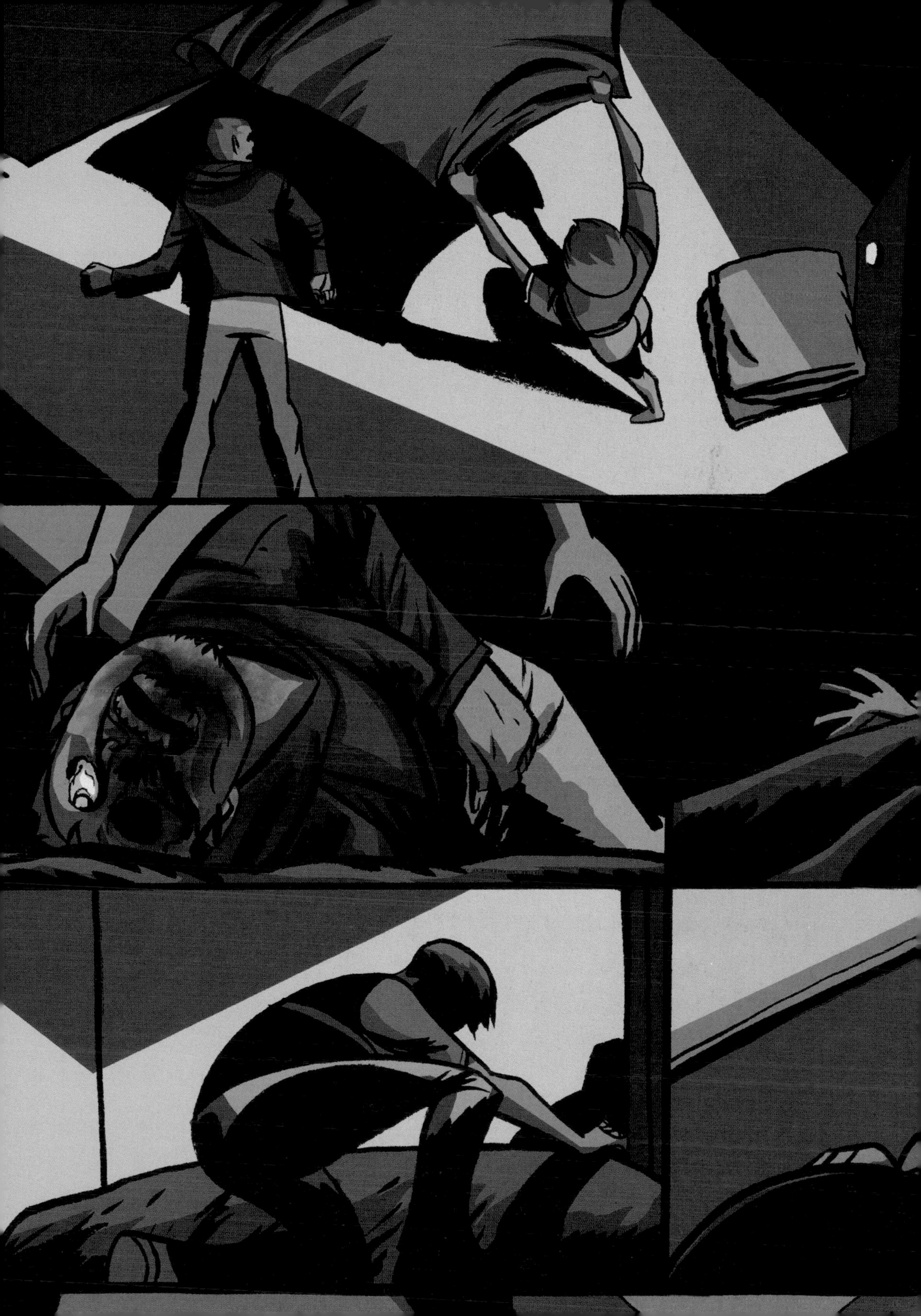

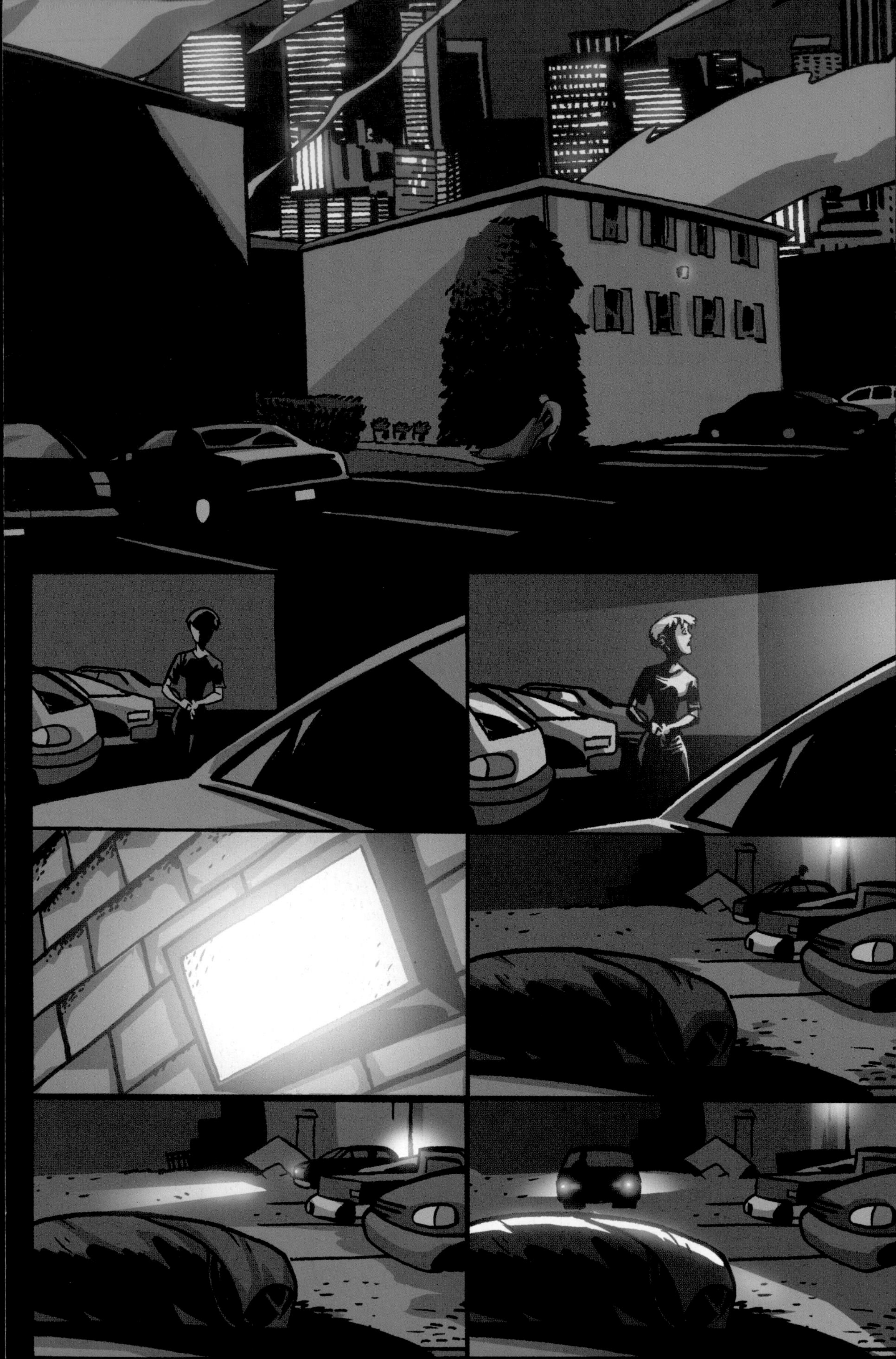

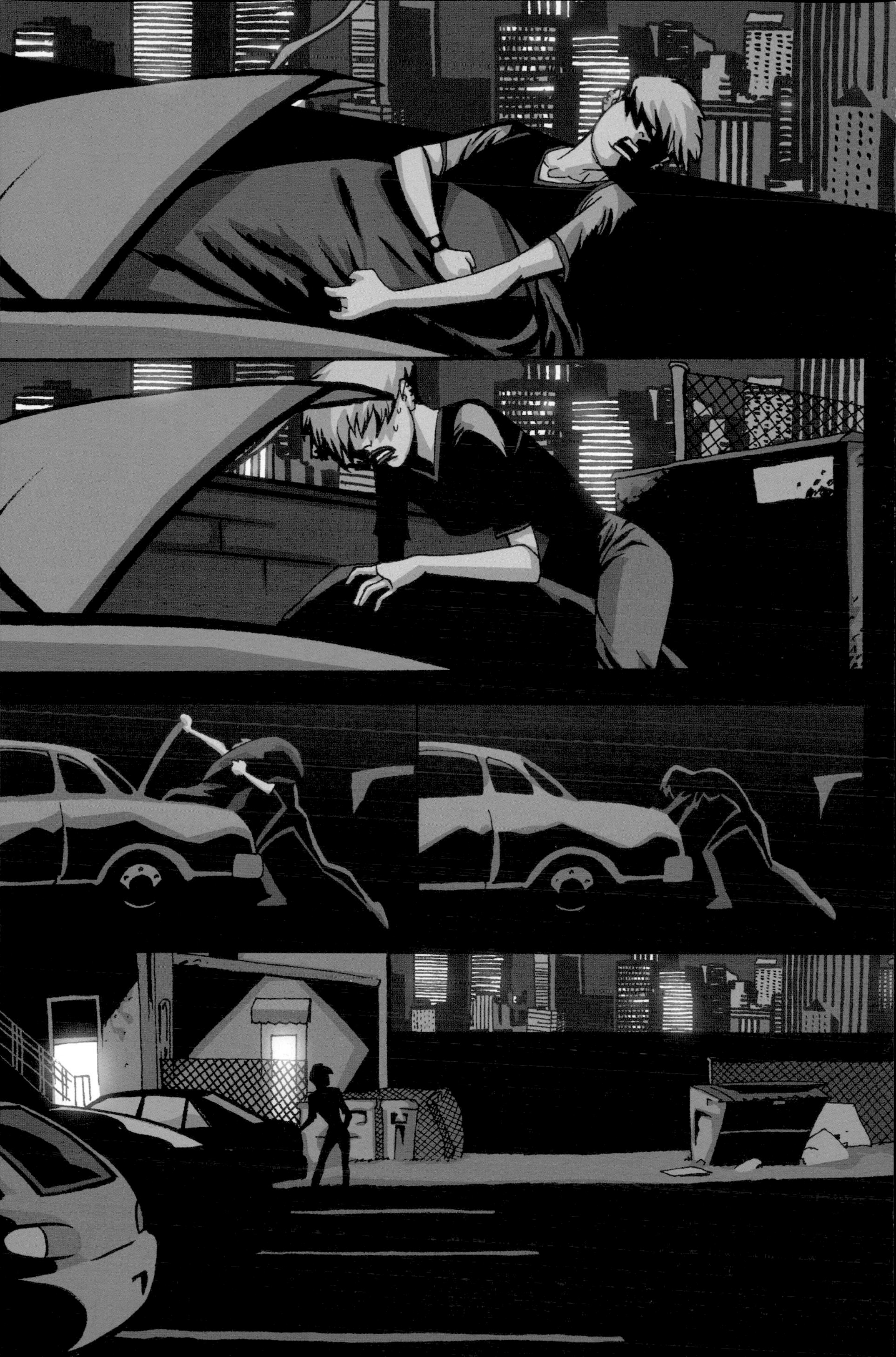

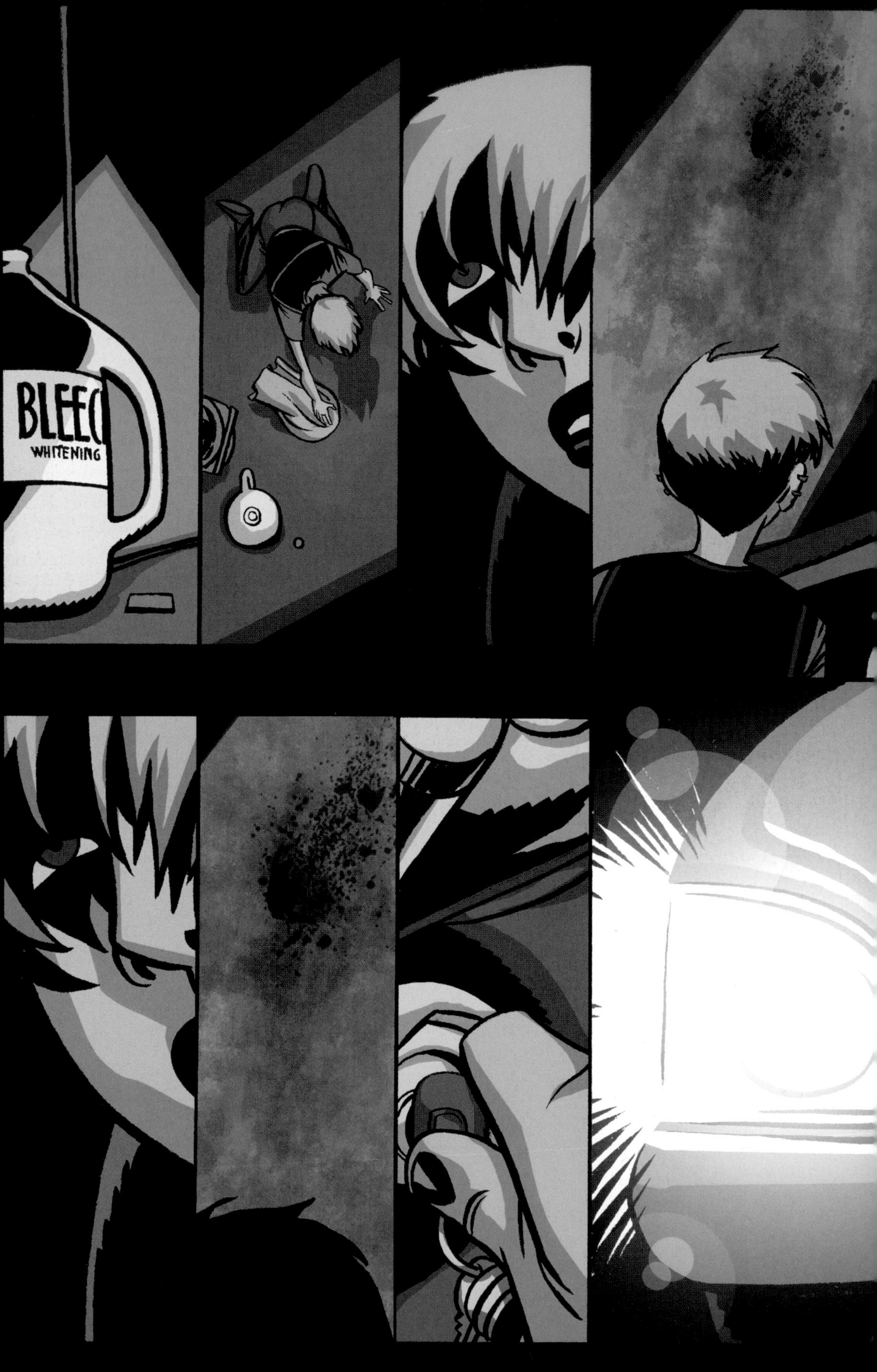
BLEEC
WHITENING

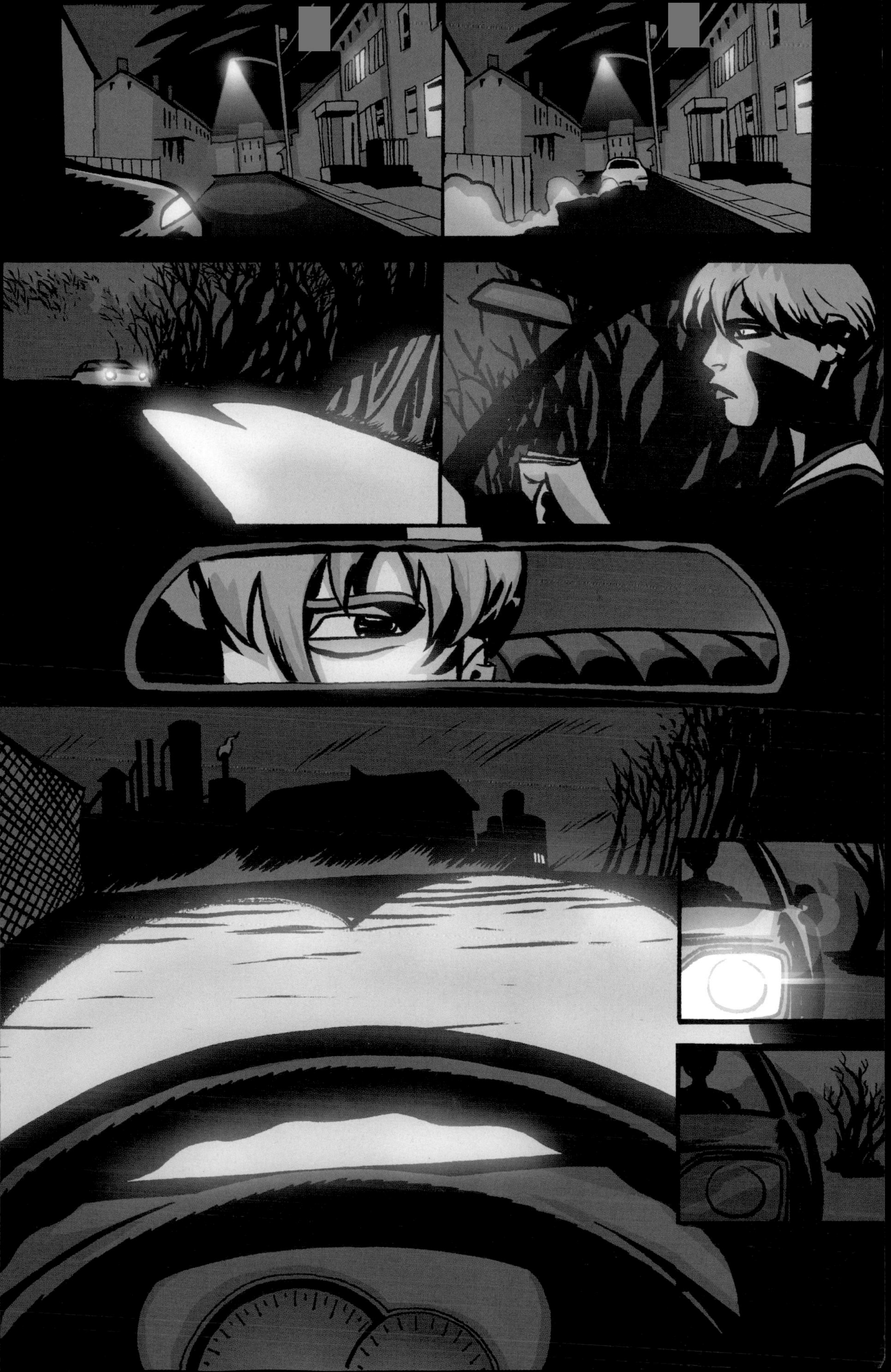

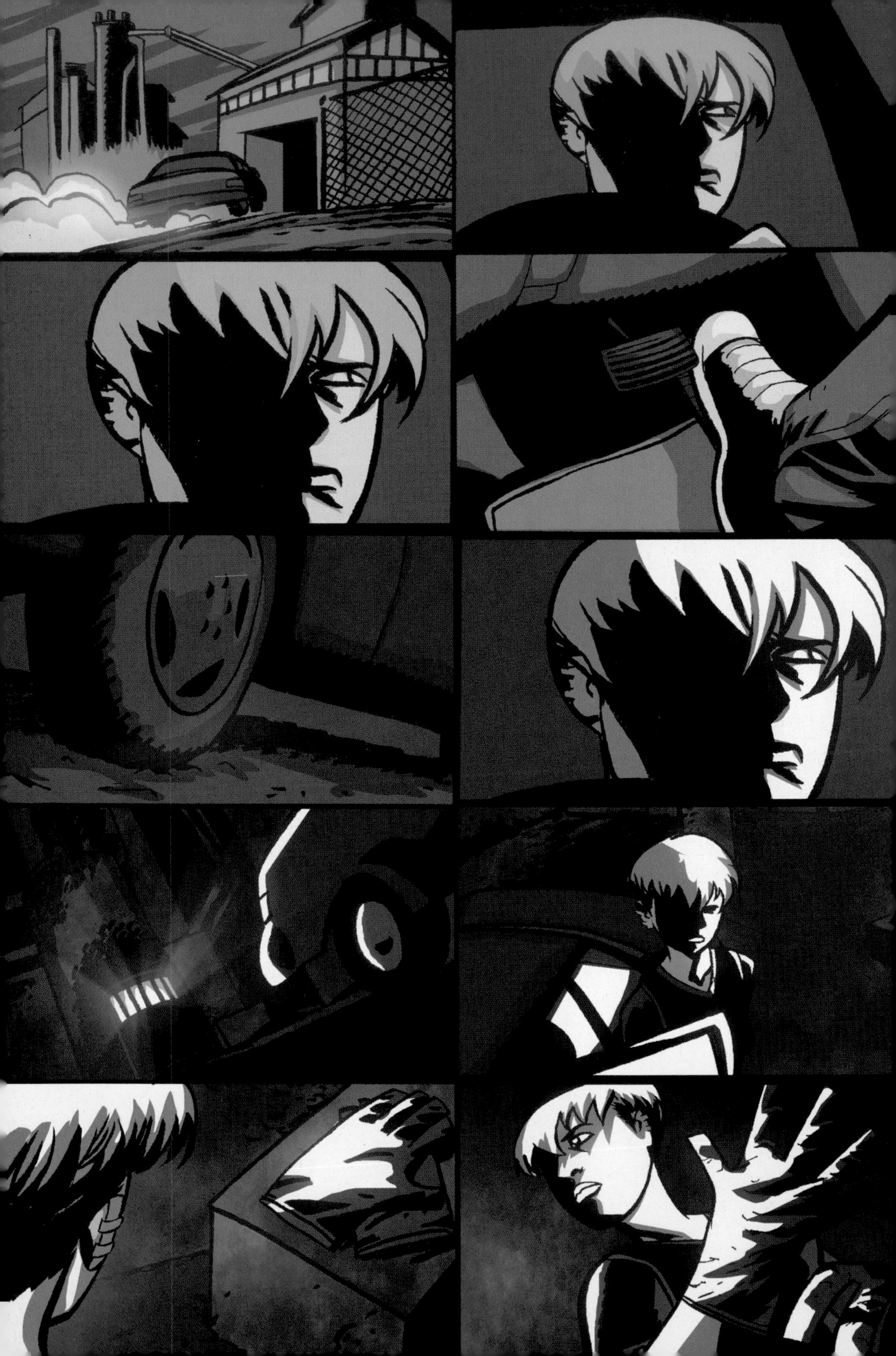

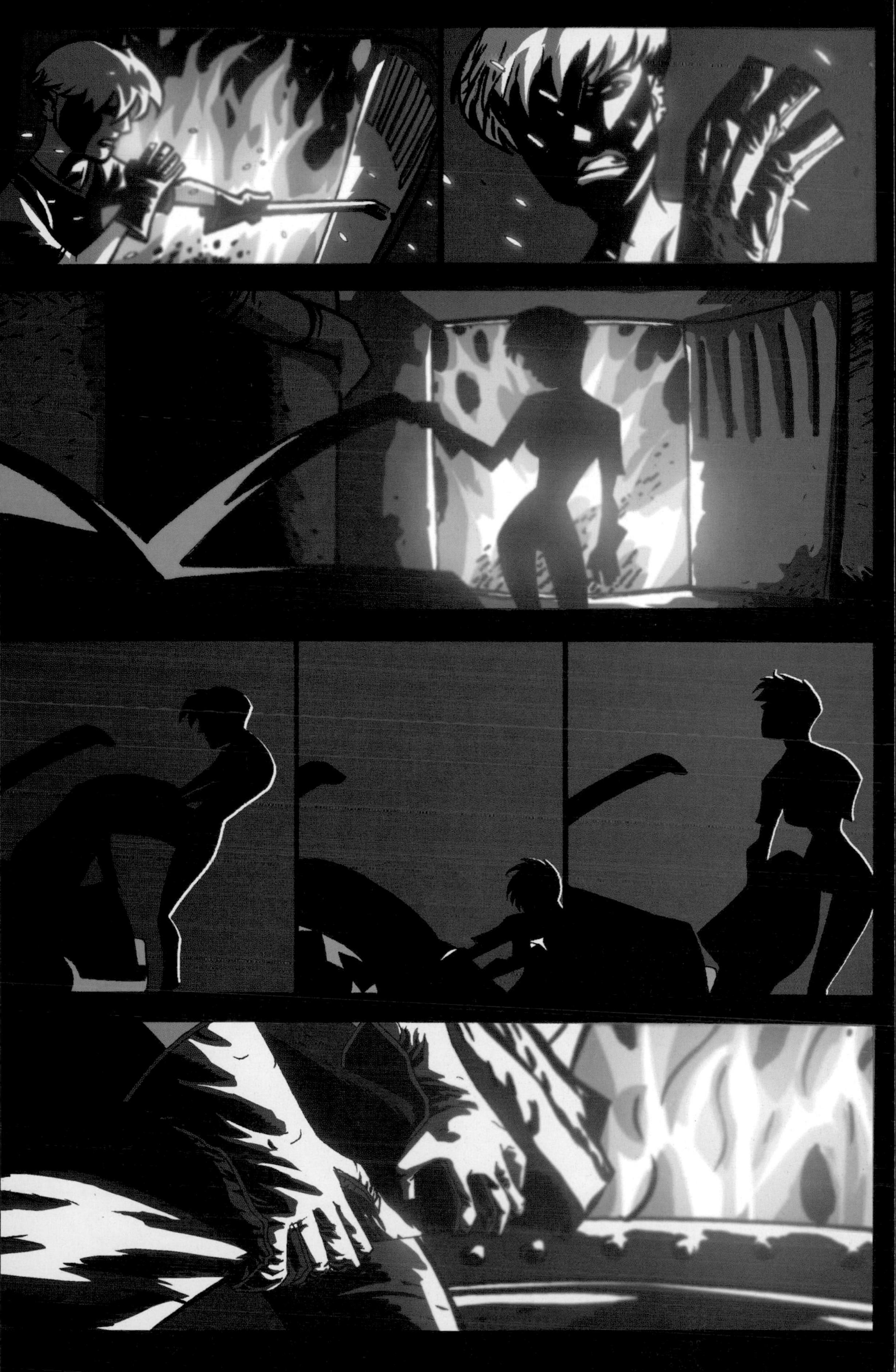

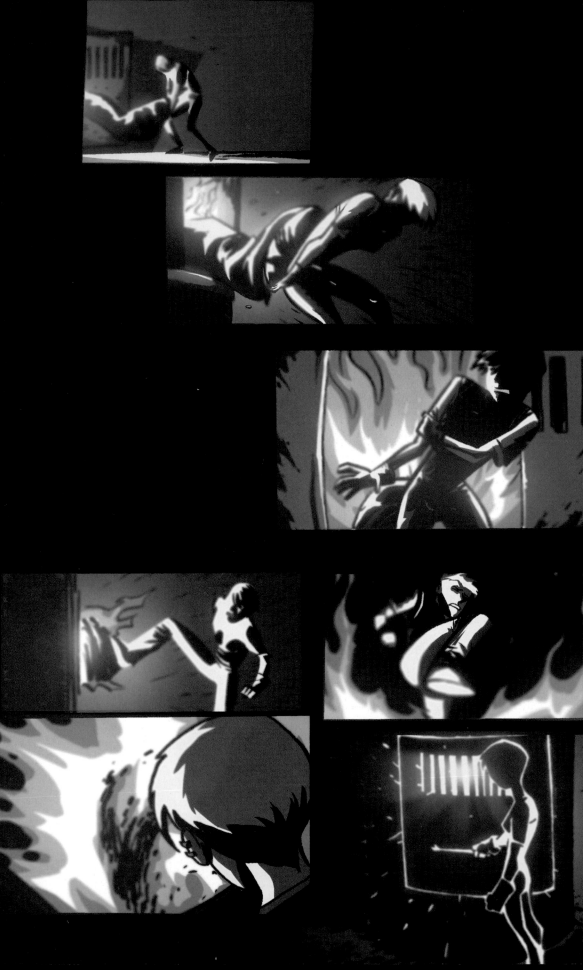

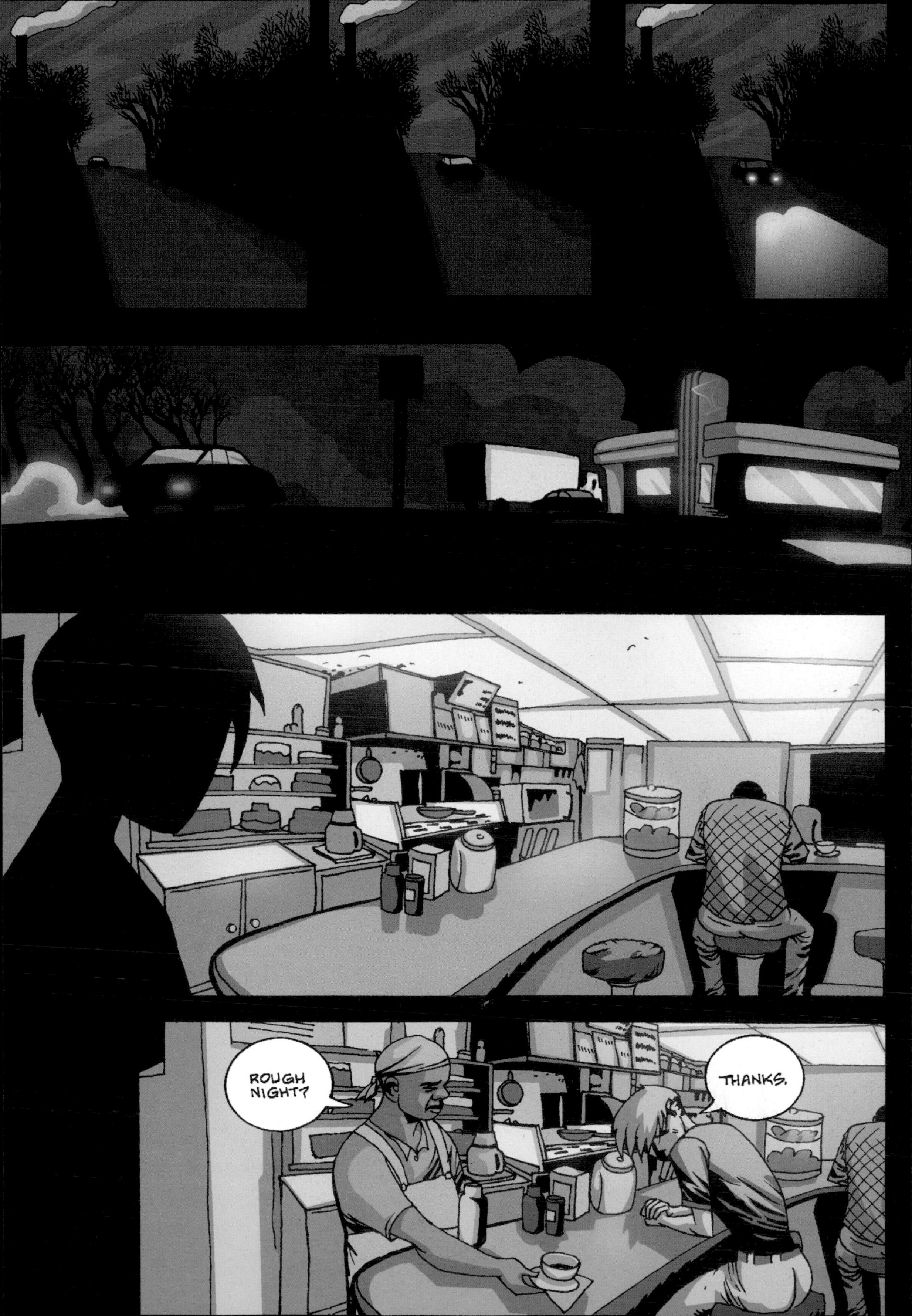
ROUGH NIGHT?
THANKS.

MENU?
NO.

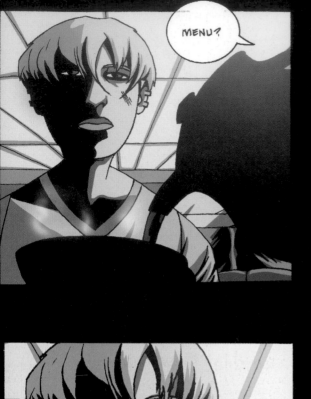

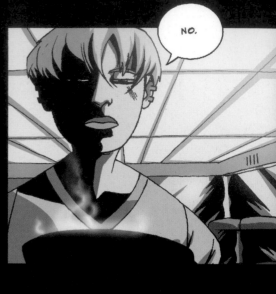

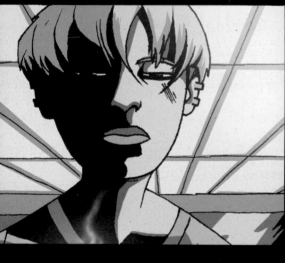

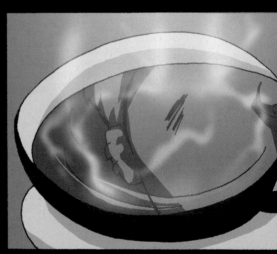

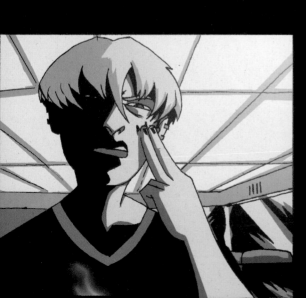

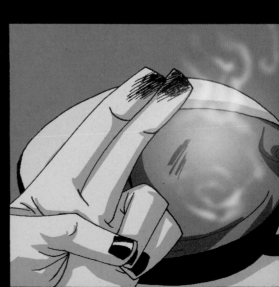

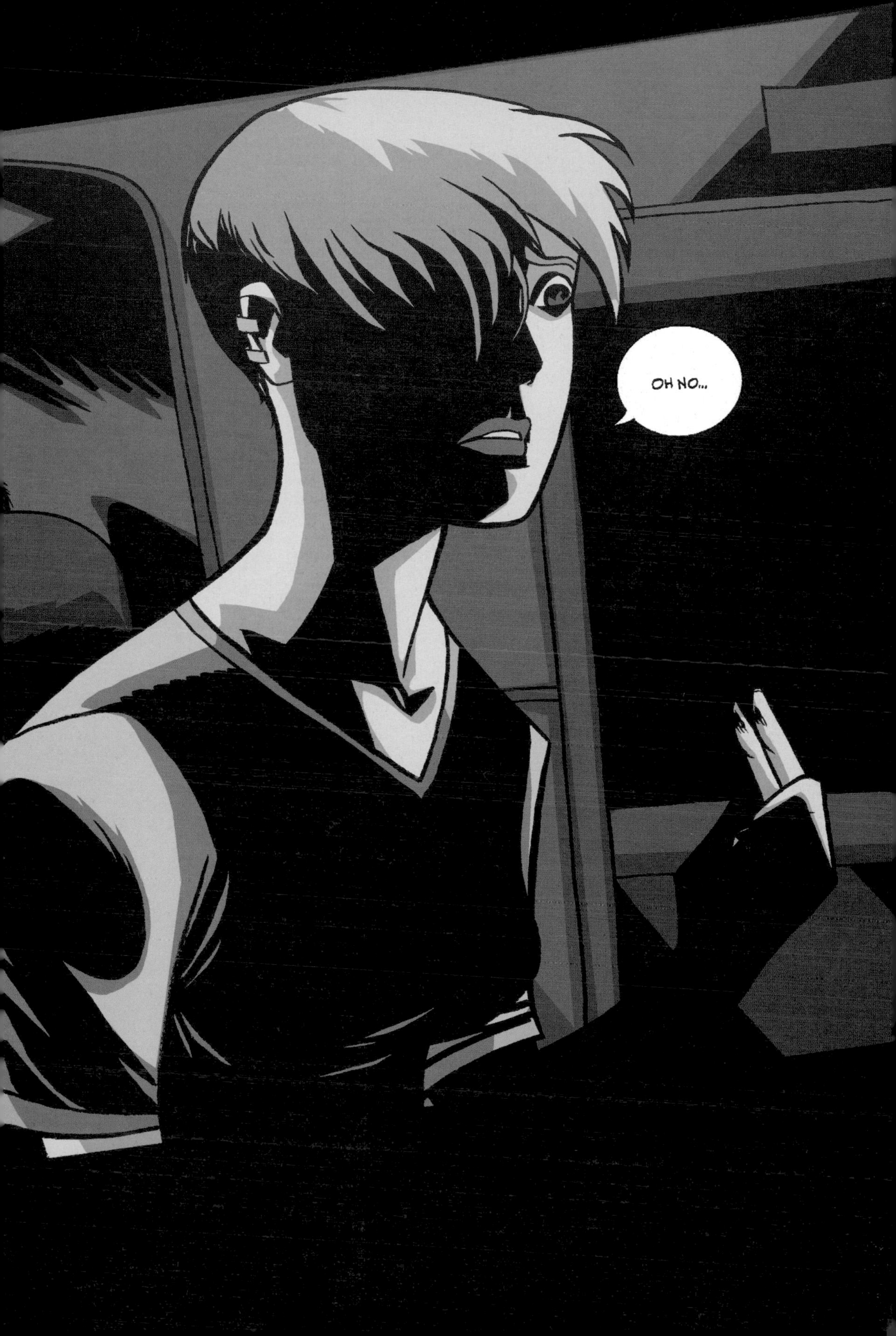
OH NO...

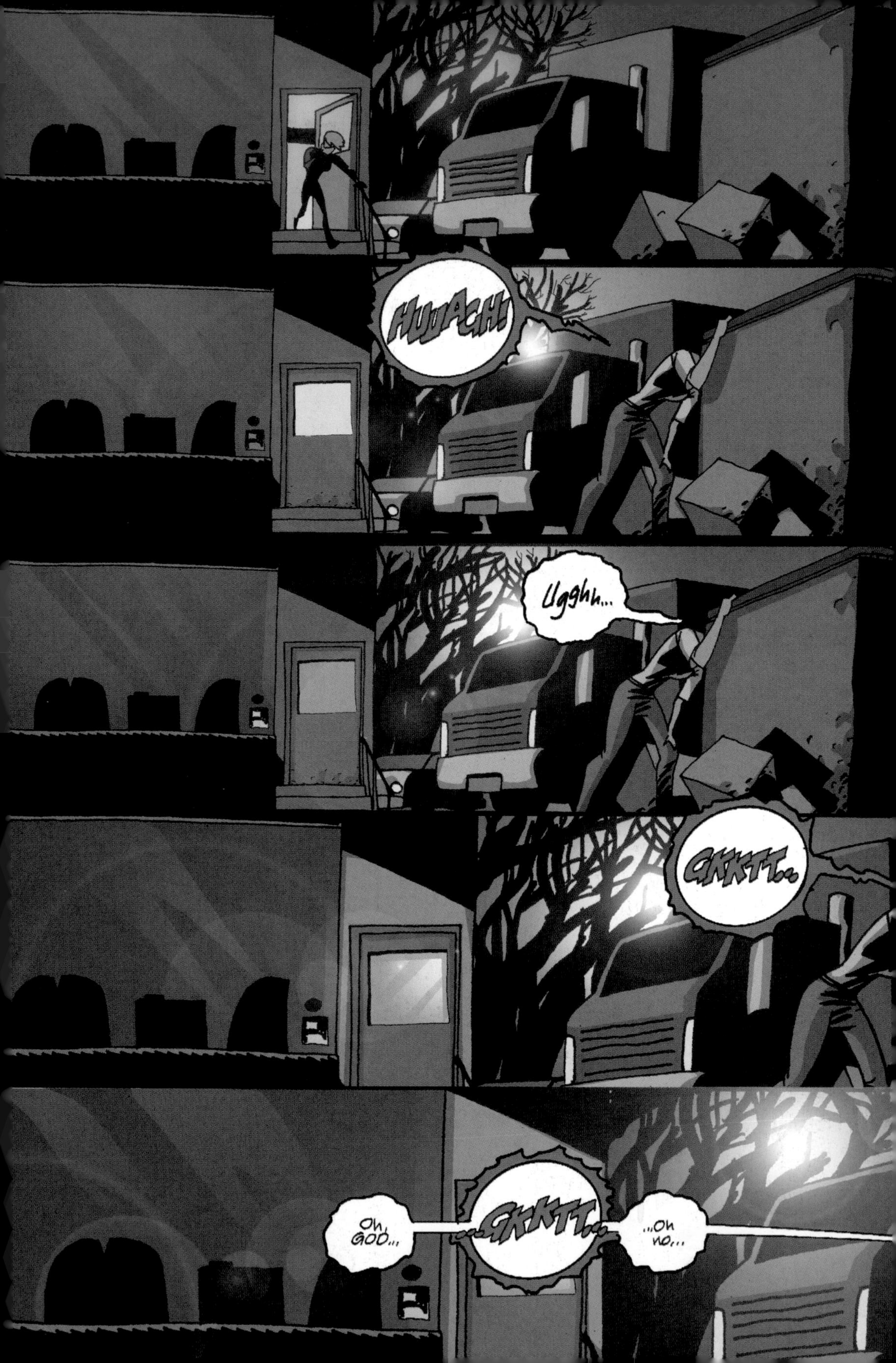
HUUACH!
Ugghh...
GKKTT..
Oh, GOD...
..GKKTT..
...Oh no...

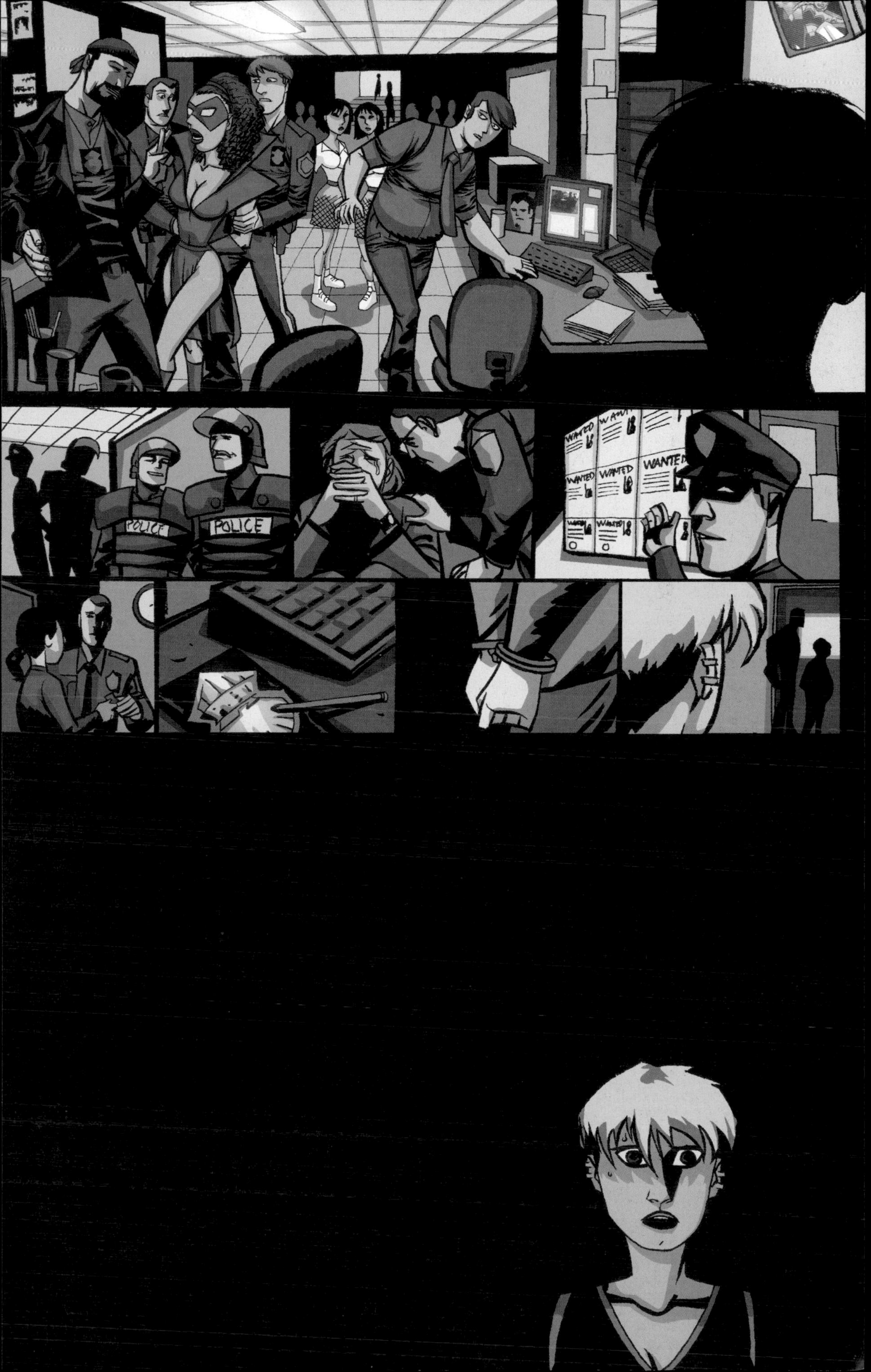
POLICE
POLICE
WANTED
WANTED
WANTED
WANTED
WANTED
WANTED

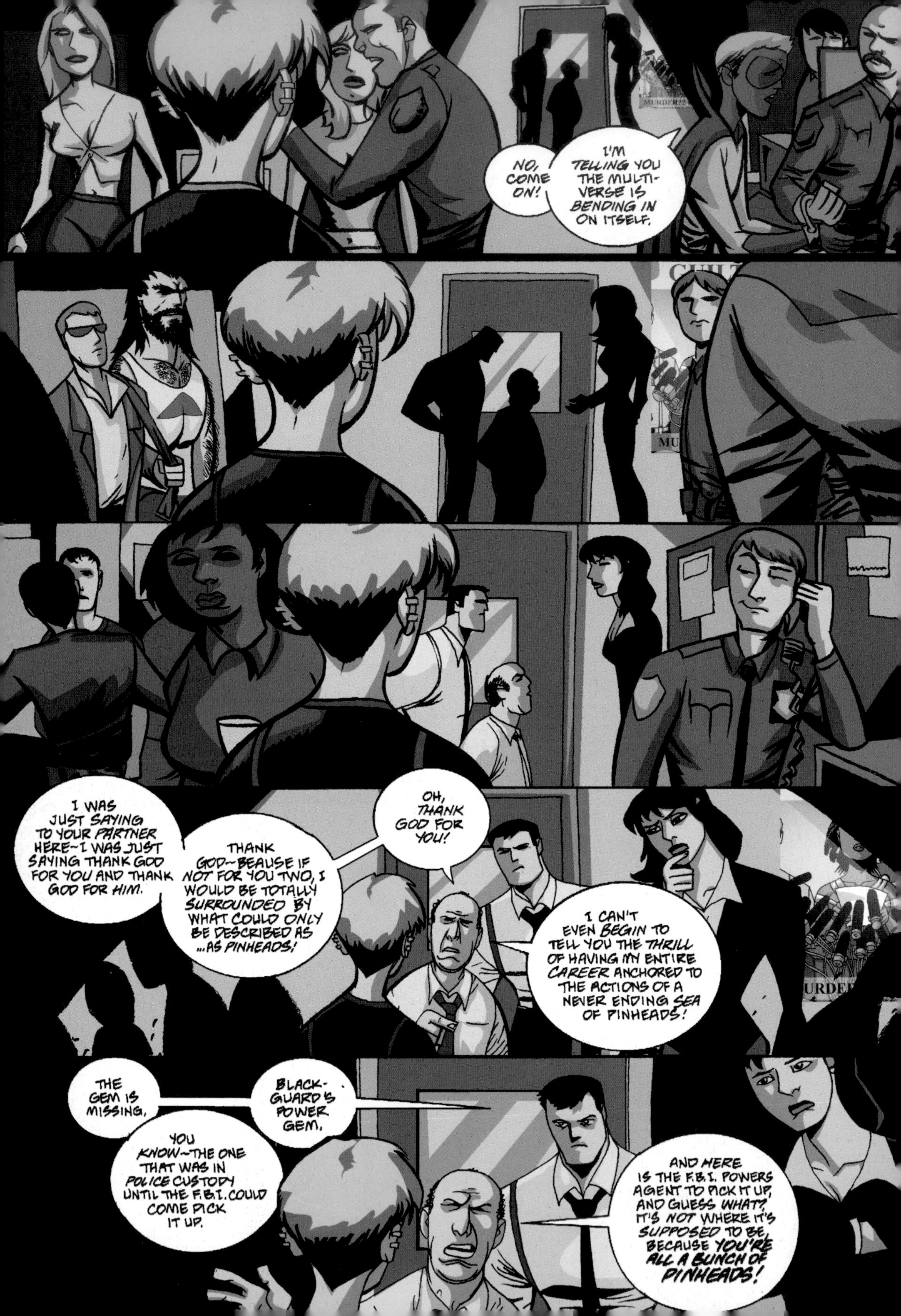
MURDER22
NO, COME ON!
I'M TELLING YOU THE MULTI-VERSE IS BENDING IN ON ITSELF.
I WAS JUST SAYING TO YOUR PARTNER HERE-- I WAS JUST SAYING THANK GOD FOR YOU AND THANK GOD FOR HIM.
THANK GOD-- BEAUSE IF NOT FOR YOU TWO, I WOULD BE TOTALLY SURROUNDED BY WHAT COULD ONLY BE DESCRIBED AS ...AS PINHEADS!
OH, THANK GOD FOR YOU!
I CAN'T EVEN BEGIN TO TELL YOU THE THRILL OF HAVING MY ENTIRE CAREER ANCHORED TO THE ACTIONS OF A NEVER ENDING SEA OF PINHEADS!
THE GEM IS MISSING.
BLACK-GUARD'S POWER GEM.
YOU KNOW-- THE ONE THAT WAS IN POLICE CUSTODY UNTIL THE F.B.I. COULD COME PICK IT UP.
AND HERE IS THE F.B.I. POWERS AGENT TO PICK IT UP, AND GUESS WHAT? IT'S NOT WHERE IT'S SUPPOSED TO BE, BECAUSE YOU'RE ALL A BUNCH OF PINHEADS!

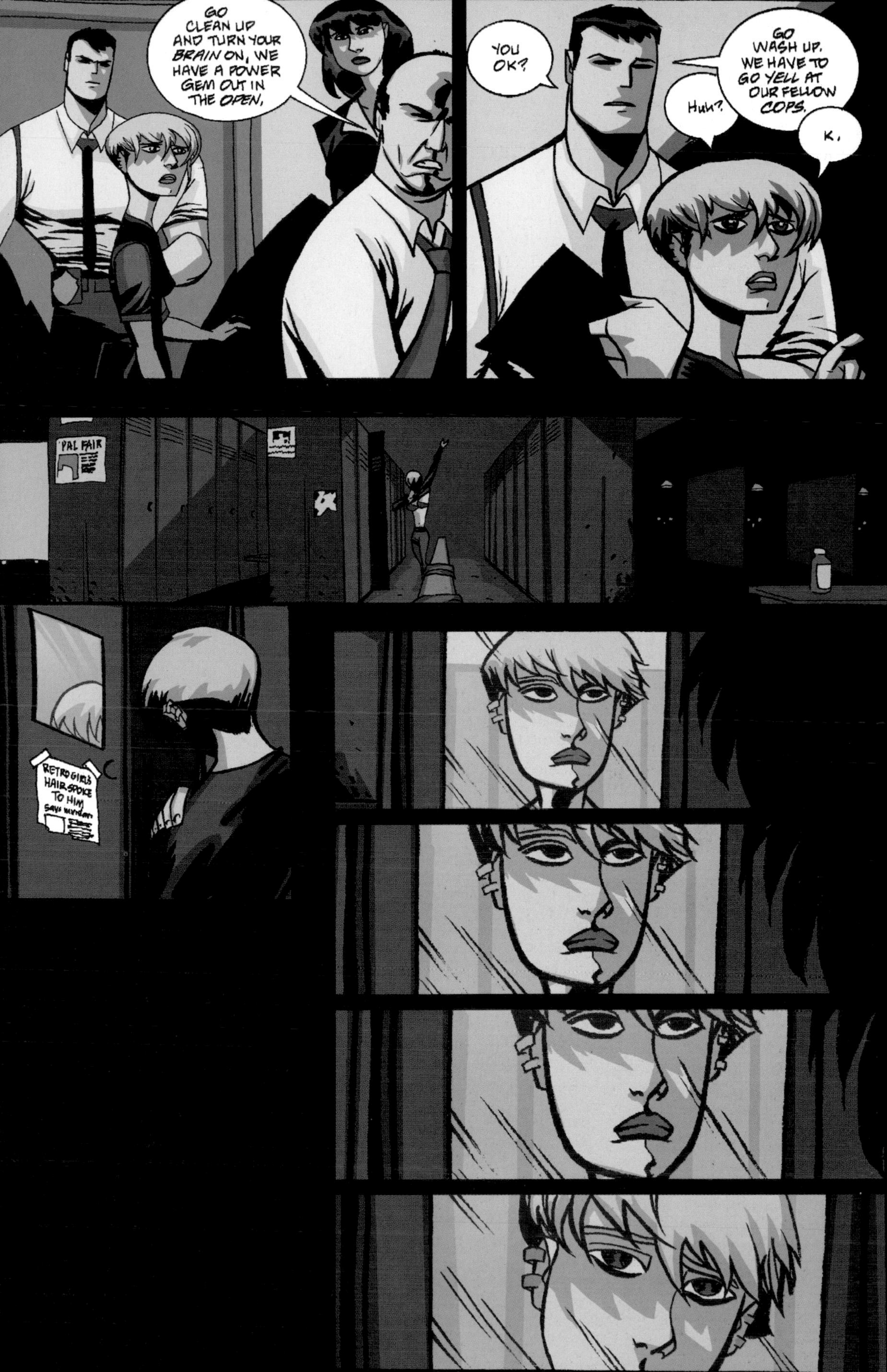

GO CLEAN UP AND TURN YOUR BRAIN ON, WE HAVE A POWER GEM OUT IN THE OPEN.
YOU OK?
GO WASH UP. WE HAVE TO GO YELL AT OUR FELLOW COPS.
HUH?
K.
PAL FAIR
RETRO GIRL'S HAIR SPOKE TO HIM

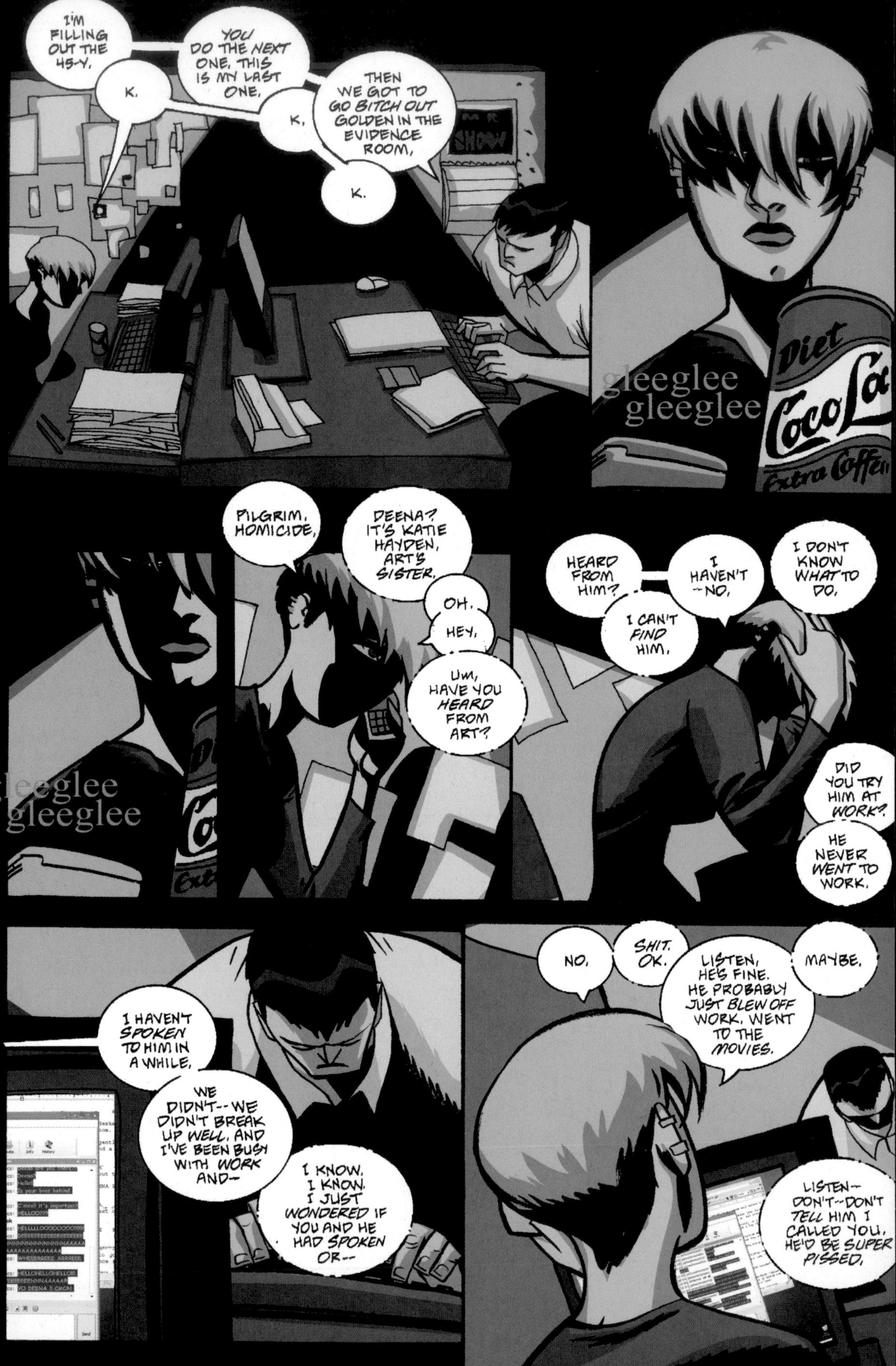
I'M FILLING OUT THE 45-Y.
K.
YOU DO THE NEXT ONE. THIS IS MY LAST ONE.
K.
THEN WE GOT TO GO BITCH OUT GOLDEN IN THE EVIDENCE ROOM.
K.
PILGRIM. HOMICIDE.
DEENA? IT'S KATIE HAYDEN. ART'S SISTER.
OH.
HEY.
UM, HAVE YOU HEARD FROM ART?
HEARD FROM HIM?
I HAVEN'T --NO.
I CAN'T FIND HIM.
I DON'T KNOW WHAT TO DO.
DID YOU TRY HIM AT WORK?
HE NEVER WENT TO WORK.
I HAVEN'T SPOKEN TO HIM IN A WHILE.
WE DIDN'T--WE DIDN'T BREAK UP WELL. AND I'VE BEEN BUSY WITH WORK AND--
I KNOW. I KNOW. I JUST WONDERED IF YOU AND HE HAD SPOKEN OR--
NO.
SHIT. OK.
LISTEN. HE'S FINE. HE PROBABLY JUST BLEW OFF WORK. WENT TO THE MOVIES.
MAYBE.
LISTEN-- DON'T--DON'T TELL HIM I CALLED YOU. HE'D BE SUPER PISSED.

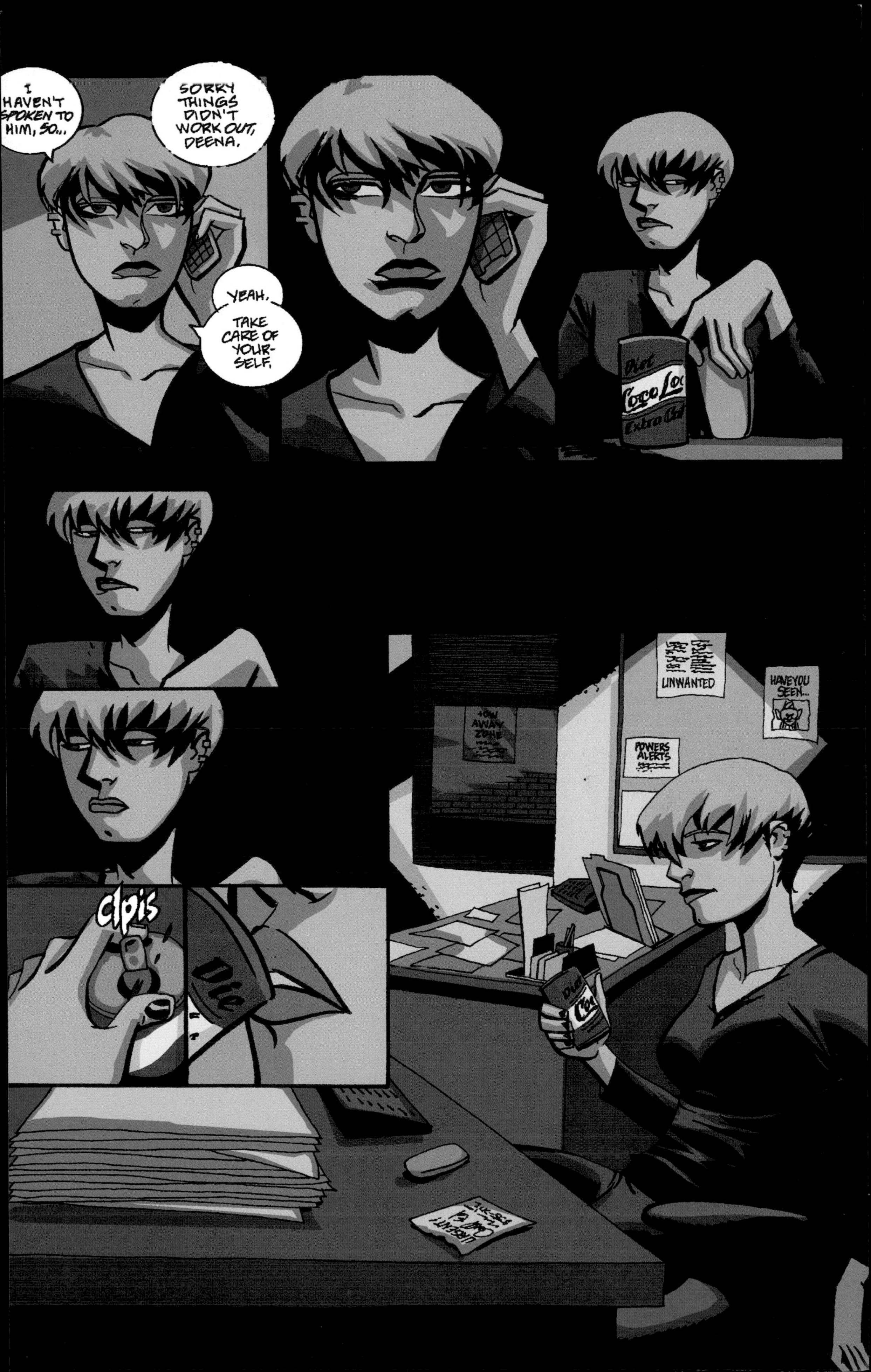
I HAVEN'T SPOKEN TO HIM, SO...
SORRY THINGS DIDN'T WORK OUT, DEENA.
YEAH.
TAKE CARE OF YOURSELF.
Diet
clpis
TOW AWAY ZONE
UNWANTED
HAVE YOU SEEN...
POWERS ALERTS

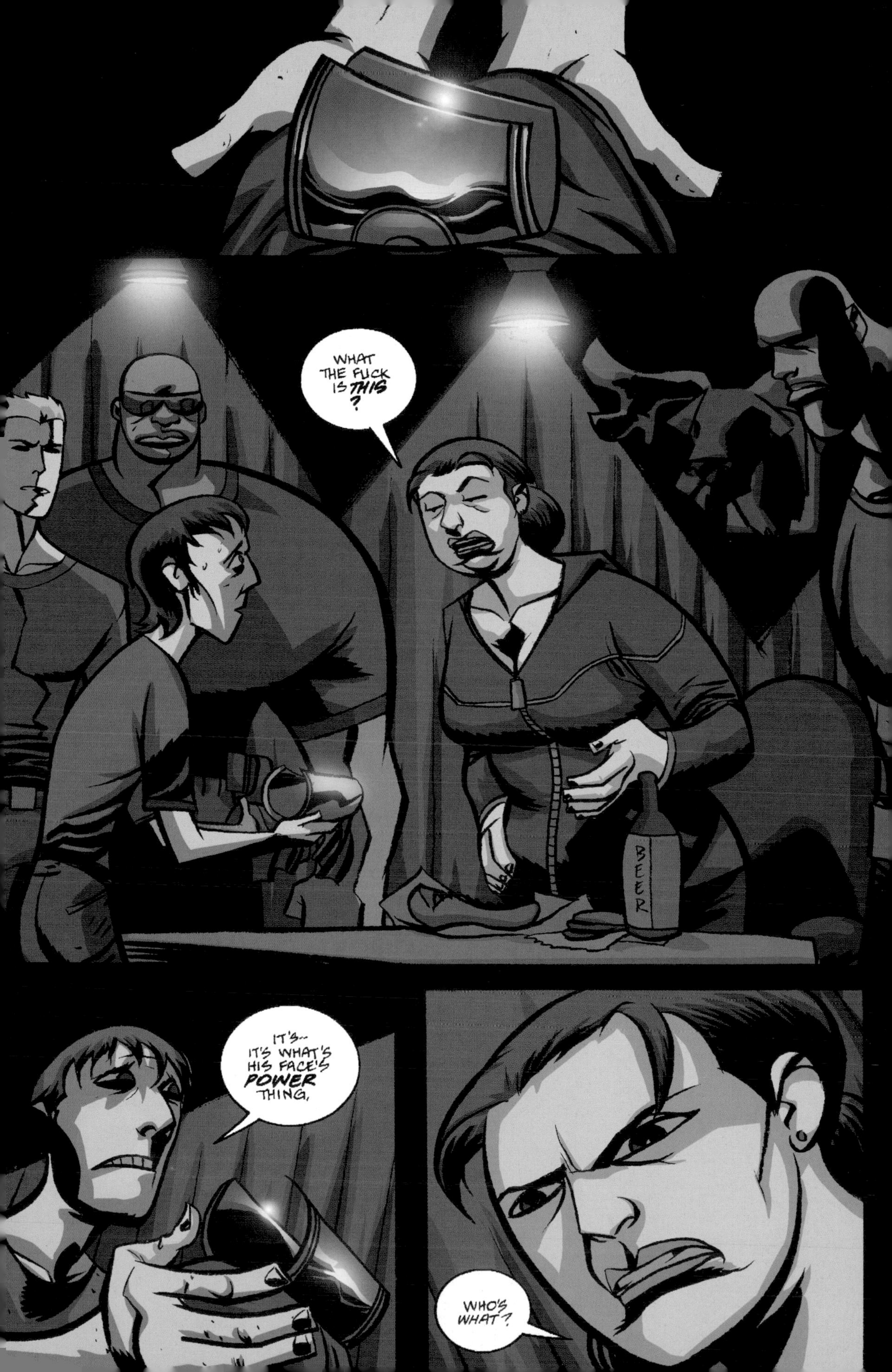
WHAT THE FUCK IS *THIS* ?
BEER
IT'S-- IT'S WHAT'S HIS FACE'S *POWER* THING.
WHO'S WHAT?

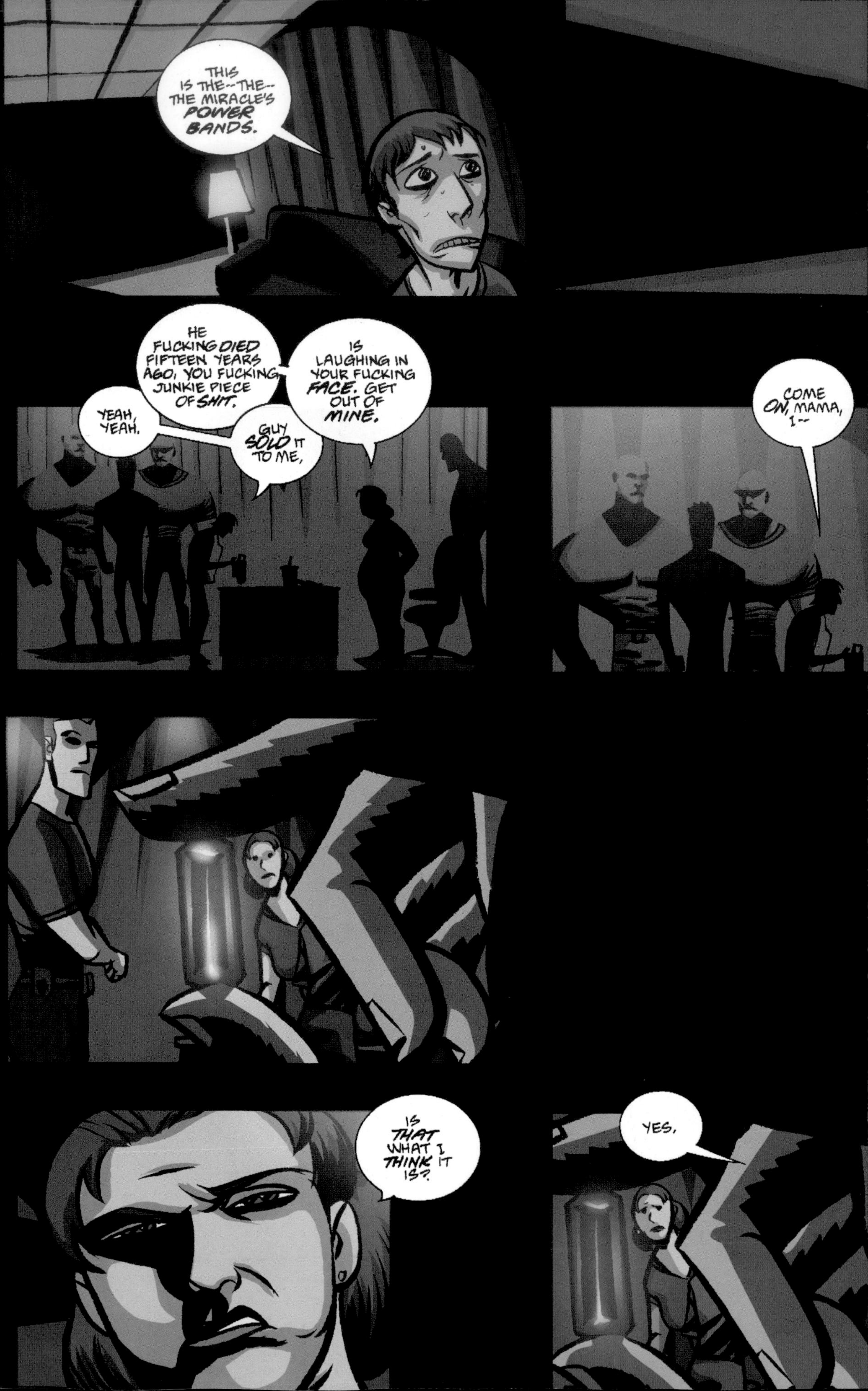
THIS IS THE-- THE-- THE MIRACLE'S POWER BANDS.
HE FUCKING DIED FIFTEEN YEARS AGO, YOU FUCKING JUNKIE PIECE OF SHIT.
YEAH, YEAH.
GUY SOLD IT TO ME,
IS LAUGHING IN YOUR FUCKING FACE. GET OUT OF MINE.
COME ON, MAMA, I--
IS THAT WHAT I THINK IT IS?
YES.

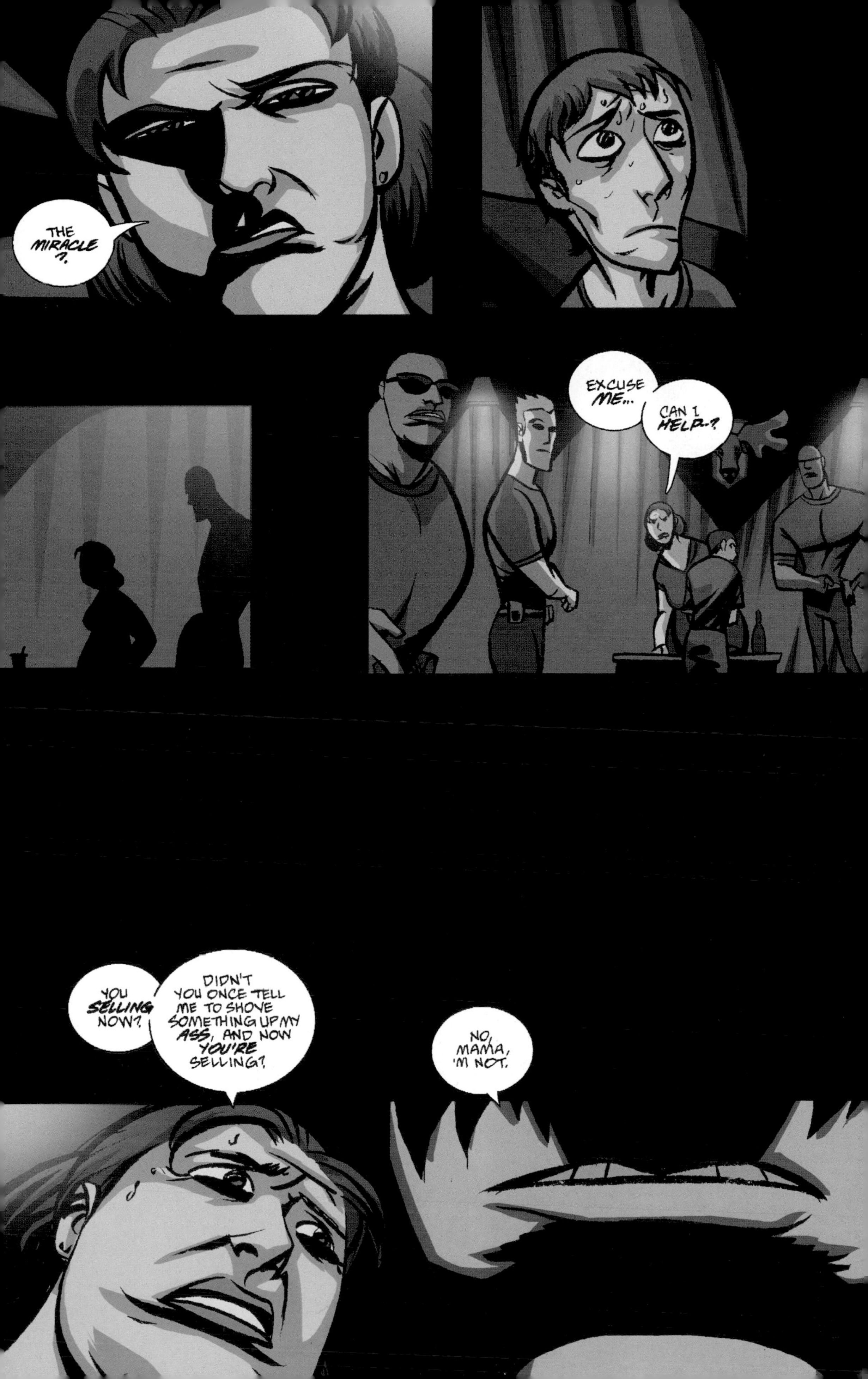
THE MIRACLE ?.
EXCUSE ME...
CAN I HELP..?
YOU SELLING NOW?
DIDN'T YOU ONCE TELL ME TO SHOVE SOMETHING UP MY ASS, AND NOW YOU'RE SELLING?
NO, MAMA, 'M NOT.

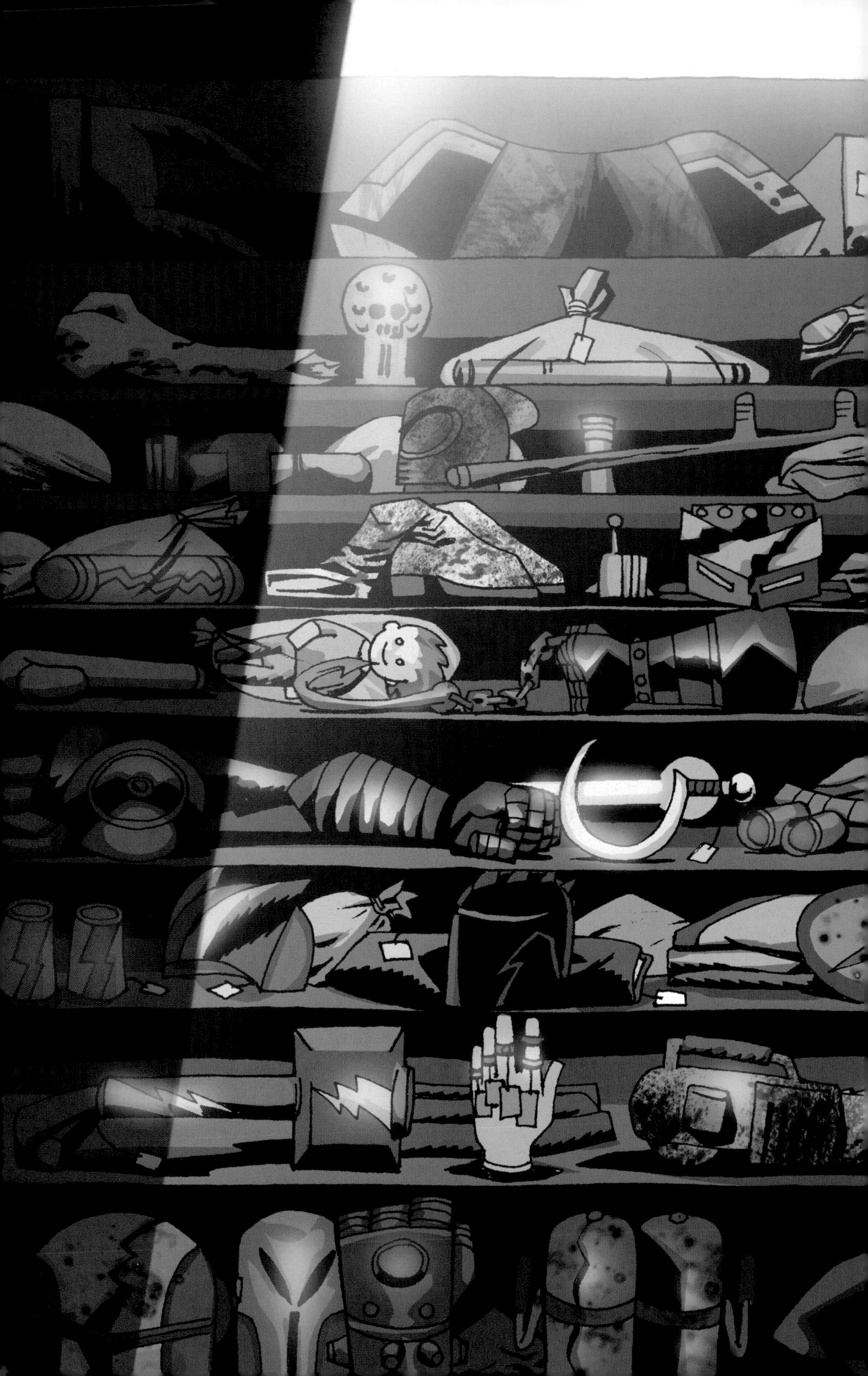

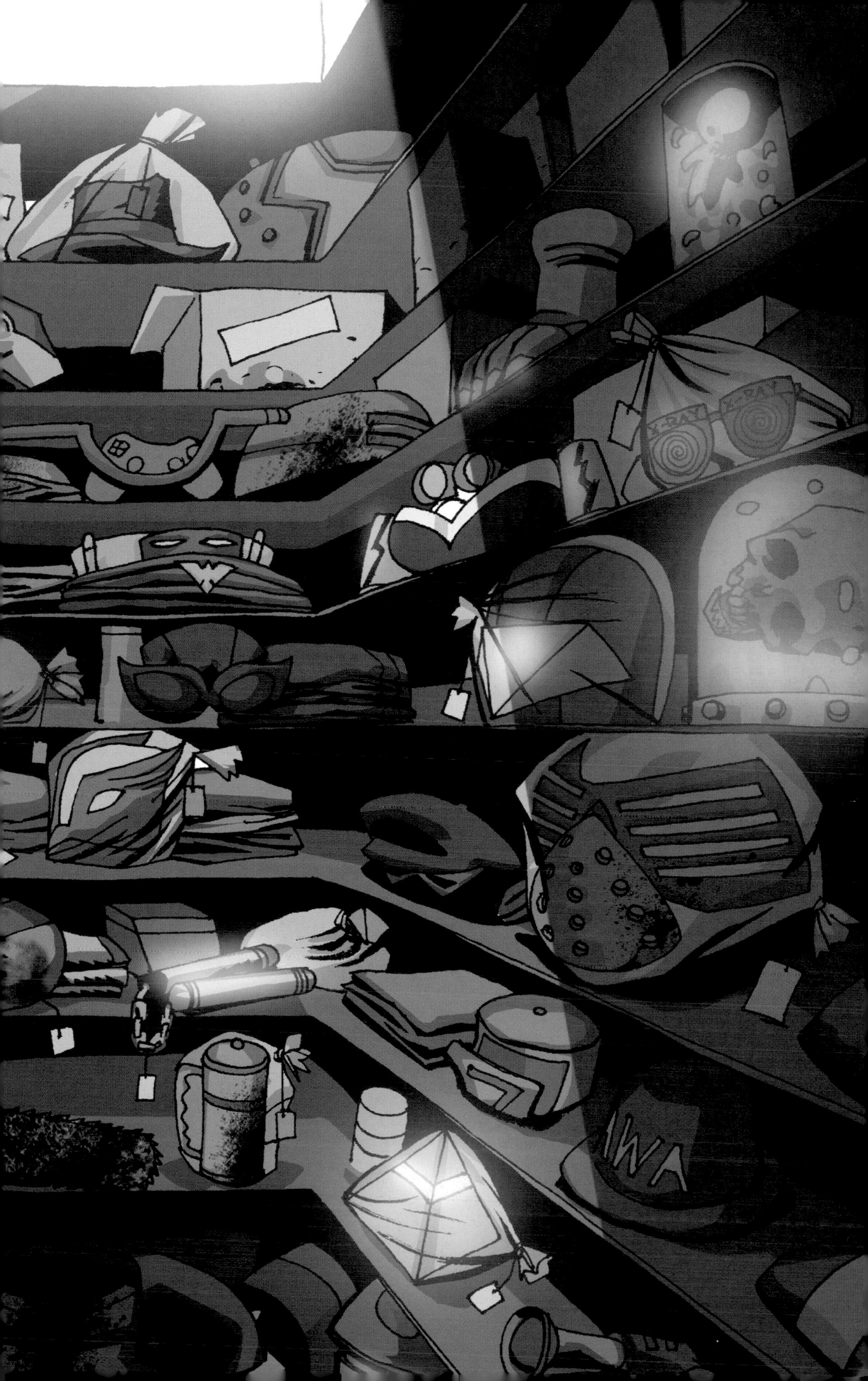
X-RAY
X-RAY

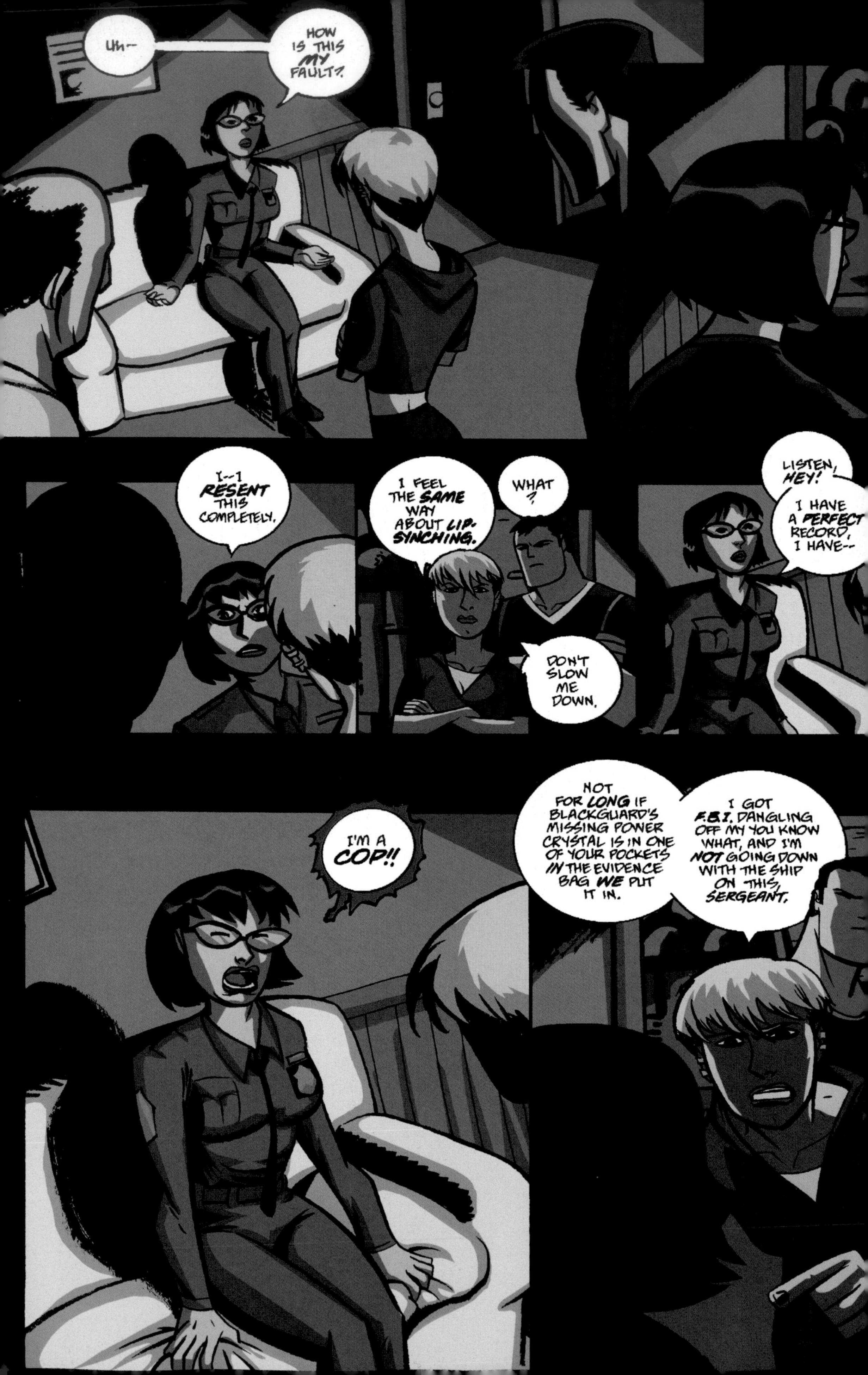
Uh--
HOW IS THIS MY FAULT?
I--I RESENT THIS COMPLETELY.
I FEEL THE SAME WAY ABOUT LIP-SYNCHING.
WHAT?
DON'T SLOW ME DOWN.
LISTEN, HEY!
I HAVE A PERFECT RECORD, I HAVE--
I'M A COP!!
NOT FOR LONG IF BLACKGUARD'S MISSING POWER CRYSTAL IS IN ONE OF YOUR POCKETS IN THE EVIDENCE BAG WE PUT IT IN.
I GOT F.B.I. DANGLING OFF MY YOU KNOW WHAT, AND I'M NOT GOING DOWN WITH THE SHIP ON THIS, SERGEANT.

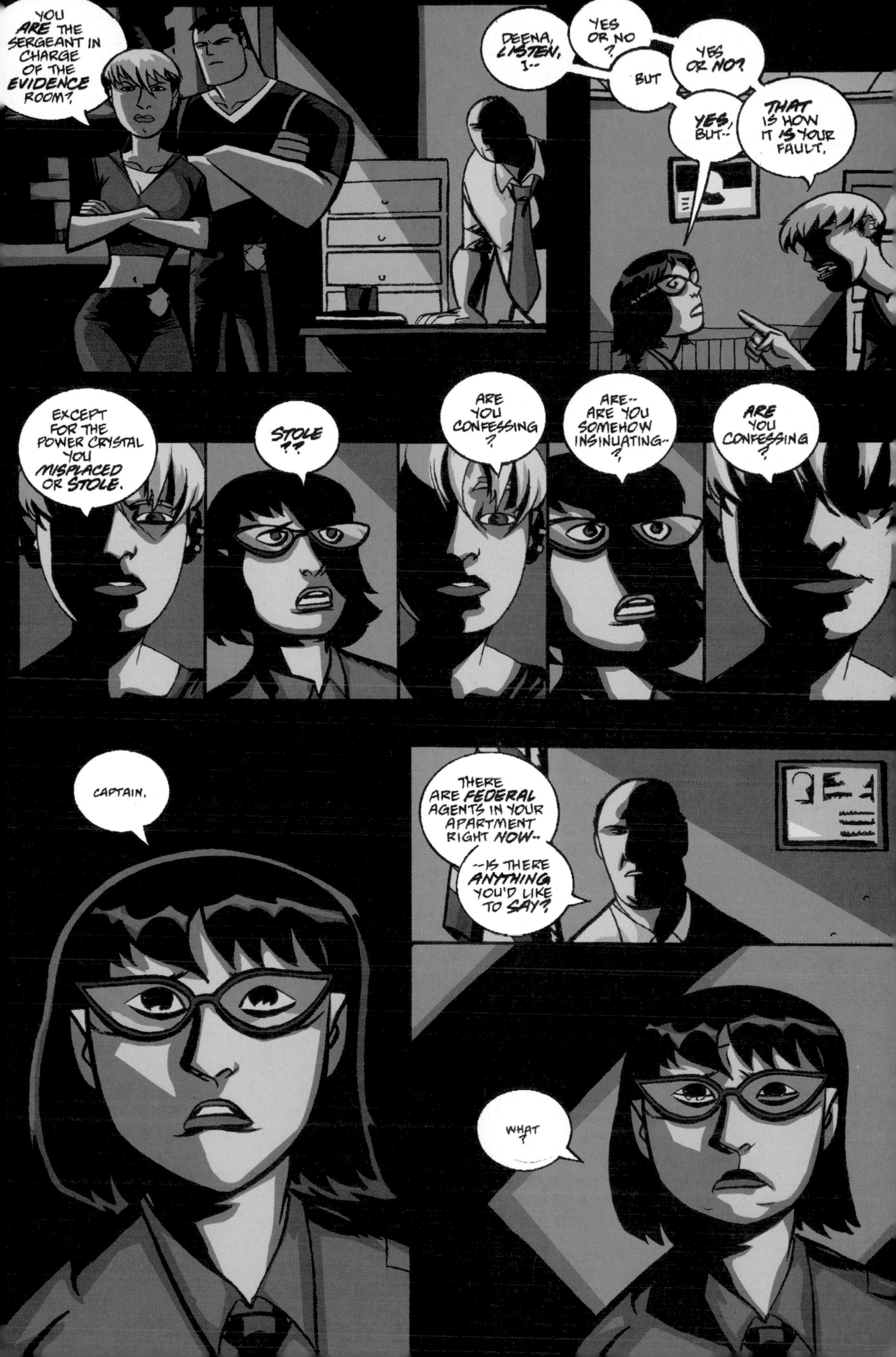
YOU ARE THE SERGEANT IN CHARGE OF THE EVIDENCE ROOM?
DEENA, LISTEN, I--
YES OR NO?
BUT
YES OR NO?
YES, BUT--!
THAT IS HOW IT IS YOUR FAULT.
EXCEPT FOR THE POWER CRYSTAL YOU MISPLACED OR STOLE.
STOLE??
ARE YOU CONFESSING?
ARE-- ARE YOU SOMEHOW INSINUATING--
ARE YOU CONFESSING?
CAPTAIN.
THERE ARE FEDERAL AGENTS IN YOUR APARTMENT RIGHT NOW--
--IS THERE ANYTHING YOU'D LIKE TO SAY?
WHAT?

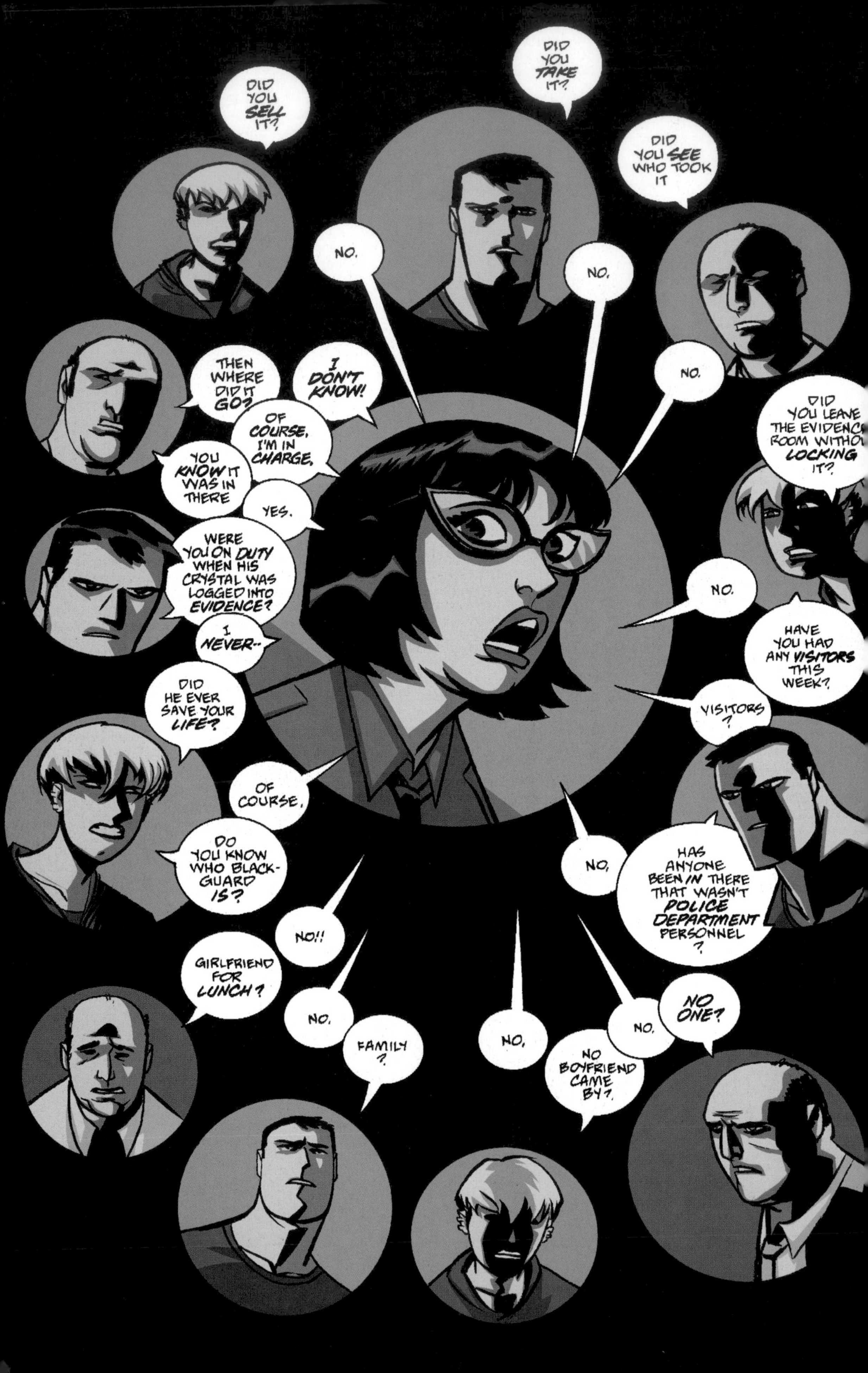
DID YOU SELL IT?
DID YOU TAKE IT?
DID YOU SEE WHO TOOK IT
NO.
NO.
NO.
THEN WHERE DID IT GO?
I DON'T KNOW!
DID YOU LEAVE THE EVIDENC ROOM WITHO LOCKING IT?
OF COURSE. I'M IN CHARGE.
YOU KNOW IT WAS IN THERE
YES.
WERE YOU ON DUTY WHEN HIS CRYSTAL WAS LOGGED INTO EVIDENCE?
NO.
I NEVER--
HAVE YOU HAD ANY VISITORS THIS WEEK?
DID HE EVER SAVE YOUR LIFE?
VISITORS?
OF COURSE.
DO YOU KNOW WHO BLACK-GUARD IS?
NO.
HAS ANYONE BEEN IN THERE THAT WASN'T POLICE DEPARTMENT PERSONNEL?
NO!!
GIRLFRIEND FOR LUNCH?
NO.
FAMILY?
NO.
NO.
NO ONE?
NO BOYFRIEND CAME BY?

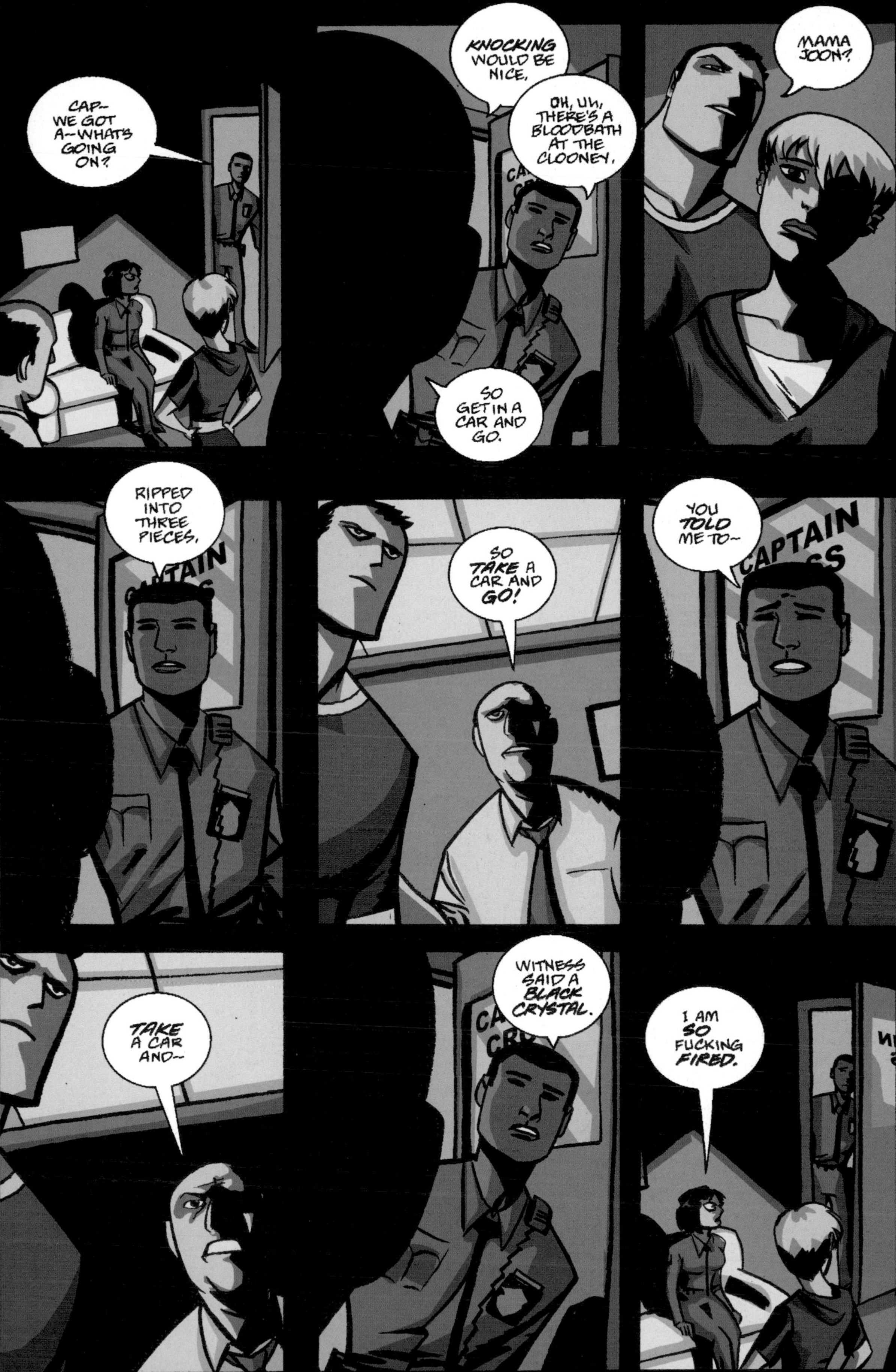
CAP-- WE GOT A--WHAT'S GOING ON?
KNOCKING WOULD BE NICE.
OH, UH, THERE'S A BLOODBATH AT THE CLOONEY.
SO GET IN A CAR AND GO.
MAMA JOON?
RIPPED INTO THREE PIECES.
CAPTAIN
SO TAKE A CAR AND GO!
YOU TOLD ME TO--
CAPTAIN
TAKE A CAR AND--
WITNESS SAID A BLACK CRYSTAL.
I AM SO FUCKING FIRED.

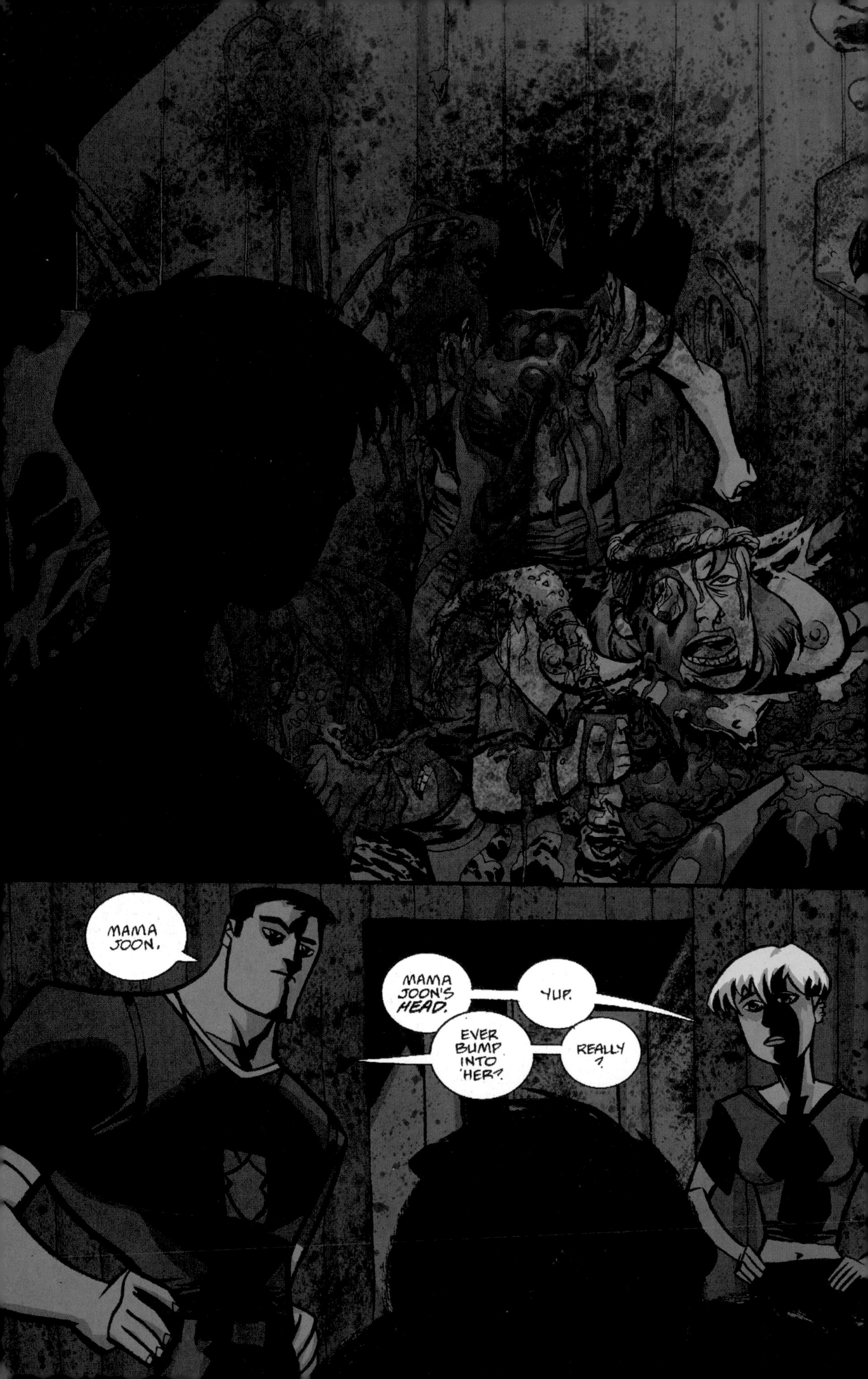
MAMA JOON.
MAMA JOON'S HEAD.
YUP.
EVER BUMP INTO 'HER?
REALLY?

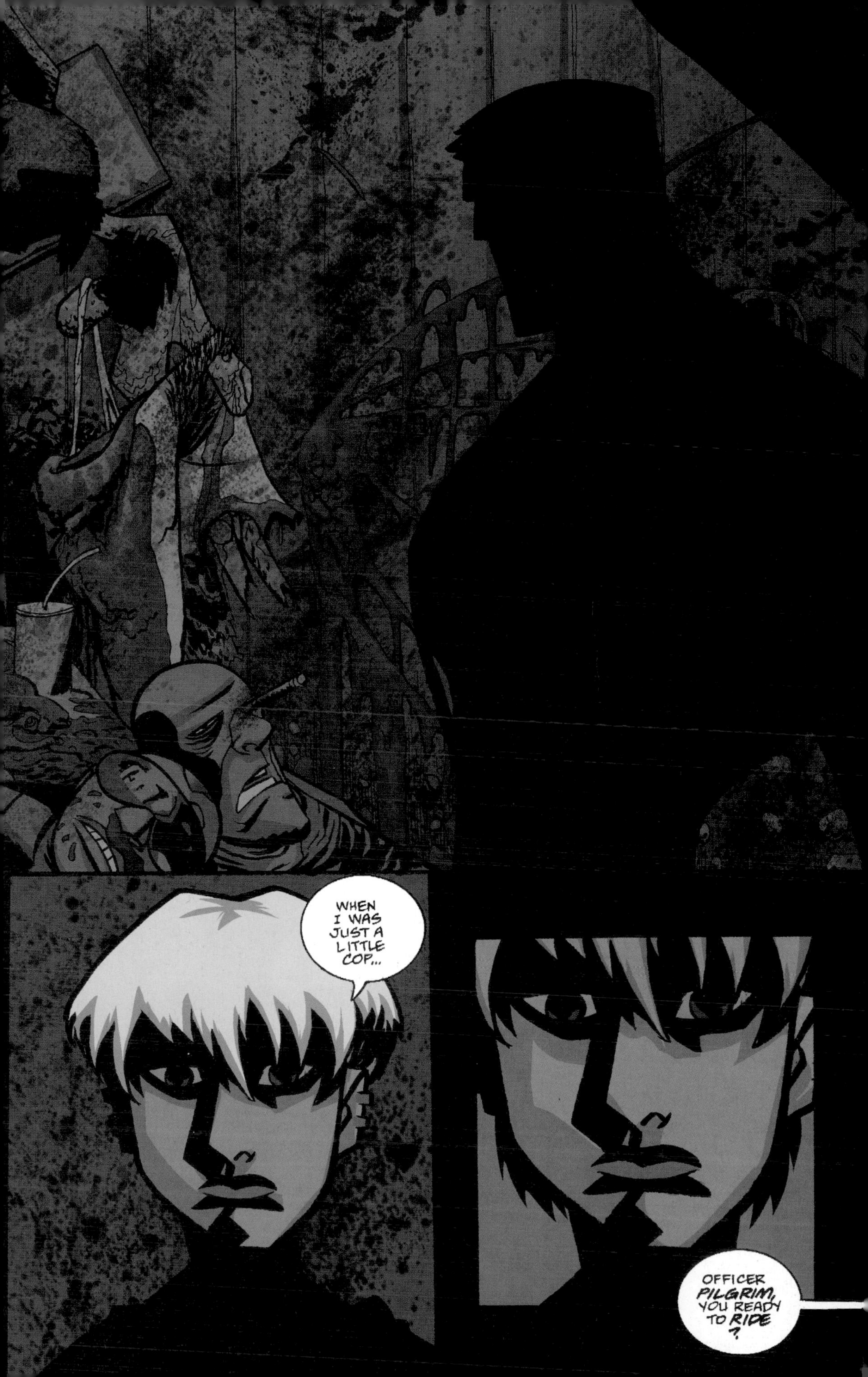
WHEN I WAS JUST A LITTLE COP...
OFFICER PILGRIM, YOU READY TO RIDE?

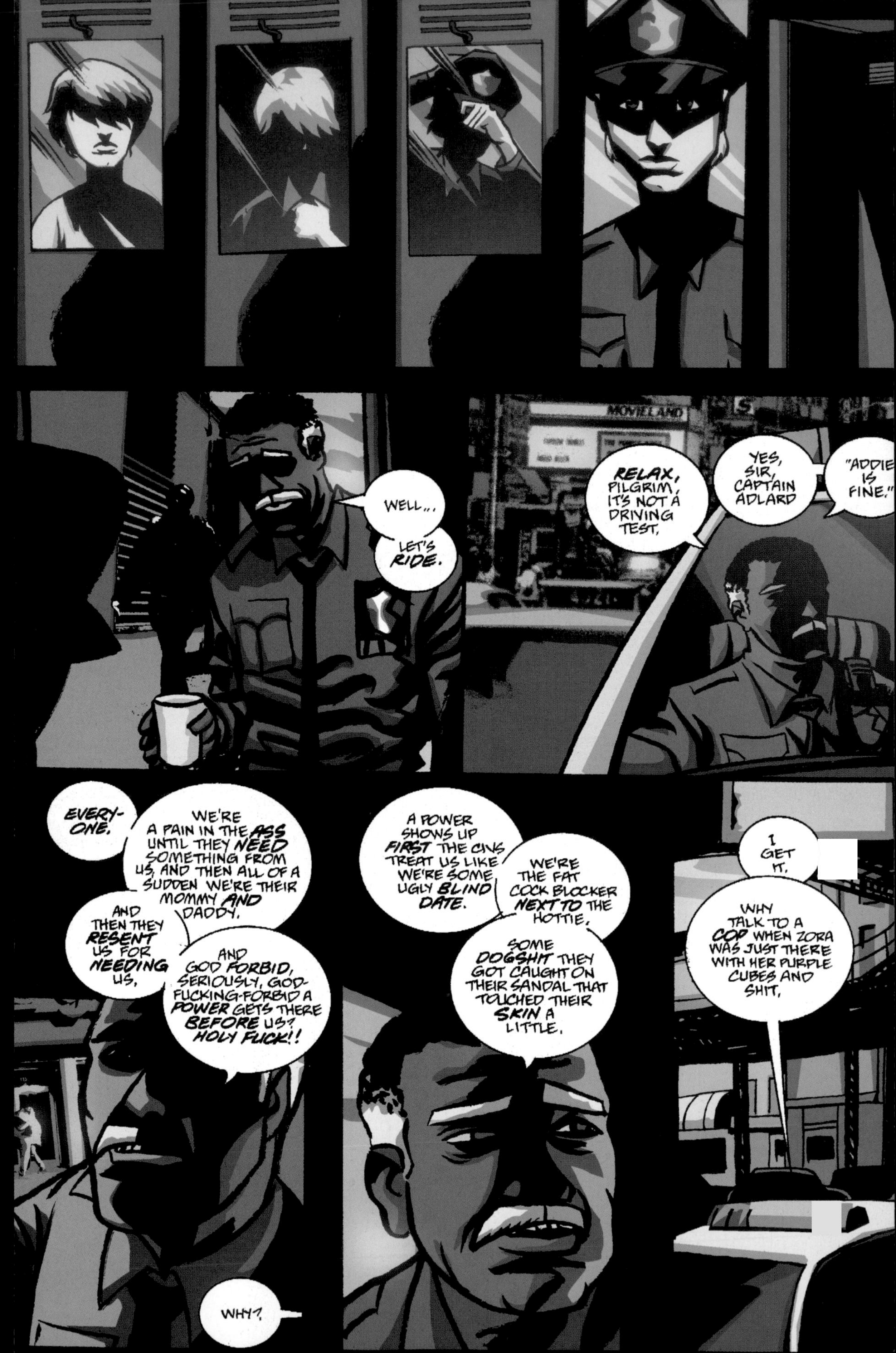

WELL...
LET'S RIDE.
MOVIELAND
RELAX, PILGRIM, IT'S NOT A DRIVING TEST.
YES, SIR, CAPTAIN ADLARD
"ADDIE IS FINE."
EVERY-ONE.
WE'RE A PAIN IN THE ASS UNTIL THEY NEED SOMETHING FROM US, AND THEN ALL OF A SUDDEN WE'RE THEIR MOMMY AND DADDY.
AND THEN THEY RESENT US FOR NEEDING US.
AND GOD FORBID, SERIOUSLY, GOD-FUCKING-FORBID A POWER GETS THERE BEFORE US? HOLY FUCK!!
WHY?
A POWER SHOWS UP FIRST THE CIVS TREAT US LIKE WE'RE SOME UGLY BLIND DATE.
WE'RE THE FAT COCK BLOCKER NEXT TO THE HOTTIE.
SOME DOGSHIT THEY GOT CAUGHT ON THEIR SANDAL THAT TOUCHED THEIR SKIN A LITTLE.
I GET IT.
WHY TALK TO A COP WHEN ZORA WAS JUST THERE WITH HER PURPLE CUBES AND SHIT.

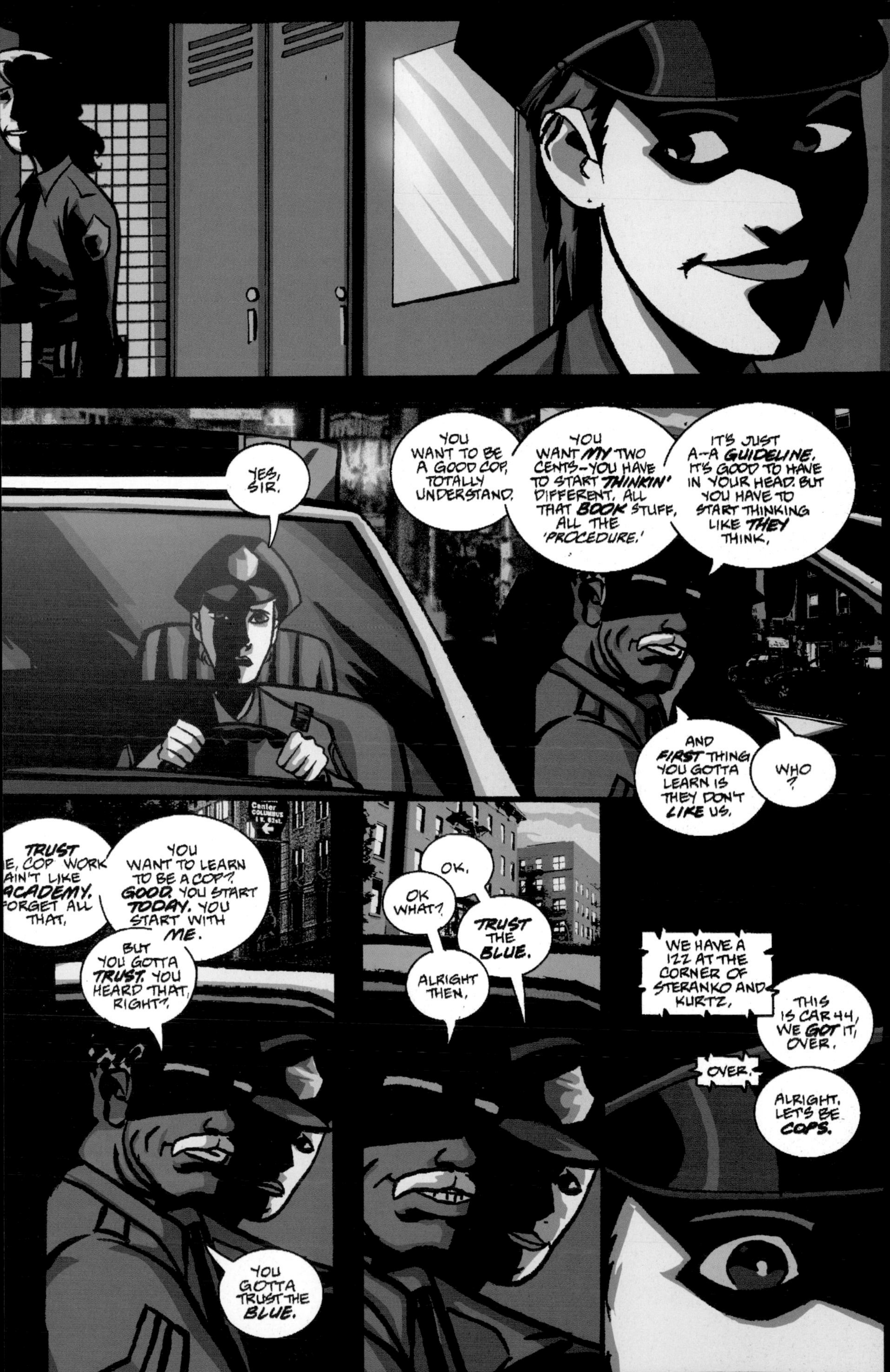
YES, SIR.
YOU WANT TO BE A GOOD COP, TOTALLY UNDERSTAND.
YOU WANT MY TWO CENTS--YOU HAVE TO START THINKIN' DIFFERENT. ALL THAT BOOK STUFF, ALL THE 'PROCEDURE.'
IT'S JUST A--A GUIDELINE. IT'S GOOD TO HAVE IN YOUR HEAD. BUT YOU HAVE TO START THINKING LIKE THEY THINK.
AND FIRST THING YOU GOTTA LEARN IS THEY DON'T LIKE US.
WHO?
Center COLUMBUS
TRUST E, COP WORK AIN'T LIKE ACADEMY. FORGET ALL THAT.
YOU WANT TO LEARN TO BE A COP? GOOD. YOU START TODAY. YOU START WITH ME.
BUT YOU GOTTA TRUST. YOU HEARD THAT, RIGHT?
YOU GOTTA TRUST THE BLUE.
OK.
OK WHAT?
TRUST THE BLUE.
ALRIGHT THEN.
WE HAVE A 122 AT THE CORNER OF STERANKO AND KURTZ.
THIS IS CAR 44, WE GOT IT, OVER.
OVER.
ALRIGHT, LET'S BE COPS.

FUCK!

STEP AWAY FROM THE BUILDING-- STEP AWAY FROM THE BUILDING!

IS ANYONE INSIDE?

THAT LITTLE PRICK!! THAT LITTLE PRICK!

WHAT PRICK?

THE PRICK!

CALM DOWN! TALK TO ME.

I'LL KILL THE FUCKER!

THIS IS MY LIFE!

WHAT THE HELL HAPPENED?

ALLENTOWN
MEMORIAL DAY
PARADE
DATE: MONDAY, MAY 30TH, 2005
TIME: 10:00 A.M.
PLACE: MAIN & HIGH STREETS

POWERS?

LET HIM TELL IT,

BUT IT--

K.

YOU DON'T PAINT THE PICTURE FOR THEM. YOU LET THEM TELL YOU.

PAINT A PICTURE FOR MY OFFICER,

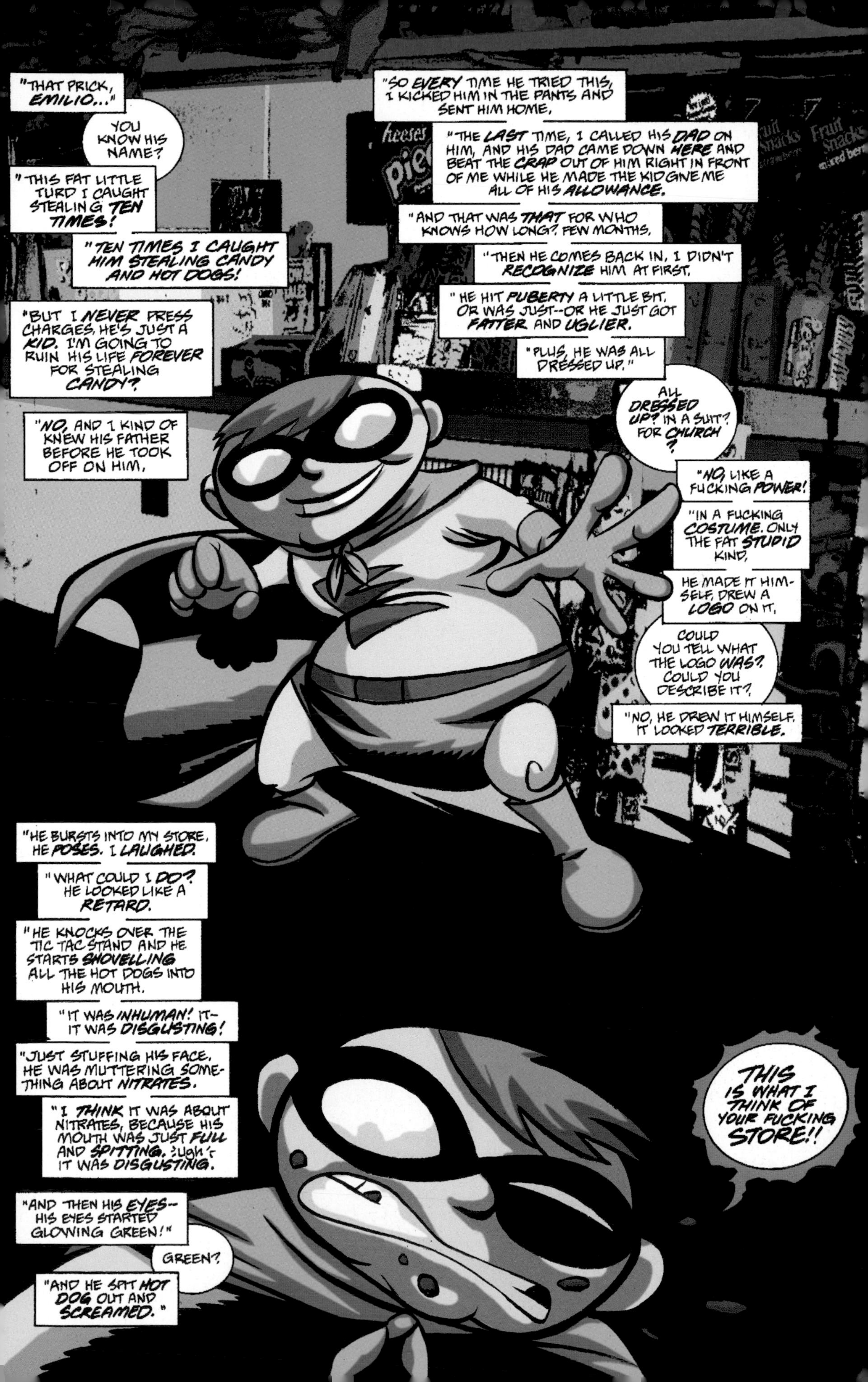
"THAT PRICK, EMILIO..."
YOU KNOW HIS NAME?
"THIS FAT LITTLE TURD I CAUGHT STEALING TEN TIMES!
"TEN TIMES I CAUGHT HIM STEALING CANDY AND HOT DOGS!
"BUT I NEVER PRESS CHARGES, HE'S JUST A KID. I'M GOING TO RUIN HIS LIFE FOREVER FOR STEALING CANDY?
"NO, AND I KIND OF KNEW HIS FATHER BEFORE HE TOOK OFF ON HIM.
"SO EVERY TIME HE TRIED THIS, I KICKED HIM IN THE PANTS AND SENT HIM HOME.
"THE LAST TIME, I CALLED HIS DAD ON HIM, AND HIS DAD CAME DOWN HERE AND BEAT THE CRAP OUT OF HIM RIGHT IN FRONT OF ME WHILE HE MADE THE KID GIVE ME ALL OF HIS ALLOWANCE.
"AND THAT WAS THAT FOR WHO KNOWS HOW LONG? FEW MONTHS.
"THEN HE COMES BACK IN, I DIDN'T RECOGNIZE HIM AT FIRST.
"HE HIT PUBERTY A LITTLE BIT. OR WAS JUST--OR HE JUST GOT FATTER AND UGLIER.
"PLUS, HE WAS ALL DRESSED UP."
ALL DRESSED UP? IN A SUIT? FOR CHURCH?
"NO, LIKE A FUCKING POWER!
"IN A FUCKING COSTUME. ONLY THE FAT STUPID KIND.
HE MADE IT HIM-SELF, DREW A LOGO ON IT.
COULD YOU TELL WHAT THE LOGO WAS? COULD YOU DESCRIBE IT?
"NO, HE DREW IT HIMSELF. IT LOOKED TERRIBLE.
"HE BURSTS INTO MY STORE. HE POSES. I LAUGHED.
"WHAT COULD I DO? HE LOOKED LIKE A RETARD.
"HE KNOCKS OVER THE TIC TAC STAND AND HE STARTS SHOVELLING ALL THE HOT DOGS INTO HIS MOUTH.
"IT WAS INHUMAN! IT-- IT WAS DISGUSTING!
"JUST STUFFING HIS FACE. HE WAS MUTTERING SOME-THING ABOUT NITRATES.
"I THINK IT WAS ABOUT NITRATES, BECAUSE HIS MOUTH WAS JUST FULL AND SPITTING. ugh IT WAS DISGUSTING.
"AND THEN HIS EYES-- HIS EYES STARTED GLOWING GREEN!"
GREEN?
"AND HE SPIT HOT DOG OUT AND SCREAMED."
THIS IS WHAT I THINK OF YOUR FUCKING STORE!!

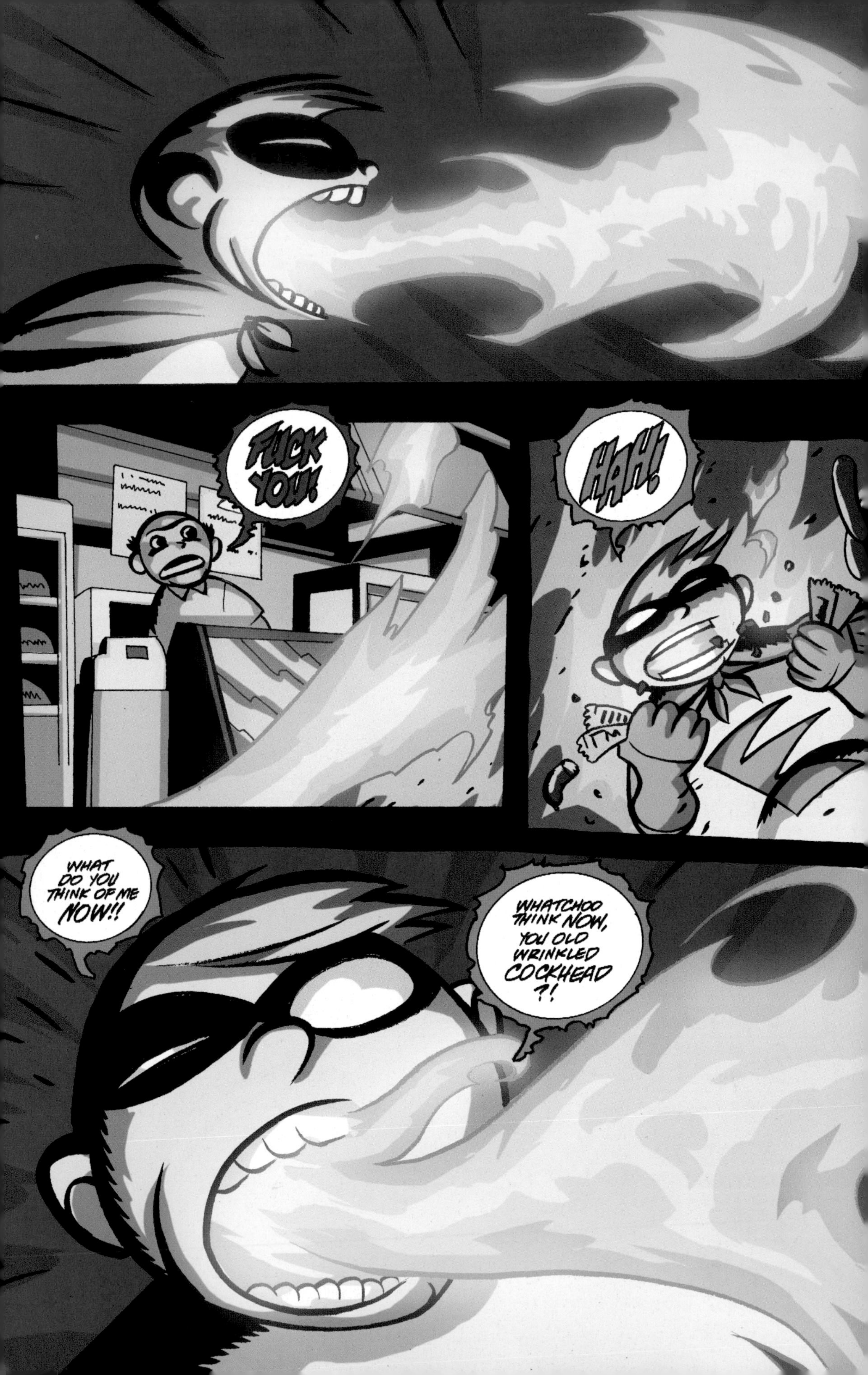
FUCK YOU!
HAH!
WHAT DO YOU THINK OF ME NOW!!
WHATCHOO THINK NOW, YOU OLD WRINKLED COCKHEAD ?!

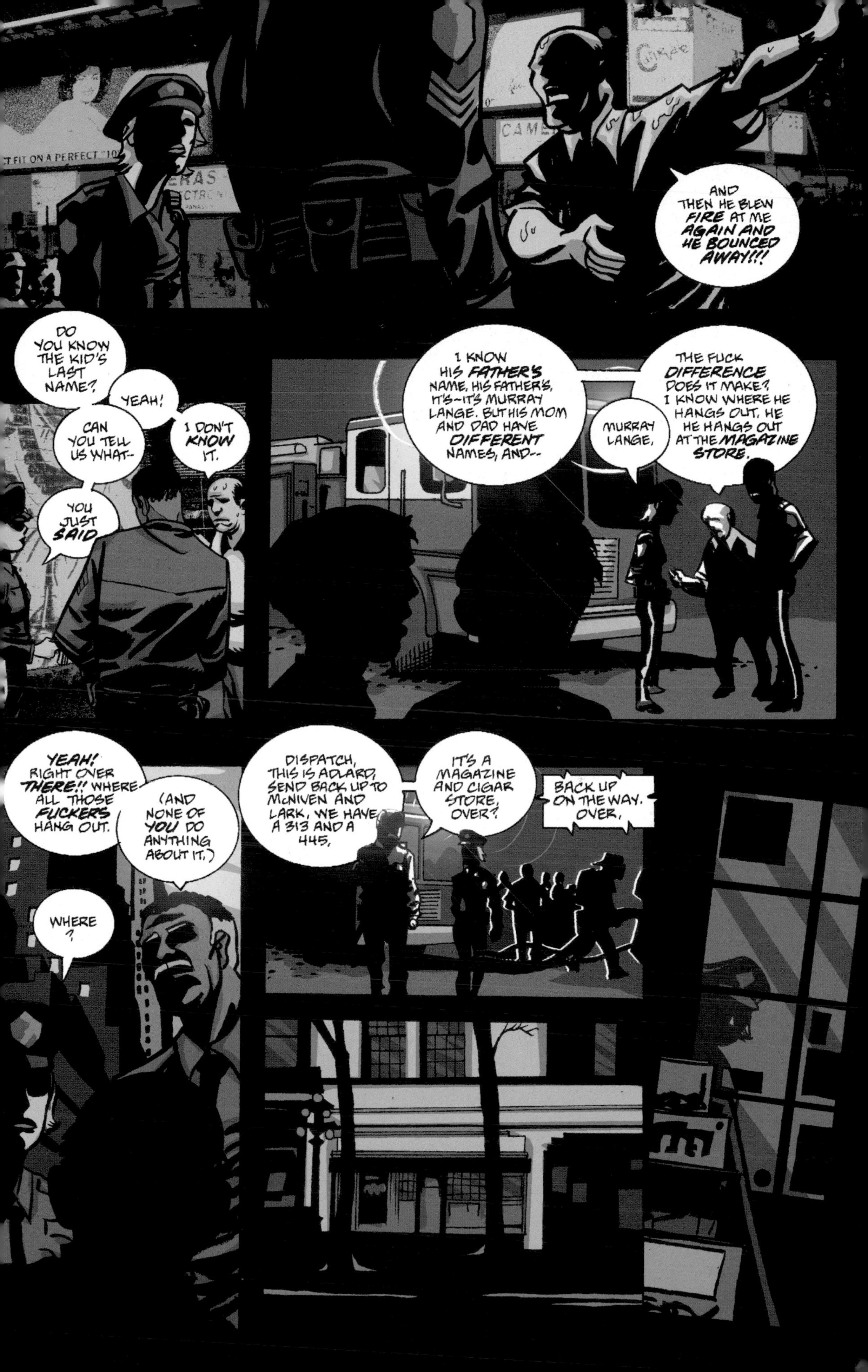

AND THEN HE BLEW FIRE AT ME AGAIN AND HE BOUNCED AWAY!!!
DO YOU KNOW THE KID'S LAST NAME?
YEAH!
CAN YOU TELL US WHAT--
I DON'T KNOW IT.
YOU JUST SAID
I KNOW HIS FATHER'S NAME, HIS FATHER'S, IT'S--IT'S MURRAY LANGE. BUT HIS MOM AND DAD HAVE DIFFERENT NAMES, AND--
MURRAY LANGE.
THE FUCK DIFFERENCE DOES IT MAKE? I KNOW WHERE HE HANGS OUT. HE HE HANGS OUT AT THE MAGAZINE STORE.
YEAH! RIGHT OVER THERE!! WHERE ALL THOSE FUCKERS HANG OUT.
(AND NONE OF YOU DO ANYTHING ABOUT IT.)
WHERE?
DISPATCH, THIS IS ADLARD, SEND BACK UP TO McNIVEN AND LARK, WE HAVE A 313 AND A 445.
IT'S A MAGAZINE AND CIGAR STORE, OVER?
BACK UP ON THE WAY. OVER.

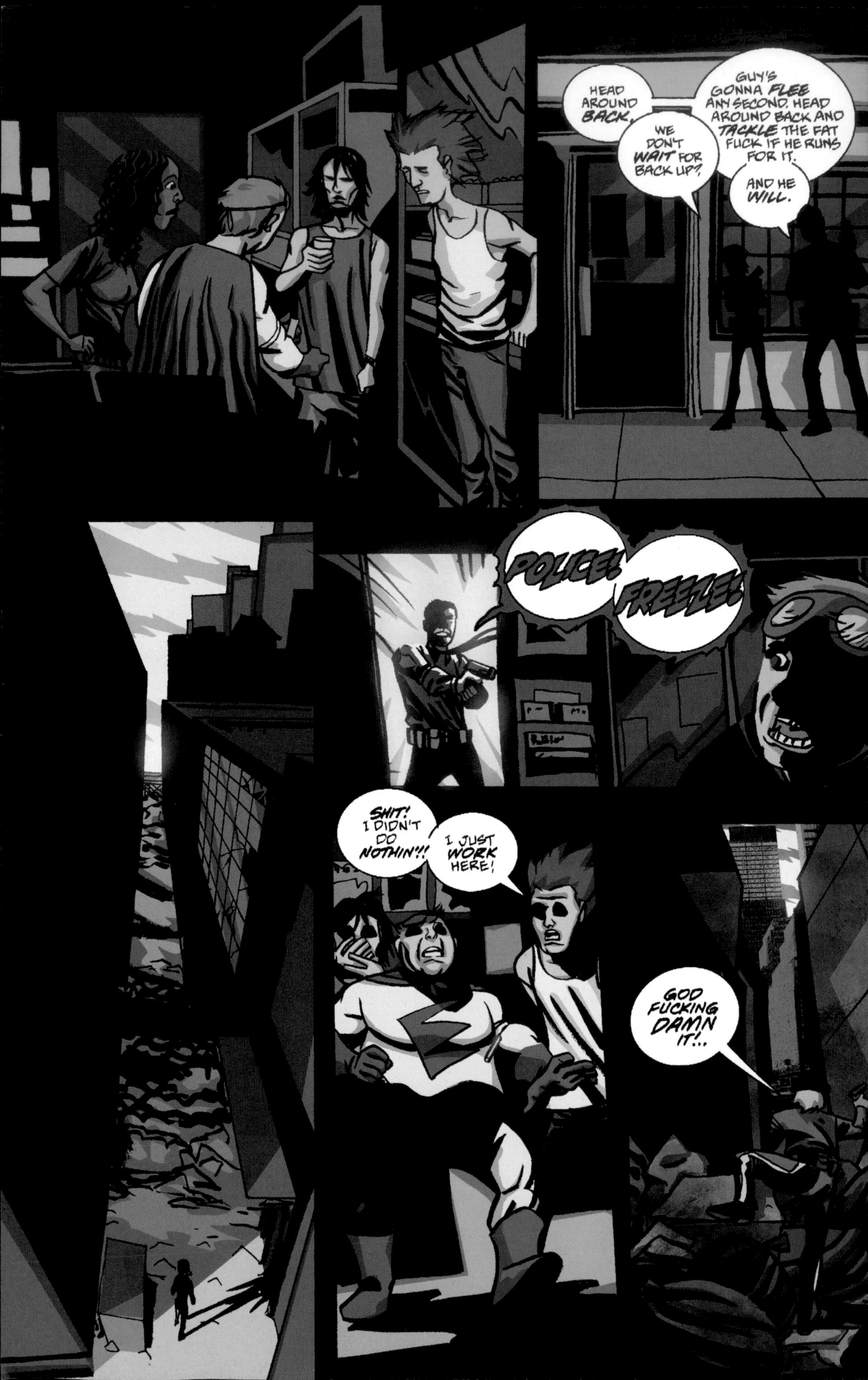
HEAD AROUND BACK.
GUY'S GONNA FLEE ANY SECOND. HEAD AROUND BACK AND TACKLE THE FAT FUCK IF HE RUNS FOR IT.
WE DON'T WAIT FOR BACK UP?
AND HE WILL.
POLICE!
FREEZE!
SHIT! I DIDN'T DO NOTHIN'!!
I JUST WORK HERE!
GOD FUCKING DAMN IT!..

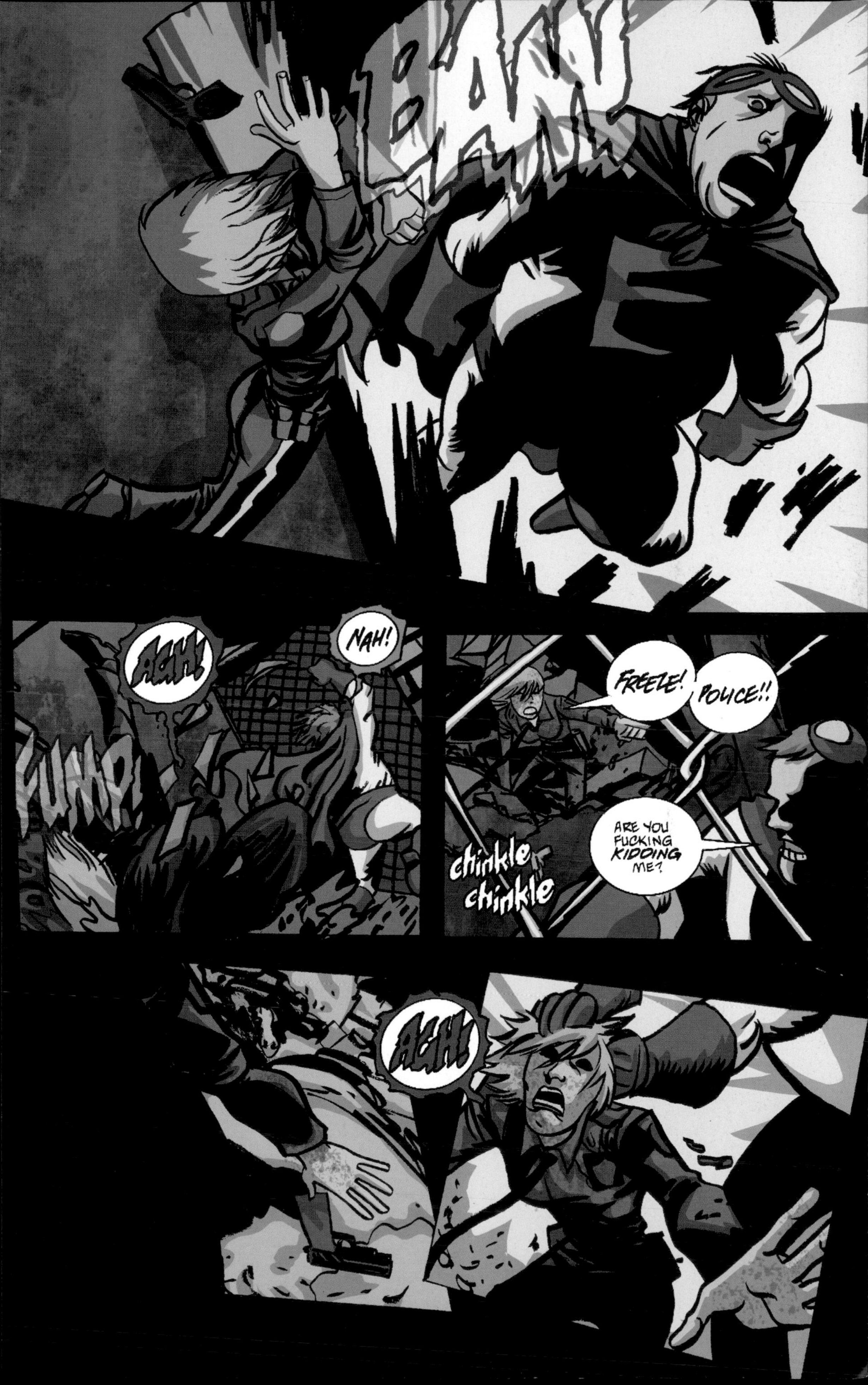
AGH!
NAH!
FREEZE!
POLICE!!
ARE YOU FUCKING KIDDING ME?
chinkle chinkle
AGH!

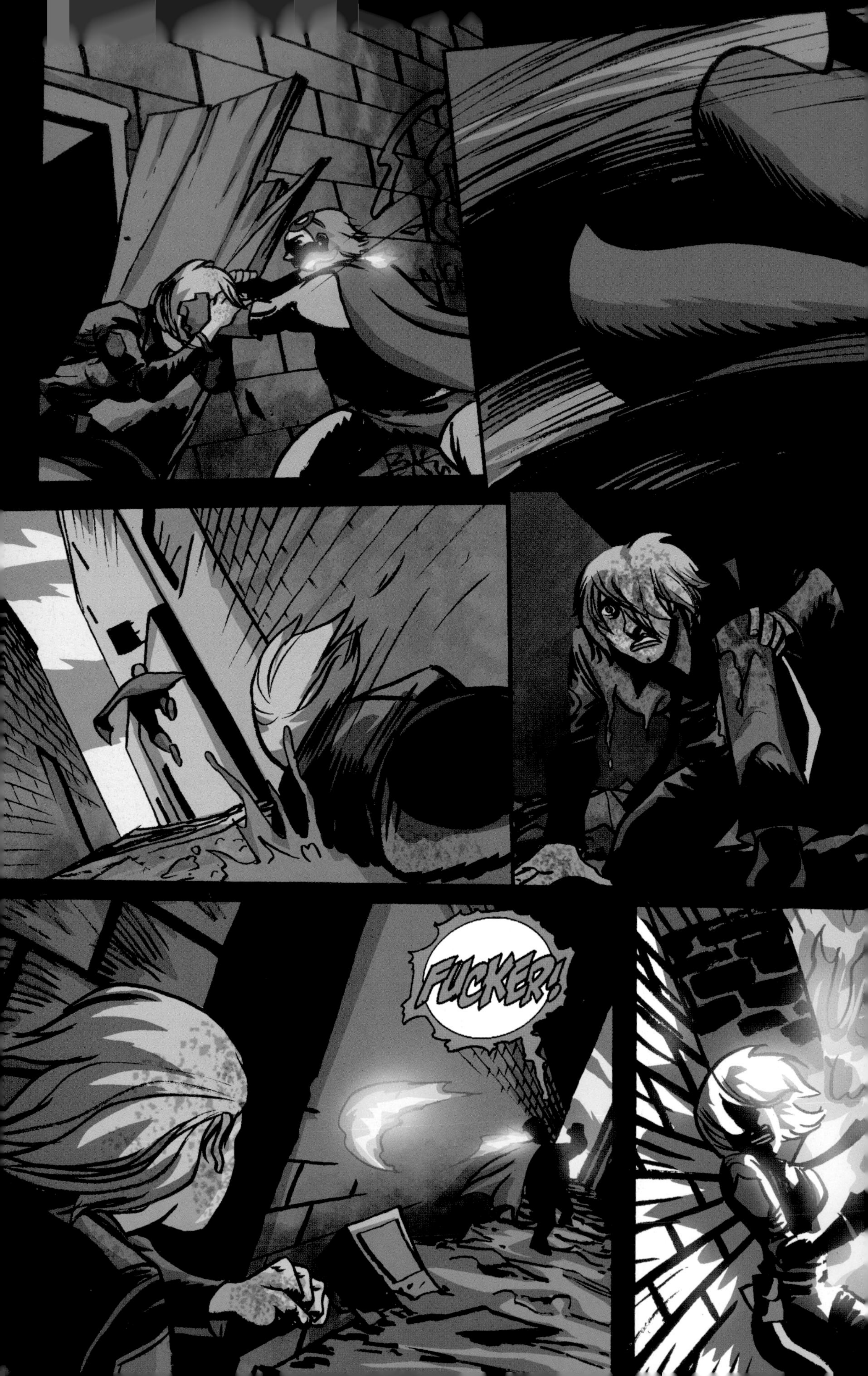
FUCKER!

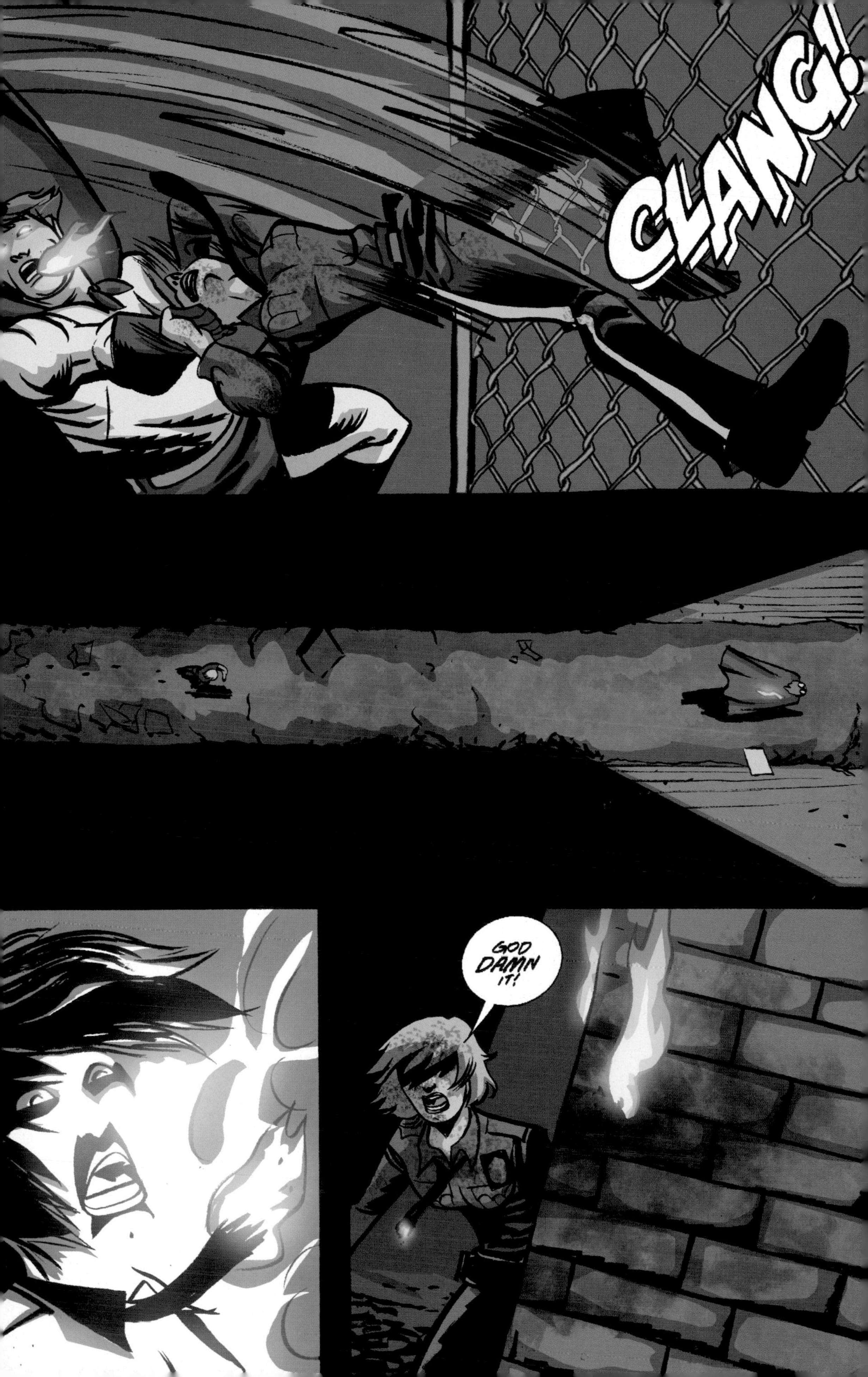
CLANG!
GOD DAMN IT!

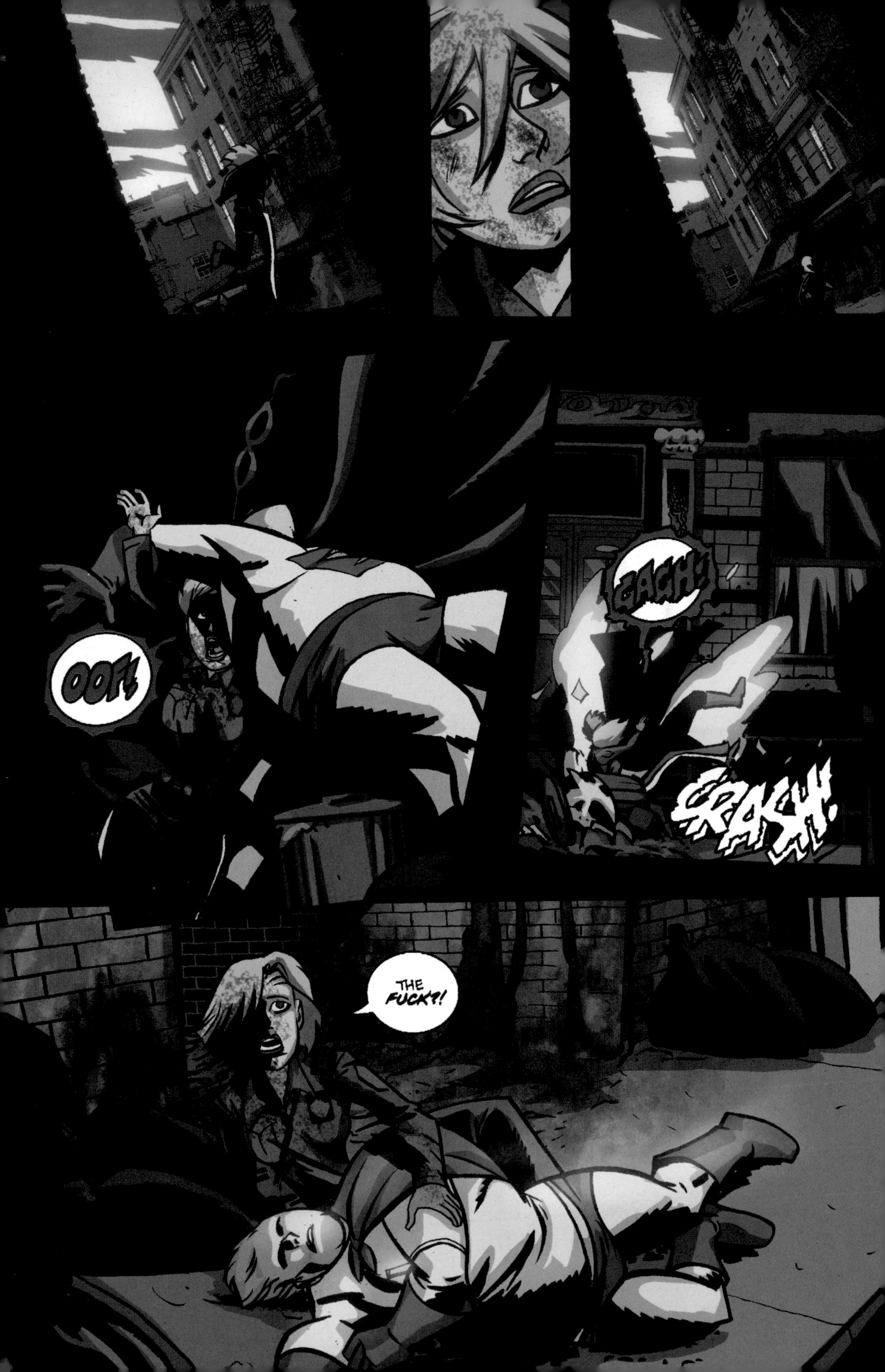
OOF!
GACH!
CRASH!
THE FUCK?!

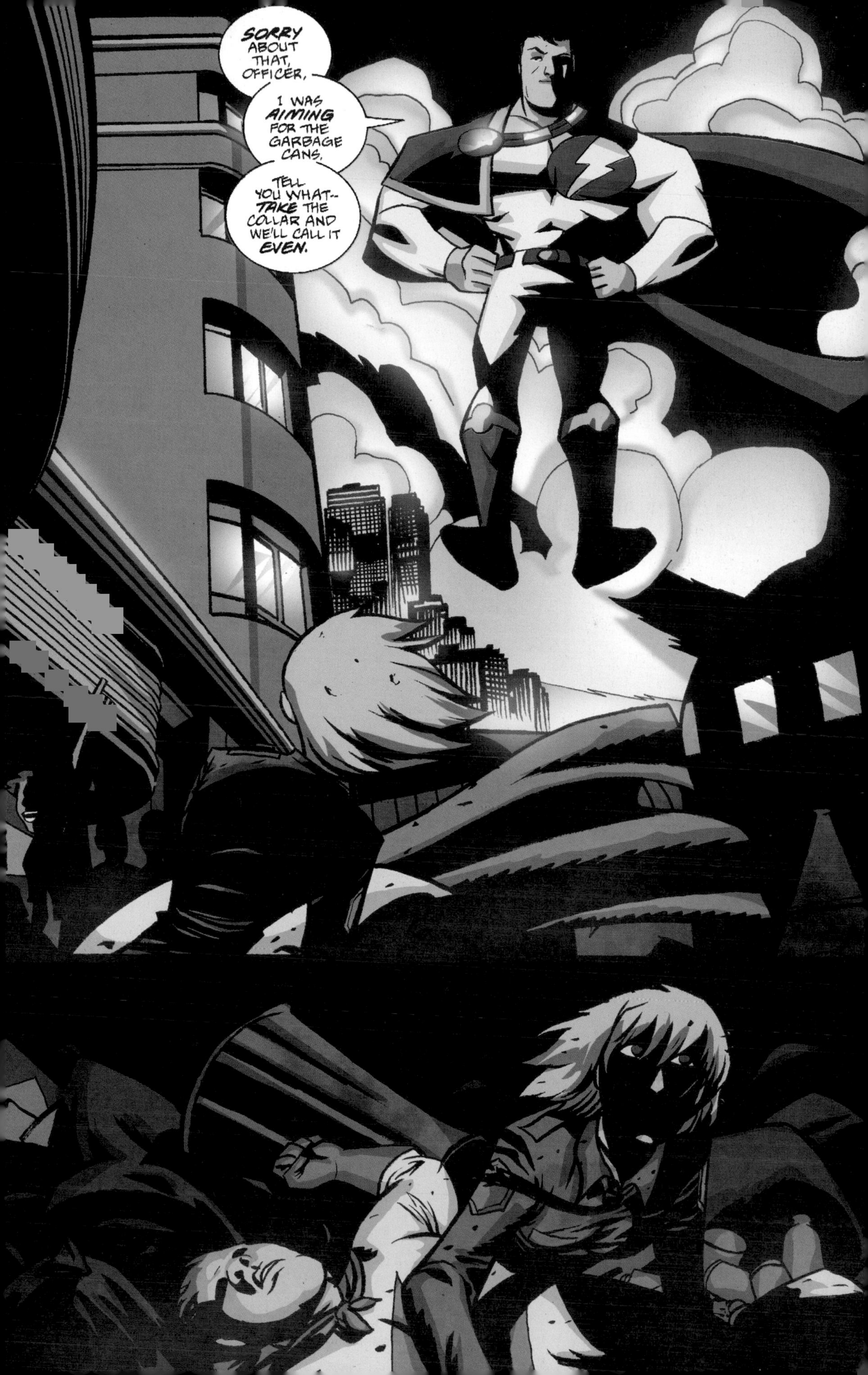
SORRY ABOUT THAT, OFFICER.
I WAS AIMING FOR THE GARBAGE CANS.
TELL YOU WHAT-- TAKE THE COLLAR AND WE'LL CALL IT EVEN.

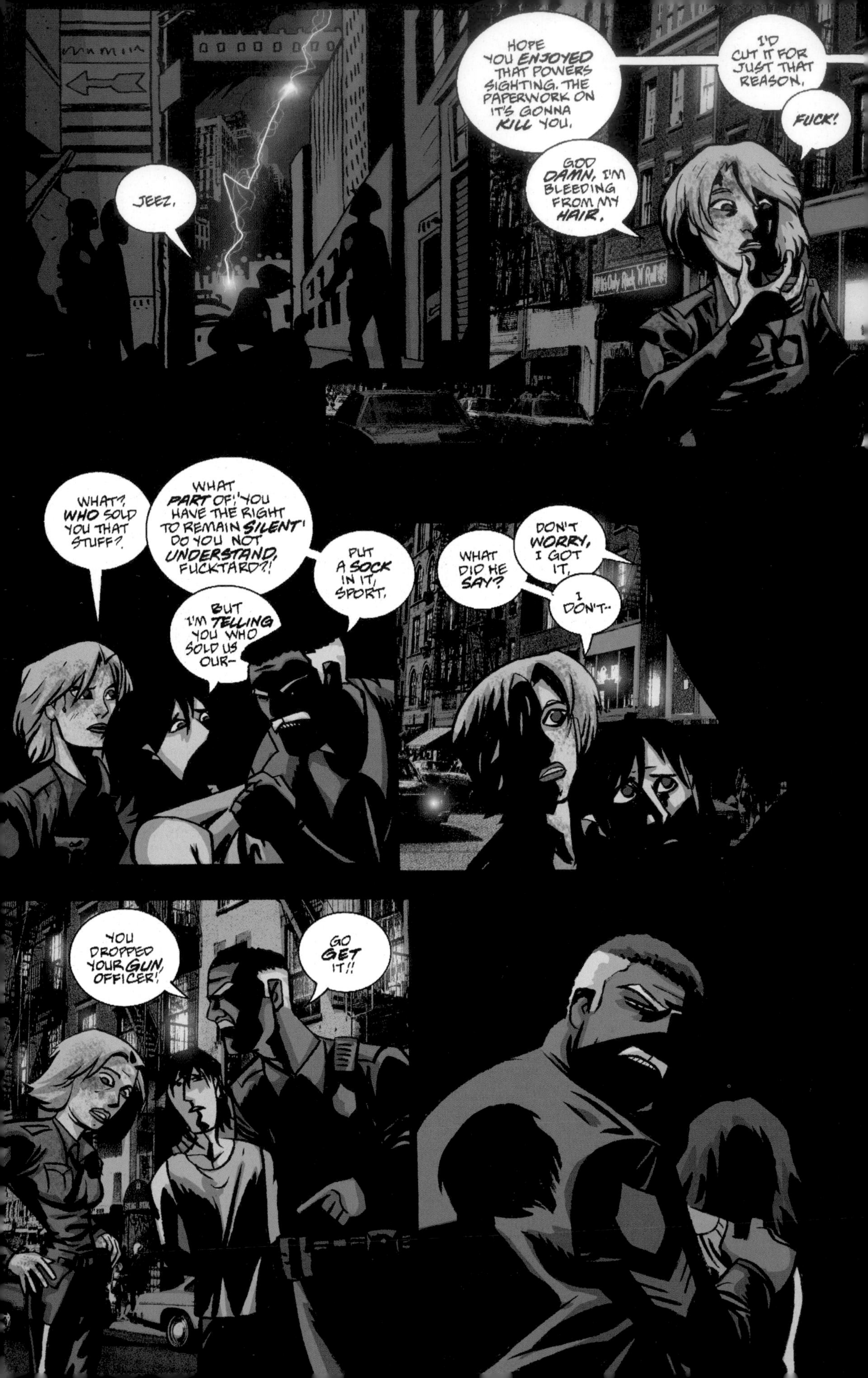
JEEZ.
HOPE YOU ENJOYED THAT POWERS SIGHTING. THE PAPERWORK ON IT'S GONNA KILL YOU.
I'D CUT IT FOR JUST THAT REASON.
GOD DAMN, I'M BLEEDING FROM MY HAIR.
FUCK!
WHAT? WHO SOLD YOU THAT STUFF?
WHAT PART OF: 'YOU HAVE THE RIGHT TO REMAIN SILENT' DO YOU NOT UNDERSTAND, FUCKTARD?!
PUT A SOCK IN IT, SPORT.
BUT I'M TELLING YOU WHO SOLD US OUR--
WHAT DID HE SAY?
DON'T WORRY, I GOT IT.
I DON'T..
YOU DROPPED YOUR GUN, OFFICER!
GO GET IT!!

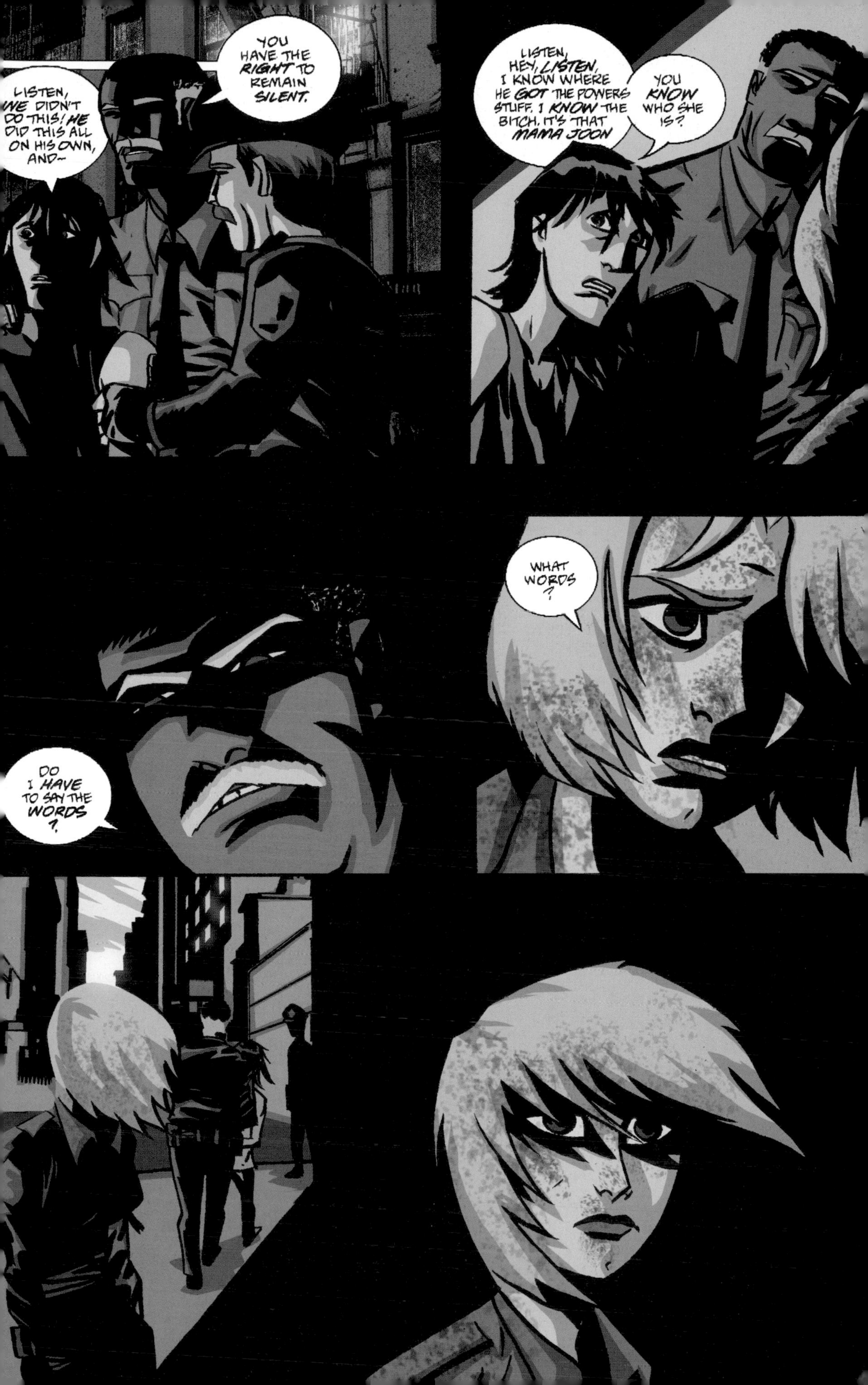
LISTEN, WE DIDN'T DO THIS! HE DID THIS ALL ON HIS OWN, AND--
YOU HAVE THE RIGHT TO REMAIN SILENT.
LISTEN, HEY, LISTEN, I KNOW WHERE HE GOT THE POWERS STUFF. I KNOW THE BITCH. IT'S THAT MAMA JOON
YOU KNOW WHO SHE IS?
WHAT WORDS ?
DO I HAVE TO SAY THE WORDS ?

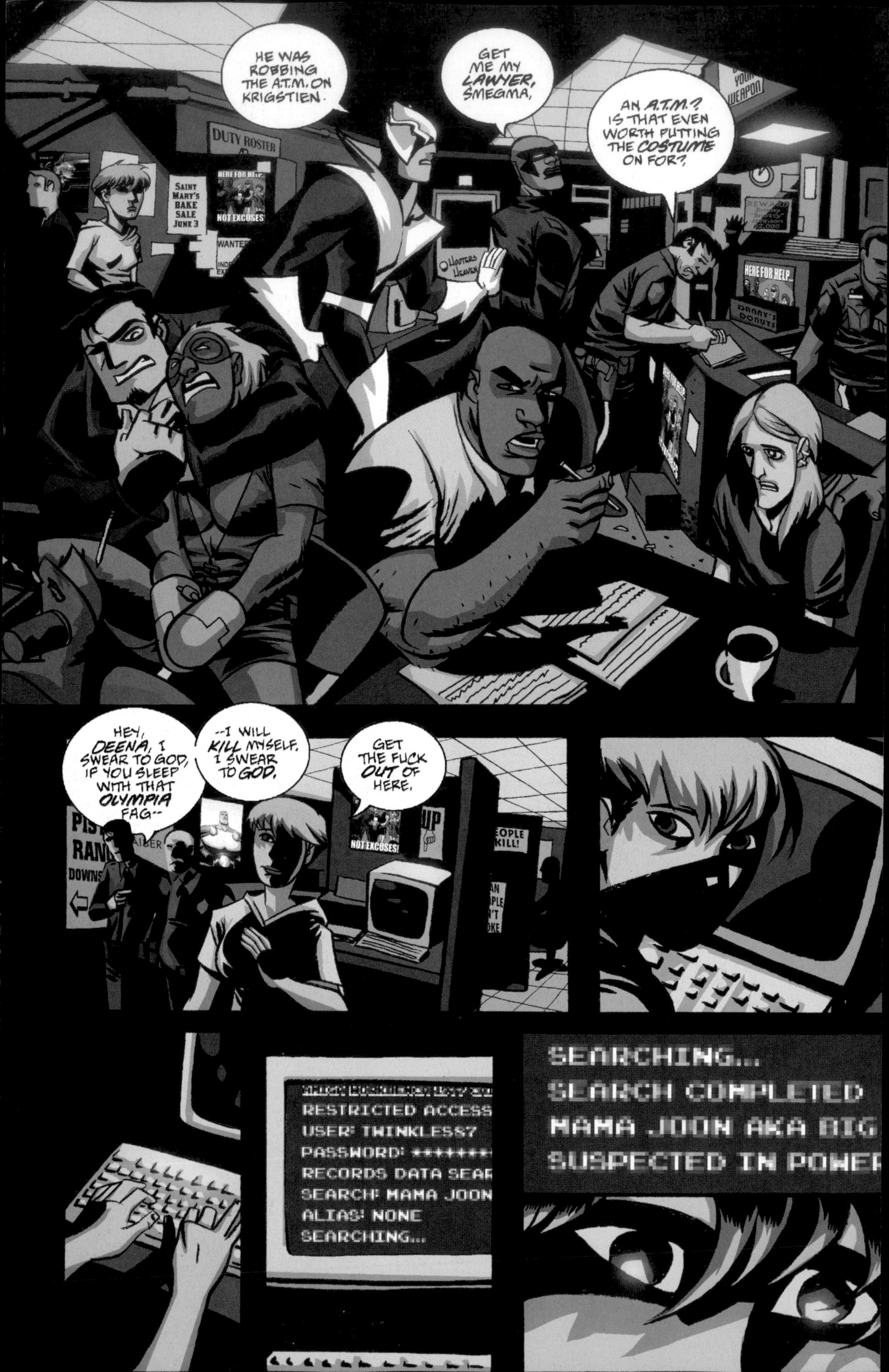
HE WAS ROBBING THE A.T.M. ON KRIGSTIEN.
GET ME MY LAWYER, SMEGMA,
AN A.T.M.? IS THAT EVEN WORTH PUTTING THE COSTUME ON FOR?
DUTY ROSTER
HERE FOR HELP... NOT EXCUSES
SAINT MARY'S BAKE SALE JUNE 3
HOOTERS HEAVEN
WEAPON
HERE FOR HELP...
HEY, DEENA, I SWEAR TO GOD, IF YOU SLEEP WITH THAT OLYMPIA FAG--
--I WILL KILL MYSELF. I SWEAR TO GOD.
GET THE FUCK OUT OF HERE.
NOT EXCUSES!
RESTRICTED ACCESS
USER: TWINKLES87
PASSWORD: *******
RECORDS DATA SEAR
SEARCH: MAMA JOON
ALIAS: NONE
SEARCHING...
SEARCHING...
SEARCH COMPLETED
MAMA JOON AKA BIG
SUSPECTED IN POWER

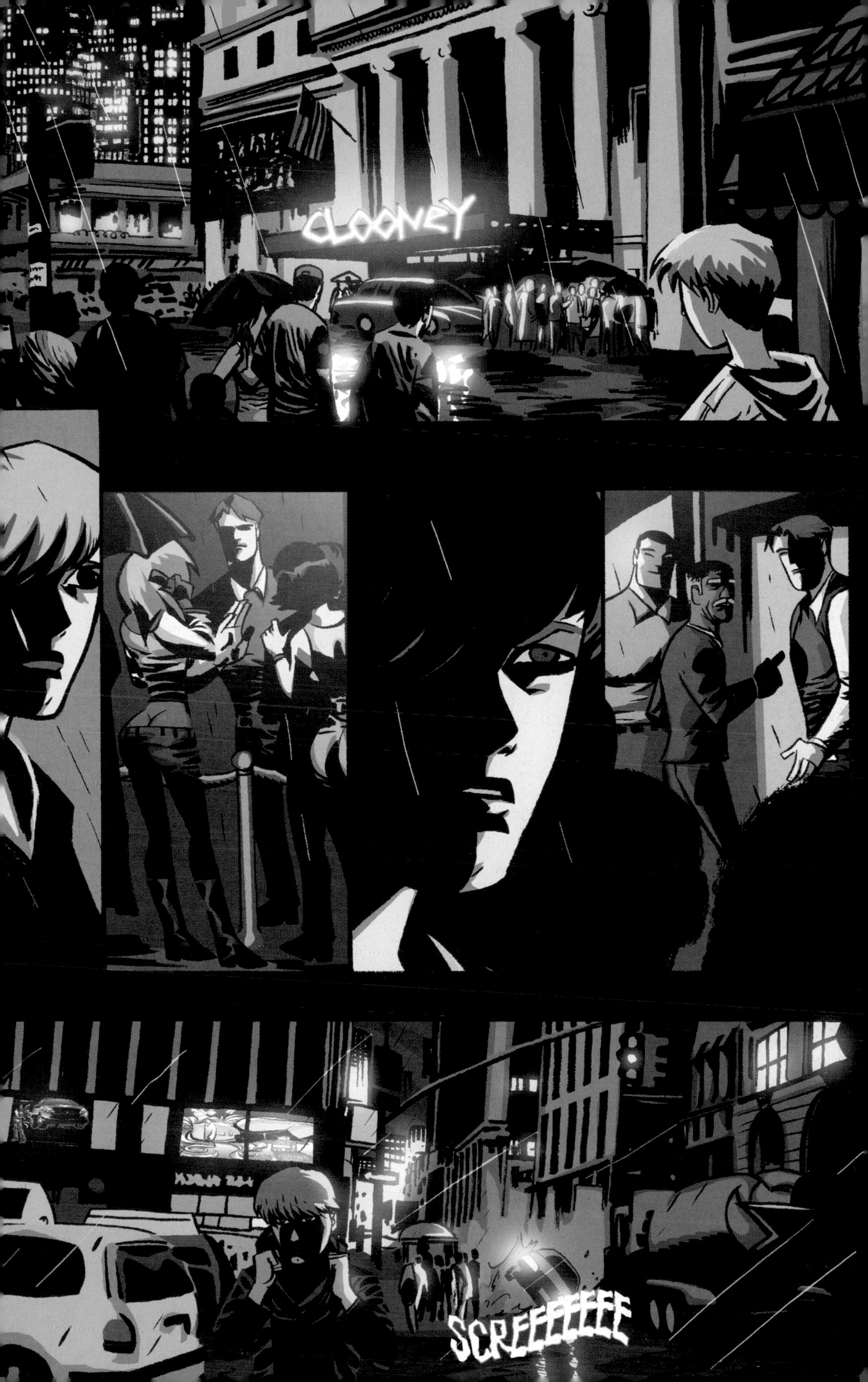
CLOONEY
SCREEEEEEE

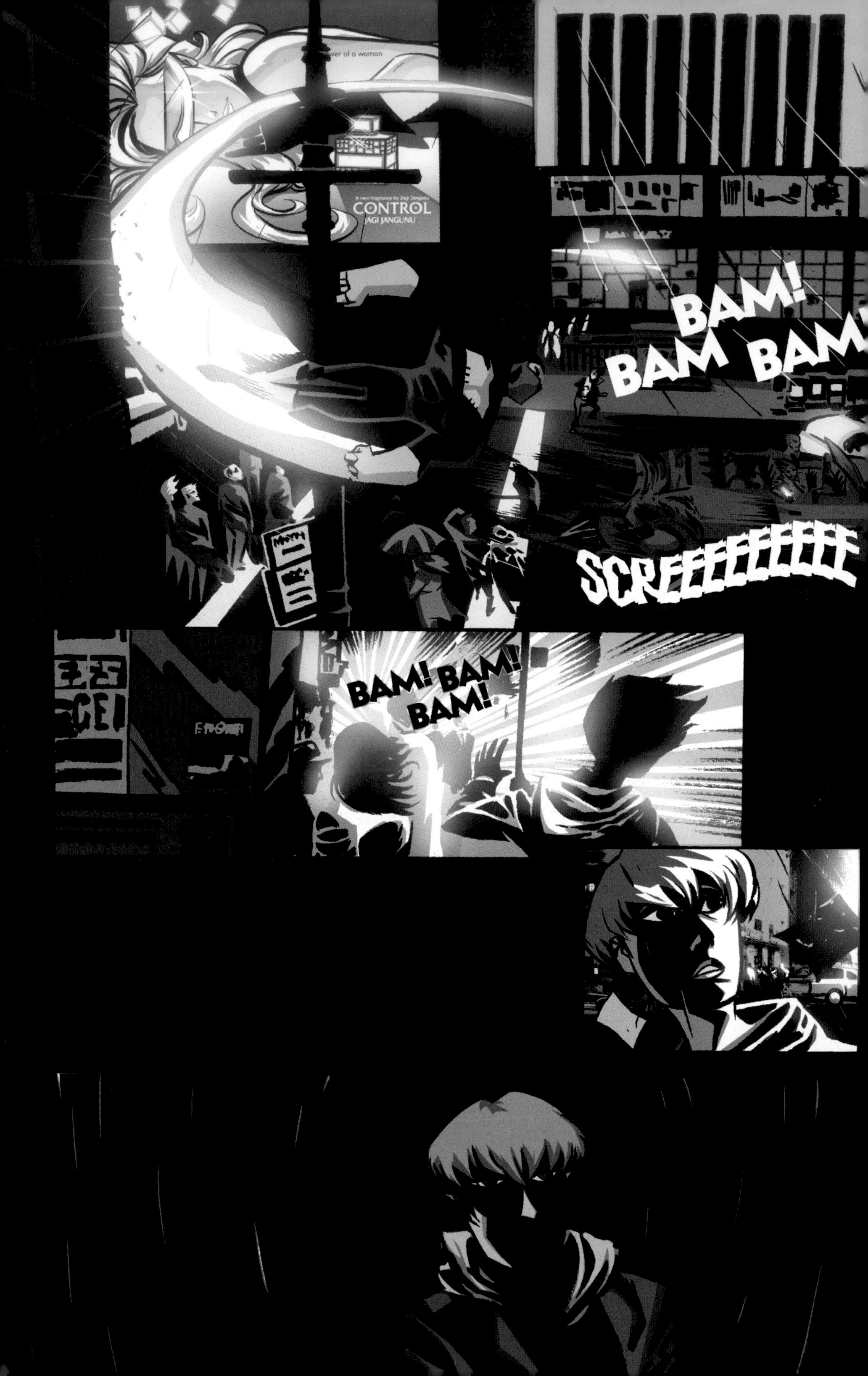
...wer of a woman
A new fragrance by Jagi Jangunu
CONTROL
JAGI JANGUNU
BAM!
BAM BAM!
SCREEEEEEEEEE
BAM! BAM!
BAM!

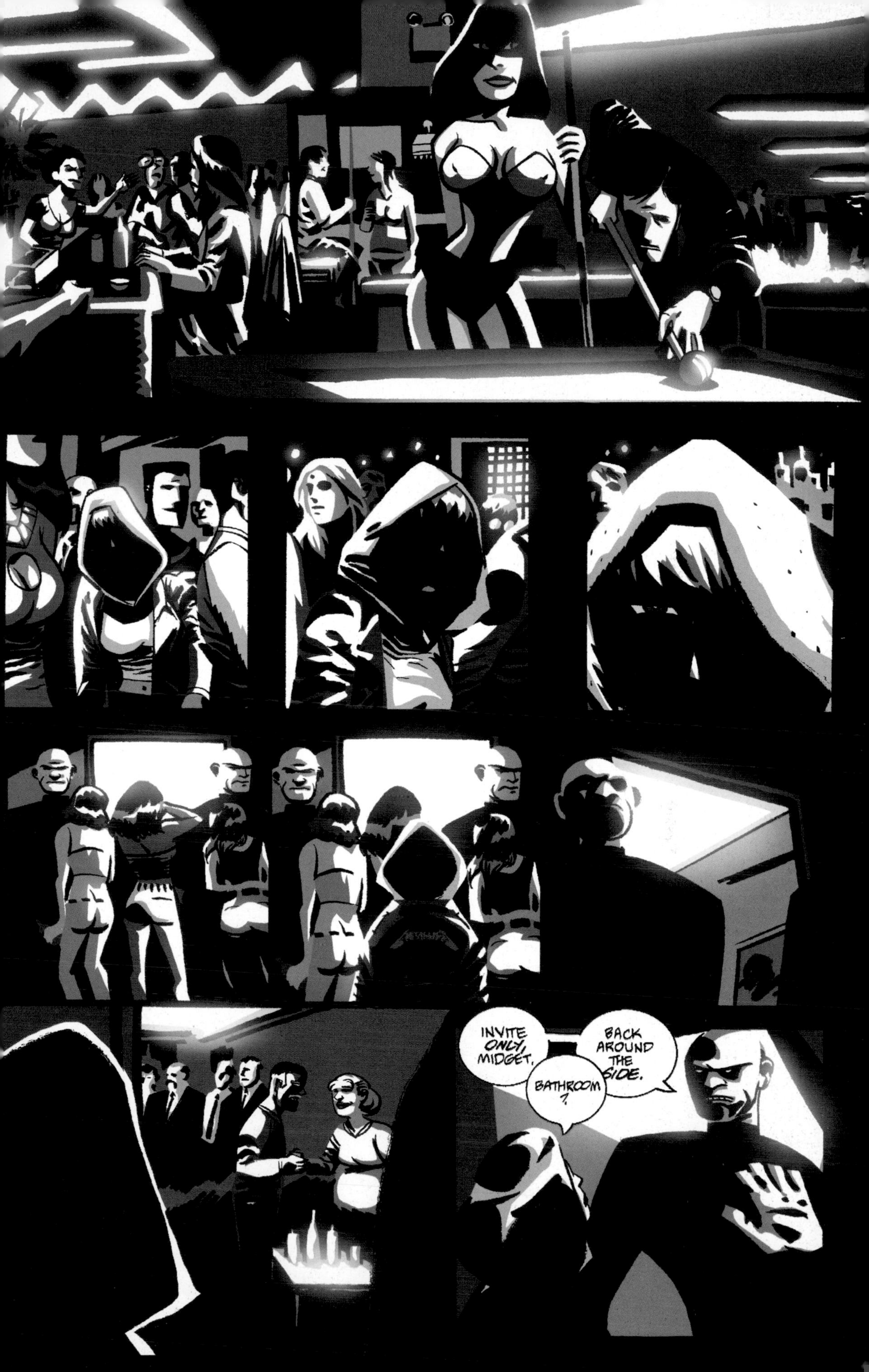
INVITE ONLY, MIDGET.
BATHROOM?
BACK AROUND THE SIDE.

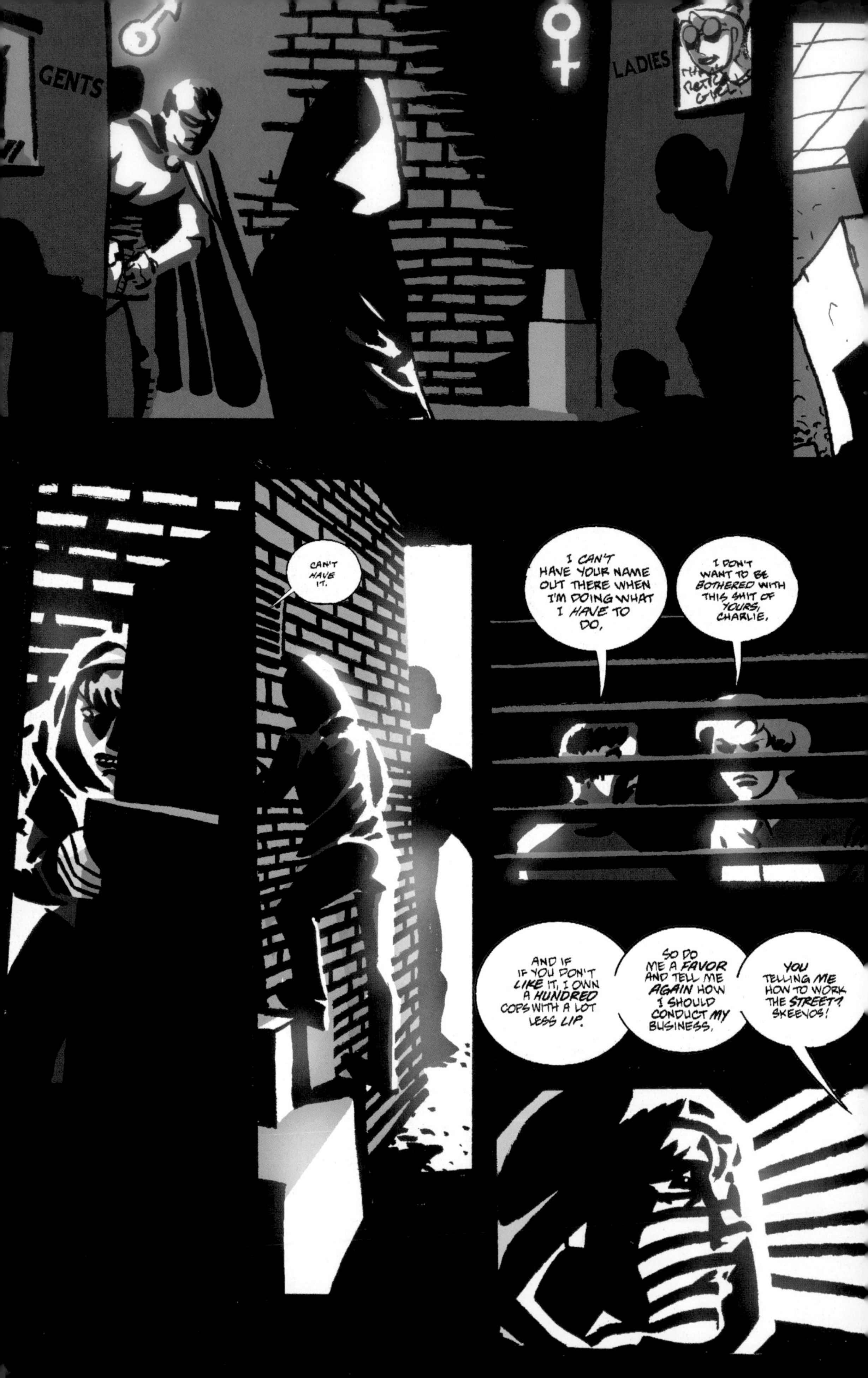
GENTS
LADIES
CAN'T HAVE IT.
I CAN'T HAVE YOUR NAME OUT THERE WHEN I'M DOING WHAT I HAVE TO DO.
I DON'T WANT TO BE BOTHERED WITH THIS SHIT OF YOURS, CHARLIE.
AND IF IF YOU DON'T LIKE IT, I OWN A HUNDRED COPS WITH A LOT LESS LIP.
SO DO ME A FAVOR AND TELL ME AGAIN HOW I SHOULD CONDUCT MY BUSINESS.
YOU TELLING ME HOW TO WORK THE STREET? SKEEVOS!

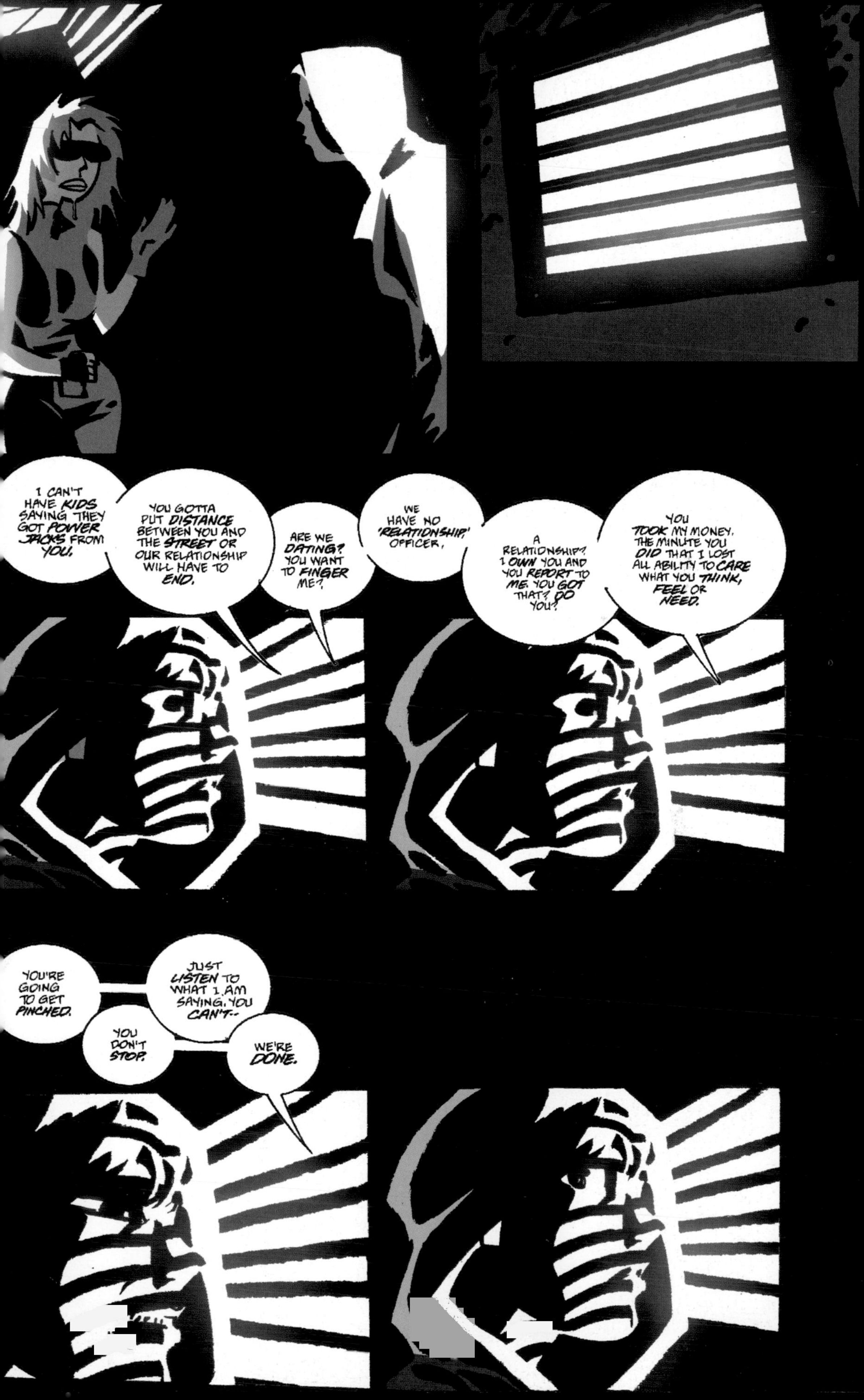

I CAN'T HAVE KIDS SAYING THEY GOT POWER JACKS FROM YOU.
YOU GOTTA PUT DISTANCE BETWEEN YOU AND THE STREET OR OUR RELATIONSHIP WILL HAVE TO END.
ARE WE DATING? YOU WANT TO FINGER ME?
WE HAVE NO 'RELATIONSHIP,' OFFICER.
A RELATIONSHIP? I OWN YOU AND YOU REPORT TO ME. YOU GOT THAT? DO YOU?
YOU TOOK MY MONEY. THE MINUTE YOU DID THAT I LOST ALL ABILITY TO CARE WHAT YOU THINK, FEEL OR NEED.
YOU'RE GOING TO GET PINCHED.
JUST LISTEN TO WHAT I AM SAYING. YOU CAN'T--
YOU DON'T STOP.
WE'RE DONE.

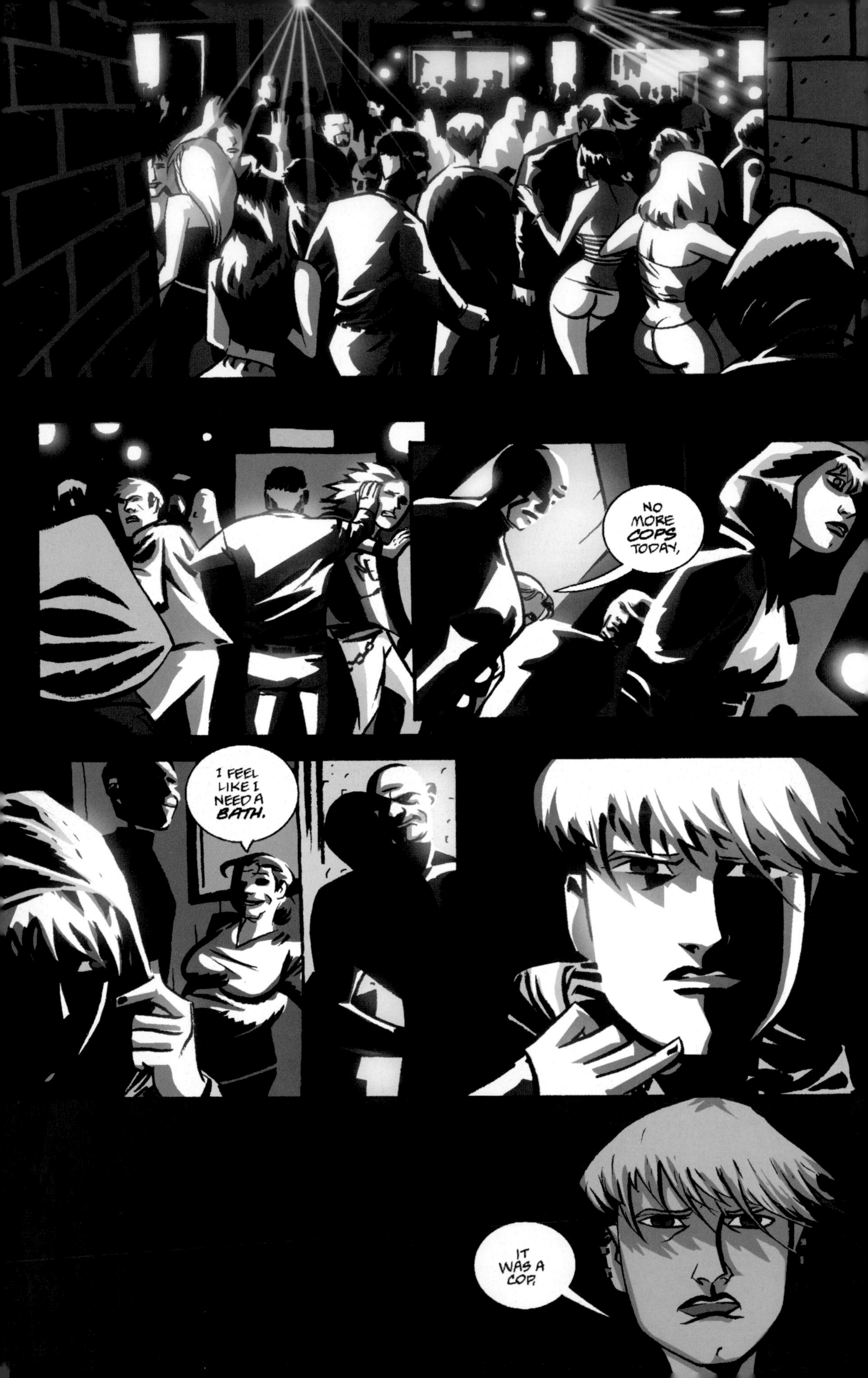
NO MORE COPS TODAY,
I FEEL LIKE I NEED A BATH.
IT WAS A COP.

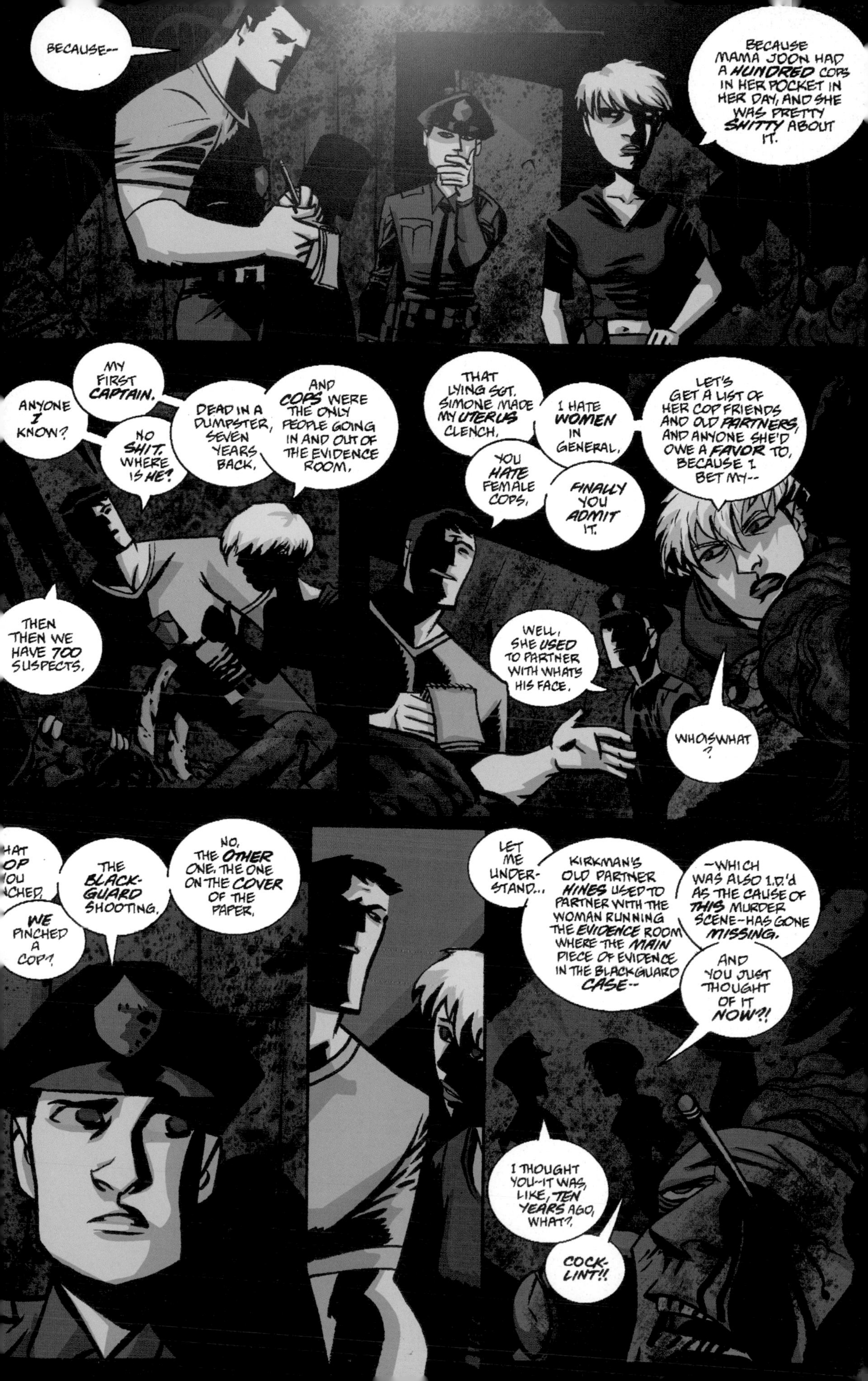
BECAUSE--
BECAUSE MAMA JOON HAD A HUNDRED COPS IN HER POCKET IN HER DAY, AND SHE WAS PRETTY SHITTY ABOUT IT.
ANYONE I KNOW?
MY FIRST CAPTAIN.
NO SHIT. WHERE IS HE?
DEAD IN A DUMPSTER, SEVEN YEARS BACK.
AND COPS WERE THE ONLY PEOPLE GOING IN AND OUT OF THE EVIDENCE ROOM.
THEN THEN WE HAVE 700 SUSPECTS.
THAT LYING SGT. SIMONE MADE MY UTERUS CLENCH.
I HATE WOMEN IN GENERAL.
YOU HATE FEMALE COPS.
FINALLY YOU ADMIT IT.
LET'S GET A LIST OF HER COP FRIENDS AND OLD PARTNERS, AND ANYONE SHE'D OWE A FAVOR TO, BECAUSE I BET MY--
WELL, SHE USED TO PARTNER WITH WHAT'S HIS FACE.
WHO'S WHAT?
WE PINCHED A COP?
THE BLACKGUARD SHOOTING.
NO, THE OTHER ONE. THE ONE ON THE COVER OF THE PAPER.
LET ME UNDERSTAND...
KIRKMAN'S OLD PARTNER HINES USED TO PARTNER WITH THE WOMAN RUNNING THE EVIDENCE ROOM WHERE THE MAIN PIECE OF EVIDENCE IN THE BLACKGUARD CASE--
--WHICH WAS ALSO I.D.'D AS THE CAUSE OF THIS MURDER SCENE--HAS GONE MISSING.
AND YOU JUST THOUGHT OF IT NOW?!
I THOUGHT YOU--IT WAS, LIKE, TEN YEARS AGO, WHAT?
COCK-LINT!!

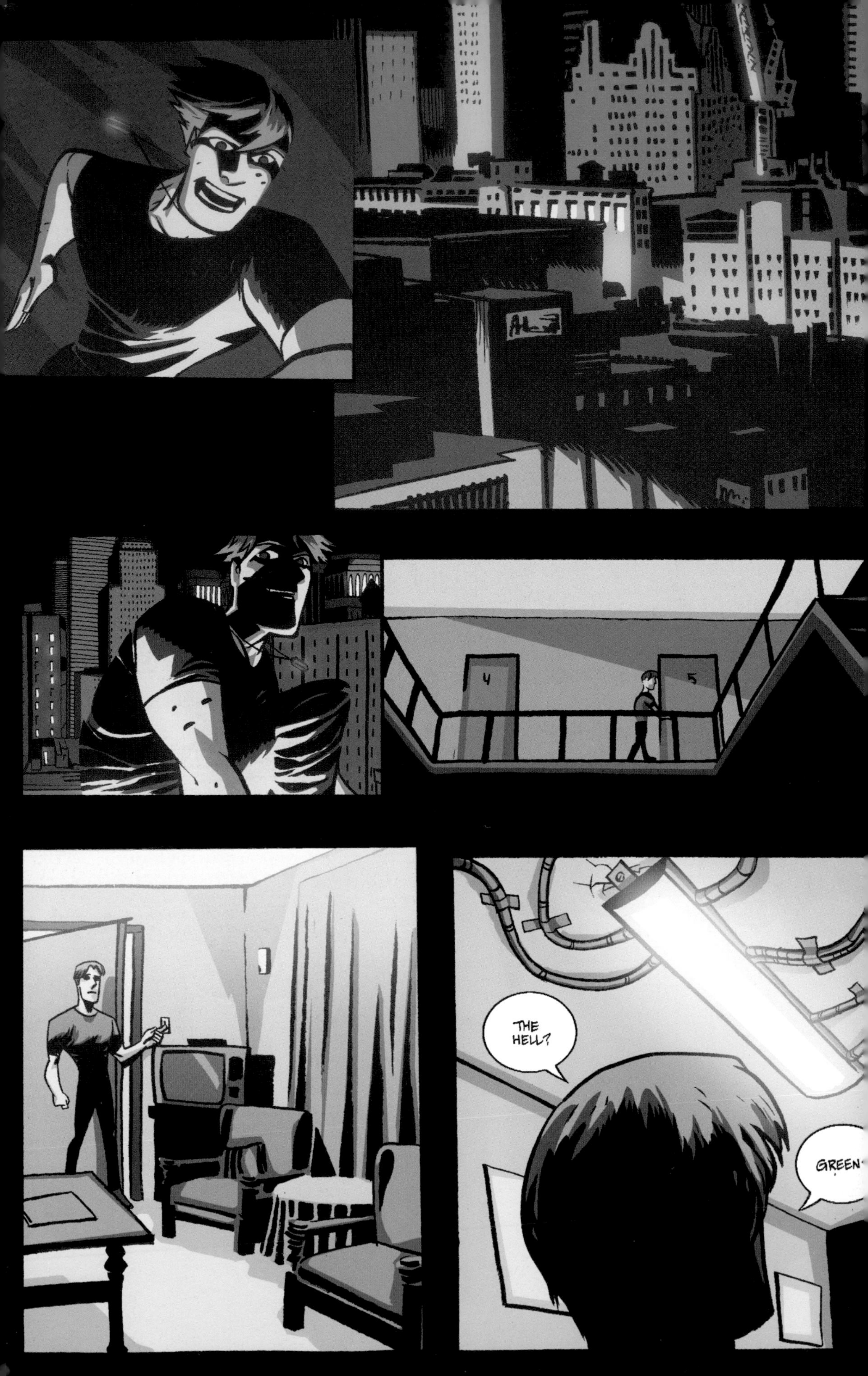

THE HELL?
GREEN-

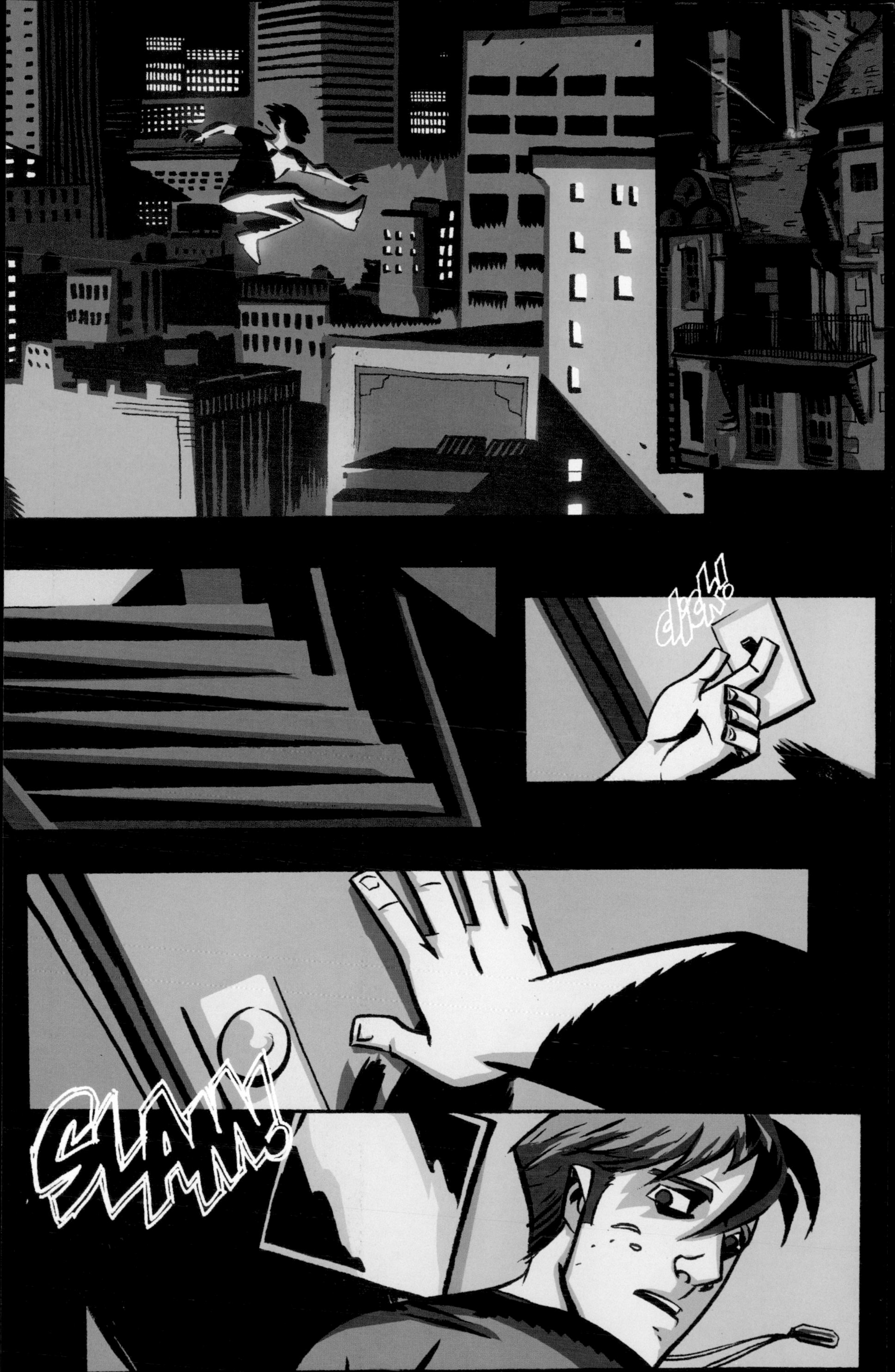
click!
SLAM!

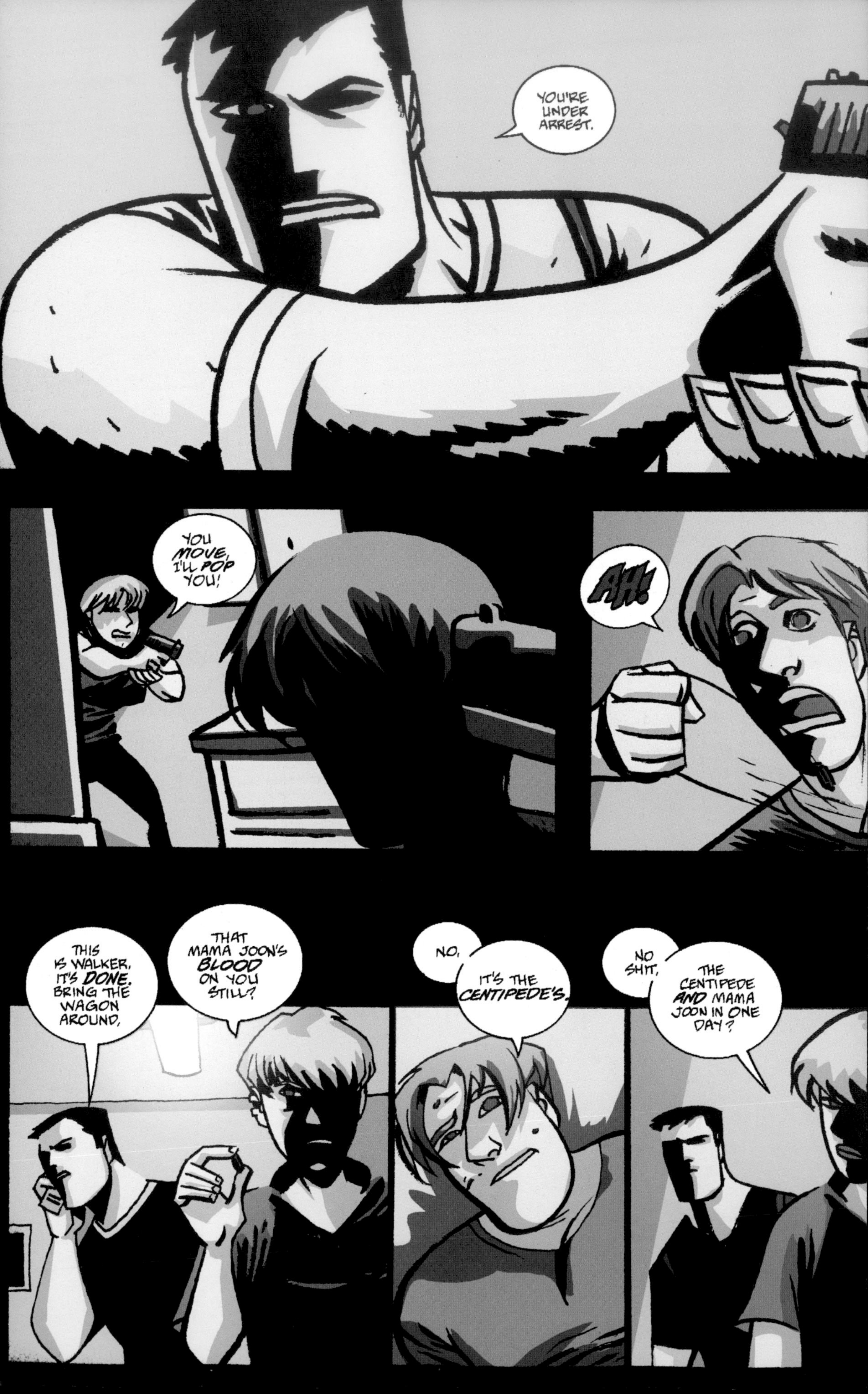
YOU'RE UNDER ARREST.
YOU MOVE, I'LL POP YOU!
AH!
THIS IS WALKER. IT'S DONE. BRING THE WAGON AROUND.
THAT MAMA JOON'S BLOOD ON YOU STILL?
NO.
IT'S THE CENTIPEDE'S.
NO SHIT.
THE CENTIPEDE AND MAMA JOON IN ONE DAY?

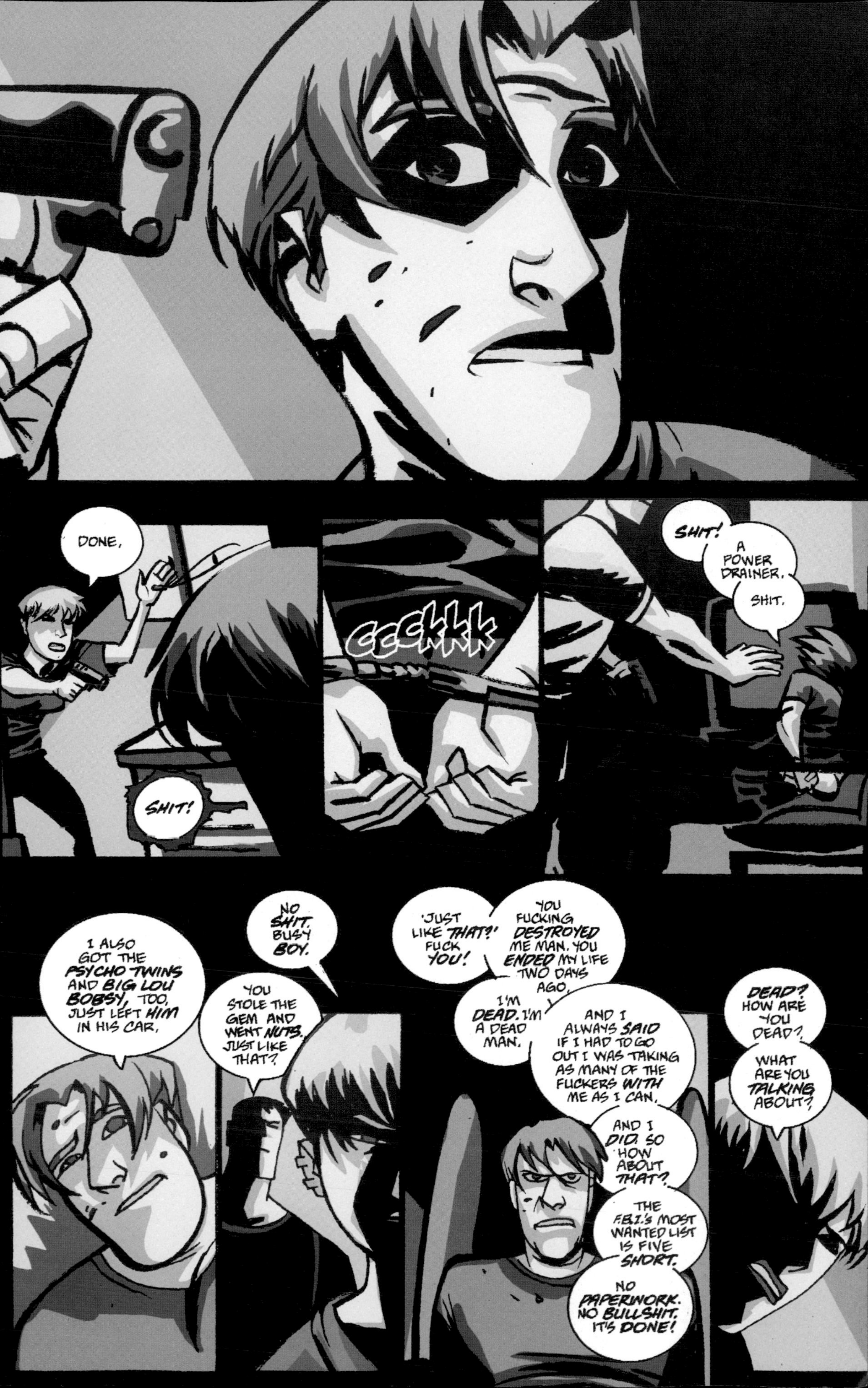
DONE.
SHIT!
CCCKKK
SHIT!
A POWER DRAINER.
SHIT.
I ALSO GOT THE PSYCHO TWINS AND BIG LOU BOBSY, TOO. JUST LEFT HIM IN HIS CAR.
NO SHIT, BUSY BOY.
YOU STOLE THE GEM AND WENT NUTS. JUST LIKE THAT?
'JUST LIKE THAT?' FUCK YOU!
YOU FUCKING DESTROYED ME MAN. YOU ENDED MY LIFE TWO DAYS AGO.
I'M DEAD. I'M A DEAD MAN.
AND I ALWAYS SAID IF I HAD TO GO OUT I WAS TAKING AS MANY OF THE FUCKERS WITH ME AS I CAN.
AND I DID. SO HOW ABOUT THAT?
THE F.B.I.'s MOST WANTED LIST IS FIVE SHORT.
NO PAPERWORK. NO BULLSHIT. IT'S DONE!
DEAD? HOW ARE YOU DEAD?
WHAT ARE YOU TALKING ABOUT?

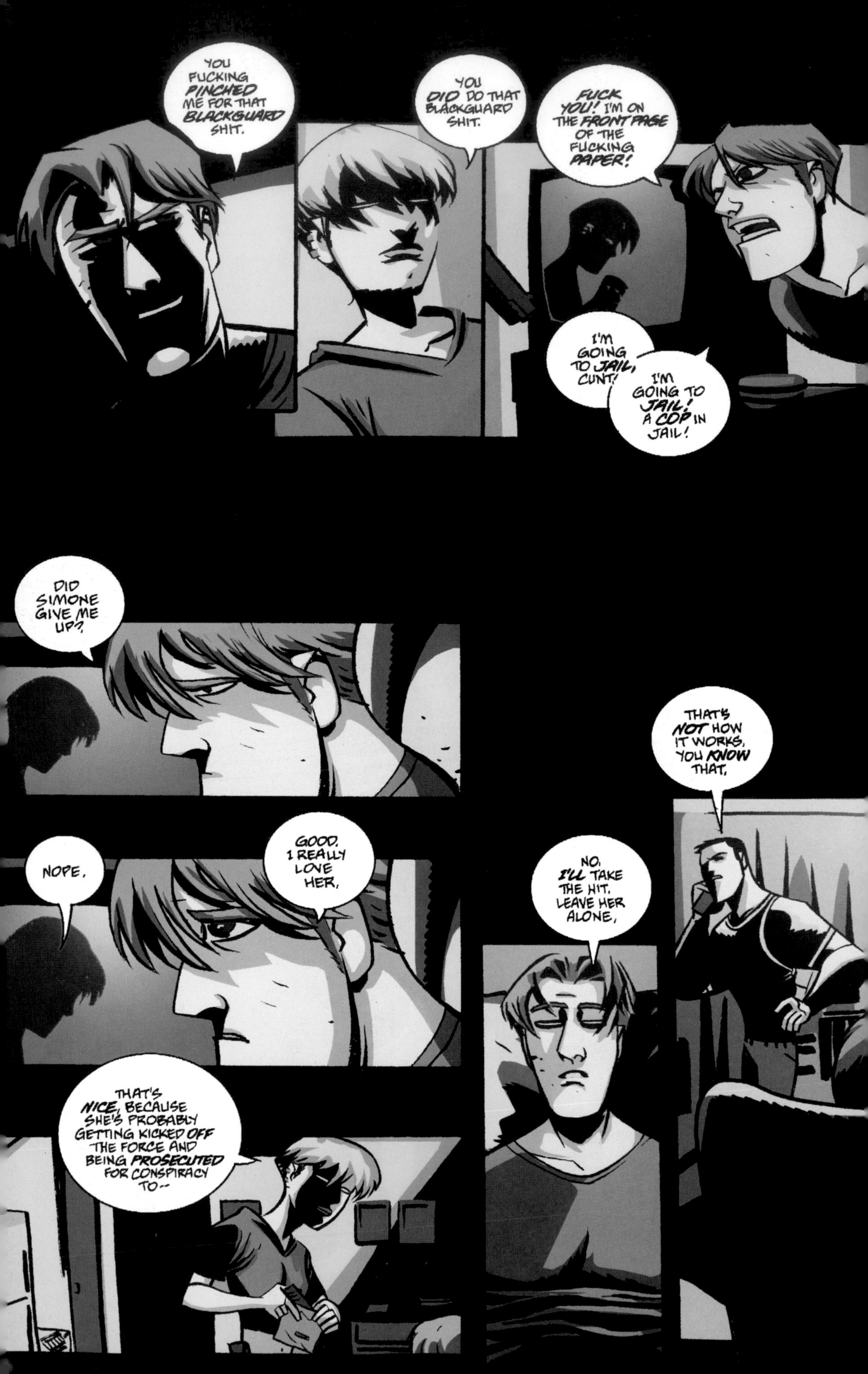
YOU FUCKING PINCHED ME FOR THAT BLACKGUARD SHIT.
YOU DID DO THAT BLACKGUARD SHIT.
FUCK YOU! I'M ON THE FRONT PAGE OF THE FUCKING PAPER!
I'M GOING TO JAIL, CUNT!
I'M GOING TO JAIL! A COP IN JAIL!
DID SIMONE GIVE ME UP?
NOPE.
GOOD. I REALLY LOVE HER.
THAT'S NICE, BECAUSE SHE'S PROBABLY GETTING KICKED OFF THE FORCE AND BEING PROSECUTED FOR CONSPIRACY TO--
NO. I'LL TAKE THE HIT. LEAVE HER ALONE.
THAT'S NOT HOW IT WORKS. YOU KNOW THAT.

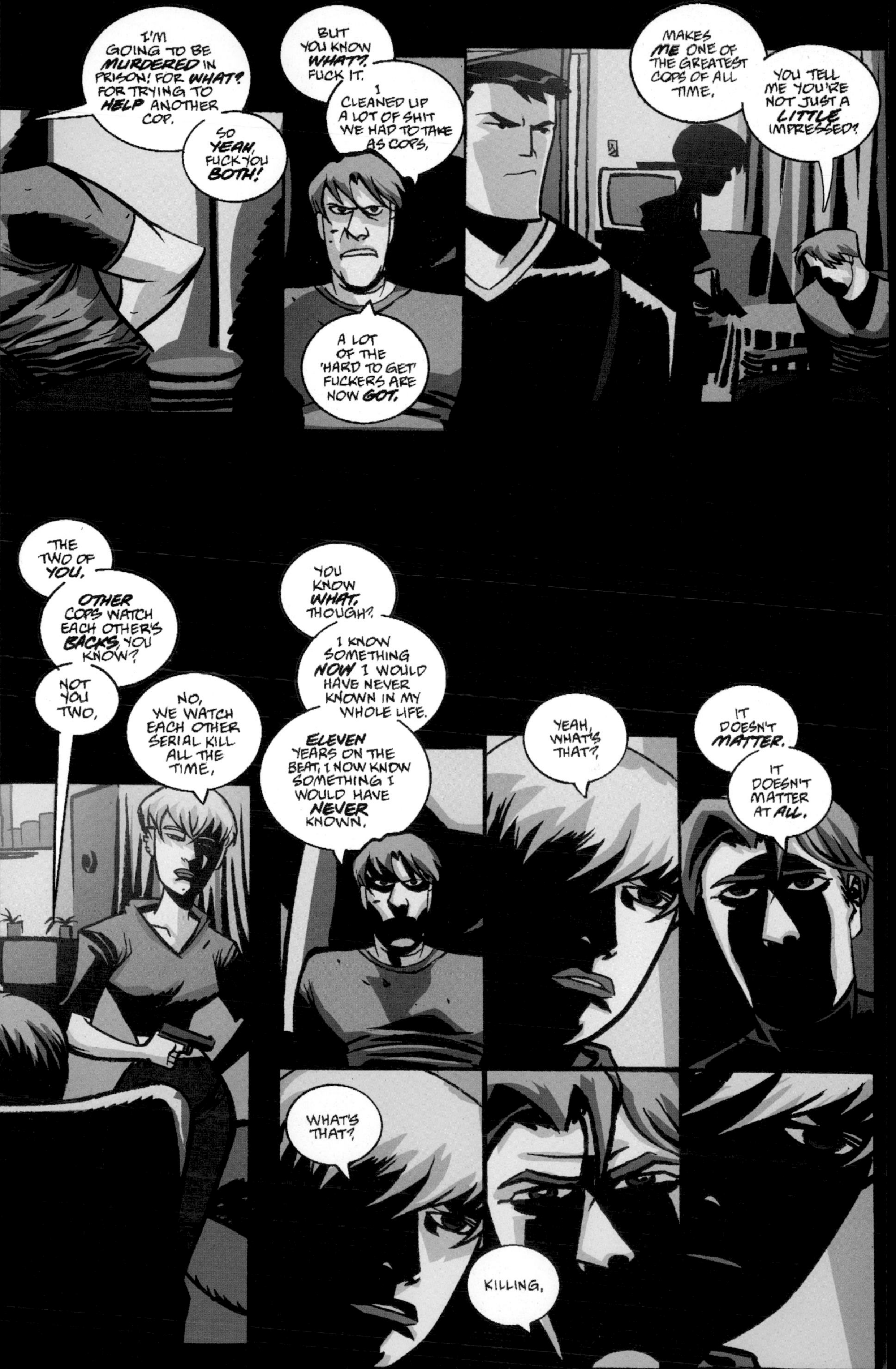
I'M GOING TO BE MURDERED IN PRISON! FOR WHAT? FOR TRYING TO HELP ANOTHER COP.
SO YEAH, FUCK YOU BOTH!
BUT YOU KNOW WHAT? FUCK IT.
I CLEANED UP A LOT OF SHIT WE HAD TO TAKE AS COPS,
A LOT OF THE 'HARD TO GET' FUCKERS ARE NOW GOT.
MAKES ME ONE OF THE GREATEST COPS OF ALL TIME.
YOU TELL ME YOU'RE NOT JUST A LITTLE IMPRESSED?
THE TWO OF YOU.
OTHER COPS WATCH EACH OTHER'S BACKS, YOU KNOW?
NOT YOU TWO.
NO, WE WATCH EACH OTHER SERIAL KILL ALL THE TIME.
YOU KNOW WHAT, THOUGH?
I KNOW SOMETHING NOW I WOULD HAVE NEVER KNOWN IN MY WHOLE LIFE.
ELEVEN YEARS ON THE BEAT, I NOW KNOW SOMETHING I WOULD HAVE NEVER KNOWN.
YEAH, WHAT'S THAT?
IT DOESN'T MATTER.
IT DOESN'T MATTER AT ALL.
WHAT'S THAT?
KILLING.

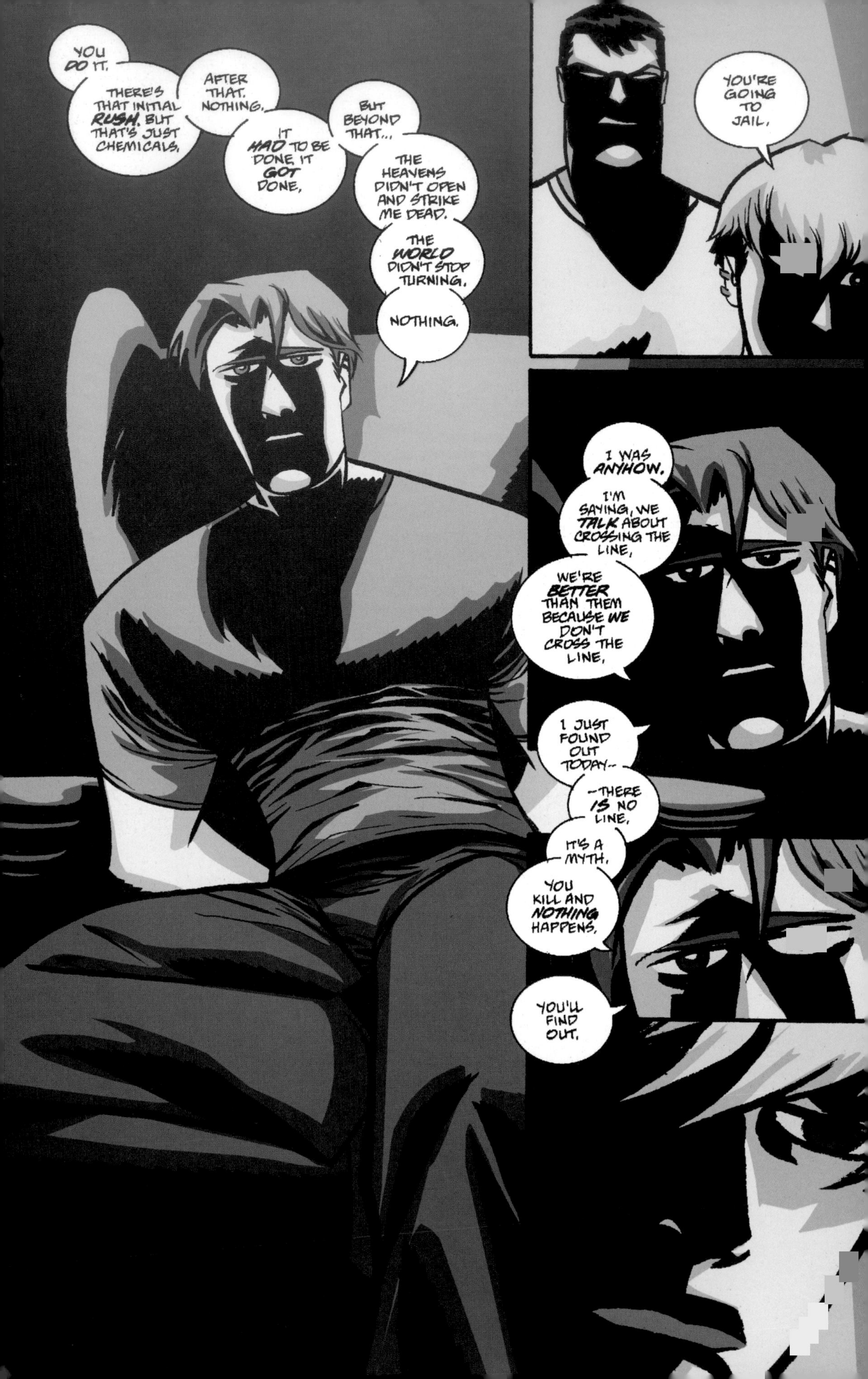
YOU DO IT.
THERE'S THAT INITIAL RUSH. BUT THAT'S JUST CHEMICALS.
AFTER THAT. NOTHING.
IT HAD TO BE DONE. IT GOT DONE.
BUT BEYOND THAT...
THE HEAVENS DIDN'T OPEN AND STRIKE ME DEAD.
THE WORLD DIDN'T STOP TURNING.
NOTHING.
YOU'RE GOING TO JAIL.
I WAS ANYHOW.
I'M SAYING, WE TALK ABOUT CROSSING THE LINE.
WE'RE BETTER THAN THEM BECAUSE WE DON'T CROSS THE LINE.
I JUST FOUND OUT TODAY--
--THERE IS NO LINE.
IT'S A MYTH.
YOU KILL AND NOTHING HAPPENS.
YOU'LL FIND OUT.

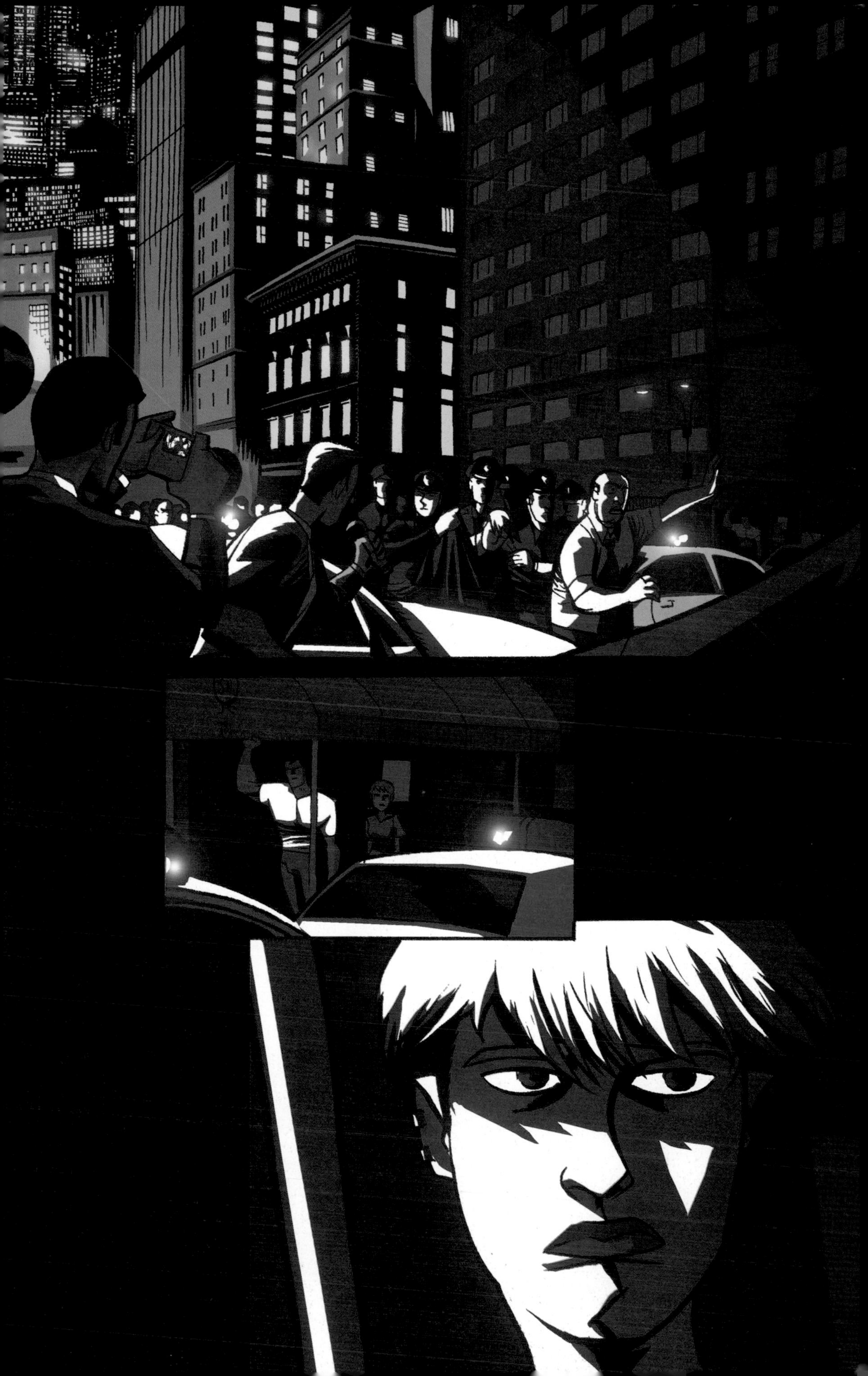

# THE DEFINITIVE POWERS INTERVIEW

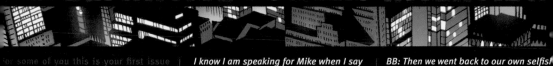

For some of you this is your first issue of POWERS, but hopefully you've either caught up on the trades or like me, have proudly read each and every single issue since the debut. You've become part of the mass who demands a higher standard out of their comics since discovering Brian Michael Bendis, one of the most exciting voices in this high-level writer-centric age of comics. Whether you were fond of his early crime comics or lured by his Marvel work, we all know he is in his element with in POWERS. And over the past 49 issues, we've all been eyewitnesses to the development of Mike Oeming who has come into his own and has become one of the best storytellers in the business, end of discussion!

If this really is your first time holding an issue of POWERS, it's likely the first time you will experience the infamous Lineup, the best letters column in comics and where the following interview will see print for the first time. That's right, Brian didn't have to steal it from some website without their permission.

The Lineup is one of the last of its kind, an endangered species in the age of Internet message boards, an old-fashioned letters column. But this is no ordinary mailbox. Where else can you read words in print like, "Fucktard," or expressions like, "Lick my taint!" Where else can you read a forty-year old fanboy come out of the basement to write a hate-filled letter while professing their love for a fallen Avenger? Your letters have made this place as fun as the pages that precede it.

This super-sized interview was conducted specifically for all of you who have been here for the ride. Take a look back at the stories that have brought us here and go behind-the-scenes of their inspiration. It is filled with laughs, pop culture references, and revelations. Go sit on your porcelain thrones, find a spot on the subway, and kick back with the Definitive POWERS interview. Thank you, Brian, Mike, and all of you for getting us to 50.

Ernie Estrella: What's it like to hit issue fifty?

Mike Oeming: It feels kind of late, we should have had it a while ago. If it were 2003 it would have been great!

*Brian Bendis: [Laughs] Honestly, even though we're now published by Marvel, it is by all definitions, an independent book*

*I know I am speaking for Mike when I say that we are so appreciative of the readership. POWERS was a bubble book when we first started. Prior to POWERS, neither Mike nor I had what you would call a hit—a book that could sustain itself financially. We did a lot of books even in black and white that were on the verge of cancellation. For this to have worked out is really awesome.*

MO: It is amazing. The main books I read were NEXUS and SPIDER-MAN when I was young—especially NEXUS. It was NEXUS # 50; a double-sized perfect-bound book that was one of those special books in my lifetime that helped form what I wanted to do in comics. To be able to reach that same landmark is a pretty big deal.

*BB: I remember when I read NEXUS, I said, "One day, I hope I get to offer Steve Rude an issue of MARVEL TEAM-UP and he hangs up on me."*

MO: That's great!

[All laughing]

MO: Did you call him "The Dude"?

*BB: I think the phone call was, "Hey would you like to do an issue of Marvel Team-Up and John Totleben is doing one and so is Bill Sienkiewicz ..." and he said, "The only Ultimate Marvel is the one that Jack Kirby created!" and then he hung-up. I kid you not. But I love him; he's still one of my favorite artists.*

EE: Can either of you recall the first conversation about POWERS?

*BB: I'm pretty sure I do more than Mike.*

MO: I remember saying, "No!"

*BB: First of all, there are a lot of memories that happened between Mike and me that I am the sole owner of because of whatever Mike does on his free time. We first met officially in a store signing in Philadelphia; David Mack was there with a few other guys. David and me were blown away by Mike's portfolio, which was filled with all sorts of different styles and very bold line work. Both David and I said privately, "Jesus Christ Mike's portfolio is so much better than the comics he's getting to draw—no one's really using him. There's nothing wrong with the comics Mike is doing but this guy needs that special thing that's gonna let him really be who he really is." He's a very unique comic book artist.*

*BB: Then we went back to our own selfish lives and forgot about him. Then Mike was developing what would be the POWERS style. He would fax us a pin-up of Jinx and one of Kabuki. To see Jinx drawn in that very bold line style really excited me. I got really-really excited. I said, "Jesus Christ I want to see a crime book like this." And uh—so we did a couple of short pieces together. While this was going on, I was cooking up this idea of a homicide book in a superhero universe. I may have been the fiftieth writer to come up to him with a pitch that never went anywhere and he just handles it like, "Whatever, man! Send it over!" When the ball started rolling and we had a publisher for it, he was kind of stuck because he politely agreed and now he actually had to do it.*

MO: What was really funny was when the publisher said, "We'll do this and who's Mike again?" and Brian said, "Well, he drew Ship of Fools" They said, "Well, I hope he's not drawing it like Ship of Fools because no one liked that book."

EE: Aw man.

*BB: Jim Valentino was our publisher and he totally believed in us, we both had good relationships on prior projects and we came to him with this one. I had this whole color theory for the book, which we've shown quite often, that the book is very mono chromatic saturated color but when the heroes show up it becomes almost garish full color.*

MO: Which was another thing I was against. First he convinced me to do POWERS, and then when he said color, I said "Fuck it. We're never going to make any money." Doing a color is like suicide.

*BB: And Mike wasn't wrong. TORSO was selling 2200 copies...*

MO: Yeah, and SHIP OF FOOLS was doing less than that.

*BB: And I'm sitting there going, "Let's do a book that you need at least 14 (thousand) to keep afloat."*

[Mike laughs hysterically]

*BB: And I'm going, "No-no. I think this one might be the ONE," meanwhile after twelve years in the business where I've yet to have one. Listen, I really had this color idea that I really thought was interesting and I saw the interrogation room in green so clearly in color. And that was so rare for*

or almost everything. You know, I never saw JINX in color—ever. But this one I did and thought we'll make a pinky pact and if it doesn't work we'll make it in black and white. At the time people thought, 'Was this the right style for a crime book?' 'Is this the right style for a superhero book?' And even people were commenting 'Is Brian's writing style interesting for a superhero book?' People pulled me aside and told me I should cut it out with the stuttering if I'm going to do a superhero book. So we just pushed ahead. When we first got our orders they were like 12,500 which was bubble, right on the bubble. Privately both of us were like, 'Oh my god, 12 and a half that's a miracle!'

MO: We also both knew that wasn't going to cut it either. Typically if your book is coming in at 12 and half, issue two would be ten, issue three is going to be nine, and if you're lucky you'll level out around eight. In other words the numbers go down, they don't go up. So right there, we knew we were done.

*BB: By the way this is the only business that that's the case by the way. Let's say you're going to put out a new magazine and first issue does 200,000 and sells out. The next issue they order more of. In comics, it's hal[illegible]half, half and hopefully you'll level out at a decent place and that goes for any comic.*

EE: Which issue did either of you believe you had a h[illegible]rst of all on the creative side when both of you said, "We've got a hit here," and secondly, when did the readers grab onto the series?

*BB: Well I was having a weird year where everybody was pulling me aside and telling me I was going to breakout soon.*

MO: Yeah, the second he started working with me, his career went on an upswing.

*BB: I was literally starving to death, with no money. And everyone kept telling me how I was going to break out. So I was like, "WILL SOMEONE HIRE ME?" No one's hiring me and no one's buying my books. It's not happening. It's nice when people say that, it's a compliment but I was literally starving to death. So you're hoping this is the one. Though we were a bubble, I was kind of thrilled at the twelve and a half because it was like ten thousand more than the last book. Maybe I was being a half-cup full kinda guy. What happened was once the book came out, Jim and (Anthony) Bozzi read the first three issues. I think Bozzi had a meeting at Image said, "If we can't make a book like POWERS sell we really should stop making comics." And I was like, goddamn, that's nice. And they offered to double ship the second issue.*

MO: That was a big part of it, the double shipment of issue two.

*BB: The good news is our second issue numbers weren't bad. They were a little over ten which is not a bad fall off for a second issue. So there was hope. And the numbers kept coming and we went back to a second print of issue one so we were officially in print. Issues 3-11 saw an upswing of 5,000 new customers every issue till about issue 11 or 12. It was shocking and neither one of us had ever come near that.*

MO: Absolutely! I was still working part time in security at the time till issue four or five.

*BB: That surprises a lot of people that Mike drew the first three issues of POWERS in a security booth. Which if anyone gives Mike shit from anyone online—He gets a gold key; that is dedication. At the same time I was doing SAM & TWITCH for McFarlane and they were letting me promote the book in the back so that was helping a little. I had just started getting work at Marvel but none of it had come out. ULTIMATE SPIDER-MAN was announced but it wasn't received very favorably.*

MO: I remember when Ultimate was announced it was exciting it was SPIDER-MAN but at the same time there was all those--

*BB: No, there was a shit-load of animosity that doesn't come near the crap I get for AVENGERS. There was press and it would mention POWERS a lot. "Who's this asshole fucking up SPIDER-MAN? Oh it's the POWERS guy." So people would check out POWERS to see who the hell I was and if I could start SPIDER-MAN from scratch.*

EE: The POWERS fan base is probably different than any of the other work you guys currently work on—

*BB: I would agree with that.*

EE: Do you feel that a certain point of time that you're making the book for this audience?

*BB: It's difficult to think like that.*

MO: We've been making it for us, really. If we were always thinking what the people want from us we would have never done the monkey issue.

*BB: [Laughing Loud]*

MO: Brian and I did it for ourselves, hoping that we're in tune with what people want.

*BB: It's amazing when you get someone on with something you genuinely like but from day one, as soon as they meet any new character they like, that you know you're going to kill in six issues it's always difficult. You can't start playing that game of making people happy. You'll always fail. The tide turns in pop culture every six months so by the time you've produced whatever it is you were trying to make people happy it could be onto something else and now you have something you don't even like. The one thing I'm most proud of with POWERS it kind of changes genres every year. Whether it's a shift in tone or whose point of view we're telling the story, or what kind of story we're telling, that's what an independent comic should be regardless of its genre.*

MO: There is something different in the POWERS stories from what we were telling early on to what we're telling now without it really changing the definition of what Powers is about. That is what's kept if fresh so far. If we kept doing the same story lines that we did for the first three stories I think we'd be ready to hang it up next week. That's it. We would have done about all the dead superhero investigations we can do.

*BB: And also POWERS gets an inordinate amount of mail and plus the message board is very high traffic. We hear from a lot of people more than most comics. We get more mail than ULTIMATE SPIDER-MAN even though it sells three times more than what POWERS sells. The only thing I do know for sure, and it's hard to generalize an audience's attitude, but our audience seems to predominantly be, "Just show me something different, I know what to expect from this book and that, I'm not exactly sure what I'm going to get from you guys every month, but I know you mean it, I'll take the ride unless you guys kill Deena and then fuck it, I'm going." And I also know that an inordinate amount of readers find the AVENGERS hate mail as funny as I do.*

MO: [Laughs] Do you think that a lot of the readers are cynical superhero readers?

*BB: No, no it's not at all because I know a lot of them read superhero comics but I do know they go, "Okay, I do like my Ultimate fix, but I also need something adult." What makes me happy about that reaction, if I have a mandate accomplishing every issue, I say "Would Marvel or DC be able to do this?" and if the answer is, no, then we did something special.*

MO: The main thing I find about POWERS special is we don't know—and this isn't a line or anything—we don't know what's going to happen next. When issue # came out for Marvel and we knocked off one of the main characters, that wasn't planned. He wasn't designed to die. It came to a shock to both of us to do it. It made sense, so let's do it. At any moment anything can happen in the book.

EE: So what exactly led to the killing off of [censored for those who aren't caught up]?

*BB: Don't give it away! SPOILERS!*

MO: Oh my goodness. The people who wait for the trade are going to kill you!

EE: Sorry

BB: No. I'll tell you what is more exciting. The thing I'm most excited about is that I have not yet in the script, written the words, "naked breast" yet I have seen in the art, [Oeming begins laughing] hundreds of naked breasts. I never added them, but they always show up.

MO: And genitalia.

BB: But there were a lot of bloody removed naked breasts, and if there was a decapitation, someone's breast is yanked off. That was Mike's contribution and I think it's special, and I think they should make an Eisner category specific for it.

MO: I think America is in deep denial about its love of sex and violence right now.

BB: [Sarcastically] Yeah, that's right.

MO: I think it is! I think it's pretty strange we live in a world where people pretend to be shocked by violence. And five to ten years ago, god, it's been longer than that, I'm sorry, the 80's, [Laughs] you saw a movie in the 80's, and you saw breasts and nowadays you get one of the two. You don't get nudity next to violence anymore.

BB: I smell a Mike Oeming-Bon Jovi haircut picture being placed next to that quote.

MO: There's a couple of them out there.

BB: That hair was sex and violence, wasn't it? I'm making hair jokes, really uncalled for.

EE: Brian, you took it upon yourself to script, letter, and layout the first three issues, what was it about POWERS that you felt the need to control so much?

BB: Well I clearly have issues but at the time I was doing it to Alias as well in other stuff and it became very clear from my peers and collaborators that I was being a bit of an asshole about it.

MO: I think it clearly just came from doing creator-owned books where you do everything.

BB: It's your book and you have to put it together. I don't think people realize that when you do a creator-owned book you do book design yourself; you do the cover design yourself. I actually like doing it, it's a lot of fun to do and it's not something you get credit for. I've been doing it for years. I didn't know not to.

MO: And there's some real skill to that. One of the main things I do when I get a book from Marvel or DC for the first time is I ask myself, "Can you read the title?" I'm shocked how many books—

BB: I know I know—

MO: If it takes you more than a split sec-

ond to read the title, it's a bad cover design. I'm shocked at how many books you have to decipher the logo.

BB: I agree.

EE: Mike, what was going through your head because you had to be coaxed into to doing the project and here you have Brian juggling all of these tasks including the layouts?

MO: I'm really proud of it. It wasn't that hard to be coaxed into it. Initially when Brian and I first talked about doing stuff we wanted to do a crime thing. So he faxes over this idea called POWERS and it has this superhero backdrop and I was hesitant because I didn't want to do superhero stuff. I wanted to do serious hardcore crime shit like JINX and TORSO and GOLDFISH.

BB: He wanted to do decapitated bosoms.

[Everyone Laughs]

MO: When we first started doing the book there was definitely a visual language that we wanted to get across. I was more than happy to take the layouts from Brian. Eventually it quickly rolled into its own thing. We speak the same language now. He taught me how to speak.

BB: No! Honestly, Mike knew it wasn't coming from, "Do what I say," It was coming from, "I don't know where the writing stops." Because when I would write the books that I draw, the layouts would be part of the visual language of the storytelling.

MO: If the person doesn't click on it and I've seen this a couple of times in some of the books with his artists—

BB: Whaaaat?

MO: There's balance. They don't know how to handle twelve panel pages.

BB: Don't talk about David Mack that way.

MO: C'mon now. He's still learning, give him a break.

BB: Mike's got a very good attitude about collaboration and that comes from—

MO: I'm lazy.

BB: No-no. People don't know you've been in comics since you were 14 no joke or exaggeration. He was inking Daredevil when he was 14 is that right?

MO: It was actually NEWSTRALIA but I'll stick with DAREDEVIL.

BB: What was it? What were you inking?

MO: It was called NEWSTRALIA?

BB: What's NEWSTRALIA?

MO: It was this book that Tim Truman put out through Innovation Comics, then it was CHILD'S PLAY, then DAREDEVIL.

BB: Child's Play... [snickers] And let's not forget Edward Penishands.

MO: It was actually EDWARD WHIZZER-HANDS.

BB: I'm sorry, but that was funnier.

MO: Okay, but DR. HOOTERS was the best. Anyways.

EE: Brian, you've mentioned in past interviews that Deena's voice comes from your wife. I'm going through a few of the other characters and see where they were conceptualized. First is Walker:

BB: There's no specific person that he's based on. There's two David Macks. One is... [Oeming giggles] the very quiet and introspective but you–can-tell-the-wheels-are-turning David Mack. And one is this wild maniac David Mack and it's a little based on, it started off based on the quiet David Mack when he's sitting there thinking. He's kind of got this detective look on his face. And Deena isn't based on my wife, she's based on both my wife and Mike's wife. They're both kind of rambunctious, funny, and constantly say stuff that is shocking. I think both of our wives are very funny women. But my wife rarely says taint. That I added myself.

MO: Or cunt sandwich?

BB: Or cunt sandwich, my wife hasn't said that since my kid was born. That's inappropriate motherly talk.

EE: Who came up with the looks of Deena and Pilgrim?

BB: That is all Mike with very little prompting from me. He did a bunch of sketches that will be published in the new hardcover as well. He got Walker instantly and we went back and forth a little bit on the line weight to define the line for the character? And Deena was all about the hair.

MO: We tried changing her hair a couple times but it never really worked.

BB: Deena keeps the bowl.

EE: She even had those Pippy Longstocking braids for a while.

BB: Yeah we tried it for a little bit but nah-she's Dorthy Hammill, put it back.

MO: I wanted to say something interesting about Walker's voice. Here's this immortal dude who's been around forever and he still doesn't know how to communicate. He's so locked up in his own brain. I think that's typical of something only a male character would be guilty of.

BB: I can't tell if it's repression or if—um...

you ever meet older guys and they just don't want to bother with finishing a conversation?

MO: [Laughing] Yeah.

BB: They've had the conversation so much they know how it's going to end before it starts. And they go, "Feh," and just forget about it. There's a little bit of that in Walker. He's had every one of these goddamn conversations. It's not worth continuing. And Feh is Jewish by the way if you look it up.

EE: What About Calista?

BB: Calista is Mike Oeming.

MO: Because I still don't know what a clitoris is.

[Everyone Laughs]

EE: Cutter?

BB: I always have an id character who is all id. There's no self-editing, you know what I mean?

EE: Yeah.

BB: It's someone who is constantly saying inappropriate things only to not care about the reaction or act shocked at the reaction. Like the midget joke to Deena, he is literally shocked that she's insulted. I think we all have people like that in our lives. Who knew he was so popular? That was the funny thing. I thought he was one of those characters when he shows up people groan.

MO: Well, Brian writes such great asshole characters.

BB: I do, I wonder why? Where does that come from? Seriously.

MO: What I find is a lot with these characters that come off as assholes often reveal themselves to be more honorable and truthful than some of the so-called heroic characters that Brian is writing upfront.

BB: Woody Allen always said to write what you can't say in real life. So there is always a character speaking the way I'd like to speak but clearly cannot without being slapped in real life.

EE: What about EG 9?

BB: I am very upset at the breakup of the Fugees. I continue to be upset about it. [Oeming Laughs] I read this whole big article about it and was very, very upset. A lot of people don't know I make references to VH1: BEHIND THE MUSIC with an inspiration for POWERS. Almost every single arc has very close connections to some pop icon or famous story in music history. I'm a big, big fan of musician biographies. And almost every murder has been based

on an actual musical biography that I really care about and that one was the closest we came to pointing to them and saying it is The Fugees. This one I had to get off my chest. At first I was upset I would never be in the Fugees, I really wanted to be in the Fugees—For a myriad of reasons that wasn't going to happen. And now that they broke up and aren't speaking and not making albums it's very upsetting.

EE: If these deaths are related to the music world, whom does Retro Girl go back to?

BB: I've actually never said who it is, shall I say who it is in this 50th anniversary issue?

MO: Absolutely!

BB: It is Janis Joplin. I read PEARL: THE OBSESSIONS AND PASSIONS OF JANIS JOPLIN, the biography and was very moved by it. Clearly Janis Joplin wasn't murdered, but there was ambiance to her. And I replaced her with a hottie in a miniskirt but that was the inspiration for her.

EE: What about Olympia?

BB: Olympia really didn't have a voice. Olympia was based on Pamela Des Barres' book, I'M WITH THE BAND, which is a really cool book. She was this famous groupie; you've probably heard of her, she's slept with EVERYBODY. Her book is amazing it's very colorful and it doesn't hold back.

MO: It was more about the groupies than the bands.

BB: If people would fuck the guy from Weezer, then they'd certainly fuck superheroes.

MO: That whole story arc was built for me [Bendis Laughs] cause it's built on an idea of a girl who swallowed a superhero's cum and getting powers for fifteen minutes.

BB: Every once in a while you have to do something specifically for the artist. For Bagley I add something that will make him happy, for Mike, it's cum and clitoris. And if I don't put a sex scene in, he'll just draw one in. [Oeming Laughing]

EE: HOMICIDE has been the inspiration for the book, Mike, how much did you reference or study the show for visuals whether it be [interrogations, crime scenes, etc.?

MO: For visual references there wasn't any specific television shows or if we'd talk about TV shows early on, HOMICIDE was definitely up there, but I think it was more about films that relate to the storytelling not specific scenes. I think one of the biggest films for us was TAXI DRIVER. The storyboards in the special edition DVD and the slow paced storytelling was

a big thing for Brian and I and just for the noir feeling was these old detective flicks like the T-MEN and a couple other ones by, Brian what was the cinematographer's name?

BB: John Alton.

MO: If you see this film, T-MEN, it's the most black and white noir-ish film that there ever was.

BB: [Impersonating Alton] John says, "Don't be afraid of the black, be afraid of the white" and I got chills.

MO: So those two things for me were the largest, strongest influences. Brian wigged our colorist, breaking him over the coals for specific stuff. For the monkey-fucking issue, Pete had some trouble figuring out the color scheme. Brian referenced the scenes in Mexico from the movie TRAFFIC.

BB: I kept going, "Yellower—More Yellow!" and "Burn it out some more!" and I couldn't think of a word and Jaime Rich (former POWERS editor) goes, "He means the Benicio Del Toro scenes in TRAFFIC." I'm in love with the work of our great cinematographers and Vittorio Storano, his work had a lot to do with the coloring for POWERS and they were very specific and thankfully we've had very talented people able to accomplish this.

MO: I've picked up a lot of that language and brought it over to my other books. Especially since I don't have a good sense of color.

BB: And you don't have to draw backgrounds.

MO: [Laughs] Well you know I'll get that digital camera out—

BB: Haaah.

MO: Because I can't think in specific color, I started thinking in color schemes and scenes that are bluer than yellow, or warmer and colder. That's one thing I've picked up from POWERS, the general language we throw around. Colors, and how they affect mood of a scene.

BB: Most mainstream comics, (not mine), are very coloring-book style coloring where the grass is green and the sky is blue. It doesn't hinder the story but it isn't furthering the story.

MO: A lot of it is generically good coloring as far as the colors don't clash but it's pretty rare that you find colorists that help tell the story and Pete does an amazing job of that.

BB: He does do an amazing job. And he is very in tune now with what we want or what kind of experiments we can try that even if don't end up using it he gets excited and uses it for something else. I've been very

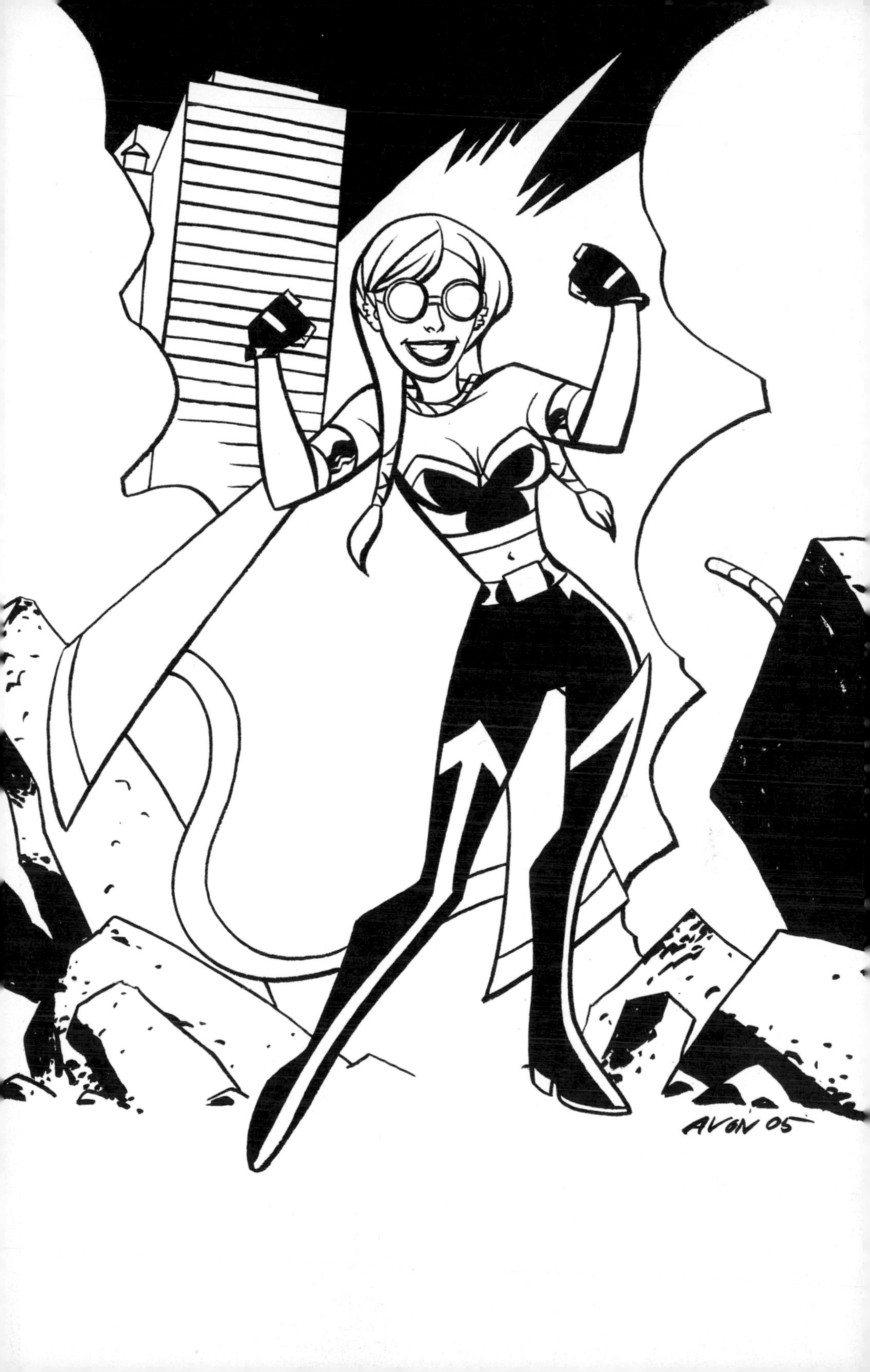
AVON 05

...cky we had Matt Hollingworth, and now Dave Stewart has done some other stuff with me. Frank D'Armata does NEW AVENGERS and you see there is storytelling in the color choices. It's not just filling it in to make it all shiny that actually accentuates the tone. We've both been involved with books where the color choices actually make the story worse—

MO: Don't get me started!

BB: Where you'd have a person all yellow and blue and you can't figure out. 'Why do I hate this? Why is this ugly?'

MO: I've had stories, and some pin-ups just destroyed to the point that I wish I'd never done them.

BB: Most people who are reading a comic, they can't nor should they even have to know the difference. They should be able to read it as a complete experience and be moved or blown away by it. Coloring, lettering, font choices and font placement, can affect or adversely pro-affect a person's enjoyment of a story. That's another reason why I get so involved, is because I know most people can't tell the difference where the writing, the art, and the coloring begins or ends, nor should they. And it's up to us to make sure that it's a complete experience.

I do think that the execution of those elements is what helps set POWERS apart from most books out there.

BB: Thanks. We're definitely one of the few books left with hand lettering.

MO: Yeah, Ken Bruzenak!

BB: I've loved him for years. He was (Howard) Chaykin's go-to-guy on all of the comics I loved that they did together. When we needed a letterer I thought, 'I would love to get Ken Bruzenak' and I forget who called him but they said he was available. Oh my god...what a pleasure. You guys should pick up American Flagg! when it comes out soon. That's some of the best lettering—

MO: And to think he hand letters all of Brian's dialogue.

BB: Oy, can you imagine? Sometimes I see the pages and I actually feel bad.

Also, Brian have you designed Deena and Walker as your version of Pembleton and Bayliss from the Homicide TV series?

BB: No, you know what, the book, HOMICIDE: A YEAR OF KILLING on the Streets by David Simon, which is an amazing book that people should look for, is a non-fiction book about true crime. This started my absolute love affair for the idea of a homicide detective and his life. In theory, Powers has evolved. The characters are unlike anything I've seen anywhere. Now

---

we know that there's a secret history of Walker and we know that Deena has this dark secret she's carrying around. You've never seen anything like this in any TV show or movie. But I've always been a fan of the partnership, the uneasy partnership. Or the partners thrusted together by geographic location and then have to figure out a relationship. What I like the most about Deena and Walker is that they're not close. They don't really like each other. They generally have affection for each other, they understand each other, but there isn't a lot of connection there, which I enjoy it immensely because I'm never going to spoon feed it. I think it's going to get worse over the next year and I enjoy that. They also know they do good work together, they're best work, so that's enough.

MO: I think it's fascinating. I think there's a really close bond there but it's not the emotional brother-sister relationship.

BB: He would kill for her but I don't think he wants to hang out with her.

MO: They would die for each other but they're not going to have beers ever after work.

BB: No one seems to want it. On the HOMICIDE TV show, Pembleton was that way but Bayliss really wanted to get in Pembleton's head. And neither of them (Deena or Walker) seems to want to be involved with the other at this point.

EE: A side thought while we're on HOMICIDE, let's take a quick look at GOTHAM CENTRAL which came out a few years ago. POWERS was originally pitched to DC, and GOTHAM CENTRAL has some elements of the HOMICIDE show and book with the board, the shift changes, do you think that the success POWERS opened the door for a pitch like GOTHAM CENTRAL?

BB: Well GOTHAM CENTRAL was the exception. There was about fifty POWERS knockoffs books that have happened only because you guys have been cool enough to make POWERS do so well. Yeah, we could not sell POWERS to DC. Actually DC approached us at the time and asked us what we wanted to do. We said we wanted to do POWERS and they said, "Eh."

MO: I remember even a smaller publisher that rejected us.

BB: Yeah, yeah. We've got our rejections—I don't know if we should say their names but they are pretty funny. [Laughs] We were looking for a page rate. We were dying.

MO: We were in poverty.

BB: We were looking to sell either half of it or something just to get the page rate. I was working for Todd (McFarlane) and he didn't want it, even though SAM & TWITCH was doing real well. So GOTHAM

---

CENTRAL is the exception. First of all, Greg Rucka and Ed Brubaker are very close, close friends of mine and not just show biz friends but they are actual friends of mine who are amazing crime writers if no better crime writers than me.

MO: Greg's a real writer.

BB: Yeah, and Ed wrote SCENE OF THE CRIME, which is a tremendous crime novel if you ever get the chance. And they did say, "Hey we're going to do this cop book in the DC Universe," and they gave me the heads up, which was more respectful than they needed to be. So I was like, "Cool." That is a book I actually like to read. But yes, there are the ones that you read and go, "Hmm, wow, that's weird. They're doing our book." Most of them... didn't make it. The one that scared the shit out of me was TOP 10.

MO: We almost folded up the tent.

BB: When Alan Moore announced his comic super hero book we had two issues in the can but we weren't solicited yet. Then all of a sudden they announced TOP 10 and we were like, "Gahhh Fu---" The whole time we were working on it going [Whispering] "No one's thought of it yet. No one's thought of this. Shhh. Do it real fast." Alan Moore then said he was going to do TOP 10 and you can't compete with Alan Moore, c'mon. I actually went and looked into it because Zander (Cannoninker on TOP 10), and I were friends at the time. I had to see if it was actually like our book. We probably would have just folded. It was not, it was superhero cops, a different genre, and I just went, "Whew."

EE: One of the unique things about POWERS is the drainer. This is like a silent character because the first time I saw them I thought it was a cool gimmick but it winds up being a major part of Walker's story. Who came up with idea of the drainers?

BB: I believe that would be me. I just read up, as I have, on police work and what they do to sustain incarceration for certain kinds of criminals and I started making logical choices about how they would handle this.

MO: I remember seeing something about certain prisons painted their cells specific colors because they were more calming and I always assumed that was where it was from.

BB: No. Once the color was chosen—that sickly green—it definitely elevated it for some reason. Somebody emailed me and said when they see the green pages they get happy because they know there's going to be yelling. So they love those interrogation scenes, which I love writing them. Obviously.

MO: I love drawing them because there are no backgrounds.

BB: Ha ha m: I love writing them immensely. For a writer there's nothing better than
putting two people in a room and locking
the door. one of them has an agenda. One
is trying to outwit the other one. It's so
much fun to write. For a while there I was
writing interrogation scenes in every one
of my books. "Let's put Matt Murdock in
an interrogation room, and Jessica Jones
in one..." just cause it's so much fun to
put your character in a box and see what
they do. I've tried to lay off it and make it
so POWERS is very special once you get to
the interrogation scenes.

MO: They really are some of the most en-
joyable scenes to draw not because the
background thing, but it's usually where
most of the emotion comes out in characters. Usually not Walker and Deena
but the other characters and my favorite
part of working with Brian and POWERS
is getting the characters to act. There's
not a lot of real emotions going on in the
stuff I've drawn for other companies.
Everybody is acting on the same level.
And from Brian's script it's real interesting to draw things that aren't being said.
He'll write notes to me and says that
someone is feeling a certain way. "He's
saying it exactly as if he doesn't mean
it." So these little notes that he'll just
say for me are great little acting notes
for the characters. And to be able to get
that across has been the thing I've been
most proud of to come out of POWERS is
my storytelling and learning how to be
a better storyteller and specifically get-
ing 2-dimensional characters to emote.
Getting a character to think on a page
was really a rare thing and that I'm really proud of. It's something that Brian
and I developed together. It's one of the
coolest things.

BB: I agree. That's my favorite part is
getting the book and when you see that
almost indescribable thing in their eyes.
That look, that, "Uh-oh I'm in trouble.
I gotta keep it up." Mike's very good at
that. Bagley's exceptional at it and so is
Alex Maleev. And so is Gaydos and I don't
mean to mention every artist I work with.
[Laughs] I'm very lucky—

MO: We just don't get the opportunity for
the most part. For the most part comics
are written for story not for the charac-
ers.

E: Now Deena's been to the hospital
three times, in an abusive relationship,
tortured, given powers, and taken into
outer space what else can you do to her?

Bendis and Oeming laughs sinisterly]

BB: You haven't read issue 11 by the time
we're doing th[...]at's probably the
worst thing we've ever done to her.

MO: Two words, man: Cunt Sandwich.

BB: [Chuckles] Deena is carrying some
[...]

MO: A character that operates in the Powers world is going to go through a lot of
shit. I'd love to story about Captain Cross
and his younger days and I bet he's seen
some crazy-crazy—

BB: I actually have all that laid out. Captain Cross has an interesting backstory.
We'll get to it one day.

MO: So, yes I think she's been through a
lot of stuff, that happens with your main
characters like Mulder in the X-FILES
who's been abducted by aliens a million
times. [Everyone laughs] I think we've
been fairly consistent if you look at what
Walker's been through. Every girlfriend he
gets, gets run over by a car or something.
He still insists on getting another one.

BB: Exactly.

E: Could each of you tell me which story
was the most difficult to script and to
draw?

BB: I know the answer for both of them.

MO: The monkey issue, right?

BB: No it was the whole arc, "Forever".
Every issue was a different time period so
Mike had to get all kinds of new reference

MO: See that stuff I love. I had no problems with it. It's a lot more work. And I
was doing more work cause every issue
was 29 pages or 30 pages was incredible
instead of 22.

BB: [Taunting] Hah-ha!

MO: See what was interesting about that
was when we did an issue that was 31
pages, no one would say anything and
the issue where we went to the back cover
people would suddenly notice.

BB: We got complaints about that!

MO: [Sighs] Oh...God.

BB: Jaime (Rich) said, "People aren't going to like that you're doing this." I said,
"What are you talking about, the story is
so big it's pouring over to the back cover."
He goes "They're not going to like it." and
people wound up emailing us saying don't
do that again.

MO: That's insane.

BB: It was more pages; we weren't charg-
ing you extra.

MO: I think I felt the hardest thing to draw
was the monkey issue. And not because it
was stuff like monkey snatch or a monkey
masturbating in the corner—

BB: You were doing that anyhow.

MO: That was fun. I really had a lot of fun
doing that. The problem was, and this
is strange. I hate doing backgrounds...

which is a necessary evil because when
they're not there it makes the page less, i
doesn't really feel a part of the universe.

BB: [Snickering] Who are you convincing
with that mantra you just spilled?

MO: It's true, absolutely. I'm serious!

BB: [Repeats Mike in a lethargic tone,
"Backgrounds are a necessary..."

MO: That's my weakness, that and dogs.

BB: [Laughs hysterically] He hates draw
ing dogs and I always put dogs in the
script. Dogs and cars.

MO: Yeah. Cars I've learned to do, bu
dogs... Anyway the problem with the
monkey issue was the backgrounds didn'
have buildings, cars, anything identifi
able, it was all just rocks. Not even trees
it was a rocky desert and all the monkey
kind of looked the same. It was very dif
ficult to establish any sense of place and
who the characters were. That was a rea
challenge. When I started it was great, I'l
draw rocks, a bunch of monkeys, mon
key titties and stuff, it'll be fun and ther
it was some of the hardest storytelling
had to do. There's no dialogue, there's nc
discernible backgrounds. [Bendis laughs
again] It was difficult to tell who the dif
ferent characters were. It was monkey se)
and you had to emote with monkeys anc
stuff. That I found the most difficult—

BB: I thought it was like naked storytell
ing. When I looked at the pages, see ther
was no, what Will Eisner would call, sto
rytelling pyrotechnics. You do all sort o
razzamatazz to cover things up your su
par drawing or storytelling. There wa
no place to hide. That goes to our life a.
black and white comic creators; there
was no place to hide. Your decision mak
ing process is more pure because you've
already worked out of your system all the
bad tricks you can pick up drawing main
stream comics. "Eh, the colorist will ge
it." or "The inker will pick things up fo
me." So when he's doing an issue like tha
there's nowhere to hide.

Not only was it difficult to produce tha
storyline. It was also a rough ride for the
audience because you're not telling then
why all of a sudden they're reading mon
key fucking and then what's with this bar
barian, and then by issue three they say
"Oh-oh-oh this kind of look like Walker...
We were coming out every six weeks at c
time so it had been months where we're
continually testing the boundaries of the
audience's patience. For the only real way
to do it right—not whispering to them in
the letters column, "It's Walker." You've
got to let them figure it out.

E: How scary was it to submit a stor
like that and not know how the audience
would react?

BB: That was what I thought was the whol[...]

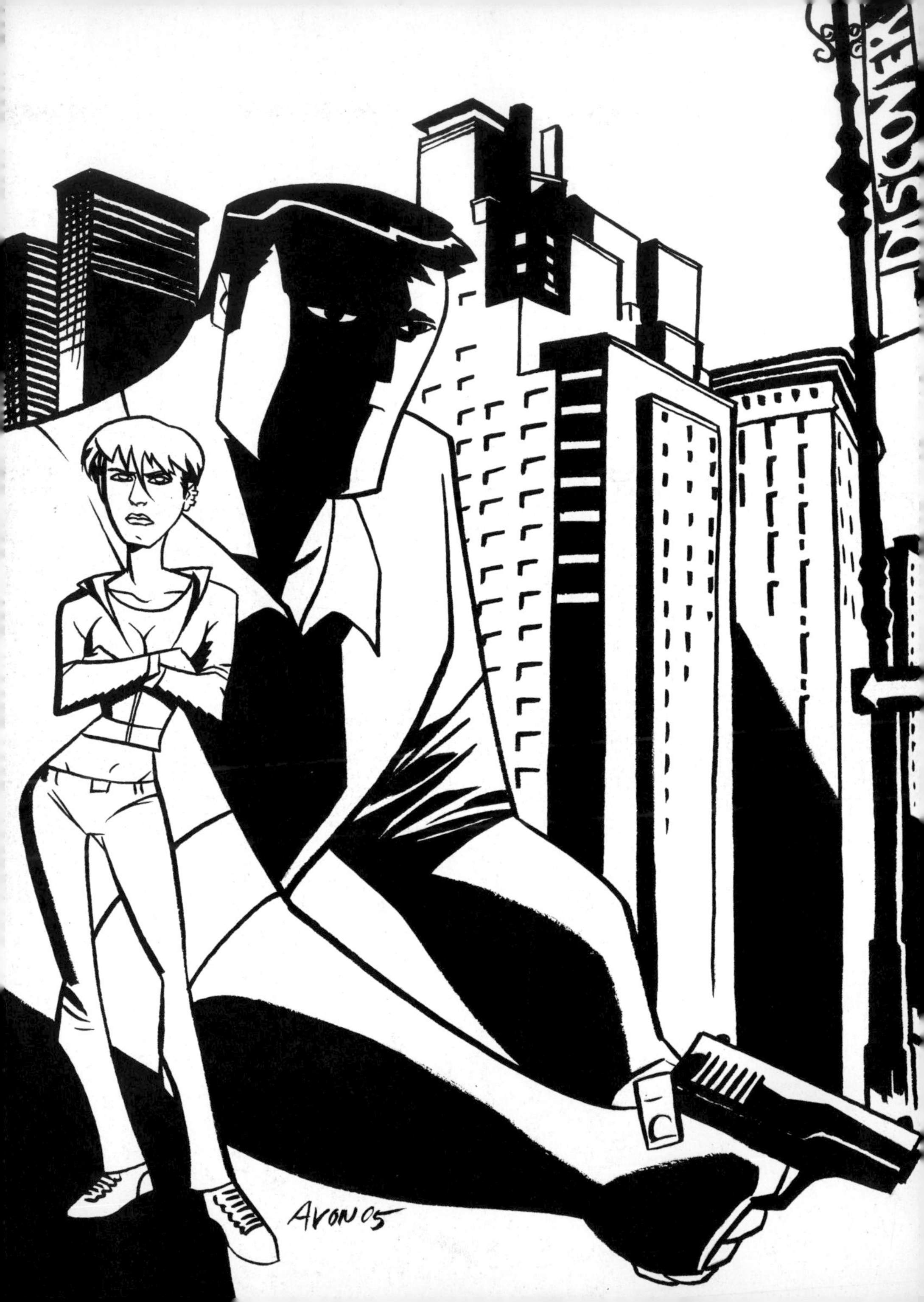
AVON 05

...agic of the book. Here's something you didn't expect to see. It was testing that. By the time we got to the monkeys the readers who have fallen in love with the characters like we had were more than happy to see Deena smack people around month after month, but here come the monkeys. It was a wild ride, man. I think it paid off. We looked at the orders and lost 1200 people from the monkeys.

MO: That knocked off anybody who wasn't sure.

BB: But then we gained 800 new readers who went, "Aw, what?" who heard about the book and thought it was a one kind of book.

MO: Which still left us 400 short if you do the math.

BB: We got them back though when we published with Marvel. But if was funny to watch the sales fluctuate because we hadn't budged in fifteen issues. Then all of a sudden there's this fluctuation of people going, "WHAT THE FUCK?!" It was funny. I've seen this about AVENGERS and ULTIMATE SPIDER-MAN, people yelling at us, I was getting yelled at for ALIAS when it first came out, I guess it's better to have that than have no reaction. It would be great to be universally loved but it's impossible. I was just watching this documentary about Air America it was on HBO, I don't know if you watched this, Mike.

MO: Is that on anymore?

BB: Y h, it's on. It's really interesting. Rand Rhod his radio person just screa ing people in her booth the whole time, just fighting with everyone said "I don't need to be loved I just need to be heard." I think I can relate a little.

MO: I just need to be loved; I don't care if anybody hears me.

EE: I'm going to go over the themes from the past storylines and maybe you can elaborate a little bit on them. For Role-Play, you had people pretending who they weren't. Did this come about from observations about gamers of RPG's?

BB: No. It was the whole wannabe aspect of life. We're just filled with them. The initial thread was, did you ever go to see one of those tribute bands, like the Back Doors? The best one is the Journey one. I actually saw them live. I remember when I was single there was this girl asked me out on a da or this famous Journey-tribute band. The guy is actually the lead sing or Journey now who sang in that band o we were sitting there watching this and literally in the middle of the date I said, "I have to go." She said, "Why," and I responded, "I can't be seen here," and left. I never saw her again. I never had done that before or since to anyone. What an asshole. So anyway it started on these tribute bands being these weird things and then got in the whole role-play-gamer lifestyle as well.

EE: What about "Anarchy" and the whole hypocrisy of superheroes.

BB: That was punk. That was something Mike and me keep coming back to, the anarchy mind-set. If there was something that stands up for truth and justice, someone's going to stand up for Fuck-You.

MO: Brian's embraced the superhero genre more, he understands it better than I do I guess. I've got a much more jaded view of the superhero thing.

BB: Way to promote your Marvel comics but yeah, go ahead. [Everyone laughs]

MO: I'm only doing a mini-series.

BB: Your Goat-headed Thor series?

MO: I have real problems with superheroes. They remind me a lot of these real-life people who put themselves on high moral plateaus judging other people. Who are they to judge us? Who are they to tell us how to live our lives, or their views are better than ours? I think that's what I see a lot in superheroes. It kind of bugs me, which explains my aversion to them for the most part.

BB: You should read more comics.

MO: No-no-no, There's more to that. I think largely when I see that I'm thinking of the archetypical Superman, Wonder Woman. So any time there's a chance to take a potshot at superheroes for the most part I'm for it.

EE: How about "Sellouts"?

BB: [Laughs] Well "Sellouts", and we're getting back to Journey again, the greatest VH1 BEHIND THE MUSIC episodes are not just the single artists, but the bands that CAN'T STAND EACH OTHER! It gets funnier as it goes on.

MO: Funny and shocking. I remember Steve Perry said he never felt like he belonged in Journey. This guy controlled the band for 25 years. Same thing with the dudes in Styx with Dennis DeYoung, they're both outsiders in their own bands that they took over.

BB: Yes, that's it! That's exactly it. But they act like they were there for six months they were there for decades! Those are the perfect examples. And Steve Perry says, "I was never friends of those guys, I never knew them. I was never part of the band, they didn't like me." And they cut to Neil Schon who's like "He said that?!" and he can't even fathom what the other guy's saying. It was shocking to him. And then Dennis DeYoung taking this hard rock band and turning it into space opera that none of them wanted to play, but they let him do it because it was working then he breaks up the band because they won't let him do what he wants. I go, "That's the next arc."

That was also the story we got the closes to pointing fingers at people in the comi book industry because you see a little o that mindset with some comic book pro fessionals of the generation before us What seems even funnier to me about th mindset is when you see Journey fightin it's over 50 million dollar When you se people in comics fighting, it's for five dol lars. And it's never really about the mone it's always about some other mindset so decided to take a couple of shots here an there.

MO: When you hear angry people in th comic industry or film industry abou something, nine times out of ten, they'r not angry about what they're claimin to be angry about when they're ranting Some other issue is manifesting thei anger, "I don't like the state of the indus try... These new writers... or music nowa days..." It's always about something els and usually the person who doesn't rec ognize that. I think that's interesting.

BB: in every comics article or intervie and the history of comics I've got m hands on for the last 25 years of my lif and you see this mindset. You see ho professionals behave publicly and the can't even hold it in towards their reader or other professionals. It ascinating t me and curious how they g there. Som people are like that they're six years ol because they're looking for reasons to b a jerk but there's other people where yo see the twists over time and it kind of fas cinates me.

But if you think about it, here's a bunc of people who made a whole lifestyle no having to speak to anyone or leave thei basement, and make comics. Anyon who makes a living in comics, means the spend a lot of time alone on purpose o by their nature of life, they decide to sta alone in their basement. Then all of a sud den as grown-ups they're supposed to b at a convention and be sociable and it' amazing someone hasn't been murdere yet.

EE: "Sellouts" was chock full of heav stuff. A sex scandal, a crazed Supershoc goes apeshit and nukes Utah, the Vatica is napalmed, Deena and Supershock, an this is all supposed to have been laye out before 9/11.

BB: With "Sellouts", the weird thing wa you did feel there was an escalation i world problems. Now no one could se 9/11 coming. But it was prior to 9/11 and i was December before where Supershoc just decides—

MO: Everything till the pope died. W melted the Pope!

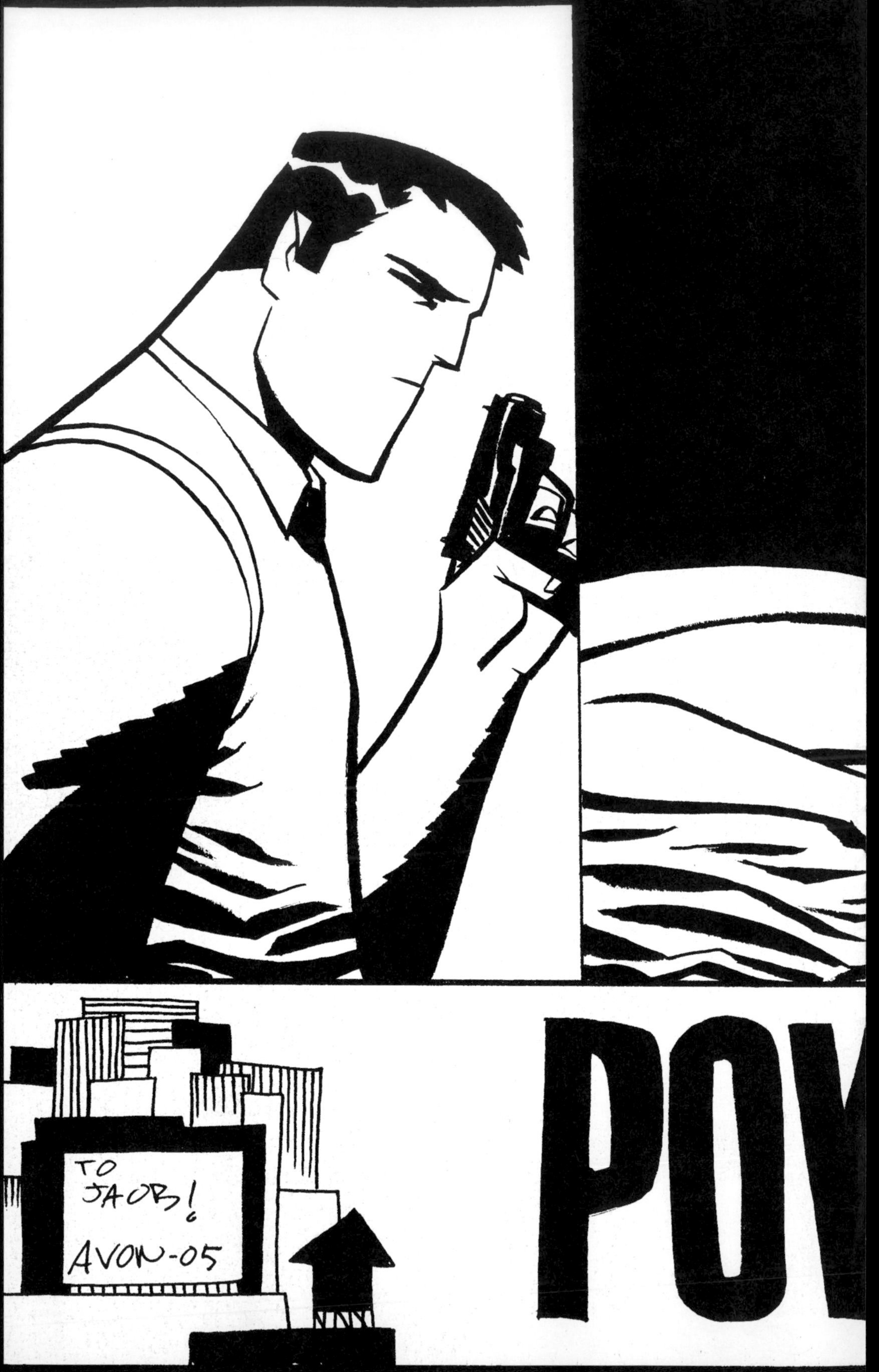
TO
JAOB!
AVON-05
POW

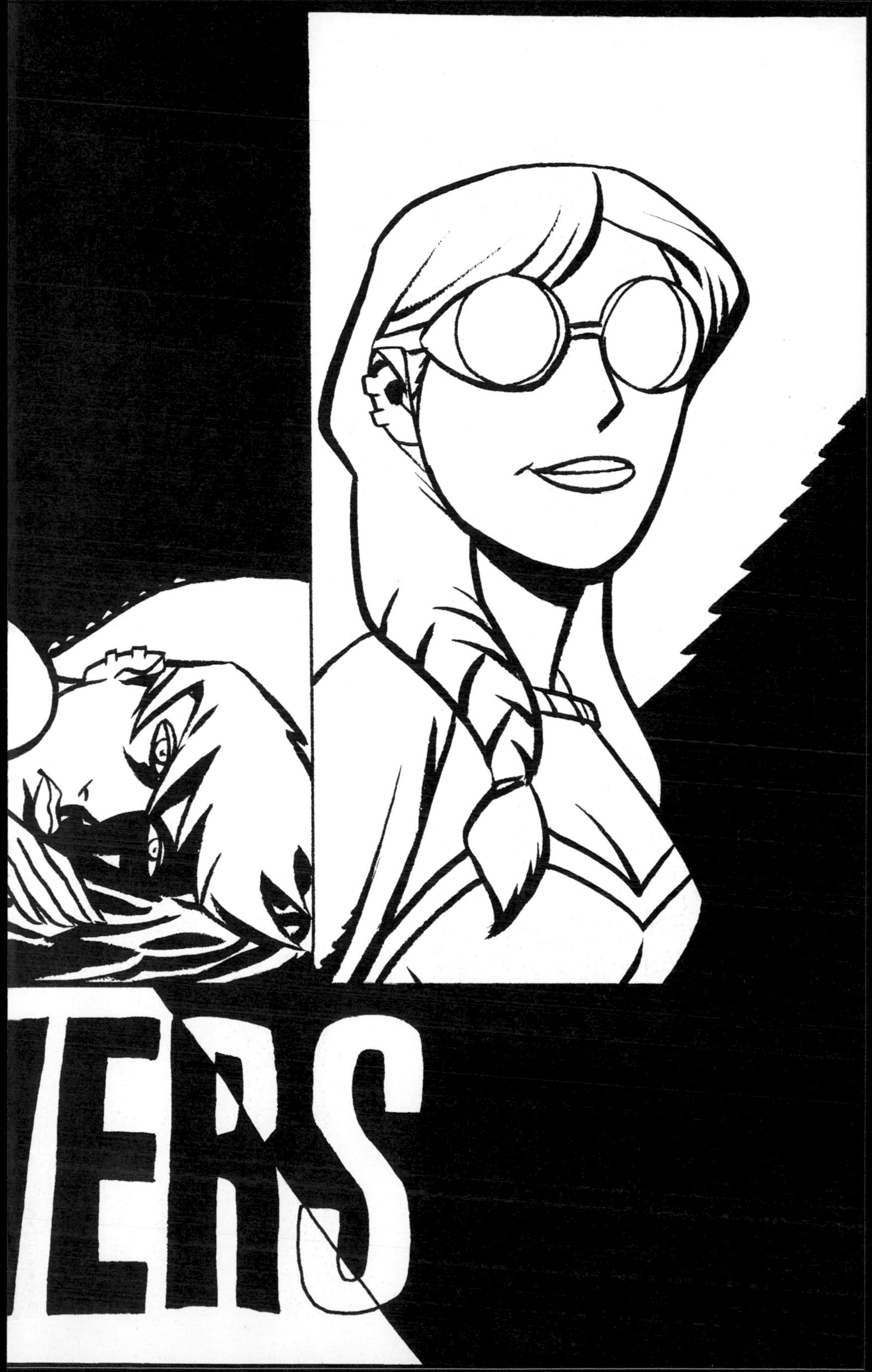
ERS

...Middle East is gone, Utah...gone!

BB: Weird. I'm rarely ever the type of writer to have premonitions of things to come, or mindsets to come. We just decided that the idea on top of all this stuff with the super-group mentality would be "What if this super powerful heroes, one of the big ones, kind of had Alzheimer's and lost his mind as he got older. "Again it was based on comedians and musicians who as they got older their mindset changes. They get angrier or a little more frustrated. There was this quote I used by John Cleese I used in a couple of places that freaked me out, who said, "When you're younger, there are absurdities in life you find hysterically funny, and then as older you get, you realize they're never going to go away, it becomes not funny at all. That's really bad."

MO: And it's never going to change, it's not a temporary state.

BB: That's the scariest goddamn thing I ever heard. I thought, well, what if like a level ten superhero just said, "You know what? Fuck it, you're done. I'm not fucking around with you guys anymore. I'll just wipe out the Middle East and you'll behave." There is part of a war mindset that says that.

MO: You hear it all the time. I'm hoping that when I hear people say that we should blast the Middle East or whatever, they're saying it out of frustration. But I get a sense especially in Jersey, a lot of it is they're fucking ignorant. They think that's just the way to handle stuff. So if some of these people had powers, they would do it. And they wouldn't have to be senile to do it.

And can I kind of put a message out there in Hollywood who might be reading this? No more movies about shit blowing New York up! I just saw another trailer for another fucking movie about some airplanes blowing New York up. We're fucking done with it, man. I'm so sick of that. Blow up Chicago or someplace like that! Anywhere but New York, just leave New York alone! We're done with it. It's that Jaime Foxx movie, Stealth.

BB: Mike thinks a lot of people from Hollywood are going to be reading this far into the interview.

EE: The second volume, the series became even darker. It goes back to the crime stories, was this something you were planning? The last two image storylines strayed far away and boom we're back into the crime stuff.

BB: A lot of the reasons that they're darker are two-fold. There are those reading the second volume having never read the first. They don't know any of the backstory and they're reading it like it's the first volume of Powers. It's written very carefully. But if you know all the stuff you know about...

---

Walker, it is unbelievably dark because you know a lot of stuff now. People have also gone back to re-read the Retro Girl arc having read Forever; they're kind of startled.

MO: I'm kind of proud too that stuck to our guns and took time revealing stuff about the characters. I remember the first two story arcs people were complaining that Walker was two dimensional and we didn't know anything about him or Deena.

BB: And then you said, "Honey, I'm trying to eat dinner."

MO: If only she would read them. [Laughs]

BB: My wife every couple of months will grab a stack. And she usually grabs Powers and Alias and if you read them all in a bunch she's like, 'what a perv I married!" [Laughs] Can you imagine our kids? I'll never show my books—

MO: I will be very proud if my child is reading twenty years from now.

BB: One day they're just going to be like on a self-discovery bandit and grab a few of our books and go to a coffee shop. Can you imagine them all reading our books?

MO: And then they'll run over to the house and tear the grandchildren from our laps.

EE: Now when the fans wanted you guys to switch roles for the 30th, what was each of you thinking?

BB: I'm thinking 'I hope no one socks my eye out of the socket so I could draw.' Yeah by the time they read this, they'll see that Mike had to do it all, because my child—we were roughhousing. I had weak corneas to start with and I had a hard contact on my eye, and I got socked in the side of my eye and cracked my cornea and I can't see out of one of my eyes.

MO: I keep telling him when you're jabbing a toddler to keep your left up. [Laughs] but he doesn't listen.

BB: Sadly we were bouncing up and down to Beyonce mash music. How's that for an image killer. [Laughs]

MO: Edit that out. Point is Brian's a pussy.

BB: I planned on fully drawing like I did the cover, but I can't. Down the road, when and if my eye heals, which it hasn't—it is supposed to be four months recovery and if not we'll have to see about transplant. That's how bad it is. So I apologize it wasn't the art I had hoped to do, but I can't see. So if you're still mad at me, F-you. I can't see!

I probably could still draw panels and thought, 'This isn't feeling the way like...

---

when I did the cover. I had both my eyes for the cover and it felt really good drawing again.

MO: You can draw with one eye but you'd be surprise at how long it takes to be able to adjust to that.

EE: Were there any other hardships or difficult times in making this run?

BB: Yeah there was a time when my hot tub wouldn't go over 98 degrees. So what was I going to do? I had my houseboy, Po-Po get in there and scrub out those filters "or I'm not paying you!" Then I said: finish typing my ULTIMATE X-MEN while I go watch TV. Listen, I've had real jobs and Mike's had real jobs it's a miracle that we're doing comics for a living! And to listen to anyone whine who's actually doing what they always wanted to do for a living—

MO: They should be punched in the head.

BB: Of course, I just whined about my eye for ten minutes. A bad day at the office...making comics, c'mon, how bad can it be? I have friends with some truly atrocious jobs and I've had some truly atrocious—just truly soul-sucking jobs in Cleveland Ohio.

MO: After being sequestered in your home studio, you can fall in too much of a pattern. You just end up falling asleep instead of working. [Laughing] So it's hard to complain about that sort of thing. I don't think the hardest thing, this was something we cleared up a while ago—was me keeping on schedule had to do with a combination of stuff or working on too many projects at once, real life things and instead of being four or five issues ahead I was one issue ahead. That was during two years ago when the issues weren't coming out. One year we only got eight issues out. That was a pretty hard time for both of us. It was aggravating for us creatively and financially we were cutting our livelihood in half doing that. We got through it and before we switched companies we took time to be five or six issues ahead and make sure that type of stuff doesn't happen again.

BB: And also, Ernie you had mentioned the series taking on a darker tone, with the relaunch we had already done the first arc by the time it was done coming out at Marvel. So when people found out that Marvel was publishing it they just assumed issue three would guest-star Wolverine and that it would be a pale comparison of what it once was. It was fun to watch them come out.

EE: How good has the move been to Icon?

BB: It's been great. We gained new readers, which is great when you don't do it tacky.

MO: Yeah, no crossovers. No gimmicks.

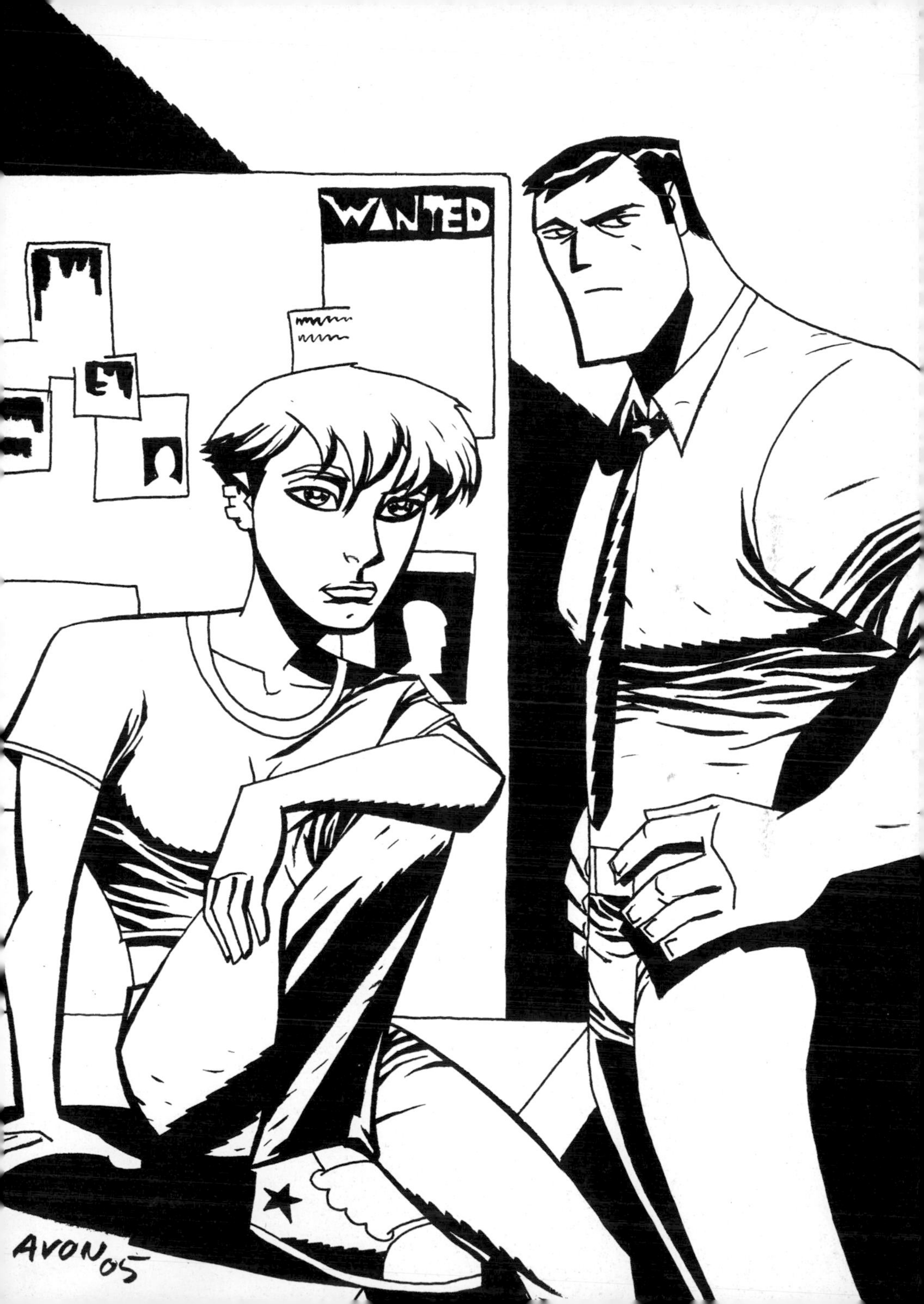
WANTED
AVON 05

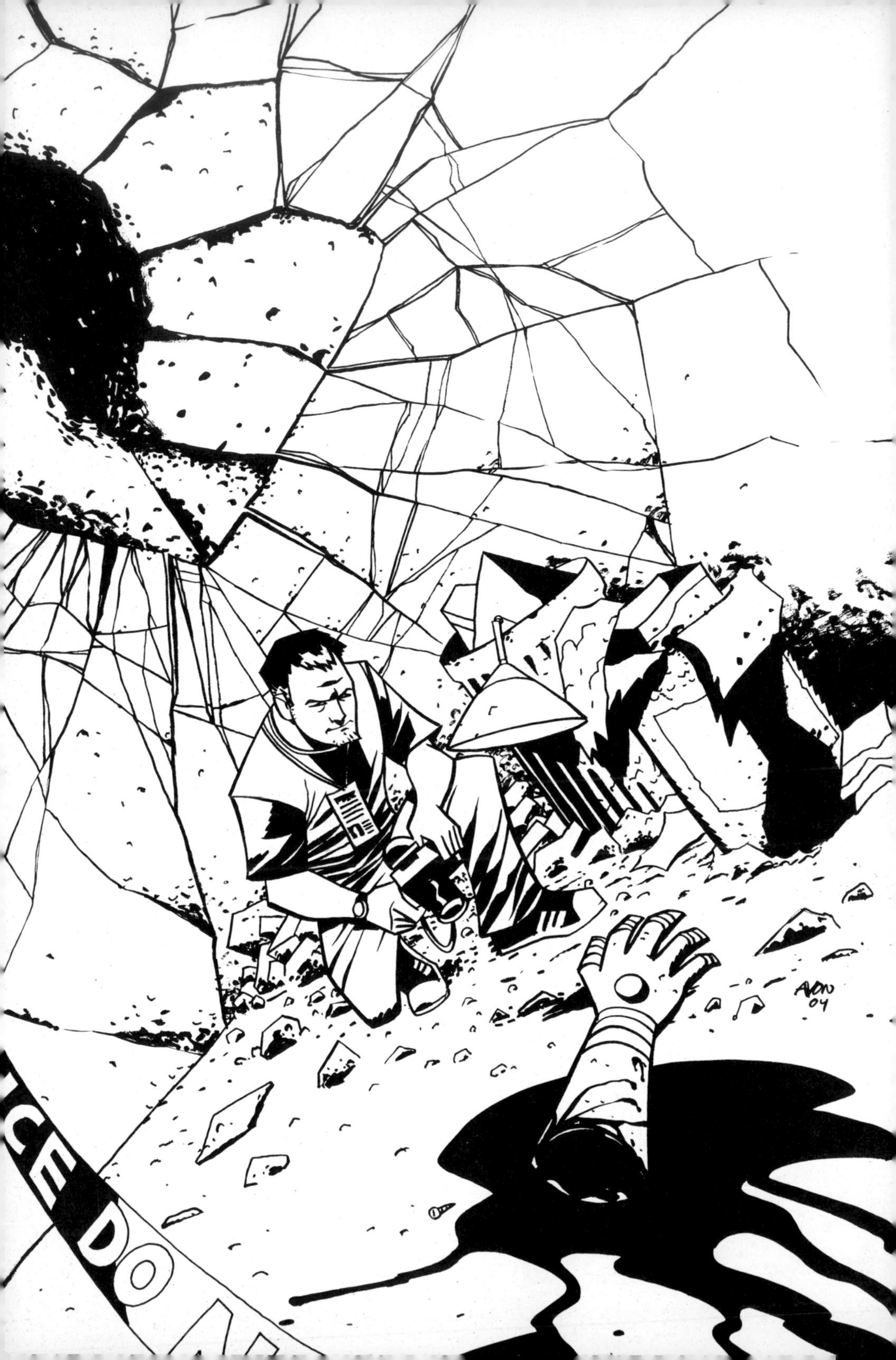
ICE DO

covers.

BB: This issue has multiple covers. Anyway...

MO: It's the fiftieth issue!

BB: It's still tacky.

MO: I thought it was a wrap-around cover.

BB: No. It's two separate covers.

MO: You too good to be on the same cover as me? I pay very little attention to what is going on.

BB: [Laughs] With the covers together, it makes a wrap-around so then people will have to buy two copies. See, what we did there?

So we picked up new readers, we have a safe home, it's the exact same situation as Image, we produce the book solely on our own, we hand them a disc. There's nothing being mandated to us as an independent book.

MO: It's such a good thing going on I feel like we're going to be punished in some way. It's awesome, it really is.

EE: Ultimately, how does Jim Valentino feel about the move because he was so instrumental in the early going?

BB: Part of the reason we moved on was Jim was no longer the publisher at Image. My relationship at Image was entirely my relationship with Jim. Jim's an awesome guy. I support Jim in all of his endeavors. Jim's a true patron saint of comics. There are guys who talk a good game; this is a guy who quietly gave a lot of people a home to safely publish a comic. Safe is the big word. There are plenty of publishers; there are not a lot of safe publishers. There are not a lot of publishers who will give you the money you earned. There are a lot of publishers that take your money and try to give it back to you at a later date or don't give you your money at all. Mike and me have worked for publishers like that. I was at Image for 7-8 years, which was twice as long as Jim Lee and (Rob) Liefeld were there which I thought was funny in some weird way. It was always a safe, warm-loving environment but my relationships are always with people, not with logos. The same goes with my relationship at Marvel. It is with the people who run it and have shown trust and loyalty. When someone is honest with me I tend to stick with my loyalty to the end of time. It's so rare for me to meet anybody who is not a lying sack of shit. And if not, you just hug them until they pry you off.

MO: Jim definitely took care of us. He was very much like a patriarchal kind of figure for us especially going out on a limb for us in the early days of POWERS when it

looked like an uphill battle. They put their money and their reputation out on the line to make sure people sell POWERS and gave us the chance.

BB: Nobody was happier with whatever mainstream success I slapped together, no one was happier than Jim. When it translated back to POWERS, finally something hit. He published JINX and TORSO, they were never going to do well and he didn't care. He never said anything about it. He never said no to any of my projects. So POWERS succeeding, I felt good that he was rewarded for his faith in me.

MO: That's what he's like, he never asks for anything.

BB: I've said before, I don't think he gets a lot of credit and the problem is he doesn't care about genre. So if he was a company like Top Shelf and doing what he had done, people would lauding him and naming awards after him because he didn't care if they were superhero books or sci-fi comics or fantasy comics, for some reason the effort put forth is less which is not the case at all. True independent comics are whatever you want it to be, not just a comic with me masturbating. I don't think he nearly gets enough credit doing what he does and what he's accomplished and giving people a safe home. The way Image started, it was almost the ultimate vanity press, for him to then turn it to this safe harbor a lot of people like Robert Kirkman and David Mack, Phil Hester the list goes on and on of people who needed it.

MO: There's no place else in the industry where you can get that kind of deal where you basically stand on your own success, if you fail, you fail. You reap all your own rewards, they weren't leeching on to you, and they weren't trying to get your movie money, or huge chunks off your book. They just wanted to do good commercial product.

The Jim story is way too common. People who have done great things for other people in the industry and then they don't get the recognition for it and you see it a lot and it sucks.

EE: How with great collaborations sometimes come with great friends. Powers has been a major period in both of your lives as well as the fans with the message board, the Lineup, what special place does Powers have for each of you?

MO: For me, I want POWERS written on my tombstone. No matter what else I do, and I want to do other things that are even bigger and more successful than POWERS, because you always want to set your goals pretty high, but I always want to be remembered for POWERS. I always want POWERS to be the thing that's associated with my name in the industry. And that goes back to reading a book like NEXUS. I felt what (Mike) Baron and (Steve) Rude did one of the best comics of all time and

no matter what either of them do, from here on out, they'll be attached to NEXUS. There are those few books like NEXUS, CONCRETE, SIN CITY, HELLBOY, those creators will always be willing to put those specific projects in front no matter what comes afterwards. We were really proud to do something like this. Truth be told not only have Brian and I become friends but this circle of us who have become friends and our families are actually close because of these projects. You can't really measure that kind of success.

BB: I was having dinner with (Greg) Rucka yesterday and he's going through what I went through AVENGERS when I first started, which is "You killed Blue Beetle, you motherfucker!" I told him that it occurred to me about a month ago that the word Hawkeye might appear in my obituary and got very scared. [Laughs] That was never in the planning. When you're thinking more seriously of course, this is probably one of the most important things I do is this book. When I mentioned earlier about our kids reading POWERS, I was waging with the funny but when my kid was born I was overwhelmed with the feeling to not suck even more than I already had.

With my kid I was overwhelmed with that feeling even more so about how my kid is going to read this in twenty years, do something that you'd really like to see and do it well.

EE: And now... we'll get to the Bernard Pivot Questions

BB: Gravitas!

MO: Gravitas!

EE: Brian, What is your favorite word?

BB: [Long pause] Taint. I wish I was joking

EE: Mike?

MO: Hawkeye

EE: What is your least favorite Word?

BB: Hawkeye...no. My least favorite word is smegma.

MO: Bankrupt. [Bendis laughs]

EE: Mike, What turns you on?

MO: Sex. No one says that.

BB: [Sighs] The reach-around.

EE: Mike what turns you off?

MO: People who squander their opportunity. They have a gig and they fuck it up.

BB: The sound of children laughing... No. Not just ignorance, but the proud-to-be-ignorance. The, "I'm thrilled with my ignorance."

EE: Brian what is your favorite curse word?

BB: It's not just the word, fuck. Jake Johannsen did this. It going, Fffffffffff-UCK! You gotta build the steam up and let it out. What bugs me is you can't write this in comic book language. It would have been Jessica Jones' catch phrase. Fffffffff-UCK!

MO: I like the word, cunt but with a Scottish accent, so it sounds nice.

EE: "Count."

MO: Yeah. Ask Mark Millar and—

BB: You don't have to ask, he'll just say it.

EE: That's true.

MO: It's funny because we've allowed Ethan (Mike's son) to start saying the word, "shite" because he's been to England. It's so cute when it comes out of an eight-year old mouth.

BB: They're going to take your kid away.

EE: Brian, what sound or noise do you love?

BB: The real answer is so douchy I can't even say it. I do like the accidental queef. [Everyone laughs] Not the people on Howard Stern (who can queef on command), those aren't funny.

MO: I like the sound of a woman moaning to be honest.

BB: The muffled sound or the actual sound? [Laughs]

MO: Not muffled. The actual—

EE: Do you like it when a woman moans your name?

MO: No. More of the moaning that's not a particular word—

BB: Any moaning, from any woman for any reason. Stomach virus—

MO: Yeah!

EE: Mike, what sound do you hate?

MO: I know this is supposed to be intellectual questions but I hate to go here but the sound of diarrhea. It hurts, the sound. Or vomiting, I'd say vomiting is worse. I actually had a pathological fear of vomiting but having a kid cleared that up.

BB: You've got to have thicker skin.

MO: I used to get violent when people threw up; I just wanted to attack them.

BB: [Laughs] That's nice. One minute people are vomiting and the next you're punching them. Mine would be... I just had it and lost it... Hang on for a second

MO: Go political. Go political.

BB: No-no I had a real answer. SHIT I had an answer!

MO: Was it the sound of your eyeball falling out of your head?

BB: Ohhhh man. I had it!

EE: We'll get back to that. Mike, what profession other than your own would you like to undertake?

MO: Um. I have a real answer but I'm going to hide that one.

BB: No. What's your real one?

MO: My # 2 answer would be a policeman.

BB: What's your real answer?

MO: I can't say. I'll tell you off the air. Sorry.

BB: What's your real answer? Why is it a secret?

MO: Because I don't really know what it is, I'll tell you later.

BB: Wow. Way to be honest in your interview.

MO: No. It's just a bullshit thing, I'll tell you later. You'll understand.

EE: We were about to get a serious revelation.

BB: I know. C'mon. Be honest. We're not those other guys.

MO: I just don't want people to be asking me this forever. It's just something I'm making up.

BB: Mine's reporter.

EE: What profession would you not like to attempt?

BB: Lawyer.

MO: I'll compile it with the sound I don't like, so someone who has to clean up vomit, like a nurse.

BB: Except my lawyer, he's awesome.

MO: He's scary. I like him. People flinch at the sound of his name.

BB: Isn't that the best?

EE: You must have paid a pretty penny for that.

BB: Worth every penny.

MO: We couldn't say his name in print otherwise the magazine would burst into flames.

EE: Last Pivot question, if heaven exists, what would like to hear God say to you when you arrive at the pearly gates?

MO: "Come on in and pick any of your sinful friends who want to come through."

BB: "Anal in a Marvel comic? BACK OF THE LINE!"

MO: You're an atheist aren't you?

BB: I'm a card-carrying Jewy Jew man. You can imagine the pride of my rabbi. [Laughs]

EE: Brian you think about that sound yet?

BB: Hold on, it's coming. [Everyone laughs]

EE: How long do you guys plan on doing Powers?

MO: We love POWERS in every imaginable way that a creator can. We never want it to get stale; it should never be less than what it should be.

BB: The good news is we have a lot of fun ideas left. You'll see by the end of issue # 11 we have a whole new can of worms. I was putzing through my POWERS idea-list which I haven't looked at in a while. It was stuff I wrote two years ago and said, Oh, that's a good idea. I forgot about that." So we have enough stories left in us, and thankfully the audience to keep the book going. My promise to Mike and the world was to wrap it up before we repeat ourselves or get stale and we are pretty good judges of that. We'll keep it going for a while. And we've got a killer ending.

EE: One last question, are the two of you planning on any creating any other projects together?

BB: Yes. We have created a new project together, recently and we will be putting it out in the near future.

Ernie Estrella is the Film Editor, DVD Reviewer and Interviewer at Buzz Scope. Check out www.buzzscope.com for more interviews like this, comic reviews, previews, and all things pop culture. What he hopes to hear from God at the pearly-gates, "Schultz, Eisner, and Kirby are all at their drawing tables and they'd love to talk."

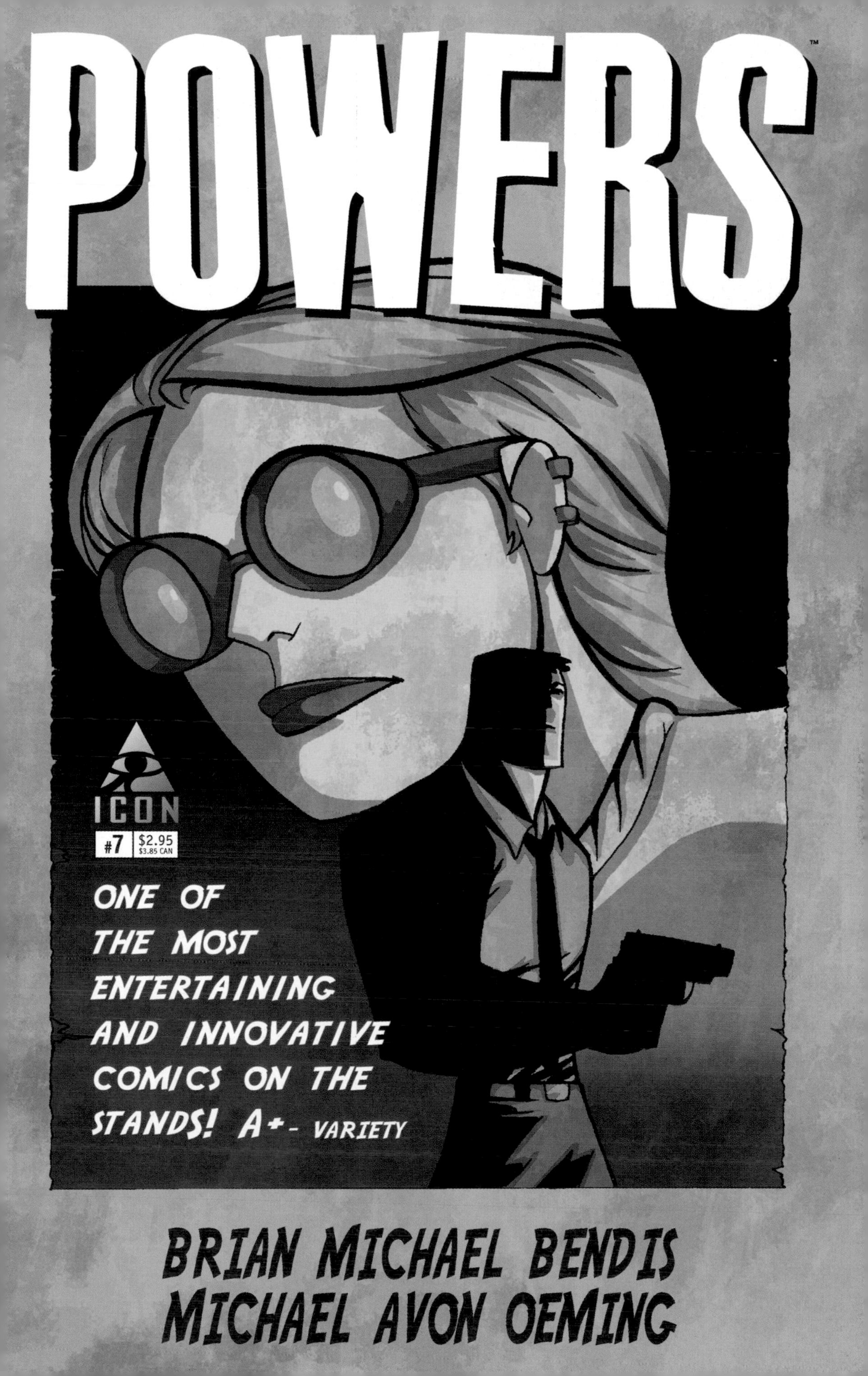
POWERS™
ICON
#7 $2.95 $3.85 CAN
ONE OF THE MOST ENTERTAINING AND INNOVATIVE COMICS ON THE STANDS! A+ - VARIETY
BRIAN MICHAEL BENDIS
MICHAEL AVON OEMING

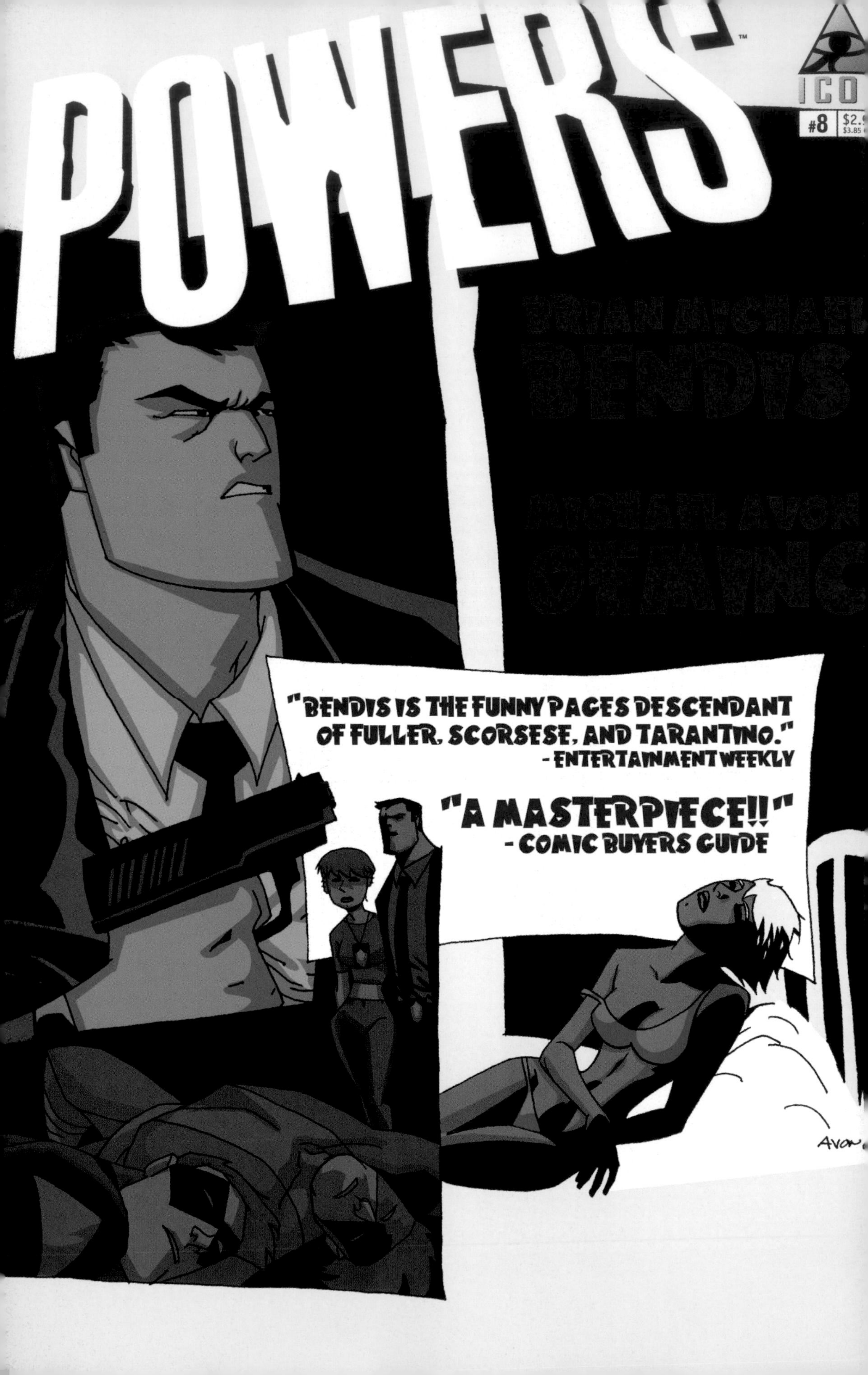
POWERS
#8
"BENDIS IS THE FUNNY PAGES DESCENDANT OF FULLER, SCORSESE, AND TARANTINO."
- ENTERTAINMENT WEEKLY
"A MASTERPIECE!!"
- COMIC BUYERS GUIDE
AVON

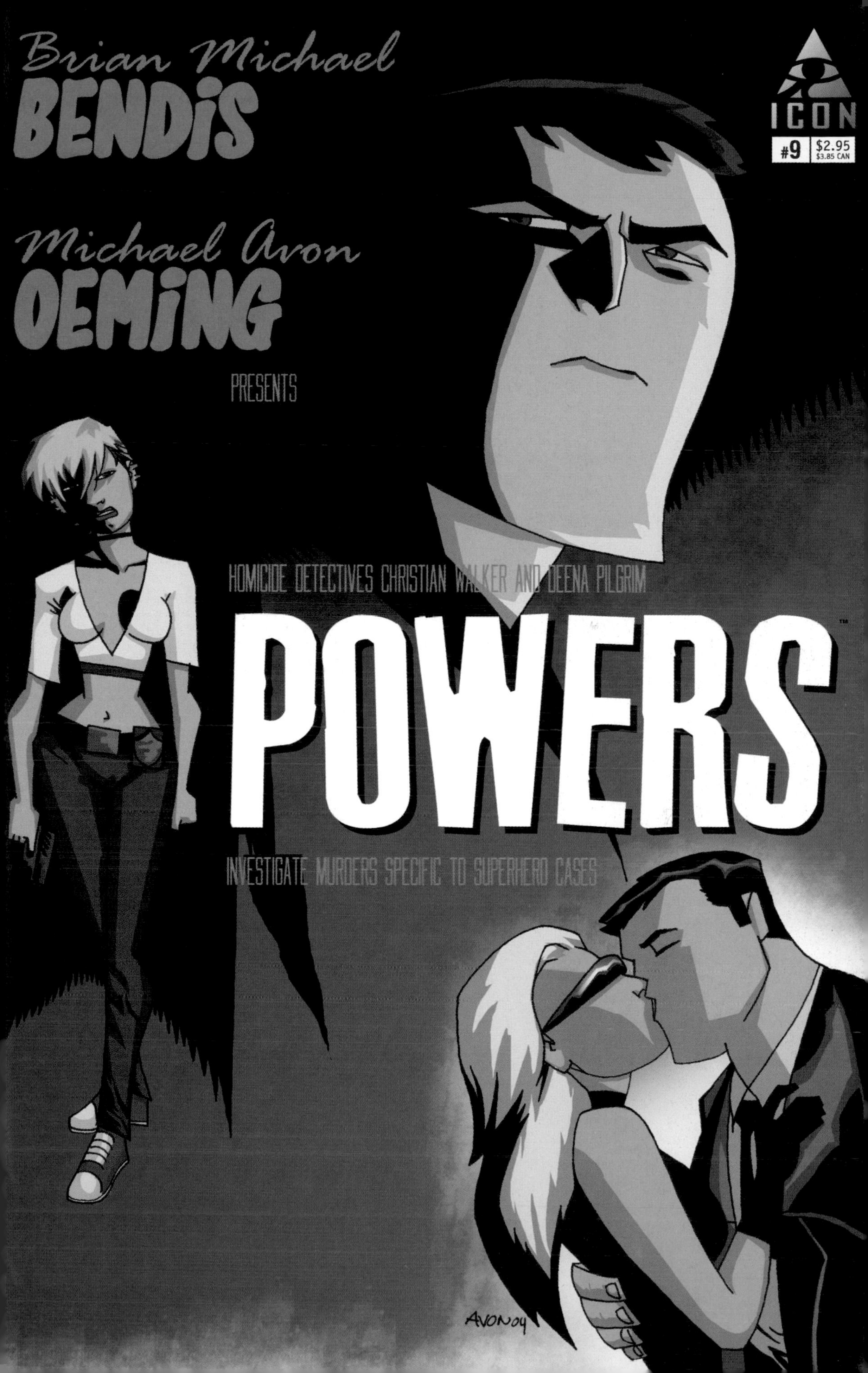

Brian Michael
BENDIS
ICON
#9 $2.95
$3.85 CAN
Michael Avon
OEMING
PRESENTS
HOMICIDE DETECTIVES CHRISTIAN WALKER AND DEENA PILGRIM
POWERS™
INVESTIGATE MURDERS SPECIFIC TO SUPERHERO CASES
AVON04

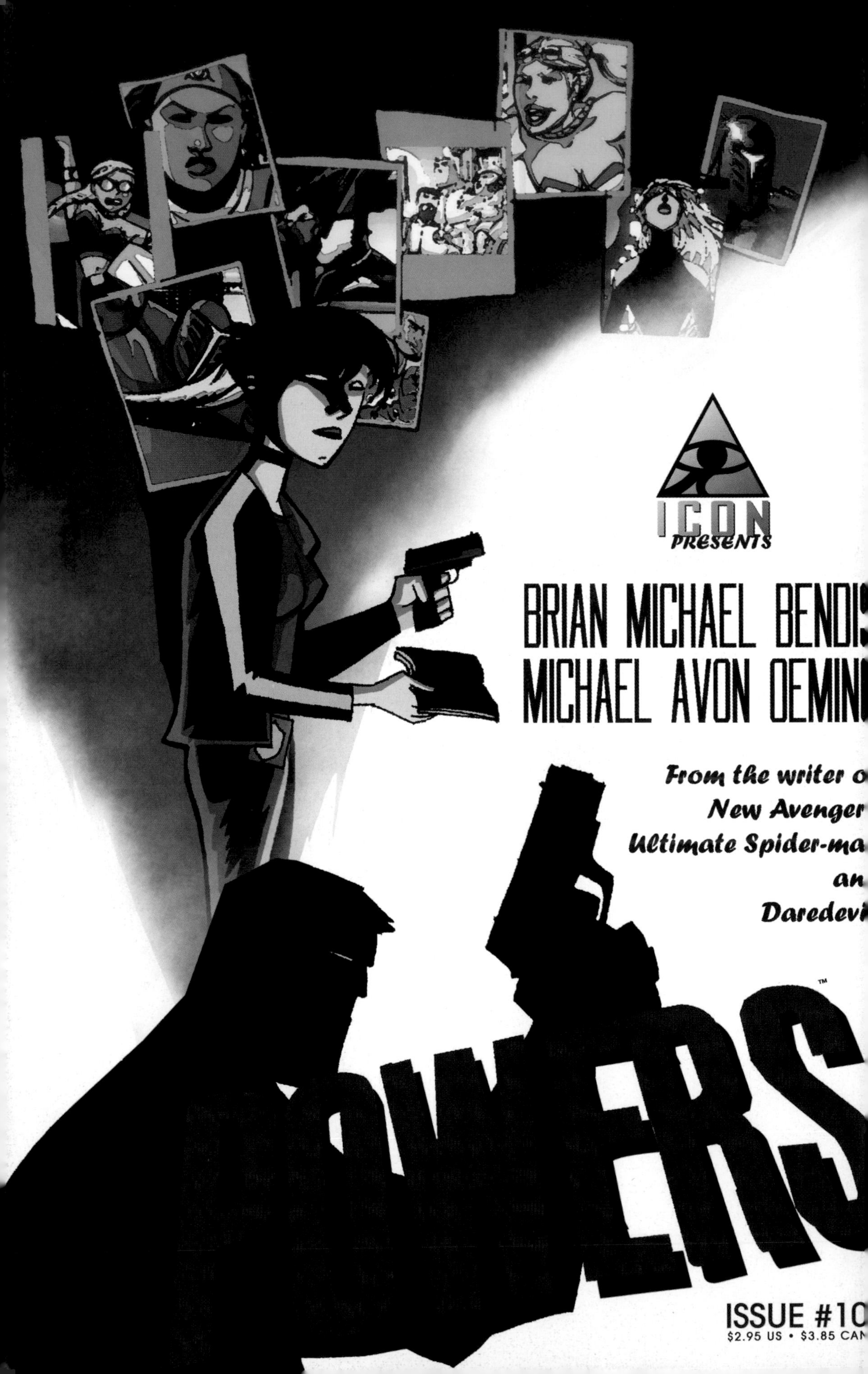

ICON
PRESENTS
BRIAN MICHAEL BENDI
MICHAEL AVON OEMIN
From the writer o
New Avenger
Ultimate Spider-ma
an
Daredevi
ISSUE #10
$2.95 US • $3.85 CA

ICON

11 | $2.95
$3.85 CAN

# POWERS

FROM THE WRITER OF
NEW AVENGERS AND DAREDEVIL

BRIAN MICHAEL BENDIS

MICHAEL AVON OEMING

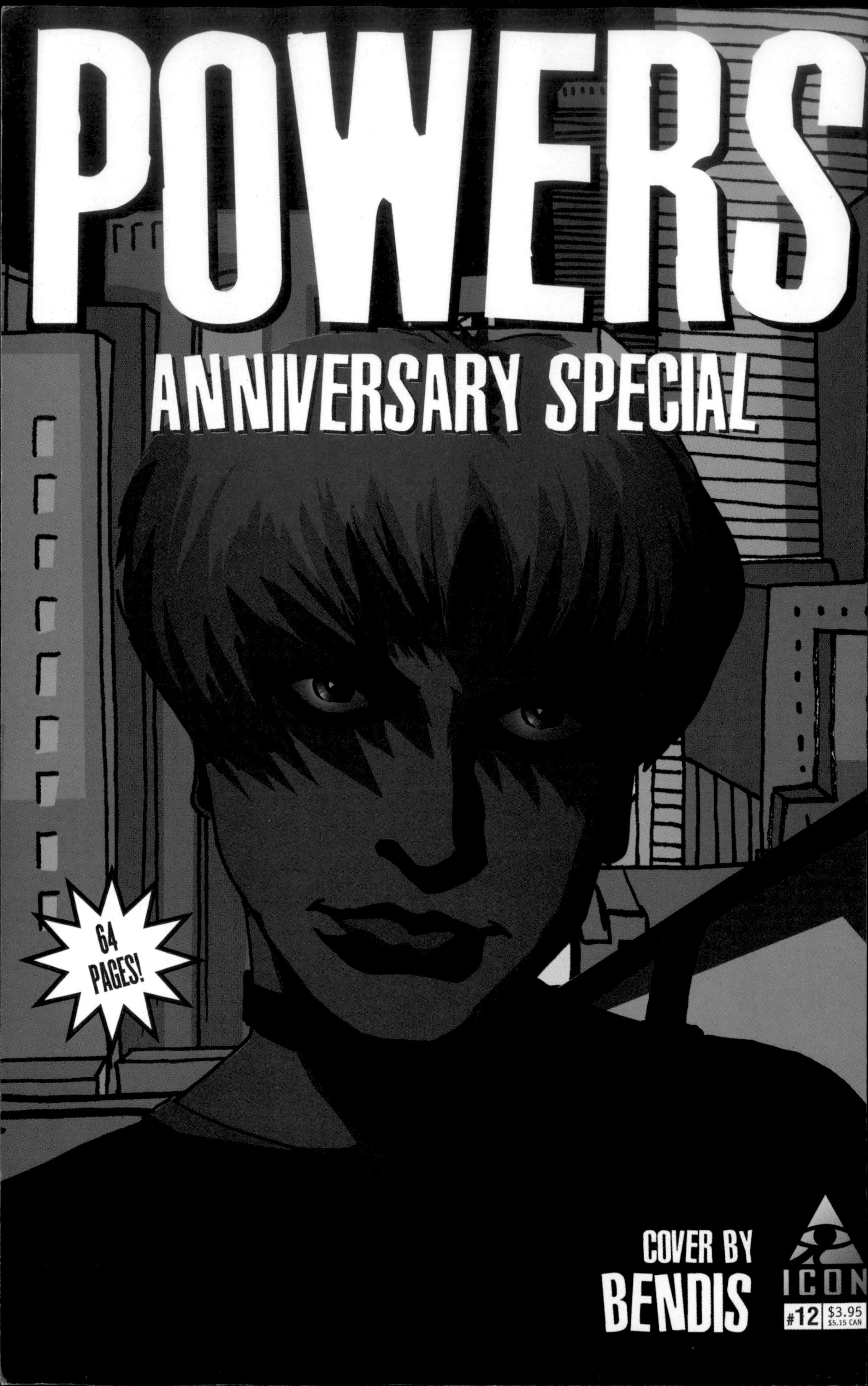
POWERS
ANNIVERSARY SPECIAL
64 PAGES!
COVER BY BENDIS
ICON
#12 $3.95 $5.15 CAN

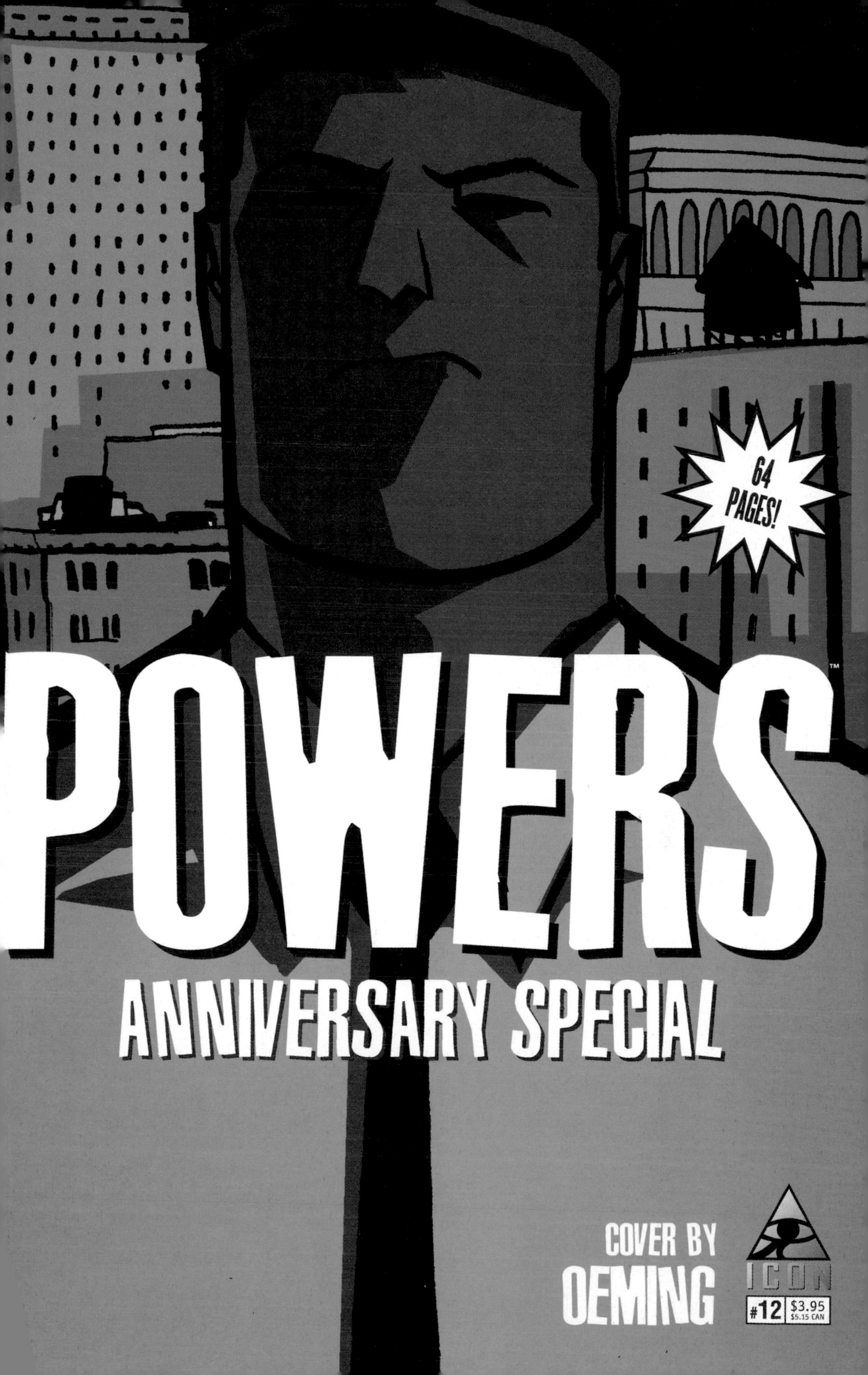
64 PAGES!
POWERS™
ANNIVERSARY SPECIAL
COVER BY
OEMING
ICON
#12 $3.95
$5.15 CAN

## By the authors...

**POWERS**
- Who Killed Retro Girl?
- Roleplay
- Little Deaths
- Supergroup
- Anarchy
- The Sellouts
- Forever
- Legends
- Psychotic
- Powers Script Book

## By Bendis...

- Jinx
- Goldfish
- Fortune and Glory
- Torso
- Alias / The Pulse
- Secret War
- Ultimate Spider-Man
- Daredevil
- New Avengers
- House of M
- Total Sell Out

## By Oeming...

- The Six
- Bastard Samurai
- Hammer of the Gods
- Ship of Fools
- Parliament of Justice